THE GORE-BOOTHS OF LISSADELL

DERMOT JAMES

'Lissadell Court, the Seat of Sir Robert Gore-Booth, Bart'. Francis Goodwin's depiction of the mansion in his '*Domestic Architecture*' published in 1833.

THE GORE-BOOTHS OF LISSADELL

DERMOT JAMES

The Woodfield Press

This book was typeset by
Orchard Publishing Services, Portadown, Co. Armagh for
The Woodfield Press
17 Jamestown Square, Dublin 8
www.woodfield-press.com
e-mail: terri.mcdonnell@ireland.com

Publishing Editor
Helen Harnett

House Editor
Aidan Culhane

Printed in Ireland by
ColourBooks, Dublin

ISBN 0-9534293-8-5

A catalogue record for this title is available from the British Library.

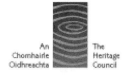

An
Chomhairle
Oidhreachta

The
Heritage
Council

This publication has received support from the Heritage Council
under the 2004 Publications Grant Scheme.

To Eric Montgomery and Risteárd Ó Glaisne, each of whom generously assisted the author in the preparation of this volume and took a great interest in its progress. Sadly, neither lived to see it published.

Descendants of Robert Gore-Booth, 4th. Bt.

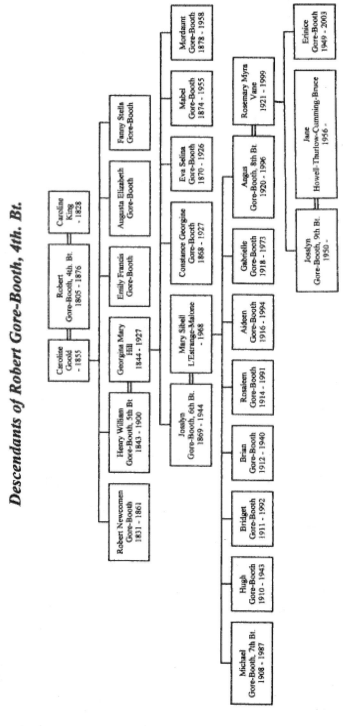

Basic family tree showing the line from the fourth baronet
to the present (ninth) baronet.

CONTENTS

Also published by The Woodfield Press

The Gore-Booths of Lissadell
DERMOT JAMES

Differently Irish: a cultural history exploring twenty five years of Vietnamese-Irish Identity
MARK MAGUIRE

Documenting Irish Feminisms
LINDA CONNOLLY & TINA O'TOOLE

Royal Roots – Republican Inheritance: The Survival of the Office of Arms
SUSAN HOOD

The Politics and Relationships of Kathleen Lynn
MARIE MULHOLLAND

St Anne's – The Story of a Guinness Estate
JOAN USSHER SHARKEY

Female Activists: Irish Women and Change 1900-1960
MARY CULLEN & MARIA LUDDY (eds)

W & R Jacob: Celebrating 150 Years of Irish Biscuit Making
SÉAMAS Ó MAITIÚ

Faith or Fatherhood? Bishop Dunboyne's Dilemma
CON COSTELLO

Charles Dickens Ireland: An Anthology
JIM COOKE

Red-Headed Rebel: A Biography of Susan Mitchell
HILARY PYLE

The Sligo-Leitrim World of Kate Cullen 1832-1913
HILARY PYLE

John Hamilton of Donegal 1800-1884
DERMOT JAMES

The Tellicherry Five: The Transportation of Michael Dwyer and the Wicklow Rebels
KIERAN SHEEDY

Ballyknockan: A Wicklow Stonecutters' Village
SÉAMAS Ó MAITIÚ & BARRY O'REILLY

The Wicklow World of Elizabeth Smith 1840-1850
DERMOT JAMES & SÉAMAS Ó MAITIÚ
(Now back in print)

ACKNOWLEDGEMENTS

As this book is addressed to the general rather than to specialists, footnotes have been kept to a minimum throughout and it is hoped that readers will appreciate the fact that points requiring elaboration are almost invariably covered directly in the relevant text. Concerning secondary sources, where an author is mentioned or quoted, the actual source may be found by reference to the bibliography. As to other sources, the primary source of the material used in this work is the archive of Gore-Booth papers, currently lodged by the family at PRONI, the Public Record Office, Northern Ireland.

The reference to the Gore-Booth Papers at PRONI, deserves some elaboration: This archive represents one of the largest single deposits currently lodged there, where it has been painstakingly and very thoroughly catalogued. Despite the size of the archive, there are unfortunate gaps, notably the lack of seventeenth and eighteenth century correspondence, which partly accounts for the fact that the earlier history of the family is treated rather briefly in this volume. Dr A. P. V. Malcolmson, who wrote the introduction and synopsis to the archive while he was Director at PRONI, speculated that the most likely reason for the comparative lack of older material was the fire, thought to have been deliberate, in the Lissadell Estate Office in 1941. Happily, what has survived is an exceptionally extensive collection of correspondence and other material covering a period of more than two centuries, making it possible for the nine members of the family featured in this book to 'come alive.'

I am most grateful to Sir Josslyn Gore-Booth, the ninth baronet, for his help in the preparation of this book, for his permission to quote from the family archive, and also from Eva Gore-Booth's poetry. I am also grateful to the Chief Executive of the Public Record Office, Northern Ireland, Dr Gerry Slator and to the Deputy Keeper of Records at PRONI for permission to publish extensively from the Lissadell archive lodged there. And it is appropriate here to express my general thanks to the staff at PRONI, especially to David Huddleston, whose assistance while researching this archive was so very helpful.

My thanks are additionally due to Sir Josslyn for his assistance in providing – and for his permission to reproduce – all but a few of the illustrations used in this volume. The exceptions are noted in the respective captions. In this connection, Messrs Hamilton Osborne King

Fine Arts kindly facilitated the author by providing the digitalised photographs which had previously appeared in the catalogue produced jointly by them with Christies of London for the Lissadell contents sale.

I must also record my appreciation to the institutions that provided research facilities. These included: The National Library of Ireland; the National Archive; the Royal Irish Academy; the National Botanic Gardens; The Irish Times Library, the Royal British Legion (Dublin) and the Sligo County Library. In Northern Ireland: the Linenhall Library, Belfast and the Royal Irish Fusiliers' Museum, Armagh. In London: the Ministry of Defence; the Royal Naval Historical Records Office, and the Public Record Office at Kew.

My thanks are also due to the following for permission to reproduce material from other sources: To Eimer O Broin for the quoted extracts from three books written by his late father, León O Broin. To A.P. Wyatt and to Michael Yeats, for their permission to quote from W. B. Yeats' poetry. To Mark Bence-Jones for permission to include the story related to him about the visit of the King-Harman brothers to Lissadell, and to Dr Michael Purser for kindly granting permission to reproduce Sarah Purser's well-known painting of Constance and Eva. Special thanks are also due to those others – experts in their various fields – who have checked individual chapters or specific parts of the text. These include Marcus Wheeler, Professor Emeritus, Slavonic Studies, Queen's University, Belfast and Gifford Lewis. The latter additionally granted permission to quote from her biography of Eva Gore-Booth and Esther Roper, and kindly gave permission to reproduce her photograph of Eva Gore-Booth's grave. Others who assisted by checking chapters or sections of the text included Sarah Ball, Librarian at the National Botanic Gardens, Commander Con Glanton, ex R.N., Adrian Glover, Charles Lysaght, Eric Montgomery, Risteárd Ó Glaisne, Andrew O Rorke, and Cecil and Brid Tams. My special thanks are due to Donal Nevin for drawing my attention to the existence of a sealed letter written by Stainslas Markievicz concerning his father's alleged title. I am also grateful to the several hundred authors whose works, listed in the bibliography, have been consulted and, in many cases, have been quoted in the text.

Other individuals were generously helpful in a variety of ways. These included Kingsley and Claire Aikins, Dublin and Boston; Angela Alexander, Dublin; Dr Brian Barton, Belfast; Hannah Dangel-Dowling, Dublin and Warsaw; Irene Grace, Dublin, Frances Homan, Kilcoole;

Professor Fergus Kelly, Dublin; Dr Noel Kissane, Keeper of Manuscripts, National Library of Ireland; Dr Michel Kostecki, Geneva; Mary McDowell, Clones; Seamus Martin, Dublin and Perpignan; Joan Montgomery, Cultra; Esther Murnane and Irene Stevenson of *The Irish Times* Library; Julie Marshall of HOK Fine Arts; Gregory O'Connor, Archivist, the National Archives; The O'Morchoe, Gorey; Elizabeth Petch, Kilbritain; Nicholas Prins, Sligo (who, while manager of Lissadell Estate, originally suggested the undertaking of this work); and Bob Purdie, Ruskin College, Oxford University. Also my wife, Gladys, who typed most of the text and who cheerfully supported me throughout the five years spent preparing this volume.

Dermot James
July, 2004.

INTRODUCTION

Ask the proverbial man or woman in the street what he or she knows about the Gore-Booth family and the most likely reaction will be some general recollections about Constance Markievicz. Others may recall something of the Yeats' connection or, perhaps, about the Ward of Court case that lasted for several decades. For many people, however, the family name will simply be a reminder of a visit to the old, grey mansion beside the sea during what might have seemed at the time, to be its declining years.

It may appear to be something of a contradiction to state that the Gore-Booths simultaneously represent one of the best-known and yet one of the least-known of all the Anglo-Irish families, yet there is more than an element of truth in the assertion. While the Gore-Booths were, for a time, one of the most prominent of all the Anglo-Irish families in the north-west, most of the individual members – certainly over the past 200 years or so – led relatively quiet, unobtrusive lives. They also steered clear of sectarianism and (with one notable exception) took little interest in politics. It could be claimed that virtually any interest that these Gore-Booths showed outside the walls of their estate was wholly admirable, while their interest within the estate was, in the main, beneficial not only for the property but also for their employees and tenants as well.

In general, they were decent, benevolent proprietors, a class that for nearly a century and a half has been excised from Irish history books in order to depict landlords – all landlords without exception – as cruel evictors. Benevolent landlords may have been a minority but there is some evidence that they were more numerous than has, as yet, been generally acknowledged. As Professor J.C. Beckett expressed it in *The Anglo-Irish Tradition*: 'A good many landlords – more than is commonly recognised – did, in fact, try to improve the lot of their tenants and promote the general welfare of their neighbourhood.' He also wrote that 'It is only recently that historians have begun seriously to question the justice of the charges usually levelled against them.' Two such historians, D. George Boyce and Alan O'Day, have made the point that the landlords had only limited control over the terms on which they let their land. They have also quoted various authors making the case that the relationship between the proprietor and tenant 'was more nuanced and less heavily weighted in favour of the landlords than had been assumed.' While it cannot be denied that the majority of the nineteenth century landlords ruthlessly evicted tenants, it seems grossly unfair to the memory of those who did their best for their tenants – sometimes resulting in bankruptcy – that their actions have gone virtually unrecorded.

Nine members of the Gore-Booth family have been chosen here to tell the family story, covering between them a period of almost 200 years. These individual chapters are preceded by a Prologue very briefly describing what happened after the family arrived in Ireland towards the end of the sixteenth century. Some of the details about this earlier period are vague, but much of what took place at that time is unlikely to be of great interest to the general reader, reflecting as it does England's attempts at the time to conquer and settle Ireland.

What makes the rest of the narrative so interesting is the sheer diversity of their individual interests. The nine family members whose lives are detailed here were, between them, Arctic explorers, artists, botanists, campaigners for women's rights, explorers, farmers, game hunters, horticulturists, landlords, literary agents, musicians, ornithologists, painters, plant hunters, playwrights, poets, railway company chairmen, sailors, soldiers, suffragettes, trade unionists, and yachtsmen. Among their number was a very prominent republican who became the first woman to be elected to parliament and the first woman to be appointed a Minister of State. The Gore-Booths were all of this – and much more besides.

While most members of the Gore-Booth family shared a retiring disposition, content to keep to themselves, Constance was certainly a notable exception, seeking from an early age to be the centre of attention. Although she has been the subject of more than half a dozen biographies, the chapter in this volume devoted to her life contains details not previously published in any of these works. Further material included here draws together from some little-known sources certain aspects concerning her that will also be new and perhaps surprising to many people.

Many of the Anglo-Irish families had their share of 'black sheep.' Obvious examples include that of Maria Edgeworth, some of whose forebears led what Julian Moynahan termed 'dishevelled lives' that came to be recorded in *The Black Book of Edgeworthstown*. The Gore-Booths had Sir Robert's brother Henry and his sister Anne, whose wild antics fall outside the scope of this volume but may yet be chronicled by some enterprising author in a work that might perhaps be entitled *The Black Book of Lissadell*.

Writing in 1976, Professor Beckett expressed the rather forlorn hope that the Anglo-Irish might once again play some part in Irish politics, but added that even if this was not possible, 'their record will remain a major element in Ireland's past.' It was probably inevitable that the record did not, in fact, 'remain,' largely because most of those whom he had in mind believed that the connection with England was essential to Ireland's well being. In the newly emerging independent Ireland, there was little sympathy for or interest in their record, so that if they were remembered at all, it was simply as tyrants and usurpers – to recall a phrase used by Constance.

Yet, reading through the record of the Gore-Booths, it is clear that as a family they were kindly, considerate, and often generous towards their tenants, for which they were repeatedly praised not only by their tenants but also by local priests and by some of the local newspapers. It was inevitable that the tide eventually turned against them so that, like most of the Anglo-Irish families, they lost all the power, most of the land, and much of the wealth that they once possessed. How this came about, and how they subsequently tried to cope with the changed political and economic situation is told here in detail for the first time.

Sir Henry's sketch drawn for his log-book, which he captioned: 'Lap [p] hut, Pasvig river, 1866. H.G.-Booth weighing a salmon just killed in Averuus.'

Nathaniel Gore meets Letitia Booth

These first few pages set the scene for what follows, and if the reader finds them difficult to follow (the Gore-Booth family connections are incredibly complicated), or boring, or both, then the author can only plead that the details in this section have been kept as brief as possible.

According to the Annals of the Four Masters, the O'Donnells and the O'Connors fought for the control of the territory around Lissadell in the fourteenth century, a battle which was won by the latter. But when the O'Connors were forced to forfeit their lands because they supported the rebellion of 1641, various Elizabethan officers, some of whom had already received grants of lands elsewhere, became the beneficiaries of this forfeiture. One of these was Paul Gore, the first significant ancestor of the Gore-Booth family. His father, Gerald Gore, had moved from Surrey to London where he became an alderman, and his eldest son, John, became a Lord Mayor of London. Following Paul's arrival in Ireland in 1599, he was awarded lands for his services as captain of a troop of horse under the Lord Lieutenant, the Earl of Devereux. After the collapse of the rebellion led by Hugh O'Neill and Hugh O'Donnell, Paul Gore escorted Rory O'Donnell (brother of Red Hugh) to Athlone and after the Irish chieftains made their submission to Queen Elizabeth, Gore was granted further lands – at Boylagh and Bannagh – in south Donegal.

Paul Gore had only just completed building a house on his new property when for reasons not now understood, King James II granted Paul's property to the future Earl Annadale. Paul received inferior land at Magherabeg, near Donegal town in lieu. He can hardly have been pleased with this turn of events but set about constructing his second house, calling it Manor Gore. He had married a daughter of Francis Wickliffe, a niece of the future Earl of Stafford, Lord Lieutenant of Ireland, and they raised a family of 13 children, nine of whom became members of the Irish parliament. When Ballyshannon was created a borough by Royal Charter in 1613, Paul became its first M.P. and a Justice of the Peace. In 1621 he was created a baronet.

Sir Paul died eight years later and was buried in Donegal Abbey, and his fourth son, Francis, succeeded to the title. All of Sir Paul's seven sons 'married well.' His eldest son, Ralph, became the ancestor of the earls of Rosse. Arthur, the second son, became the ancestor of the earls of Arran, a family that subsequently inherited the very large Saunders Court estate near Ferrycarrig in County Wexford. A third son, Henry, married the eldest daughter of Robert Blaney of Monaghan and was the ancestor of the earls of Kingston. Two further sons settled in County Kilkenny, giving the family name to Goresbridge, and the seventh son settled in County Mayo and, according to a memorial tablet in Killala cathedral, married Ellinor St George of Carrick, County Leitrim, by whom he had four sons, Paul, Arthur, William and George, and eight daughters. He died at his residence, Newtown Gore, later renamed Castle Gore, near Killala, in 1697.

The Books of Survey and Distribution show that when Francis succeeded to the title from Sir Paul, he held over 4,000 acres. Most of this, however, resulted from his marriage to Anne, daughter and heir of Robert Parke of Newtown, County Leitrim, a place now more generally known as Parke's Castle which is attractively situated on the shore of Lough Gill. He managed to keep on good terms with both the Cromwellians and the Royalists during the Civil War, avoiding an engagement in either cause. After the Restoration, Charles II dealt with claims and counter-claims in connection with forfeited lands and 'as the political party comprising the soldiers and adventurers had been that to which he was indebted ... he was morally and legally bound to confirm these grants.' The list of petitioners included 'Gower, Francis, alias Gore, who had made no less than 62 petitions'. He was rewarded with grants of land in Sligo, Mayo and Kilkenny under the Acts of Settlement and in 1661 he was knighted and also became M.P. for Sligo.

Sir Francis then settled at Ardtarmon, two miles west of Lissadell, close to Raughley Point with its yellow strand of which Yeats was to write: 'I have walked to Sinbad's yellow shore and never shall another take my fancy.' According to family tradition, Francis built his castle there but most accounts aver that the castle had been erected earlier by the O'Hart's, who had long been in the possession of these lands. Whether Francis Gore built Ardtarmon Castle or took it over and enlarged it, or whether the O'Hart castle was not actually at Ardtarmon at all, but situated a couple of miles away at Lissadell, is uncertain. On the early Ordnance Survey maps a ruined castle is shown situated on the shore close to where the first house at Lissadell was subsequently built. Named as Bunbrenogue Castle, nothing remains of it now, possibly because the masonry was utilised for the new building.

Anyway, Francis Gore was the first member of the family to live in the neighbourhood of Lissadell and when he died in 1713 he was succeeded by his eldest son, Robert, of Newtown, County Leitrim. Robert had, 35 years earlier, married Frances, the eldest daughter of Sir Thomas Newcomen. Little is known about this Robert, but one of the oldest surviving documents among the Lissadell Papers is a letter from King James II, dated 1686, and addressed to the earl of Clarendon. The letter authorised Clarendon (who had been appointed Lord Lieutenant earlier that year) to create Robert as a baronet of Ireland, but the king's instructions were never carried out.

Robert was succeeded by his eldest son Nathaniel who was born in 1692, and had married a wealthy heiress, Lettice (or Laetitia), only daughter of Humphrey Booth, who as Controller of Customs was an important official in Sligo town. It was this union that later resulted in the incorporation of the two surnames, Gore and Booth, into the family name and the establishment of the subsequent dynasty. Although the very substantial financial consequences of this marriage were not to become apparent until later, it proved to be the most significant single event in the history of the Gore-Booth family when the extremely prosperous Booth estates in the English midlands were added to the Sligo property.

The second son of this marriage, John, succeeded to the Booth estates near Manchester, while the eldest son, Booth Gore was created a baronet of Ireland in 1760, becoming Sir Booth Gore, First Baronet of Lissadell. He married a cousin, another Newcomen, Emily or Emilia, a wedding briefly reported in the *London Evening Post* dated January 10, 1744: 'Last week, Sir Booth Gore, Bart. was married to Miss Newcomen, daughter of Brabazon Newcomen of the County of Lowth, Esqr., a beautiful young lady of fine Accomplishments and a large Fortune.' It seems that the male members of the family continued to have not only a good eye for attractive looking women, but unerringly picked those beauties most likely to bring with them handsome dowries.

Some time between 1750 and 1760, Sir Booth built the first Gore house at Lissadell (usually spelt Lissadill or Lisadill at this time). Erected close to the sea and directly in front of the site of the present mansion, no documents survive about this house. Fortunately, a painting of this dwelling have survived, thought to have been the work of James Gore-Booth, depicting the property as a three-storey building standing on the seashore. It shows that alongside and to the rear of the house, a large garden had been laid out, surrounded by a high wall, and sections of this wall have survived to the present day. The painting also depicts extensive stands of trees on either side and behind the house, but the front was exposed to the full force of Atlantic storms, which may explain the rather ugly box-like porch which appears to have been a later addition.

Sir Booth died in 1773 and was succeeded by his eldest son, also named Booth Gore, who became the second baronet. It was he who, some sixteen years later, inherited the extremely prosperous Booth estates in and around Manchester following the death there in 1789 of his unmarried uncle, the aforementioned John Gore. As Dr Malcolmson expressed it in his synopsis to the Lissadell archive: 'So after a bewildering series of childless marriages and deaths, the Gore baronets of Lissadell succeeded to the Booth estate in Salford and Manchester in addition to their patrimonial Gore estate in Sligo.' Sir Booth Gore had been an absentee, living for the most part in England while his brother, Robert, lived at Lissadell – very probably on a caretaker basis – and when the second baronet died in 1804, also unmarried, the title devolved on to his brother who then became the third baronet. In that same year he assumed by sign manual the additional surname and arms of Booth, thus becoming the first Gore-Booth.

Although a bachelor in his sixties, Sir Robert decided to establish a family line of his own and wasted no time getting married. His wife was Hannah Irwin from Streamstown, County Sligo, a property which was to become part of the Gore-Booth estate some 90 years later. They had three children, two sons and a daughter, and the eldest later became the second Sir Robert, but the younger son, Henry, turned out to be a very colourful, and probably the most outrageous member of the family. As Henry was only five when his father died, his behaviour may have been partly the result of a lack of paternal direction during his formative years. He joined the Scots Guards and married a Scottish sculptress, Isabella Smith, and commissioned Francis Goodwin, the architect of his brother's house, to design a house for himself (which was never built) at Cullamore. Instead, he set up a shipping business in Glasgow and when he found himself in financial difficulties, he abandoned both his business and his unfortunate wife and family, embarking on a life of recklessness involving one or more mistresses in the Far East and resulting in numerous illegitimate children.

However, the real story of the Gore-Booths of Lissadell commences with Henry's more conventional elder brother, Robert, whose active if less colourful life is described in the first of the following chapters.

Lady Gore-Booth's

SCHOOL OF NEEDLEWORK,

LISSADELL, Sligo.

Ladies' and Children's
Hand-made Underclothing.

Children's Frocks, Robes,
Pinafores, &c.

Tea Cloths, Handkerchiefs, &c.
In Drawn-Thread Work and Embroidery,

Hand-knitted Woollen Gloves.

For Illustrated Price List and Samples, apply to—
THE MANAGERESS,
Lady Gore-Booth's School of Needlework,
LISSADELL, Sligo.

96

Sir Robert Gore-Booth, Fourth Baronet (1805-1876)

Building Lissadell

Sir Robert Gore-Booth, the fourth baronet, was born on August 25 1805, the eldest son of Sir Robert Newcomen Gore-Booth and Hannah, daughter of Henry Irwin of Streamstown, County Sligo. His father had assumed the additional surname of Booth almost exactly a year before his heir was born, and it is with this fourth baronet that the real story of the Gore-Booth family begins. Robert was only seven years of age when his father died. As a minor he had to wait 14 years to inherit the property. He was educated at Westminster School and went on to Queen's College, Cambridge gaining an M.A. degree in the same year that he came of age. Eight years later he was admitted to an *ad eundem* degree by Dublin University. On attaining his majority in 1826, he succeeded not only to the Lissadell Estate, but also to the very prosperous Booth estates at Salford and Manchester, an area in the English midlands then rapidly becoming heavily industrialised. These family acquisitions enabled him to indulge freely in his interests in architecture and travel, a combination that eventually led him to make the decision to replace the old house at Lissadell.

Just four months after coming into his inheritance, he married the Honourable Caroline King, second daughter of Robert King, the first Lord Lorton, whose wife was a daughter of the first earl of Rosse. Caroline brought with her a dowry of £10,000 but sadly she died in childbirth along with her first-born child. Two years later, Sir Robert married again, this time to another Caroline – Caroline Goold, noted for her beauty and for her entertaining, whose father, Thomas Goold of Dublin, was a Sergeant at Law who went on to be a Master in Chancery. Caroline brought with her a considerably smaller dowry of between £2,000 and £3,000, but both marriages – especially the first – were considered 'advantageous,' bringing additional wealth and prestige to the family. In that same year, the ties between the Gore-Booth and King families were further strengthened when Robert's sister, Anne, married Caroline's brother, Robert King of Rockingham.

Henry Coulter described Lissadell before Robert inherited the estate as 'wild and miserable and poor looking.' But within a few decades Sir Robert had demonstrated 'the immense improvement which may be made in the appearance of the country and the quality of the soil by the judicious expenditure of capital.' Coulter considered the estate to be:

> one of the most highly cultivated and beautiful in the United Kingdom…. If the excellent example set by Sir Robert Booth as a resident country gentleman – living at home and devoting himself to the improvement of his property – were more generally followed by Irish landlords then indeed the cry of distress which is so often raised … would never more be heard, even in the west of Ireland.

Sir Robert deserves to be remembered as an innovating landlord whose treatment of the Lissadell tenants seems to have been generous and humane, especially during the Great Famine, though there were some later attempts to smear his record during those years, as will be seen. Some of his actions as a younger man during an earlier famine were also the subject of allegations casting doubt upon how well he treated his tenants at that time. He was a man of many interests, which included travel, painting, music; horticulture, and hunting. He was fond of sailing and is known to have cruised to the Outer Hebrides and to the Mediterranean. He was an accomplished musician, owning a Stradivarius 'cello with which he 'used to give three or four recitals in London during the season' and he installed an organ, built by Hull of Dublin, when his new house was completed. A keen hunter and a good rider, he founded and was master of the Lissadell pack of harriers, and actively supported local race meetings as well as field sports. Over and above all these interests, he enjoyed nothing better than fishing in the nearby rivers and lakes.

These activities had to take second place to his responsibilities after his marriage. Besides his family commitments and his work developing the estate, various local institutions, organisations and charities needed attention as did, later on, his duties as a magistrate, as governor of the local mental hospital and the infirmary, as the Lord Lieutenant of the County, and as a Member of Parliament.

As a young man, he was fond of travelling, visiting Italy while still in his twenties, and he also visited the Holy Land. While the new house was being built, Sir Robert and Lady Caroline embarked on a Grand Tour of Europe, collecting mementoes and items to furnish the mansion, including a number of seventeenth-century Italian paintings. Twenty years later, after the death of his wife, he went on a further extensive European tour but only the sketchiest details are now known about any of his travels. One old passport that has survived among the family papers shows that he travelled widely throughout Europe and the Mediterranean. It was stamped in almost a dozen countries including France, Spain, Italy (both in Rome and Naples), Turkey, Saxony and on board a Danube steamer. When Robert's son, Henry, was asked what he knew about his father's travels, his replied: 'We can, so far, trace little of his grand tour abroad, only that he purchased the pictures in Italy that are in the Gallery, also the stones, shells and other objects.' More than a century later, Sir Paul Gore-Booth wrote rather unkindly in his autobiography: 'My great-grandfather, Sir Robert Gore-Booth, went on the Victorian Grand Tour and strained the family fortunes by buying mediocre Italian paintings at high prices.'

Sir Robert's various tours abroad, along with the fact that his father had spent little of his time at Lissadell, gave rise to rumours locally that he might be considering moving to his English estates, abandoning or downgrading his property in Sligo. On his return from one such tour, accompanied by his mother, the relief among his tenants is apparent from the following account published in the *World of Fashion* in 1824:

> Lady Gore-Booth and family have arrived in Lissadell….We rejoice to find that the Lissadell family, who spent a princely fortune in their native country during many generations, have given the surest pledge of their intention to reside in it [and] in Lady Booth's having lately caused considerable additions and improvements to the Mansion house. The return of this old and respectable family was hailed, and deservedly hailed, with the usual expressions of joy, exhibited by a grateful tenantry to a liberal landlord on similar occasions, such as bonfires, music, and taking the horses from the carriages for the purpose of [the tenants] drawing them the last mile of the journey.

The reference to improvements being made to the old mansion in or around 1824 is interesting as this was only a decade or so before it was demolished following Robert's decision to erect an entirely new house. The earlier mansion had, in fact, been standing for less than 80 years. The original house at Lissadell, which Sir Robert had inherited from his father was a relatively modest, bow-fronted building dating from the previous century. It stood quite near the present house but almost on the seashore, so that it was very exposed to the Atlantic weather. His decision to rebuild was probably prompted by the fact that he simply wished to own a more substantial mansion more in keeping with an estate of over 30,000 acres, and one which would reflect the family's greatly improved circumstances. Certainly the reason sometimes advanced for replacing the house – that its situation was too exposed – was hardly sufficient in itself.

Sir Robert decided to allocate the sum of £10,000 for the construction of his new house, and this tight budget was probably a factor when he decided not to commission an architect from the first rank, engaging Francis Goodwin, a relatively little known English architect. His choice was almost certainly influenced by noticing, in the course of his visits to the Booth Estates, the newly-built town hall at Manchester and several public buildings in Salford and Macclesfield which had been designed by Goodwin and which represented this architect's finest works to date. Fortunately for Goodwin, Sir Robert had also been greatly influenced by what he had seen during his travels in Italy and Greece, where he had acquired a taste for neo-classical architecture and desired to have his new house built in that style.

Portrait of Sir Robert as a young man

It may have been no coincidence that the substantial dowry of £10,000 brought to Sir Robert by his unfortunate first wife precisely matched the amount which Sir Robert fixed as his original budget figure. When Goodwin's initial designs for Lissadell exceeded this budget by nearly 50 per cent, Sir Robert made it clear that the plans, rather than the budget, would have to be amended. Goodwin, for his part, was reluctant to omit too many of the features which could make the required £4,500 reduction possible, so his second attempt brought the figure down to £12,256. This was still not enough and Sir Robert forced Goodwin to make two more attempts, until a tender for a total of £11,701 submitted by James Nowell, the contractor, was finally accepted.

As directed, Goodwin designed the house in the neo-classical style, its severe appearance based on Greek revival – the whole in the shape of an uneven letter 'H,' though he managed to make this less than obvious. Goodwin thought very highly of his plans for Lissadell but tactfully wrote that some of the ideas were adaptations of suggestions made by Sir Robert. In fact, Sir Robert had, for his part, borrowed several of his own ideas from Rockingham, where Lord Lorton, the father of his first wife, had commissioned the famous John Nash to build the then new house overlooking Lough Key near Boyle some 20 years earlier. Among the suggestions adopted were the bow front, the top lit gallery, and the tunnel access for the delivery of supplies to the house. This latter feature has been described by Anne Pakenham as the most elaborate in Ireland.

In her *Discourse* on the Lissadell estate, Sophia Chambre outlined Goodwin's career in some detail, especially noting the various influences – including his design for Manchester Town Hall – which were brought to bear in his plans for the house. The fact that he had faced this building with limestone and that it also lacked ornamentation produced, as Chambre noted, 'a very stark effect similar to the effect the Ballisodare limestone creates at Lissadell.' She took the view that the house bore a striking similarity to a public building and perceived that, having been involved in designing churches and other public buildings, Goodwin at this stage wished to turn to domestic architecture and was trying to set up an architectural practice in Ireland.

At Lissadell he had been commissioned by an exacting client who continued to request alterations and modifications to the plans throughout its construction. Anxious to complete his first major domestic assignment, it must have been frustrating for him to have to abandon some of the various elements of his original designs (and some of the revisions too) because of Sir Robert's determination to control costs. Describing the exterior of the house, Goodwin wrote that 'the nature of the material employed in its construction will in great measure account for the plainness of the design, since the working of architraves to the windows, and other ornaments, would have proved very expensive.'

While the house at Lissadell was still under construction, Goodwin published his *Domestic Architecture* in two volumes in order to demonstrate 'a series of designs for mansions, villas, rectory houses, gardener's lodge, gamekeeper's lodge, park gate lodges, etc., in the Grecian, Italian and old English styles of architecture, with

Observations.' It also included a description, with plans, of Lissadell House referring, perhaps tongue in cheek, to the fact that the house 'had been erected for less than the estimate by a considerable sum,' and describing its various features, notably the porte cochiere:

> The principal thing to be remarked in the external design, is that the lower part of the projecting centre of the North front forms an entrance for carriages to drive into, which is closed by gates, because the violence of the wind on this coast is at times so furious that it was necessary to provide shelter against it; and it is accordingly intended, that whenever such is the case, one of the gates shall be closed in order that visitors may alight without being annoyed by it.

Many years later, this was to have an additional, defensive function (along with some other features, such as the spy-hole in the hall door and the iron bars in the basement windows), when agrarian unrest became a serious cause for concern for many Anglo-Irish families. Goodwin also laid great emphasis on the placing of all the domestic quarters out of sight, stating that:

> Another great recommendation attending placing the offices as has been done at Lissadell, is that an unobstructed view may be obtained from every front of the house, and also that the pleasure grounds may be continued quite round it, without interruption from out-buildings, courts, &c. In order to secure this advantage to his mansion in the fullest extent, it is Sir Robert's intention to form a convenient subway to the offices for the conveyance of whatever the establishment requires … .

Goodwin's two volumes of plans included his estimated costs for the various suggested buildings but in the case of Lissadell, he was careful to point out that:

> As it would be improper for us to state the exact cost of this mansion, we shall only observe that a similar one might be erected in England, in brick with stone dressings, for a sum between £14,000, and £15,000, or with all the fronts faced with stone, for about £18,000.

Also included in his volumes were drawings and plans for a gate lodge and ornate gates for 'the Principal Park Entrance to Lissadell Court,' complete with what he called a telegraph tower. This feature was:

> hereafter to be attached to this entrance into the park, besides forming, as it will, a pleasing architectural object as beheld from the country around, [it] will command an extensive prospect from its upper part, while it will prove of direct utility by affording the means of telegraphic communication with the adjoining estates.

Goodwin's estimate of the cost of the lodge and cast iron gates was £2,270 but this work was never undertaken. Indeed the fact that the cost was specifically stated while that of the house was not, suggests that he already knew Sir Robert had turned these plans down. As a result of completing Lissadell, Goodwin secured two or three further contracts in Ireland including an ornate gate lodge at Markree Castle near Colooney. Its castellated design, complete with a tower, has caused some people to assume, wrongly, that it was constructed from his rejected plans for a gate lodge at Lissadell.

At first sight Lissadell House seems to lack any ornamentation because the architectural detail is so subtle. Each of the four facades is different, the north exterior, which meets the eye on approaching the house, has been described as having the appearance of a Greek temple, with an imposing facade designed to impress the visitor. The bow windows, which form the main feature of the south façade, and which afford a wonderful view from the library, have been immortalised in Yeats's often quoted lines: 'The light of evening, Lissadell,/Great windows, open to the South ...'

O'Rorke thought that the house had a 'simple but classic elegance ... without turret or pinnacle, without pier or buttress, without crocket, niche or canopy, without any of those semi-detached appendages which architects sometimes tack onto their work to arrest attention.' In his biography of Yeats, Roy Foster described Lissadell as 'that austere neo-classical mansion on the Roughley peninsula, lost among woods and avenues' while Yeats himself thought it 'an exceedingly impressive house inside with a great sitting room as high as a church ... but outside it is grey, square and bare.' Seán O'Reilly commented that 'neither the pocket of the patron ... nor the taste of the architect suggest any further inclination to enrich the exterior' and added that 'Lissadell remains the fixed testimony to [Goodwin's] abilities as a domestic architect, if also to his limitations.' Maurice Craig's description bore more than a hint of some reservation when he wrote that the house was 'distinguished more by it solidity than by suavity, and more by literary association than by either.' His view might appear to echo the irony that when the house was being built, the Wynnes – not the Gore-Booths – were the most prominent local landed family. Yet, when the Gore-Booths subsequently overshadowed the Wynnes, the area became almost universally known not as the Gore-Booth country, but as 'the Yeats country,' notwithstanding the fact that the Yeats family could hardly have been classed as landowners.

If the exterior of Lissadell House is seen by some to be disappointingly plain, Goodwin's design ensured that the entrance to the interior was all the more unexpected and dramatic. The visitor is met by a spectacularly high entrance hall decorated with Doric and Ionic columns from which there is an impressive staircase of Kilkenny marble with cast iron ballustrades leading to the building's most important feature, the great gallery, lit by sky-lights high above. On Goodwin's plans, the gallery is marked as the music room, reflecting one of Sir Robert's tastes, where an organ was installed. In the main, the house then remained largely unaltered for more than a century and a half.

Lissadell House. Goodwin intended that the height of the hall should give 'some idea of the grandeur intended in the Imperial Procession to the bedrooms'.

There is some suggestion that after Sir Robert decided to replace the original house and when the contract for the building work was being prepared, Thomas Goold, his father-in-law by his second marriage, may have financed the cost of the specially commissioned new furniture. Mark Bence-Jones noted that Goold stayed at the house as it neared completion, and quoted a letter sent by him to Lord Dunraven describing how he found himself: 'greatly benefited by it. The air is balmy to a degree and a more gay and joyous party could not be. Sir Robert's house is really beautiful, the demesne has all the great features of sea, mountain and by varying form of ground.'

While the house was still being completed, Sir Robert set-off for an extensive tour of Europe with Lady Gore-Booth, leaving his agent in charge of affairs. It was fashionable at this time for wealthy people to embark on what came to be known as 'The Grand Tour,' usually incorporating visits to the major European cities and often concentrating on classical Greece and Italy. For the duration of this 1836 tour, Sir Robert appointed the agent, George Dodwell, a power of attorney to act in his absence. Various difficulties with the builders presented Dodwell with a whole series of problems, causing him to write several times to Sir Robert while he was abroad. In one of his letters, which reached Sir Robert in Rome, Dodwell informed him that 'the greater part of the rendering of the roof is either come off or is quite loose,' besides which, he added that the window sills 'admit a great quantity of wet.' Dodwell's anxiety is obvious at the end of the letter: 'I would not wish to see either meddled with in your absence ... I do not wish to go near the house, there are so many matters to complain of.'

Even while the house was still under construction, Sir Robert was hoping for an opportunity to acquire more land near Lissadell. No suitable property came on the market until the Fitzmaurice family, earls of Orkney, decided to sell their Ballymote estate in the south of the county. The resulting enlargement of the family holding in Sligo was achieved by considerably reducing the property at Manchester and Salford, thus diminishing a dependable source of revenue from the industrial English midlands in order to invest in Irish land, the income from which was heavily dependent on factors over which Sir Robert had limited control. Poor harvests resulting from bad weather were a recurring problem for all landlords even without the unforeseen and disastrous onset of the potato blight little more than a decade later. Following the purchase of the Ballymote estate, which included most of the town, a patent for the holding of fairs there was granted to Sir Robert, which for a century before had been held by the Fitzmaurice family, having been held originally by Sir James Fullerton since 1604.

Most the original furniture for the main rooms of the house was commissioned in a single order at this time from the highly regarded Dublin firm of Williams and Gibton. Angela Alexander, who wrote the introduction to the auctioneer's catalogue in 2002, when surplus items from Lissadell were sold, referred to the company's unparalleled standing at the time, supplying furniture for the Vice-Regal Lodge, Dublin Castle, the Chapel Royal, the Four Courts and other significant buildings in Dublin. She recounted how Williams and Gibton had produced for Lissadell 'furniture in a wide variety of styles to suit the different spaces and uses.' She also noted that the mansion 'is an important survival of the firm's work for a country house at this date and shows the amount and variety of furniture considered necessary to furnish a house of this size. As such it is a large and significant collection.

When the mansion was finally completed, Lissadell was the first in Ireland to be lit by its own gas supply. This was produced in a plant installed by Sir Robert about a quarter of a mile to the west of the mansion, complete with a house for the manager in charge of the works. The cost of the 'gas appliance' was just under £500. Each evening, gas men lit all the rooms and remained in attendance in case of an escape of gas. Thomas Kilgallon, who was to become Sir Henry's valet and whose story is dealt with in the next chapter, once described Lissadell on the night of a ball:

> When fully lit up, to me it looked like what fairyland could be like in my imagination at the time, with all the different coloured dresses of the ladies flitting about. The great number of footmen in their red plush breeches and vests, the music from the band over the door as you entered the gallery, the pillars wreathed with flowers. It was a sight worth seeing. Sir Robert had all the gassaliers fully lit in all the reception rooms.

Almost three decades after the house was completed, Frazer's handbook for travellers described the house as a spacious, modern mansion, surrounded by an extensive park where:

> the corresponding plantations and the arrangement of the grounds which constitute this large demesne will not only interest those fond of rural improvements, but [will] at the same time show how much may be achieved by industry and perseverance, even in places such as Lissadill, which are greatly exposed to the fury of the Atlantic.

The site for the house was a sloping hillside which, before construction began, was excavated to provide a level platform for the house and its immediate surroundings, and the surplus soil was carted forward to provide what was later to become a croquet lawn. Sir Robert had a special interest in horticulture and as soon as the house had been completed, he provided it with shelter belts which as they matured enabled him to introduce less hardy ornamental trees and shrubs. Sir Robert established a large walled garden, two acres in extent which, besides providing the household with vegetables and fruit, was stocked with shrubs and plants. From very early on, he took a special interest in the many exotic trees and shrubs which were then being imported into Europe for the first time. Records exist of plants and seeds sent to him by others having a similar interest, including the future prime minister, Lord Palmerston, whose Classiebawn estate lay about ten miles to the north, and by Owen Wynne, at Hazelwood, a few miles to the south. Palmerston sent what he called 'Indian seeds' to Sir Robert in 1826, with the suggestion that he might like 'to add some of these evergreens to the groves of Lisadell.' A year earlier, Palmerston had sent seeds of what he called the 'Deodara Cedar tree' in the hope that 'they may contribute to the future adornment of Lisadell.' According to the dendrologist, Edward Step, the Deodar Cedar (*Cedrus deodara*) was first introduced into Britain from the western Himalayas in 1831, a fact confirmed in the seminal work on the subject by Elwes and Henry. This is interesting as it indicates that its introduction into Ireland seems to have occurred at least six years earlier.

Elsewhere in the demesne there is an ice-house, a bee-hive like structure built of brick and stone, which probably pre-dated the present Lissadell House. A major addition to the property was a quadrangle of two-storey stable buildings which included a large riding school for exercising horses under cover. When the idea of an annual 'Harvest Home' was introduced, at which the estate workers and tenants were liberally entertained by, and attended upon by the family, this took place in the riding school. The Estate Office, where the estate records were kept, was located in this same block of buildings.

* * *

Sir Robert became, in turn, a Magistrate, Grand Juror and Lieutenant of the county, and after successfully standing for election at the end of the Famine, he held the seat for the remainder of his life. He was also involved in many aspects of local business. When the Sligo Savings Bank was set up, Sir Robert became a trustee for some time, as did two of his agents, George Dodwell and Vernon Davys. Another agent during Sir Robert's time was Edward Bailey, the sculptor (1777–1869), who had fallen upon bad times. Reputedly careless with money, he was declared bankrupt in 1836, and while nothing about his term at Lissadell seems to have survived in the family papers, it seems probable that Sir Robert employed him for a time out of sympathy for his situation.

As already mentioned, north of Lissadell, near Cliffoney, lies Classiebawn Castle which Lord Palmerston, then Minister for War, had commenced building a few years earlier. Despite being largely an absentee landlord, he was certainly an improving one, and commentators at the time spoke highly of him, though there are doubts about how he cared for his Irish tenants during the Great Famine. In 1822, he engaged the well known engineer, Alexander Nimmo, for some of his construction work including the building of a harbour at Mullaghmore as well as estate houses in Cliffoney village. Palmerston's improvements, his cultivation methods, his housing and schools, the new harbour, etc., are interesting because some of his ideas influenced the young Sir Robert Gore-Booth to embark upon similar projects. One of these was the building of a small harbour at Raghley for which he too engaged Nimmo.

Population levels continued to rise alarmingly in Ireland despite regular visitations of famine and disease, a situation that was already a cause for concern as early as 1831 when the government decided to set up the Poor Law Enquiry Commission. Apart from the obvious fact that the fast-growing population could not be matched by any appreciable increase in the amount of suitable land, there were additional problems caused by the lack of employment, poverty and vagrancy. The commission came to the conclusion that emigration offered the only solution and suggested that those who could not find sufficient money should be given free passage to one of the colonies. Nothing came of this at the time, because government intervention of this nature was deemed politically unacceptable, but a decade later the Devon Commission of Inquiry into land tenure came to a similar conclusion, seeing emigration as the only feasible solution to the problem.

Many proprietors having a large percentage of tenants who habitually found difficulty in paying rents, decided that it made economic sense to re-organise their estates by increasing the size of individual holdings. This could only be done by reducing the number of tenants. If this ensured the landlord's income, it was not only good for him but also for the tenants who remained. For those displaced, however, the result was drastic. If the landlord made no provision for them (and he was under no legal obligation to do so), their situation was at best wretched and at worst fatal. Some landlords offered the evicted tenants alternative holdings almost invariably on inferior, marginal land. The best hope for dispossessed tenants was an offer of compensation, along with the payment of the cost of a voyage across the Atlantic and an additional sum to help the ex-tenant to start a fresh life in the New World.

Only a minority of landlords were prepared (or were in a position) to be so generous. Evictions were not confined to Ireland, and the experience in nearby Scotland, where clearances were often no less ruthless, serves as a reminder of this. Evictions in the two countries actually differed in several respects – notably in that the removal of tenants in Scotland was usually effected, not to facilitate the re-ordering of the tenants' holdings, but in order to replace human beings by Cheviot sheep. These clearances forced so many evicted Scotsmen to find a new living by enlisting in the Highland regiments that, as John Prebble wrote concerning the clearances, 'the great Cheviot Sheep won more battles in the Napoleonic Wars than regimental historians have acknowledged.'

The estate surrounding the new Lissadell House comprised more than 30,000 acres spread across 40 townlands. It soon began to show the effects of Sir Robert's improving works, though one of these schemes was to cause controversy and put a question mark over his generally humane treatment of the tenants.

When famine struck in 1831, he provided food for his starving tenants, but a few years later Sir Robert engaged in his first attempt at removing tenants from the Ballygilgan part of the estate. During 1836 he decided to annex these 800 acres of good cattle grazing lands adjoining Lissadell, known locally as the Seven Cartrons, because the lease, which had belonged to a middleman, had fallen-in. He arranged with Lord Leitrim, who also had an interest, to get possession from the various tenants, most of whom were farmers and fishermen with holdings of no more than one or two acres. Concluding that such plots were too small to enable the occupiers to make a reasonable living, and that the inevitable consequence of this was an inability to pay the rents, he decided to take what he regarded as remedial action. By way of compensation, he offered the 52 families that he wished to remove a choice of taking land elsewhere on the estate or, alternatively accepting paid passages to North America. Not one tenant chose the first option, as the alternative land was inferior. Although the second option included £2 per head for 'disturbance' and £4 for every improved acre of land – somewhat better than the going rate at the time – claims were made that the tenants were ruthlessly evicted.

Many years later, Sir Robert had to give evidence to the Devon Commission about this matter and he asserted that 'all the tenants, except two or three, gave permission [their agreement] to Martin [the middleman involved] and, to those who acted thus, land was offered elsewhere.' No reference was made to the condition of that land or where it was situated. While undoubtedly faced with something of a Hobson's Choice, the tenants were not simply thrown out on to the road and left to fend for themselves. When they opted to accept emigration as the lesser of two evils, the records clearly show that Sir Robert took some trouble to personally oversee the provisioning of the ship he chartered 'for the purpose.

Nevertheless, it can hardly be disputed that the Ballygilgan families were effectively evicted. The incident left a black mark on Sir Robert's name, and much capital was made of it several decades later. Some versions of the incident failed to mention the compensation offered, let alone that it was better than the average for that time, and few accounts gave him credit for the fact that he personally supervised the provisioning of the chartered ship, the *Pomona*. Incidentally, according to the local historian, John C. McTernan, Sir Robert paid the fare for Richard Yeats, the poet's grand-uncle, to travel with the Ballygilgan tenants to Canada.

After the vessel had sailed, a wild rumour circulated that it sank during the crossing, drowning all on board. In order to dramatise this story, many of the much later accounts claimed this 'coffin ship' sank before it left Sligo Bay. Such stories, without proof or foundation, when repeated often enough, gain a degree of credibility that becomes almost impossible to refute.

The allegation has continued to be related – with various embellishments – for more than a century and a half, and even during the past few decades several books have been published repeating the allegation that the *Pomona* sank and all aboard were drowned. A recent example occurred in a book about the civil war by Tim Pat Coogan and George Morrison, where the tale was repeated that 'a whole shipload of emigrants was drowned within sight of shore,' the story being then attributed to a very unlikely source, namely Gore-Booth 'family tradition.' A similar version had already been aired in two of the biographies of Constance Markievicz. Jaqueline van Voris embellished the story with the detail that the chartered ship had both a fiendish captain and a false bottom, encouraging the author to pose the question – without attempting to answer it – why the captain would contract to drown himself. In Diana Norman's biography, the claim was made 'that the

boat Sir Robert hired … was a typical coffin ship, which sank outside
Sligo Bay with the loss of all lives.' She then proceeded to damn Sir
Robert and his heirs with the afterthought: 'Perhaps not surprisingly, no
evidence for this survives in the family papers,' the intended inference
being, apparently, that the Gore-Booths deliberately destroyed any
awkward evidence. It is true that no evidence of the sinking of the *Pomona*
in Sligo Bay is to be found among the Lissadell Papers, but finding the
evidence anywhere else would be equally difficult.

Within the past decade, another book, written about the history of the
locality by Joe McGowan, gave both versions of the story, and included
a ballad based on the invented account, one verse of which ran:

> Many's the lad and pretty lass, that evening on the shore,
> Lamenting for their own sweethearts they'd never see them more,
> They're sailing on the ocean to a place they do not know,
> And they'll mourn tonight for their heart's delight.
> On board the Pomono.

The truth about the *Pomona* can be established from *Lloyd's Register
of Shipping.* In contrast to the other colourful versions, it makes for
rather dull reading, simply recording that the *Pomona* sailed from Sligo
for Quebec on May 31, 1839, returning to Kingstown, where she arrived
on August 29, and from there she sailed for Sierra Leone on October
19. The *Register* also records that the *Pomona* made several later
voyages from Ireland to the New World.

If Ballygilgan had provided Sir Robert with one kind of problem, the
coastal region around Ardtarmon and Raghley (or Raughley) provided
him with another. Before the 1845 famine, his agent had reported that,
although the former extended to 145 acres, only 40 were arable, the
remainder being 'sand and marsh.' Living in this exposed and windswept
townland at the far north-west point of Sligo Bay were over 30 families
– about 200 people – and all but two of the tenants had been in arrears
of rent since 1840, 'not one of them having paid a farthing.'

The desolate scene created by wind-blown sands along this exposed
coast, a problem that had long existed but had begun to worsen during
the 1830s, attracted the attention of a number of writers at the time.
Samuel Lewis, in his *Topography*, described the conditions endured by
the unfortunate people in the affected parts of the parishes of Drumcliff
and Ahamlish, an area comprising 'a sinuous belt of sandhills and poor
ground along the western shore.' The worst affected part was the area
around Ardtarmon and Ballintemple, west of Lissadell, and further north

at Mullaghmore where, in the space of a few years, over 1,000 acres were covered in sand, in some places deep enough to bury cottages and even a church. In 1841, the *Sligo Champion* recalled that this part of the Gore-Booth estate had formerly been:

> one of the most flourishing in the county, and the soil could not be surpassed for richness and fertility. By contrast, however, some 800 acres is no more than a sand bank [and] most of the miserable occupants can only enter their cheerless dwellings by the chimneys.

This encroachment had been watched helplessly by landlords and tenants alike until Lord Palmerston began experimenting at Mullaghmore with the planting of bent-grass. This had been found to be effective along the Atlantic coast of south-west France, trapping and binding sand and thus reducing drifting for long enough to allow other vegetation to form a more permanent cover. The fact that Maritime Pine trees were also introduced into the same Camargue region with considerable success, would seem to lend credence to the possibility that Palmerston had heard about the effect these trees had in stabilising sandy soils and providing effective shelter belts. His success prompted several other landlords in the area, including Sir Robert, to adopt the same methods, but the latter had a further problem at Raughley. The land to the west of Ardtarmon tapers and curls around the northern extremity of Sligo Bay, and terminates at Raughley Point and its small harbour. The neck of Raughley Point, which had been protected for centuries by a high shingle bank, was threatened at this time when severe Atlantic storms began to erode the protective shingle at the rate of one foot per annum. During a further storm, the bank was actually breached, allowing the tide to overrun the sand hills that formed the neck of connecting land. Bent grasses, hurriedly planted, once again provided the answer, and these have been augmented in modern times by large boulders, deposited by heavy machinery, to prevent the point from being converted into an island.

During the period between the Ballygilgan evictions and the Great Famine, Sir Robert continued his programme of improving his estate, encouraging and assisting the emigration of tenants in order to facilitate the enlargement of individual holdings. Between 1838 and 1841, he assisted more than 250 of his tenants to leave, paying their passage along with additional allowances. Most of those removed by Sir Robert were either tenants who had been unable to pay rents for between three and ten years or who indicated that they wished to emigrate voluntarily.

The two decades preceding the Great Famine saw the first serious attempts at large-scale land improvement. The benefits of land drainage was only then becoming generally recognised and the more progressive landlords embarked upon ambitious schemes to bring the poorer parts of their estates into better production. These schemes involved much road building, and Pentland Hart, one of the Commissioners appointed to enquire into the 'conditions of the poorer classes in Ireland' in 1853, noted that Sir Robert had built 68 miles of roads. About 20 miles north of Lissadell, another landlord, John Hamilton at Ballintra, spent on an extravagant scale both in building roads and draining land on his large estate. During the summer of 1845 he had toured around parts of Ireland, mostly in Galway and Mayo but also in parts of Sligo, to observe the methods being utilised by other landlords and to assess their effectiveness. Just as Hamilton had, by 1845, built up an efficiently run estate populated by a contented tenantry, so too had Sir Robert Gore-Booth, though while the latter's endeavours brought increased wealth, in Hamilton's case his reckless expenditure ultimately led him to the brink of bankruptcy.[1]

Just over a year before the onset of the Great Famine, the Devon Commission of Inquiry was set up to investigate land tenure, and over 1,000 witnesses made oral submissions. The Commissioners, who included among their number John Wynne of Hazelwood, sat in Sligo during July, 1844 and among the witnesses called was Sir Robert Gore-Booth who, as already mentioned, was questioned about the events at Ballygilgan a decade earlier. Several of Sir Robert's tenants were also questioned at length, including Francis Barber of Rahelly, near Carney. He informed the Commission that he held 160 acres on a lease of three lives at what he considered a fair rent, and he had made improvements to his holding costing £1,300 over the previous 20 years. In his memoirs, Barber wrote that he was 13 years old when his father died, leaving his mother to raise eleven children. Young Barber set about improving the holding, which he described as being in a wretched condition and, after several years of hard work, Sir Robert's agent informed him that, because of his perseverance, he was entitled to a larger farm, and 50 acres were added to the original 27. After further improvements Sir Robert gave Barber a lease at a reduced rate of four shillings and sixpence an acre, and the farm was extended to 160 acres. Barber wrote of this period:

---

[1] See Dermot James, *John Hamilton of Donegal* (Dublin, 1998).

> The whole of this land I have improved, and have laid out upon it no less a sum than £1,300, every shilling of which was created by my own industry. I have paid my father's debts and supported my mother and her family and, according to the custom of the country here, have given portions befitting their station as farmer's daughters, to six of my sisters.... From having a small farm at will, much of it swamp and feeding snipe and wild duck, I have now got a large well cultivated farm on lease, which will amply repay me all my outlay. I am now a substantial farmer.

Francis Barber's remarkable success story attracted much attention, especially from several newspapers. According to *The Times* (in March 1881), Barber was the largest tenant in the Lissadell estate. That article described how, over a period of 40 years, Barber had transformed his enlarged holding and so pleased was Sir Robert Gore-Booth with this hard working and efficient tenant that 'he granted him, unasked, a lease for three lives.' Barber's reaction to this was the building of 'a handsome three-storey house ... in the Elizabethan style ... entered by a gateway with a lofty tower and gilt cock on the top which forms a conspicuous object.' By this time, Barber had a further holding at Castlegarron as well as mountain pasture at Gleniff.

He branched into other enterprises, notably road contracting, giving substantial employment in the area, but when he secured the tender for a major sewage system in Sligo town, it unexpectedly involved rock-blasting and Barber was faced with claims for damage caused to various properties. Already over-stretched by borrowings, he had to mortgage his farm at Rahelly and accepted a loan from his landlord, by then (in 1880) Sir Henry Gore-Booth. Barber surrendered his interest in his farm for the sum of £3,250 – the amount he owed – with the stipulation that the property would be handed back once the indebtedness, including the interest, was repaid. He moved to Castlegrove where he lived for eight years, and died at the age of 88. Rahelly House was subsequently occupied by the Lissadell agent, James Cooper, until his departure in 1918, and it was destroyed by fire during the civil war in 1922.

Before the onset of the Famine, the tenants at Lissadell were benefiting from greatly improved holdings, and the fact that Sir Robert had managed to put the estate in good order was to prove crucial for both its survival, and for the survival of the tenants when the hitherto unknown potato blight struck over the next three or four years. Long before the blight arrived in Ireland, Irish newspapers carried reports of the phenomenon in America, and during the month of June 1846, disturbing news appeared in some newspapers about a potato disease which had broken out, first in Belgium and then in other European countries. Two months later, there were reports of the mysterious disease spreading across England and it arrived in Ireland during September, when it continued to spread in a south-east to north-west direction so that Sligo was one of the last places to be affected.

Some landlords had learned lessons from the experience of the severe, though short-lived famine of 1831, enabling them to cope more effectively when the 1845 famine struck, but there is little indication that any such lessons were learned by the government. Hopes that the blight was to be a one-off attack were dashed when, in 1846, rotting tubers began to be noticed much earlier in the season and the situation was aggravated because, following a change of government, Sir Robert Peel's 1845 remedial measures were cancelled by Lord John Russell.

When Sir Robert had asked the Board of Works to send a representative to inspect the situation locally, a Captain O'Brien arrived and wrote a detailed report which confirmed the situation as Sir Robert saw it. The very first farm that O'Brien visited comprised 12 acres and supported no less than 32 people. The three families involved had been offered £60 to give up their land a year earlier but had decided to continue to live in wretched conditions described by O'Brien who saw there:

> A widow lying on the ground in fever, and unable to move. The children were bloated in their faces and bodies, the limbs were withered to bones and sinews, with rags on them. They had been found that day gnawing the flesh from the bones of a pig which had died in an outhouse.

Conditions similar to these were encountered by Captain O'Brien throughout those properties lying between Lissadell and Cliffony where the landlords either could not be bothered or simply did not have the means to do anything for their unfortunate tenants. The social condition of these people, O'Brien noted, 'must at all times have been wretched in the extreme. From Sligo to Ballyshannon it is like a rabbit warren.'

When Russell's government shifted the responsibility for the tenants away from itself and on to the landlords, it probably considered that it had arrived at a perfectly logical solution. One of the reasons why this policy failed was because of the decision to administer the scheme on a basis that divided the whole country into Poor Law Divisions that lumped well-run and badly-run estates together. John Hamilton, whose estate at Ballintra has already been mentioned, campaigned to have the system changed so that each individual landlord would be responsible for his own tenants. Like Sir Robert Gore-Booth, Hamilton's estate was in a sound condition when the potato blight arrived in the north-west. Both men had undertaken large-scale schemes to improve their property. The majority of their tenants were relatively well off and able to pay their rents, and both landlords had reacted quickly to the crisis by importing food, establishing food kitchens and setting up mills, etc. Hamilton made repeated submissions to the Chief Secretary and to the Lord Lieutenant, and he had also travelled to London to make the point to the Treasury that it was grossly unfair to expect what he called the 'willing' landlords to take care of their own tenants in addition to those of the neighbouring landlords who would not or could not look after their own. Such a system, he argued, simply encouraged those who were doing nothing to continue doing nothing.

Lissadell House: The Gallery—generally considered to be the most impressive feature of the mansion—drawn by T.P. Flanagan.

While surviving correspondence does not indicate the same level of campaigning to change the system on the part of Sir Robert, there can be no doubt that his views broadly accorded with those of Hamilton. When Captain O'Brien reported to the Board of Works he mentioned that 'Sir Robert Gore Booth's estate is large and the supplies he has procured would keep those of his own estate well enough, were he not pressed to feed his neighbour's tenants.'

If Sir Robert did not campaign as actively as Hamilton in order to persuade the government to alter its policy of lumping good and bad landlords together, he more than made up for this, as far as his own tenants were concerned, by procuring food supplies, installing and running soup kitchens, and by the provision of seed. He was helped in this by Lady Gore-Booth, who not only assisted in distributing the food to the tenants' cottages and at the soup kitchens, but also raised money for relief from friends and acquaintances – she even managed to persuade the prime minister, Lord John Russell, to contribute £100. In a letter to the Select Committee, her husband attested to Lady Gore-Booth's work on behalf of the poor, relating how she had been distributing food and medicine, and had, on one occasion, gone out alone because of his own illness.

Even leaving aside his generosity in providing food, clothing and medicine at his own expense, he made a particular point of supervising everything which he arranged, ensuring not only a fair distribution but also preventing the misappropriation of scarce materials. His strong presence would have been a deterrent to anyone who might have thought of making-off with a sack of provisions, a fairly common occurrence elsewhere at this time. Besides serving on several local relief committees, he was a member of the Board of Guardians and Chairman of the Grand Jury, and could thus implement government policy in his area in tandem with his personal responses in both effort and money. He was also well placed to influence proposals regarding plans to run local relief works, if necessary, in his own interest. For example, he rejected a plan to build a new relief road from Sligo to Raughley that, in his view, was too close to Lissadell House. Road building formed by far the greater part of relief works, a policy widely criticised because so many of the new roads 'began nowhere and ended nowhere.'

In 1847, the government decided to replace the relief works by soup kitchens, and Sir Robert became Chairman of the Central Finance committee formed to provision the new food relief centres. During the period from August 1846 to July 1847, he had expended around £35,000 of his own money on importing and distributing food, and while he was able to record a small profit in the early stages, from then on his relief schemes were run at a loss. After a period of trying without success to persuade the government to subsidise the transportation of food, the government eventually changed its policy – possibly through the intervention of Captain O'Brien of the Board of Works. It seems that O'Brien had given a favourable report to his superior, Lieut. Col. Jones, about the work being done at and around Lissadell, and had strongly recommended that assistance should be given to Sir Robert and others acting like him. The Quaker, James Hack Tuke, reported to the Society of Friends on the efforts being made by Sir Robert:

> He has established soup boilers, which make 140 gallons of soup. He gives, gratuitously, 280 gallons per day, every day including Sundays. He sells, six days in the week, 150 loaves a day, each being four ounces larger than the four pence loaf sold in Sligo, and sold by him at two pence per loaf. From what I have stated it is no exaggeration to affirm that the people are dying from starvation by dozens daily, but for Sir Robert Gore-Booth they would be dying by fifties.

These details were confirmed during the debate in the House of Commons on the Irish Poor Relief Bill, when part of a letter written by Captain O'Brien of the Board of Works, which referred to Sir Robert's actions in County Sligo, was read to the chamber by Mr Labouchere. After quoting Tuke, Labouchere's account then continued:

> He also sells 30 tons of Indian corn per week at a reduced price, and he gives a portion of Indian corn to 30 persons daily. In this manner he has provided for the poor, and sold through the agency of his chaplain, Mr Jeffcote, since the 28th August, Indian meal, 393 tons; barrel flour, 70 tons; white wheat flour, 40 tons; biscuit, 9 tons; rice, 3 tons; oatmeal, 12 tons; total 527 tons.... He has now in Greenock, ready to be shipped, but he is in difficulty respecting freight, 200 quarter of oats, 23 barrels of barley, 200 loads of beans, 18 tons of pease, 100 barrels of flour, 180 barrels of wheat, 99 tons of oats, 25 tons of barley meal. Much good could have been done if the government could assist Sir Robert Gore-Booth in having this large quantity of food transported to Sligo ....

Labouchere added that he was happy to say 'that the government had made the necessary arrangements for affording the required facilities for transporting the grain so provided, by means of steamboat.' (Cheers).

Father O'Gara, parish priest of Drumcliff, was another who, on behalf of the local people, attested to the good work being done by the Gore-Booth family and contrasted their actions on behalf of the poor with the poor example set by some of the other landlords in the area. The fact that Sir Robert extended his personal relief works far beyond the boundary walls of his demesne, at least as far as Mullaghmore ten miles to the north, raises an interesting point about Lord Palmerston, the proprietor there.

Palmerston's role during the Famine is unclear. He was an absentee from his Mullaghmore estate and it is easy to conclude that he was, therefore, a bad landlord. But absentee landlords were not necessarily bad, notably those who, though absent locally, lived elsewhere in Ireland. Henry John Temple, the third Viscount Palmerston, was already Secretary of War when Sir Robert succeeded his father, and he became Secretary of State for Foreign Affairs in 1830 when he was largely responsible for the creation of Belgium as a separate state. Under Lord John Russell's Whig administration he became Foreign Secretary, living for the most part in the family estate at Broadlands in Hampshire. Following the return of the Whig government in 1846, he was serving as Foreign Secretary under Prime Minister Russell, and eight years later he was to become Prime Minister, a post he was to hold on three separate occasions. His estate at Mullaghmore, as noted earlier, appears to have been well run and his reputation has survived as that of an innovating landlord. He co-operated with Sir Robert Gore-Booth in chartering a number of ships to transplant families to Canada, and chartered further vessels on his own account. He also shared in Sir Robert's arrangements to import 200 tons of Indian corn in 1847, two-thirds of which Sir Robert used for his own tenants, and the remainder was sold on to Palmerston and to several other local proprietors.

The proximity of Lord Palmerston's estate resulted in friendly relationships between the two families, but Sir Robert found himself having to assist Palmerston's tenants during what came to be known as 'Black '47.' If Sir Robert was irritated because he felt obliged to come to the assistance of Palmerston's tenants, there is no evidence of it among the surviving correspondence. Conditions for other neighbouring tenants, including those of Sir Gilbert King, Captain Michael Kelly and Charles Gore Jones were a good deal worse, but even the people living on those estates were also recipients of Sir Robert's charity to some degree at least. A less benevolent man could have averted his eyes and disclaimed any responsibility for evident suffering outside the walls of his own property but, in this sense at least, Sir Robert's charity knew no bounds.

The knock-on effects of the Famine can hardly be exaggerated. Apart from the obvious fact that potatoes were almost unobtainable, most of the alternatives were, because of cost, beyond the reach of those who most needed them. The near total destruction of the potato crop also meant that there was little or no seed for sowing in the following year, and the bad harvests additionally resulted in a greatly reduced need for labourers, whose families joined the ever-growing numbers of the impoverished. Sir Robert wrote at this time:

> The distress cannot be imagined – it must be seen, but I am happy to say that very little exists on my own property or those portions of it over which I have control. Some leased lands are in a miserable state but the districts worst off are owned by absentee landlords or those too poor to give any assistance – it is not easy for those who have not received their rents to give … I find this myself, but my property being without debt, I can carry on for a little, although it is a hard case to have to burthen one's property with debt for others – but we must keep [the] creatures alive at any cost.

How Sir Robert Gore-Booth was attempting to achieve this is indicated in a news item in the *Sligo Journal* in March 1846 where it was reported that he 'had every tenant on his extensive property … profitably occupied other than on the public works.'

The relief work undertaken by the Society of Friends (the Quakers) during the Famine has often been praised and deservedly so. Though small in numbers, they organised relief in a remarkably focused manner when so much expenditure and effort – especially on the part of the government – was dissipated by red tape, mismanagement and sometimes by corrupt officials. The Quakers were careful to assess the various situations locally and kept detailed records of what needed to be done. One of their number, William Bennett, reported in March 1847 on the situation in County Sligo, where he found 1,200 destitute families in the parish of Mullaghmore 'despite the employment afforded by Lord Palmerston.' What he had to say about Lissadell during that worst year of the famine is, of course, even more interesting. He wrote: 'Sir Robert Gore-Booth had 280 men at work and there were some 300 on public works, nevertheless, 200 families were in extreme distress and the supply of Indian meal had been exhausted.'

Sligo became the main food depot for the north-west, and sub-depots were established throughout the region, the nearest one to Lissadell being at the Coastguard Station at Raughley. However Sir Robert opened a food depot at his own expense at Lissadell (as did John Wynne at Hazelwood). Landlords were responsible for paying the rates of their tenants whose rents were less than £4 a year, so when conditions worsened and tenants could not even pay the rents, let alone the rates, the landlords found themselves forced to take action or face bankruptcy. James S. Donnelly, in his contribution about landlords and tenants in *A New History of Ireland*, wrote that: 'the two most serious problems facing landlords, especially in the west and south, were those of collecting rents and finding the means, out of their diminished incomes, to discharge heavy Poor Rates, and to provide additional employment.'

Sir Robert was aware that inaction would result in bankruptcy, but he was determined to execute his own policy with humanity and generosity. His well-run estate placed him in a better position than most to do this, and he was probably anxious to avoid facing the reaction provoked by his earlier evictions in 1836. He had begun the process of reorganising his land to give the tenants holdings of not less than five acres, although he had more recently come to the conclusion that even five acres was insufficient to put a tenant into a position where he might have a reasonable chance to pay rents on time. Looking to the future, he wanted to be in a position to increase all his tenants' holdings to 25 acres, but whatever increase was arrived at could only be achieved by the removal of a percentage of his tenants. He even submitted a scheme to the government suggesting that if he was granted land in Canada, he would settle families from Lissadell on farms of 100 acres each, enabling whole families to emigrate together and to do so with other families from the area as an integrated community. Nothing came of this even though a number of other proprietors came up with similar ideas.

Conditions around Ardtarmon continued to be among the worst on his estate, and he submitted plans for dealing with this townland to the Committee for Colonisation, viewing it as a case study in the problem of over-population. Sir Robert made the point in his report that only about one quarter of the 145 acres in the district was arable, with the remainder being mostly bog or wind-blown sand. Of the 31 tenants, only two had paid their rents and all the others had been in arrears since 1840 – long before the onset of the Famine. He noted that despite all this, and the inhospitable conditions there, the population had increased by one-third and it appeared obvious to him that if the situation was left to itself, matters would simply get worse.

The Select Committee on Colonisation from Ireland had been set up in 1846 after the potato crop failed for the second year in succession. The committee favoured 'transplantation' which was emigration under another name, but with the proviso that funding should be raised locally to augment whatever was to be provided by the government. Sir Robert agreed to give evidence to the parliamentary committee, and told its representatives he considered that because of 'the smallness of their holdings, the farmers could not live in any degree of comfort.' He also informed them that he had 'at all times endeavoured to increase the size of the farm in a manner that was consistent with justice to the individuals.' When asked (possibly with the 1836 evictions in mind) whether he had effected 'voluntary emigration' prior to the Famine, Sir Robert said he had never forced any individual. 'If a man could not go back to his own farm, he had the choice of going to another farm – inferior ground, but a sufficient quantity for his means – in a different part of the estate. No man was compelled to go by me.' And asked whether any of those who had emigrated had encouraged others to follow, he replied: 'The accounts [sent back] have been such as to increase the emigration. They have been favourable.'

Despite his denials that he had forced any tenants to emigrate, it has sometimes since been argued that tenants who were offered by their landlord a chance to emigrate voluntarily did not have a real choice because they were likely to fear the consequences of a refusal. Turning down an offer of an assisted passage could result in a subsequent eviction without compensation. There is no evidence that this occurred on the Gore-Booth estate. Indeed Sir Robert allowed compensation not only for land, but also for abandoned livestock and crops, for household materials and for improvements. Such evidence as has survived indicates that there was little or no ill-feeling towards Sir Robert during the Famine, either on the part of the tenants who went or those who stayed, nor were there negative responses from the local parish priests or in the Sligo newspapers. But all this was to change a few years later.

When the Committee chairman enquired if he had any evidence from any persons to show how they had fared after emigration, Sir Robert read extracts from various letters, including one from Owen Boyle to his mother in which he wrote:

> Dear Mother, The day I left Sligo I had not a cent of money but six shillings that Mr Jeffcott [the Lissadell agent] gave me, but thanks be to God, I did not want for money after. When I landed I met Master [name unclear], he gave me 4 shillings per day for three weeks, and for the Winter if I would stay. This is a good country for smart boys and smart girls. The truth is best to be told.

When Sir Robert was asked if he recalled the case of a man of the name of Thomas McGatry, he replied that the person was 'by profession a beggar boy,' and when asked if he knew how McGatry had obtained his passage he replied:

> Mr Yeats' brother asked him on the shore to assist him in rowing out [to the emigrant vessel] and he would give him 6 pence. He was missing when Mr Yeats wanted to pull ashore. He [McGatry] lay in the vessel many hours til at last he was forced to come out from hunger. The captain found him a very

good boy on board and made a subscription for him … [The boy] wrote to Mr Yeats apologising for his conduct, sending home two pounds and ten shillings for his mother, saying he had £5, but kept the other £2. 10s. hearing it was cold [in Canada] in winter.

When questioned about the measures he had taken to supply food to the people remaining in the area, he recounted how he had imported a considerable quantity of corn from America, Liverpool and Glasgow, and had set up two water mills to grind the corn as well as a steam engine, but even with these he had found the demand for food was greater than he could supply.

From his submissions to this Select Committee and from the family papers that have survived, there is a considerable body of evidence to show that Sir Robert personally took great care in his preparations to remove around 1,000 persons from his estate to Canada in 1847. He involved his brother, Henry, who was engaged in the importation of Canadian timber into Scotland, to charter three returning ships to take the emigrating families to New Brunswick. He personally inspected the fitting-out and provisioning of the ships, ensuring that there was an ample stock of food, which he himself provided. As each ship arrived, he supervised the departure of the families and engaged his own doctor to medically examine each individual when tickets were being issued along with provisions for the journey and a supply of new clothes. A second medical examination was made on boarding the ship, after which Sir Robert personally entrusted each individual to the care of the ship's captain. If fever was detected, the emigrant concerned had to return ashore, and all of the vacated places were immediately taken up by others who anticipated a better life on the other side of the Atlantic Ocean.

It is interesting to note the reaction of the local newspapers at the time – especially in light of the very different views published by some of the same papers when the Famine was over. Both the *Sligo Champion* and the *Sligo Journal* saw Sir Robert Gore-Booth's emigration programme as laudable, regarding his scheme as an acceptable solution to the problems posed by the Famine. The *Champion*, which had regularly castigated the role of landlords in general and had named five locally in this context, complimented Sir Robert not only for his work in relieving distress but also for the manner in which he conducted his emigration scheme.

The three ships chartered by Sir Robert, the *Aeolus*, the *Yeoman* and the *Lady Sale*, all arrived safely in the New World after reasonably good crossings. All seemed well until the Colonial and Land Emigration Officer in London wrote to him after receiving complaints made by the government's emigration agent, Mr Perley, in the Canadian port. The master of the *Aeolus*, Michael Driscoll, wrote to Sir Robert on his arrival at St John's, Newfoundland informing him that his 500 passengers were 'scattering fast and getting good employment.' The health officer there expressed the view that Sir Robert's tenants 'could not be classed as common adventurers, or emigrants, nor the ship classed among the dirty old emigrant hired vessels' being, in fact, 'superior to many of Her Majesty's transports.' In his letter he added: 'Your Kind acts at hoam to privint famin and to Elivate the Condition of the Poor is as well nowen here as in the Towen of Sligow. Your Ever Thankful Tennants were Highley Respected on being landed in this town.'

The second ship, the *Yeoman*, which arrived about a month later, was an even larger vessel but carried the same number of passengers. The captain's wife who had travelled with him wrote to Lady Gore-Booth to tell her that she had given all on board tea and sugar every day, and a fiddler on board had made 'happy faces and nimble feet,' and while the passengers had looked squalid on arrival, they had not been overcrowded or diseased and had been well fed. The agent's report confirmed this:

> The whole of the passengers from the *Yeoman* were tenants of the estate of Sir Robert Gore-Booth, Bart. at Lissadell near Sligo, and are sent at his individual expense, they having yielded up their individual holdings on his estate in consideration for their passage and expenses. They were amply provided with provisions of the best description, in every variety for the voyage, and no pains had been spared to make them comfortable. They are to receive a week's allowances of provisions on landing, after which they must shift for themselves.

When the *Lady Sale* arrived at St John's, Mr Perley sent a further report stating that three deaths had occurred during the voyage, and added that this boat's passengers were 'of a worse class than those who have arrived by the *Aeolus* and *Yeoman* from the same estate. Many of them will become a public burthen from the moment of their landing.' The *Lady Sale*, was smaller than the other two vessels, and carried fewer passengers, one quarter of whom, it was stated, arrived suffering from fever. This brought criticism from the local doctors who said that this 'displayed the heartless character' of the person who sent out this 'freight of paupers.'

Paupers many of them undoubtedly were, but as Sir Robert had taken care to subject each passenger to two separate medical examinations before leaving, it seems unfair to blame him for fevers which were not evident to the doctors on embarkation. Furthermore, the death toll of three out of 350 passengers was almost remarkably low, given the experiences recorded elsewhere at the time. While the majority of those who sailed on these three ships had come from Lissadell, some had come from Sir Robert's Ballymote estate and others from the estates of other Sligo landlords, including, in the case of the *Lady Sale*, emigrants from Lord Palmerton's property. All three vessels chartered by Sir Robert had arrived safely, though one of the nine ships Palmerston independently chartered during 1847 sank with the loss of 87 lives.

The criticisms expressed in the reports from Canada must have disappointed Sir Robert who had taken more care than most landlords in his assisted emigration plans. Even so, these criticisms pale when viewed alongside the picture generally painted of 'coffin ships' which either sank at sea, or arrived with less than half of the passengers still alive, many of whom were likely to succumb to fever after disembarking.

When giving evidence to the Select Committee on Colonisation he had been most emphatic about the care he had personally taken to ensure that only those who were fit to travel had sailed on the ships he chartered. He countered the suggestion of pauperism among those who had landed from the *Lady Sale* by stating that those on board that particular ship had brought, between them, not less than £1,500. He took the opportunity to criticise the government for its failure to adopt his suggestion of acquiring a tract of land in Canada so that those of his tenants who wished to do so could have settled in one area to form a mutually self-supporting group.

During 1849, some newspapers prematurely declared that the Famine was over. The *Sligo Guardian* reported during August that: 'In respect of the potato crop, the crisis may be said to have passed and the country presents the cheering aspect of an abundant harvest.' However, even as the worst effects of the Famine were beginning to fade, a change of mood towards landlords in general began to become evident. Hitherto, verbal and physical attacks on landlords were confined to those who had notoriously ill-treated their tenants, but this now gradually changed to include all landlords – without exception.

* * *

There is no evidence that Sir Robert had any ambition to engage in public life until just after the Famine ended, when the sitting member of parliament for Sligo County resigned and he was persuaded to stand for the 1850 election. The whole political climate, too, had already begun to change, and Sir Robert was soon being warned that his actions during the Famine were now being re-interpreted in a manner designed to discredit him. One of the early charges being put about was that he had forcibly evicted tenants. Concerned about this, he wrote to the local parish priest, Fr Patrick O'Gara, asking him to let him have names of any parishioners who had been sent to Canada against their will. This was Father O'Gara's response:

> I feel great pleasure in stating that the Emigration of your Tenants was perfectly voluntary, and Truth compels me to say that they were all well clothed, well fed, and were supplied with good Bedding at your expense and that the deepest concern for their Welfare was manifested by Lady Gore and yourself. I may also add that her Ladyship supplied the most distressed with Monies to be expended by them in St. John's until they could procure employment. The unremitting anxiety thus manifested for the well being of the Emigrants as well as the feverish sympathy invariably exhibited by her Ladyship and yourself in behalf of the Famine-stricken Poor who were so munificently relieved without religious Distinction, has secured for you and your Family a very large and enviable amount of sincere Affection ....

In the event, Sir Robert was elected unopposed and he purchased a house in London, 7 Buckingham Gate, where he entertained during his regular visits to attend Parliament and also when the family stayed there during the summer months. Thomas Kilgallon, who later became Henry's valet, described how the family spent 'the season' in London each year, usually going in February after the annual horse fair at Catnagat, near Collooney, which he attended because it was noted at the time for carriage and hunting horses. Sir Robert's London visits were timed for the opening of parliament and the whole family, along with servants, usually followed later. Kilgallon recalled that initially travelling to London was done by stagecoach, but later they all went in two of the family's carriages:

> They took the silver plate. It was quite a business packing all up. They had boxes specially made for them. The housekeeper did not go as there was a housekeeper for the London house, a Mrs Tigwell. They took the first and second housemaids, house steward, groom chambers, under butler, and first and second footmen and steward's room boy. All the other servants were put on board [reduced] wages [but] they were allowed milk and vegetables.

Kilgallon recorded some interesting details about how the Lissadell household was then being run. The servants were managed by the house steward, Mr Ball, who engaged all the servants, paid their wages, and dismissed them when necessary. His duties included ordering all the wine for the house and acted as wine waiter at dinners. Ball supervised a small army of footmen, grooms, maids, etc. The groom chambers carved, and with the footmen, waited at all meals, despatched the post, opened the newspapers and ironed them. Their other duties included attending the hall door and polishing the furniture in the main rooms. One of the footmen was also under-butler who kept the dinner silver in order and laid the dinner table, making sure that plates intended to be hot were kept warm in a special iron cupboard heated by charcoal kept outside the dining room door.

Lissadell House: The Drawing room with its pillars and pilasters setting-off one of a pair of Williams and Gibton bookcases.

Kilgallon also recalled that the maids had to be up by four a.m. to prepare for carrying hot water to the bedrooms and carrying down the filled bath-tubs afterwards. There was a cook, a Frenchman named Fribourg, a pastry cook, kitchen maid, scullery maid, and some kitchen boys. Class distinction among the servants was strictly observed but especially during meal times in the kitchen.

> The house steward took the head of the table, the under butler the other end, as there was always two joints, one at each end. All the women sat at one side of the table, the men the other. The housekeeper sat on the left of the steward; the maids, according to their rank next to her. Sometimes there would be quarrels if the second lady's maid took the first maid's place next to the housekeeper. The same with the men .... The house steward said Grace, and when all the room servants had finished their meat, the others laid down their knives and forks, and the steward [again] said Grace. The housekeeper rising, the lady's maids following the steward taking up the rear, went to the steward's room for the next course, the under servants finishing their meals. At meal times there was a wagon on wheels with a large copper of beer on it and several horns instead of glasses for drinking .... There was beer served out to all the servants, both men and women, several times a day, at 11 a.m., dinner hour 7 p.m. and again at supper .... At night there was whiskey and wines served. Usually there was a small dance in the servant's hall once or twice a week for three or four hours. They were allowed beer and a bottle of whiskey for punch. There was an old fiddler gave them music.

According to O'Rorke, a Catholic archdeacon as well as a historian, Sir Robert 'loved a seat in Parliament,' adding that: 'his tastes were for a private station, the duties of which no one knew better how to discharge. While in London 'he was a generous, hospitable host' but back in Lissadell,

> he passed the time in patronising local sports, helping local charities, at least those of his own co-religionists, and making things pleasant for his servants, dependants, neighbours and all round. As a landlord, Sir Robert must be classed with the best; for he let his lands at their value, and never pressed for rent, as is sometimes done by others, at a moment when poor people are obliged to part with their stock or farm produce at a loss, always allowing his tenants plenty of time to wait for, and sell in, the best market.

Conflicting evidence continues to provide differing views about the role of the landlords at this time. John C. McTernan, who wrote widely about aspects of County Sligo, had this to say:

> There has been a great deal of debate and not a little disagreement on the role landlords in Famine times. The situation varied greatly throughout the country.

As regards Sligo, it can be stated that most resident proprietors assisted their tenants to a greater or lesser degree by providing employment on their estates, subscribing generously to Relief Committees, importing food to feed hungry tenants and, in a few instances, providing financial assistance to those wishing to emigrate.

If his assertions were correct, why then were the actions of the good landlords so very soon erased from the records with the result that the sacrifices they made have now been virtually forgotten? Apart from Sir Robert Gore-Booth, notable Co. Sligo proprietors who did their best for their tenants included Major Charles O'Hara of Annaghmore who purchased corn for his tenants – possibly sharing transport arrangements with Sir Robert. The latter was enabled to do so, as Noel Kissane noted in his history of the famine, 'by means of his brother [Henry, who lived near Glasgow], a ship owner, has ordered several cargoes [of corn] from America direct to Sligo.' Other benevolent landlords included Edward Cooper of Markree Castle, Alexander Crichton of Beltra (whose wife, Jane, died of cholera contracted while visiting the houses of tenants in 1847), Alexander Percival of Temple House and John Wynne of Hazelwood.

It may be no more than a coincidence that in this part of Sligo (considerably less than half the county) there were at least six proprietors known to have looked after their tenants. As the author has noted in earlier volumes, Elizabeth Smith of Baltiboys was able to list half a dozen such landlords – including her husband – living in west Wicklow, and John Hamilton at Ballintra was one of at least six caring proprietors living in south Donegal. One hesitates to attempt to extrapolate these figures on a countrywide basis because the resulting figure would account for a total somewhere between three and four hundred benevolent landlords nationwide. Professor J.C. Beckett, wrote that 'a good many landlords – more than is commonly recognised – did, in fact, try to improve the lot of their tenants and promote the general welfare of their neighbourhoods,' but one wonders if even he could possibly have had such numbers in mind?

Whatever the actual number, it must have seemed impossible at the time that the memory of what the benevolent proprietors had done during the famine would ever be forgotten – much less erased from the record. In Sir Robert's case, it may have seemed improbable that another contestant would even attempt to challenge him for the parliamentary seat during the post-famine elections. If he had any lingering misgivings, he must have taken comfort from what the *Sligo Champion* told its readers, that Sir Robert's endeavours on behalf of his people 'would never be forgotten.' However, Sir Robert's efforts in assisting tenants to emigrate were soon to be interpreted in a very different way. In his essay on emigration during in the mid-nineteenth century (published in the *The Hungry Stream*, edited by E. Margaret Crawford), Patrick J. Duffy concluded that the popular image of landlords which emerged in the post famine years was:

> one of oppression and injustice, and this image has come down in folklore to the present. Much of this was founded on eviction policies which gathered pace from the 1840s, as the population/land crisis manifested itself at the level of the estate. Emigration also became an emotive issue from this period [which resulted in] the emergence of the "exile motive" as a societal response to the loss of millions of people from the country. Encouraging people to emigrate by means of assisted passages, therefore, was a risky undertaking for the estate in these circumstances of a rising tide of public opinion.

The first rumblings of moves to tell a different story about Lissadell came when elements of the local press warned of forces of sectarianism which were now becoming apparent, and came to be ranged against Sir Robert when he stood for re-election. The *Sligo Journal* sprang to Sir Robert's defence:

> The priests of Sligo cannot forget – for it is not so long ago – the princely way in which Sir Robert Gore-Booth shared his fortune with the people in that dreadful season of famine and affliction …. They cannot forget the ships which, one after another, came laden with provisions … and all at the expense of a man towards whom they are using all their influence to turn the sectarian animosity of an ignorant and ungrateful people.

It was all the more depressing for him that one of Sir Robert's most vociferous supporters during the Famine should turn so bitterly against him just a few years later. Father O'Gara, the parish priest of Drumcliff, had fulsomely praised Sir Robert and Lady Gore-Booth for relieving 'without religious distinction, the plight of the Famine-stricken poor of the parish,' adding that it would be a source of consolation to both of them 'that they were surrounded by a grateful peasantry.' Yet, despite these and similar sentiments, O'Gara took an active part in a concerted campaign to vilify Sir Robert for allowing his name to go forward for the 1852 election.

A new element of Irish life had become eligible to vote following the passing of an Act extending the franchise to tenants holding land valued at £12 or more. This was to have considerable political significance, giving electoral power to a whole new class of middle-tenant farmers, one of the very few groups to emerge in a strong position after the Famine. It was mainly members of this group who formed the Tenant League to further their aims of achieving rent reductions, fixity of tenure and 'Tenant Right.' Landlords began to find themselves facing the combined forces of the Land League, an awakening nationalism and an increasingly powerful Catholic Church. These developments were supported by many of the local newspapers, hence the spectacular change of mind on the part of one of the Sligo newspapers which, having averred four years earlier that Sir Robert's benevolence would never be forgotten, now joined in an concerted campaign against him.

Sir Robert soon realised that the new political climate had turned the electoral contest into a campaign of exceptional bitterness. Opposing him was an independent candidate who had the support of the Catholic Archbishop McHale and, not unexpectedly, the Catholic clergy as a body, along with the nationalist press. The *Champion* called upon all Catholics to support the candidate standing against Sir Robert on the grounds that 'it would be strange if Catholics were to vote against their religion and in opposition to their clergy.'

His campaign was, however, supported by two other local newspapers, with the *Sligo Journal* entreating its readers to remember – and exhorting the priests not to forget – Sir Robert's actions during the Famine. He could hardly have complained about the unqualified support offered to his opponent, but what took him by surprise was the accompanying campaign which sought at the same time to take away his good reputation which he must have considered unassailable. A number of local parish priests were in the vanguard of those who campaigned against him and one of them, Father Noone of Ahamlish in a public speech, went back two decades to the Ballygilgan affair, and to the unfounded allegations about the sinking of the *Pomona*. He also claimed that 2,350 houses of honest and religious tenants had been razed during the recent famine; that promised farms were never provided; and that Lissadell tenants died in ditches like vermin or got a watery grave in rotten ships. Father O'Gara of Drumcliff, as already mentioned, joined in this campaign despite the fact that he had actually worked alongside Sir Robert in relief work during the Famine. He had also written a letter to the Committee on Colonisation praising the benevolent work done by both Sir Robert and Lady Gore-Booth, and had quite recently confirmed in writing that none of the Lissadell tenants had been forcibly evicted. Sir Robert felt forced to issue a poster addressed to the Electors of Sligo in which he stated that:

> During the progress of my Canvass in this country, I learned for the first time
> that a report had been most industriously circulated among my constituents
> that I am opposed to all legislation on the subject of the Land Question, better
> known as Tenant Right at present agitating this Kingdom. I had hoped that my
> past conduct among you, during a period of more than ordinary trial (to which,
> from personal motives, I wish not further to allude), would have been a sufficient
> protection against such slander, got up by interested and designing parties and
> with no other object than to render me unpopular.

He gave an undertaking that he would support any measure which would
'secure to the tenant the full and fair value of the outlay of his capital on
the improvement of the soil.' He also undertook to support all measures
'for the reduction of taxation and the amelioration of your condition,
and that of our common country.' While his reputation must have been
dented, most of the electorate stood by him and he headed the poll, and
then continued to hold the seat at every election throughout the ensuing
26 years until his death. The *Sligo Chronicle* commented:

> It cannot be a matter of surprise in this county that Sir R. Gore-Booth should
> have been placed at the head of the poll – his exertions on behalf of the famishing
> poor in '47 sufficiently account for that. The conduct of the Roman Catholic
> priests towards Sir Robert during the election has, however, created surprise,
> and a still stronger feeling in the mind of every man of unbiased judgement
> who has heard of it ....

The newspaper then published a copy of a letter written by Father O'Gara
in 1847, which he had sent to Lady Gore-Booth:

> Mr O'Gara's compliments to Lady Gore-Booth and he has the honour to inform
> her that the destitute poor are permitted the use of broth etc. every day during
> Lent.... He feels (sic) not to exert to the most extensive, indiscriminate, and
> unostentatious charities, performed by her Ladyship, and so gratefully
> remembered by the poor of God, that the respectful regard, exhibited by her
> for the religious convictions of the Roman Catholic people of this district,
> entitle her to the eternal gratitude of every friend of suffering humanity, as
> well as of freedom of conscience. It will, he trusts, be consoling to her ladyship
> to learn that the humble prayers of God's humble creatures are offered every
> night, and in every house, for the spiritual and temporal welfare of her ladyship's
> family.

That attempts were made to erase the memory of Sir Robert's generosity
so very soon after the Famine had ended, prompts the more general
question concerning the true position regarding the 1836 Ballygilgan

evictions. While the perception of Sir Robert as a landlord changed so quickly after 1850, the substantial body of surviving records covering the Famine period clearly shows that the allegations being made against him were both politically motivated and grossly unfair. The records covering the period of the Ballygilgan evictions have not survived, making it difficult to judge whether similar allegations made concerning that period were based on fact or simply represented emerging feelings against landlordism in general.

* * *

Sir Robert and Lady Gore-Booth had a great love of horses, and had introduced hunting in the area. His hounds were thought by some to have been the first in the county. After the Famine, Sir Robert revived the sport with the Gore-Booth Harriers, also known as the Lissadell Harriers, which had their inaugural meeting at Teesan towards the end of 1850. Sir William Stokes, who visited Lissadell at this time, wrote: 'What gives this place its greatest charm is that the house is truly the refuge and hope of all that are poor, sick and destitute.'

Twenty years after the mansion at Lissadell had been completed, the foundation stone of the estate church was laid by Sir Robert's mother in the presence of a large number of clergy, along with a congregation that had assembled for the special service. Beneath the stone was placed, as reported in the *Sligo Independent*, 'a case containing the coins of the present reign and a parchment with the date and particulars of the erection of the building, etc.' Prior to this, parishioners attended services at a small Wesleyan chapel. Sir Robert built a school beside the church, and a second one at Milltown, near Drumcliff. The clock in the tower was added after Sir Robert's death as a gift from the tenants in his memory. Incidentally, Thomas Kilgallon wrote that the dowager Lady Gore-Booth – mentioned above – used to go out into the gardens 'on fine days in a bath chair with shafts, drawn by a donkey and accompanied by Miss Hains, her maid, walking by her side.' The old lady, who according to some accounts 'ruled the roost at Lissadell,' also had a manservant who carried her up and down the stairs from the north bedroom where she lived and slept. This servant liked to smoke but as he did not dare to do so in the house he had to resort to indulging his craving in the old garden known to the family as St Helena.

Just over four years after work on the church had begun, Sir Robert suffered four bereavements in as many months, the final one being that of his wife in January 1855. Reporting her death, the *Sligo Journal* described Lady Caroline Gore-Booth as:

> Gentle in spirit, amiable in manner and affectionate in feeling …. Her tender sensibilities were ever engaged in promoting the objects and happiness of others with a total disregard of self. When the dark clouds of pestilence and death covered the land, Lady Gore-Booth appeared as a ministering angel among the people, her charitie was unbounded and her exertions to relieve the wants and sufferings of the distressed excited the admiration of all classes.

Tragedy stuck yet again six years later when Sir Robert's eldest son, Robert Newcomen Gore-Booth, heir to the estate, was drowned in a boating accident off Lissadell. A captain serving in the 4th. Light Dragoons, he had been married just over a year earlier, but there were no children of the marriage. He had been sailing with his brother, Henry, who narrowly escaped with his life and who subsequently inherited the estate.[2] Thomas Kilgallon, who started working for the family just after this, was to recall that Robert's young widow continued to live at Lissadell for some time. After her second marriage – to a John Ussher – she and her husband often stayed at Lissadell, where Sir Robert was 'very attached to her, and always happy with her company.'

That the Lissadell estate was well run was due in no small part to the fact that Sir Robert kept meticulous records concerning many aspects of the estate in diaries, ledgers and notebooks. Among those surviving, is a collection of Game Books in which were recorded details of game shot on the estate. Each month's total was carefully tabulated with a column for comments, and at the end of each month the total 'bag' was invariably enormous. Conservation was unheard of, either then or even as late as the early years of the twentieth century. In one shoot some 300 brace of woodcock were downed in a single week. Despite slaughter on this scale, the estate continued to be noted for its woodcock for more than half a century as shown in an entry made during 1906 when some 200 brace of these birds were taken during another week. The earliest of these surviving records dates from 1846, after which there is a gap until 1853. This gap raises the possibility that shooting for sport was abandoned during the remainder of the Famine and in the difficult years that followed. A much shorter gap in the records occurred

---

[2]   Another account states that it was his uncle, Thomas Goold, not Henry, who was in the boat.

between August and November 1855, which is helpfully explained in the Game Book: 'Returned from the Continent.'

Lissadell House: The Billiard room, which Sir Henry decorated with a collection of his sporting trophies and Arctic memorabilia.

A 'Meat from Farm' Record Book (1860) listed all the beasts killed on the estate as well as meat purchased from Sligo. Also among the family documents are a number of small account books, including one that recorded purchases, on account, from Richard Smith, Grocer, Wine and Spirit Merchant of 10 Knox's Street, Sligo. Entries for June 1846 included candles, Epsom Salts, fruit, vinegar, wax, refined sugar, pickle bottles, corks for same, hemp seed, starch, and pearl ashes, all purchased on the same day for the sum of £3. 5s.1d. Accounts were also kept with Leech and Sons of Sligo for a variety of goods ranging from pots and saucepans to feather dusters (and black lead at seven shillings a stone). Miscellaneous record books covered the consumption of milk and cream on a weekly bases – for example: 'June 12-19: 287 gallons of milk; and 7 quarts of cream in the houses daily; 42 quarts of new milk weekly.'

Records were also kept of 'Numbers of People to Dinner, Lunch, etc.', with names of 'strangers staying in the house, and when they go and come.' Many of the 'strangers' were, in fact, members of well-known families living in the area, including the Wynne's, Gethins, Parkes, Jeffcotts, Coopers, Percivals, Goolds, Kings, Irwins, 'the Enniskillens' and 'the Palmerstons.' The monthly totals of persons having dinner at Lissadell – the figures included family and servants – regularly ran to more than 1,300 during the 1850s.

Details of wages paid to the staff were recorded from 1840, the earliest entry showed that Mr L'Antoine, 'the cook,' was paid £84 per annum, J. Carew, the coachman, received £31.10s., and J. Folgate, the Footman, £25.4s. Other payments included John Tennant, the gas-man, £52; James Stewart, the House Steward, £63, and Hart, the groom, £8.8s.

Quite the most remarkable record-book was entitled 'Rat-Book' in which were recorded payments for rats killed in and around the house. It gives some idea of the huge numbers of these rodents that must have been a serious menace to food-stocks and health, not only in the mansions and larger farms but in the humblest cottages as well. One entry, for the period June 20–30, 1846, recorded that a total of £9.4s.2d. was paid out for rats killed at Lissadell, and the locations and actual numbers despatched during this short period were listed as follows: June 20: Cow House 19, Hen house 26; June 23: Stock Yard, 101; June 27: Kitchen, 109, Hen house, 34. June 30: Cow house 20.

As late as 1863, Sir Robert was still adding to his property, this time with land at Aughamore, Clogher and Mullaghgar, which he purchased from the Earl of Leitrim. When his agent died in 1866, instead of appointing a new agent, he entrusted the task of running the estate to his surviving son, Henry. However, Sir Robert lived on for a further ten years, and this family overlap must have contributed to the smooth changeover in the management of the property.

Lodged among the Gore-Booth Papers is a copy of the Memoirs of Samuel Waters, an officer of the Royal Irish Constabulary. After Waters had joined the force, his first posting was to Grange, a few miles north of Lissadell, and within a short time he became very friendly with the family and with Sir Robert in particular. Sir Robert must have taken a great liking to the young policeman within a very short time after Waters' arrival in the district, making a room available for him, and a good horse too. Waters was also invited to join in hunts, shoots and in fishing. The advantages of these arrangements were mutual – the young constable obviously enjoyed these privileges and it was no disadvantage to Sir Robert to have a young, active constable around the place – especially at a time when the Fenian Movement was beginning to become active. Something of this relationship becomes clear in the following extracts from Samuel Waters' writings:

I had at this time, the princely income of £125 a year all told to keep myself and my horse. My first station was Grange in the County Sligo, a village half way between Sligo and Bundoran. I got lodgings with the post-mistress on very reasonable terms.... This was in the year 1866 when the Fenian conspiracy was beginning to spread though the country. The mountain district around Grange was full of young Fenian enthusiasts. They assembled at night for drills, etc. and it was a great part of the duty of the Police to trace and disperse these gatherings. Fortunately they had no arms of any account and they never dreamed of facing a well-equipped body of Police. Their scouts gave the word if we approached near their meetings and they forthwith broke up and dispersed.

I always loved outdoor sports and in Grange I devoted every spare hour, and I had plenty of time, to shooting, fishing and hunting. The great man of the district, Sir Robert Gore-Booth of Lissadell, kept a pack of harriers and a fine house always open to his friends in unbounded hospitality. He was always most kind to me. I had a room at my service whenever I wished to go there in the winter months and a horse from his stable to ride to the hounds. The family spent the summer at his London residence. I almost invariably formed one of the party at his covert shoots and in walking the mountains after grouse.

The winter of 1868 was a very hard one. Snow fell heavily and travelling by road was difficult and dangerous, We daily expected a rising of the Fenians. I slept always with a pistol under my pillow, and the men in the barracks next door with loaded carbines beside their beds.... Mounted patrols went out every night and co-operated with the police. These patrols were carried out by grooms and stable attendants, and also by male members of the family, and by guests. A friend of mine, Captain Charles Wynne, son-in-law of Sir Robert, always took his turn, accompanied by a guest, usually one Capt. Martin. The patrols of these scouts usually led to Grange about midnight. They put their horses up in my stable and spend the night with me over a game of cards, with occasional refreshers of whiskey punch.

I often laughed to myself when I heard the ladies at Lissadell sympathising with them on the hardships they endured – out all night in such weather. Many a sly wink passed between Charley Wynne and me when this happened....

Some of the precautions taken at Lissadell following rumours of a Fenian rising were also recalled by Kilgallon: 'Iron plates fixed on lower bedroom shutters. Old guns and rifles carefully examined and loaded, hand grenades, pistols and swords seen to; extra powder and shot ordered ....Nothing came of it.' However, while the household continued to be on the alert, a group of friends at the house, including Captain Wynne, Captain Wood Martin and Constable Waters, decided to play a practical joke. Late one night, they made Kilgallon help them to dress up in old clothes before letting themselves outside and locking the hall door. They then knocked on the door with sticks and shouted that they wanted Sir Robert. Inside, the family and the servants thought it was a Fenian attack: After repeated calling for 'Ould Sir Robert,' he opened the door, revolver in hand. Then, led by a fiddler, the pranksters entered, dancing a jig. Sir Robert was not amused.

Despite all this, his grandson, Josslyn, was to write much later that 'the Fenian troubles did not affect Lissadell in 1867. They [the family] were offered police protection which was refused as it was not considered necessary.' However, as can be seen, some precautions were certainly taken, though it seems that no serious problems arose for the family resulting from the widespread agitation at that time.

Constable Waters referred to the unusual assembly instituted by Charles Wynne at Lissadell, of which Wynne was 'perpetual Grand Master.' This was the Pig and Whistle Club, which Waters described as:

> An institution which arose in this way. Sir Robert Gore-Booth had a strong prejudice against smoking in the house. He would not allow it even in the Billiard Room, and there was no smoking room. When reasoned about this he would say that smoking was only fit for servants and grooms, and if gentlemen chose to indulge in it at Lissadell they might go to the kitchen, where they would find congenial company. Charley Wynne took him at his word, and he instituted the Pig and Whistle Club, the members of which were any gentlemen residing in the house who wished to smoke before going to bed. The place of assembly was the large kitchen in the hours after the ladies had retired for the night.... Lissadell was infested with rats, and a common amusement in the Pig and Whistle Club was to destroy some of them in this fashion. Next to the kitchen range was a large hot plate in which there had worn a hole near the floor. The smokers used to make a pool by putting a coin a-piece. Then each in turn took a large kitchen knife, and, with luck, the rat lost its head. The game was that each subscriber got five minutes with the knife and the one who killed the most rats took the pool....

Thomas Kilgallon wrote what is probably the only description of Sir Robert's appearance in his master's old age. 'Sir Robert had good sight, although his legs looked very weak and inflamed.... He was a small man, slightly round in the shoulders, very quick in speech, fond of company, especially that of ladies.'

Sir Robert's health began to fail in 1876, suffering from 'bad turns.' He died, aged 71, on December 21 of that year at seven in the evening in the presence of his son, Henry William Gore-Booth, daughter-in-law, Georgina Mary Gore-Booth, Augusta Gore-Booth, Elizabeth Gore-Booth, William Hamilton Esq. M.D., and Thomas Kilgallon. While the family was still in mourning and preparing for the funeral, his niece, Isabella McCaul Gore-Booth, who had been staying at Lissadell along with her brother and sister, also died suddenly, 'her death occasioned by the shock of her uncle's death and the fatigue she underwent during his illness.' She had appeared to be in normal health and had participated in the family's annual Harvest Home festivities just over a week earlier, as had her uncle. Kilgallon recounted how, when Sir Robert's health declined, 'one of the Scotch Miss Gore-Booths' [Isabella] came on a visit from her married sister's place in Liverpool. He remembered her saying 'good-bye' to Sir Robert as she departed to her room. He died that night and she died on the following day.

Sir Robert's death was reported in considerable detail in the local newspapers, including the *Sligo Independent*:

On Thursday night the painful intelligence reached this town that this worthy gentlemen, a good landlord, and honourable member of the British House of Commons had breathed his last at his residence, Lissadell. When the sad news became known it created throughout the town and county a universal gloom, and sincere expressions of regret were heard everywhere. His death was rather sudden; for, although he had been complaining for a few days previous, a fatal result was not apprehended. His general health had not been very good during the past year, and, by directions of his medical advisers, he abstained from taking any part in public life by attending in Parliament or otherwise. He retained his faculties up to the last, and on Wednesday the 13th he was present at the annual festive gathering amongst some of his tenants and labourers, called the Harvest Home. Not alone was he present, but he seemed to enjoy very much the re-union amongst his people, and he seemed well pleased and delighted – as he always was, that all present were happy and enjoying themselves. He complained of a slight illness a few days before his death and on Wednesday evening at about seven o'clock, his spirit gently departed, and he breathed his last, surrounded by several members of his family, to whom he was endeared, and by whom he was beloved by reason of his many domestic virtues, goodness of heart, and kindness of disposition. So has passed from us a gentleman whose reputation as a landlord was of that high degree of excellence that his name was revered in the home of every tenant on his estates, which are extensive, and he was held up as a pattern to every landlord in Ireland. Indeed, as a landlord,

Sir Robert Gore-Booth could not be excelled, as it seemed to be his special delight to deal fairly – nay, indulgently, with his tenants, and no case of harshness could ever be brought against him. Even incorrigible tenants he found excuses for, and, if the late baronet had any failing at all, it was that he was too indulgent to some of his tenants. As a Magistrate, Grand Juror, and Lieutenant of the County, he was found to act impartially, considerately, and with a desire to carry out what was best suited for the public good…. A more popular resident country gentleman could not be found anywhere, and in the neighbourhood of Lissadell and amongst 'his own people' as he used to call them, he was as greatly beloved, revered, and esteemed, as he is now sincerely regretted.

Sir Robert's funeral took place on a dreadfully stormy and cold St Stephen's Day, during which there was a continuous downpour. To add to the sombreness of the occasion, the coffin of his niece, Isabella Gore-Booth was also in the cortege. The weather did not deter a huge attendance following the two coffins from the house to St John's Church in Sligo. The funeral service was conducted by Sir Robert's brother-in-law, the Rev. Mr Goold, and the chief mourners were Sir Robert's son and heir, Henry William Gore-Booth, along with Owen Wynne and Captain C.B. Wynne, sons-in-law. The attendance included the Earl of Leitrim, Lord Harlech, the Earl of Kingston, Lord Cole, the O'Connor Don, and the Mayor of Sligo. Also among the attendance was the Roman Catholic Bishop of Elphin, Dr Gilooley, and three local parish priests.

His life had been blighted by many tragedies including the early death of his father; the death of his first wife and the simultaneous death of their first child; the deaths of two of his youngest sisters in infancy; the violent death in a carriage accident of one of his daughters; the scandalous behaviour of his sister towards her husband; the bankruptcy of his younger brother and his behaviour thereafter and, as if all that was not enough, the tragic death, in 1861, of his eldest son and heir.

His humane dealings with his tenants, especially during the awful famine years should have been what he was best known for but virtually nothing of this is now recalled. Deirdre Ryan summed up the situation in her thesis, *Lissadell Estate, Famine and Emigration, 1845–1847*:

It would appear … that all evidence of his work on behalf of the tenantry during the famine vanished into the archives … while a folk memory of doubtful provenance, focusing on the image of a coffin ship, held sway over his posthumous reputation. In this he was the victim of a changed political and social orthodoxy which allowed the reality of his outstanding contribution to be forgotten.

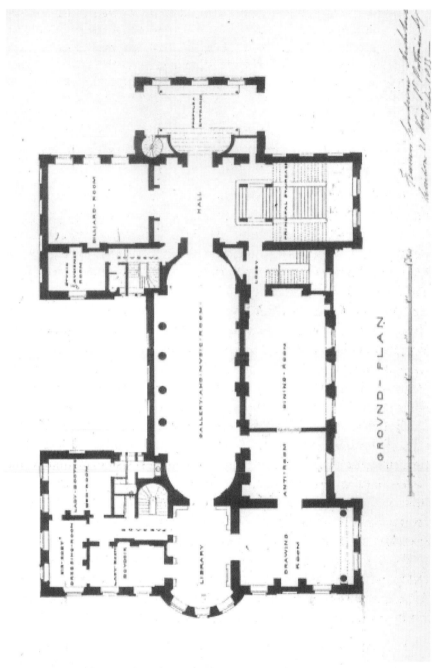

Francis Goodwin's ground plan for Lissadell House on which he called the *porte cochiere* a 'propylea entrance'. A dictionary definition of a propylaeum is 'a gateway of architectural importance leading into a temple'.

Sir Henry Gore-Booth, Fifth Baronet (1843-1900).

SIR HENRY

'He had the Passion for Arctic Travel'

Henry William Gore-Booth, the second son of Sir Robert and Lady Caroline, was born in 1843 and succeeded to the title and the family estate on the death of his father in 1876 because his elder brother, Robert, had died in a boating accident. At the age of 23, while his father was still alive, Henry had already taken over the reins of a very well run estate, and he went on to become, like his father, a popular, benevolent and innovating landlord. The historian, O'Rorke, wrote of Sir Henry that he 'inherited the virtues of his father and added to them many virtues of his own.' He also described Henry as 'large hearted and genial, a thorough sportsman, a kind and indulgent landlord who took a practical interest in the poor of the area.' Archdeacon O'Rorke added that Henry performed many noble acts and had given 'the same impartial aid to Catholic charities which they [the Gore-Booth family] extend to the charities of other denominations.'

According to his granddaughter, Aideen, Sir Henry had initially been concerned about the estate's finances because so much money had been expended in relieving famine distress, resulting in the estate being heavily mortgaged. Despite this, within five years of taking control, Henry had reduced the rents at Lissadell to the level of Griffith's Valuation – well before the Land League campaign to achieve this had commenced. He took a genuine interest in conditions for his tenants, making it his business to know each of them personally as well as their individual circumstances. They in turn came to trust him dealing in their most personal matters, depositing their wills and marriage settlements with him for safe keeping and sometimes requesting him to arbitrate in their personal differences with their neighbours. It was a matter of some personal pride to him that relations with his tenants continued to be good even during the difficult years of the Land War. A special correspondent, wrote in the London *Times*:

> Few owners or agents have such intimate knowledge of their tenantry, their holdings, or their necessities…. He has a curious, carefully kept record of the troubles, disputes, and condition of his poor neighbours. In settling difficulties, his intervention has prevented much litigation, a pugnacious pastime in which even the poorer class of Irish are too fond of indulging.

Although he took little interest in public affairs, he was appointed High Sheriff in 1872, and served for a number of years as a Justice of the Peace and Deputy Lieutenant for the county. He was, however, deeply involved in a whole range of organisations and activities locally, including his appointment as President of the Sligo Agricultural Society. His many business interests included three of the co-operative societies that he and his eldest son founded in the area, along with the Sligo Shirt Factory which he took over to prevent its closure. Under his management, this enterprise flourished for many more years providing much needed employment. He became involved in mining locally, and played a prominent role in the setting up of the railway connecting Sligo with Enniskillen, subsequently becoming the company's chairman. He also continued the oyster fishery enterprise initiated by his father who had been one of the pioneers in creating artificial oyster beds.

A year after taking on the responsibilities of managing the estate, Henry married Georgina Mary, daughter of Colonel John Hill of Tickhill Castle, Yorkshire. The marriage took place in April 1867 in Tickhill Parish Church where the ceremony was performed by the Right Rev. Dr. John George Beresford, Lord Primate of Ireland, great uncle of the bride. There were five children of the marriage: Constance, Josslyn, and Eva were born in 1868, 1869 and 1870 respectively, followed by Mabel and Mordaunt, in 1876 and 1878.

Henry was an intrepid traveller, visiting Italy and Greece as a young man, and travelling around Europe on 'The Grand Tour' after his marriage. Sadly, as was the case with his father, no accounts of these travels seem to have survived, and the few known details are to be found among a small collection of newspaper clippings in the family archive. His journeys through Europe brought him to Germany, Greece, and Italy and almost certainly elsewhere in Europe as well. He travelled to Africa for game shooting and also visited the West Indies and North America in 1894 – the latter being the only occasion about which some small detail is now known. Just before the end of his life, he travelled to South Africa and to Switzerland for health reasons.

Besides these visits abroad, between 1873 and 1898 he voyaged extensively in the Arctic Ocean, a region that was then being systematically explored for the first time. Fortunately, the logbooks of these latter trips, which he kept with the same attention to detail that he paid to his estate books, have survived. Many of the objects which he collected during his Arctic voyages remained on display at Lissadell until the property was sold – stuffed birds, walrus tusks, harpoons, geological specimens, shells, and a travelling clock which accompanied him on his polar voyages. Also in the collection there was a scale model of his vessel, the *Kara*, and a boot belonging to the explorer Leigh Smith whom Henry helped to rescue. But the object which many visitors to Lissadell most clearly remembered was the stuffed bear, standing upright on its hind legs in the entrance hall, a reminder of the quick thinking of Henry's valet, Thomas Kilgallon, who shot the grizzly[1] as it was about to attack him, thus saving not only his master's skin, but also, in different sense, that of the bear.

The stuffed bear shot by Sir Henry
during one of his early voyages to the Arctic region.

---

[1] While it seems a pity to spoil a good story, Henry actually claimed in his diary that it was he, not Kilgallon, who shot the bear – albeit after three attempts.

Thomas Kilgallon, who has been mentioned already a number of times, originally arrived at Lissadell around the same time that Constable Waters came to the district. Kilgallon, then a young boy just out of school, had been working for Captain Wynne as a boat boy, but found himself out of a job when Wynne's boat was laid-up for the winter. Henry Gore-Booth, who happily sailed all the year round, invited the lad to work for him instead. When the boy was not engaged in work about the boat house, Henry got Kilgallon to call him in the mornings, doing odd jobs including bringing him hot water for washing and shaving, and generally learning 'how to valet him.' Henry decided that when the lad had little to do he should go to school, but with no Catholic school in the vicinity, he was sent to the estate school at Ballinfull where the teacher was warned not to teach him anything but reading, writing, geography and arithmetic.

From that time, whenever Henry sailed his yacht, *Minna Ha Ha*, young Kilgallon went with him and quickly became proficient in looking after the boat. 'I cleaned her up and dried all the sails, coiled and hung up all the rigging, and passed any time between the boathouse and the house. I had eight pounds a year, one suit of clothes [and] I slept at the stables, quite comfortable rooms.'

As he grew older, Kilgallon moved up through the servant ranks until Sir Henry gave him a choice of becoming the butler or working directly and personally for him as his valet. When Kilgallon hesitated, Henry told him it was his own wish that he should become his valet because 'as I was so long with him and knew all things in connection with his boating, fishing and shooting, and knowing all his ways.' So, Thomas Kilgallon was appointed Henry's valet but, as time went by, he became close to being something of both a companion and confidante, accompanying Sir Henry almost everywhere he went. In his old age, Kilgallon wrote down his recollections of his time at Lissadell, some of which give a interesting insight into the lifestyle of the Gore-Booth family over a period of four decades or more. As Valerie Pakenham wrote, 'he ruled the household from the 1890s until the First World War and, like Honest Thady, wrote his memoirs.'

One of the first incidents which Kilgallon recalled about his earlier period at Lissadell, happened just after Henry had decided to act as his own agent. After collecting rents in the estate agent's office in Stephen Street, Sligo, Henry discovered he was too late to lodge the money in the bank and decided to bring it back to Lissadell. It was a clear moonlit night, and with Kilgallon beside him and a groom behind as he approached Tully Hill, a man stepped out of the hedge, moving towards the leading horse. Sir Henry drew his revolver but the man stumbled and fell. Kilgallon was quite certain that this saved the man's life 'for had he succeeded in catching the horse, he was a dead man, as Sir Henry was a deadly shot with all firearms.'

Thomas Kilgallon wrote of Sir Henry's wife, Lady Mary, as 'always bright and cheerful, and seemed to attract young and old around her, especially young ladies and gentlemen of marriageable age, [and had a reputation for] uniting many of those in matrimony.' He recalled that she continued to have a cheerful disposition into old age, and that she and Sir Henry were devoted to one another. Kilgallon related how, as he helped him to dress each morning, Henry would invariably sing the chorus of a fashionable music hall song. Often as not, before he could finish, Lady Gore-Booth would rush into the bedroom and throw pillows at him to curtail his performance. She also extended the annual school treats' day, originally begun by Sir Robert for the three schools established by him at Ballinfull, Muninane and Milltown, expanding the scheme to all the other national schools in the area.

It is often assumed that the ordinary people were invariably deferential to, if not in awe of the landlord class. Kilgallon witnessed an instance of a local woman, who used to bring fish to Lissadell, standing her ground and insisting on her own dignity. She was waiting at the top step as Lady Gore-Booth was saying goodbye to some friends at the hall door. Lady Mary suddenly noticed the woman and asked: 'Well, Mrs. Fish, what do you want?' She replied: 'My Lady, I am not Mrs Fish. My name is Mrs Mannion, wife of Mr Paddy Mannion, a decent man, and I have as much right to be called Mrs Mannion as you have to be called Lady Gore.' 'Of course you have as much right to your name as I have to mine – I am so sorry, I thought you were Mrs. Fish.'

No doubt the Gore-Booths, like others of their class, took advantage of their privileged position, but their employees sometimes found it advantageous to do so as well. One of these was known as 'Paddy the Market Man'. He used to travel to Sligo to collect money from the agent's office as well as the orders from the various shops in the town for Lissadell House. He went round each of these shops to tell the owners what time he would collect the orders and if they were not ready when he called back at the stated time, he would say nothing, simply walking out and driving off. His system worked well, for when the shop owners found that Paddy had left, a special messenger was quickly despatched after him for fear he would reach the mansion without the orders, the consequence of which would, in all probability, be the loss of the Gore-Booth custom.

According to Aideen, Henry took no nonsense from his staff. She told the story concerning the maids who were in the habit of putting the washing to dry on the bank opposite the front door. When they took no notice of Henry's request not to do this, he is said to have taken out his gun and shot the washing!

During one of their visits to England, Sir Henry and Lady Mary went to Aske Hall, the residence of the earl of Zetland who later became Lord Lieutenant of Ireland. On several occasions after the Zetlands came to Dublin, Sir Henry and Lady Gore-Booth visited them at the Castle, accompanied by 'Miss Constance and Miss Eva.' Kilgallon described the scene at one of the Castle levées when Constance and Eva were there:

> The Throne Room looked very gay on the night of a ball, or levee. There was a gallery overlooking the Throne Room which required a ticket from the housekeeper to admit you. I was admitted to see all the great functions that were to be seen there …. The Queen's health, Victoria, then was drunk, also the Royal Family and His Excellency and the Vicereine, which all had to be drunk standing. I quite enjoyed my stay there, there was always something new going on, and plenty of music…. Soon after we left, the Regalia [the Crown Jewels] was stolen.

Even when the family was back at Lissadell, they seemed to be perpetually visiting all and sundry. Markree Castle, near Collooney, was often visited even though there had been some rivalry (in connection with elections) between Sir Henry and Colonel Cooper. These visits continued despite the fact that Henry always found the house very cold because the colonel had a reputation for being 'stingy over fires.' Kilgallon recounted how there were constant rows in the servant's quarters because each department was allocated a single scuttle of coal per day, often causing the servants to steal from each other's allocations. The family also frequently called to see the King-Harman cousins at Rockingham, where the fine picture gallery was said to have been the inspiration for the similar feature at Lissadell.

Henry was staying with his cousin, Lord Harlech, at Derrycarne, near Dromad, in December 1878, when Mordaunt, his second son was born. As usual, his valet had accompanied him, and around two o'clock in the morning, Kilgallon was awakened by the butler who said that a man outside wished to speak to him. When Kilgallon went down, he found the man completely covered with snow, having travelled from Sligo to Dromod by a night goods train, and had continued through snow drifts to Derrycarne to break the news to Sir Henry that his wife had given birth to a son. They returned to Lissadell the following morning.

Despite a fire in the estate office in 1941, a large number of Sir Henry's farm note books and account books have survived and clearly demonstrate how, like his father, he attended to every minute detail concerning the estate. Although he had been running the estate during the last ten years of his father's life, he must have found a new sense of freedom of action after his father's death in 1876. This, combined with his own detailed knowledge, not only of the estate but also of the tenants and their families, augured well for the future of Lissadell.

In that same year, Henry purchased from Owen Wynne over 900 acres at Mullaghneane for the sum of £12,000. The Wynne family of Hazelwood just outside Sligo town, was one of the most influential in the county, and various members had represented either the town or the county (or both) in Parliament between 1725 and 1865. After that, the fortunes of the family went into decline, while those of the Gore-Booths continued in the ascendant for four or five decades. The two families were related by marriage several times over, and Owen Wynne, Sir Henry's brother-in-law, was described by Wakefield as a model landlord to whom the poor looked 'as their friend and benefactor.'

As Sir Henry continued to consolidate the position of the estate, a special correspondent from *The Times* travelled from London on a tour of County Sligo to report on conditions there. Some of his remarks about the area in general and about Lissadell (which he, like some others, spelt as Lissadill) are interesting:

> On the sudden death of his father's agent, Sir Henry undertook the charge of the estates which he now owns, and has managed them most successfully for ten years, inaugurating a very thorough system of accounts and book-keeping, which are sadly deficient on some Irish estates…. His neighbours and tenants declare him to have been a model country gentleman, kindly-hearted and liberal, ever ready to aid and improve his people…. The present baronet does not think that the Land Act of 1870 has been altogether a success. The increased security conferred on the tenant enabled him to get more credit than was good for him; commodities not always needed or fitting were pressed on both man and wife; the necessity of payment seemed far deferred; and when bad times came, other creditors were often more exacting than the landlord….
>
> A great deal has been done both by the late and present owners, to improve their property…. A surveyor laid out roads and squared the plots, allotting them

according to the numbers of holders, arranging as much as possible that a fair proportion of good and bad land went together. With Sir Henry's own assistance, a fair valuation, which has always given satisfaction, was put on the new farms; this and all the other works were personally superintended by Sir Henry.

The article went on to describe the improvements made to the other townlands in the estate, adding the comment:

The pity is that half the population of these townlands could not be deported and their holdings doubled in size. Without fishing or work independently of their farms, the families, even on the best land, have not scope for reasonable subsistence.

After noting that there were 522 tenants in the Lissadell estate and 454 at Ballymote, the writer added that: 'Rents are generally under the Government valuation, and have not been advanced for 40 years.... On whatever sized holdings, the active and thrifty seem to thrive.'

The picture given by this newspaper article largely confirms the general perception at that time of a good landlord with reasonably contented tenants. A commission was set up in 1883 to enquire into the 'Condition of the Poorer Classes in Ireland,' and one of its appointed Commissioners, Penton Hart, wrote of the Gore-Booth estate: 'As we neared Lissadell, everything bespoke the resident and good landlord. We saw comfortable cottages scattered over the face of the countryside, each with its own territory, and with the land apparently in very good condition.'

Sir Henry and Lady Mary distributing food to the tenants during the famine of 1879 - (*Illustrated London News*)

Conditions continued to be reasonably favourable for the Gore-Booths and their tenants alike until 1879 when a number of significant events were to cause serious problems for the landlords generally. One of these was the growing competition resulting from the importation of cheap grain from America, undermining the home market and forcing Irish farmers to reduce their prices. The landlords lost revenues both directly and indirectly as a result, with reduced prices for their own crops and reduced receipts from rents now that many of the tenant farmers were beginning to find it difficult to pay.

The cruel treatment of tenants by so many landlords has resulted in well-deserved criticism although, as already stated, exceptions were seldom made for those who strove to act benevolently. Boyce and O'Day have written about the more recent re-assessment of the role of landlords, quoting various writers who argued that the relationship between the proprietor and tenant was more nuanced and less heavily weighted in favour of the landlord than had been previously assumed. They also refer to the limited control that landlords, in practice, enjoyed over the terms on which they let their land, and when things went seriously wrong, only a minority of landlords had the resources to meet the resulting problems.

That same year, 1879, was to test the landlords further in a fashion that they had not had to face since the Great Famine three decades earlier, for famine struck again after two successive years of bad harvests. Only a quarter of the potato crop in the north-west was saved, and large numbers of cattle and sheep died as a result of the exceptionally wet weather. Amid scenes reminiscent of the famine of the 1840s, the small farmers were especially badly hit. Once again evictions became commonplace and Sir Henry and his wife personally distributed provisions to those in need. Archdeacon O'Rorke was loud in his praise for the efforts made by Sir Henry to help his tenants, and described Lissadell as a 'provision store,' adding that Sir Henry personally investigated the conditions of his tenantry and their crops.

Charitable organisations also did much to alleviate the plight of the hungry, but the general deprivation began to have an unexpected effect on the smallholders who, unable to pay their rents and subjected to ruthless evictions, suddenly began, with a mixture of mutual co-operation and agitation, to press for change. They needed someone to channel their fears and their anger, and they also needed a leader to co-ordinate their efforts, and they found the answer in Michael Davitt. Davitt, a Fenian who had spent many years in prison, founded the Land League earlier in 1879 with the aim of securing a 25 per cent reduction in rents, along with an end to evictions and, in the longer term, the transfer of land from the landlords to their tenants. The Land League of Ireland was formally established in October, and Davitt chose a landlord as its president, Charles Stewart Parnell.

Most of the subsequent agitation was forcibly kept under control, but a number of landlords, including William Clements, the third earl of Leitrim, and Major Denis Mahon (returning from a meeting of the local Board of Guardians), along with some of their employees were murdered. Many landlords lived in fear for their lives and even Sir Henry, despite his good reputation, found the need to take some precautions for his personal safety. Lord Leitrim had stayed at Lissadell the night before he was murdered on his way to visit his Donegal estates and Henry heard about the shooting when returning from a visit to Henry Tottenham's estate at Glenferne, Co. Leitrim. When he asked the coachman what the people of the district thought of Lord Leitrim, he was told that 'he was not too bad if you took him the right way.' Taking a second coach from Manorhamilton. Sir Henry asked the second driver the same question, and was told: 'Well, your honour, Hell would not be full if Lord Leitrim was not there.'

Sir Henry's reputation at this time spread as far as Italy when the publication, *Emporo Pittorescu*, reproduced illustrations from the *London Illustrated News* depicting scenes at Lissadell during the 1879 famine. Under the title 'La Miseria in Irlanda', there were pictures with captions like, 'Scene in Lissadell', 'In Questa di Soccors' (Applying for Relief), and 'Sir Robert a Lady Gov Boot (sic) all' opera nella loro bottera' (… at work in their shop). The secretary of the local Relief Committee wrote to several newspapers attesting to Sir Henry's recent benevolence: 'Sir Henry Gore-Booth kept an open store of food at Lissadell, giving out meal, etc., to the starving poor, free to all, at his own cost, and I believe all the members of the family assisted in doing so.' This general store had been set up in the riding school where Father Shanagher and the Rev. Mr Cosgrove (who, between them, knew the circumstances of the poor who came) gave out tickets indicating the amount of food to be given to each holder. Wearing white aprons, Sir Henry and his wife, distributed meal, flour, tea and sugar and, according to Kilgallon who witnessed the scene, 'all left with smiling faces.'

The 1881 Land Act was the government's principal reaction to the

Land League agitation, giving to the tenant farmers the right to have their rents judicially fixed by the newly established Land Commission. Many rents were, in consequence, reduced by up to 25 per cent and, in some cases, by as much as 40 per cent. Radical as these changes were, they were not enough for the Land League which pressed for the abolition of the entire landlord system, and the scene was to be set for further political unrest with the introduction of Gladstone's first Home Rule Bill five years later in 1886. During January 1887, *The Irish Times* reported a meeting of Sir Henry's tenants at Ballymote who met to consider:

> the best means of tiding over this year of depression and difficulty and to solicit a reduction in their rents. It was proposed and seconded that, as Sir Henry always held at heart the welfare of the tenants, and was never known to cause an eviction on his extensive property, we go and pay our rents as usual, and rely for an abatement on our landlord's generosity. The tenants chose the wisest method, as they all got substantial abatements unsolicited and in extreme cases most liberal terms. Such as were unable to pay got any time they asked.

Sir Henry, who maintained that his rents were at all times reasonable had, as already noted, reduced his rents both at Lissadell and at Ballymote. The reduction at Ballymote was an extraordinary 40 per cent, a decision that was greeted there with bonfires and a torch-light procession. The Ballymote tenants sent an Address to Sir Henry, part of which read: 'It is most gratifying to us to be able to bear testimony to the fact that you have always been the poor Tenant's friend, let your land for its value, and allowed us many other privileges too numerous to notice in this Address.' Thanking the tenants for this, Sir Henry wrote in reply: 'It has never been my custom to let my land to the highest bidder, but it has always been my earnest wish to see my Tenants content and comfortable, and it affords me the greatest pleasure to find, by your Address, that my wishes have been gratified, and that such is the case.'

Sir Henry continued to remain on good terms with the Land League locally, indeed when the League's Ballymote Branch organised a 'Monster Demonstration' in December 1880, he was invited to attend. Even so, he was by then aware that the writing was on the wall for the landlords and, as noted by Terence Dooley in a contribution to a recent book edited by Carla King, Henry asserted at this time that he would be 'willing to sell every acre [because] it would be a great saving to me if I could get 23 years' purchase on the ordnance valuation, one fourth added.' It seems as though he might have agreed with Elizabeth Bowen's definition of an Irish estate as 'something between a *raison d'être* and a predicament.'

* * *

Burton Irwin, a cousin of Henry's, used to stay at Lissadell about once a year, and Thomas Kilgallon recalled that before he arrived, mousetraps were always set in his bedroom as he said he would not sleep if he thought there were mice in the room. He was a bachelor and lived most of the time in the Kildare Street Club in Dublin and, after he died, Sir Henry told Kilgallon that his cousin had left him 'some money and the small estate in Streamstown.' Irwin had asked Henry on several occasions to join the Orange Order but he refused saying he did not belong to secret societies because 'you were not free to be master of your own mind, and people pestered you for influence and for help in things you might not care.'

Conservation continued to be barely understood, judging from the ongoing wholesale slaughter of game birds (and almost anything else that moved) resulting from organised shoots, whether at Lissadell or elsewhere. A brief news item in the sporting publication, *The World*, in November 1895 reported that Lord Ripon had just held his second shooting party of the season at Studley Royal where Sir Henry Gore-Booth was one of the guests. Ripon and Gore-Booth, along with four other guns, managed to shoot 'nearly five thousand seven hundred head in three days, the bag including five thousand one hundred and seventy six pheasants.' On a rather lighter note, one of the Sligo newspapers, while reporting poaching near Grange, north of Lissadell, in 1878, remarked that Sir Henry: 'has a consuming passion for shooting hares and snipe, whose souls, unnumbered Achilles-like, he yearly sends to Hades, and their bodies to the market.'

Records of shooting for sport at Lissadell continued to be kept in special Game Books which had printed columns for partridges, pheasants, snipe, woodcock, etc. One entry, under the heading 'Remarks', consisted of the single word 'Borris,' a veiled reference to a visit to Arthur McMurrough-Kavanagh, at Borris House, County Carlow, a meeting that was to be hugely significant for Henry. The 'bag' totalled a modest 19 snipe, eight woodcock and one teal, but the real significance of this visit was to emerge later.

His grandson, Hugh, related the story (though reproved for doing so by his father), about one of Henry's guests at Lissadell who expressed a wish to shoot a roe deer. His sons decided that in order not to disappoint the guest, they caught a large fawn billy-goat and, with the help of the gamekeepers, they disguised the animal as a deer by tying some antlers to the goat's horns before tethering it in a wood near the house among the rhododendrons. Then, accompanied by the head keeper, the guest was led to the wood where he spotted the 'deer.' The keeper advised a long shot and the guest, with remarkable aim, dropped the animal at a great distance. Overjoyed, the sportsman immediately sprang up and was preparing to rush forward to examine his prize, when the keeper admonished him saying that such conduct was not practised at Lissadell where it was usual for the antlers to be brought down to the house by one of the keepers. The antlers were duly produced and, as Hugh recounted, 'so complete was his delusion that until the day of his death he never dreamt of how he had fallen victim to a practical joke.'

Lightning struck the chapel at Magherow, near Lissadell House, during Mass one Sunday in 1883, killing a member of the congregation and injuring some others. On hearing the news, Sir Henry hastened to the scene 'to help and to console the afflicted,' and he later contributed to the cost of repairing the damage which, according to the *Sligo Champion*, was considerable. The same newspaper later noted that the largest contributions donated to the repair fund were those of Sir Henry and Lady Gore-Booth, and 'added to these are the donations of lesser amounts from the junior members of the Lissadell family.'

While he was, first and foremost, a landed proprietor, Henry was also something of an entrepreneur, and besides becoming involved in mining, shirt manufacture, the co-op movement, and a railway company, he also invested in property abroad. Except in so far as they had potential for the railway company of which he was to become chairman, the mines near Arigna and Ballisodare held no interest for him, but he later became involved in a mining venture in the more immediate area. This was at the instigation of another local landlord, Henry Tottenham of Glenade, Co. Leitrim, with whom he agreed to go into partnership in a barytes mining operation near Glencarbury in 1889. The partnership did not survive Tottenham's subsequent financial problems, indeed it ended in lengthy and expensive legal wrangling. Henry eventually withdrew on the advice of his solicitor who warned him: 'We are altogether averse to having any further litigation as we are afraid, from what we know of Mr Tottenham, that you would gain practically very little benefit.'

From 1895 onwards, the Gleniff Barytes firm was successfully run, first by Henry, and later by his son. Barytes had been discovered in the vicinity of Ben Bulben in 1859 and the mines were worked for 120 years, though Josslyn sold the family interest in 1911 to the Gleniff Barytes Company of Glasgow.

The journalist and author, Kees van Hoek, described the old workings and the signs warning visitors to keep away from the mines when he visited there around 1945. The valuable deposits were still being excavated and transported to the nearest roads by an aerial cableway for processing at the deep-water quay at Sligo. He scrambled up to one of the shafts high up on Gleniff and described the scene which met his eyes:

> Clatter and shake, jibber and jitter, the pneumatic drills, jerkily boring the shotholes for the dynamite charges, all in an unreal pinkish light of mud and dust, the sound, cooped up as it is, incessantly splitting and pounding one's head. To come out of this underworld right into the clouds, descending to blue hills drenched in summer sunlight as into God's own amphitheatre, gives one a sense of being born anew.

Although a Royal Commission was established in 1836 in a bid to ensure that the introduction of a railway system in Ireland would follow a coherent plan, the development of the railways proceeded in a haphazard fashion because many different interests were anxious simply to promote their own schemes. Sligo was not behind other towns in competing to join the growing network centred on Dublin and Belfast but compared to other places of a similar size, its eventual connection came late in the day. Work was actually completed from Dublin as far as Mullingar when the Midland Railway Company halted its proposed extension to Carrick-on-Shannon and Sligo because it wanted to concentrate its resources on the Dublin to Galway route. Work on the line to Sligo did not recommence until after the Famine, and the connection to Sligo was not completed until 1862 when the travelling time between the town and the capital was reduced to five and a quarter hours.

Frustrated by this long delay, several attempts had been made earlier by interests in Sligo to connect the town with Enniskillen, which had already been joined to the network at Belfast, but nothing had come of them. After Sligo was linked to Dublin, a new group of influential people, which included Sir Henry, pressed for a connection with Enniskillen through Collooney and Manorhamilton. Because of a downturn in the economy, blamed on the importation of cheap grain from America and cheap goods from England, this plan was put aside. It took Sir Henry and his backers, including his neighbour at Hazelwood, Owen Wynne, along with Francis La Touche, H. Lyons Montgomery and Loftus Tottenham a further 13 years to get a Bill as far as Parliament, and even then their proposed line had to overcome a good deal of local hostility.

A public meeting to consider the merits of an alternative route through Bundoran was held in Sligo in September 1874, and Henry was among the attendance, but did not oppose it until he heard that this line was planned to run 'down by the edge of Cartron Hill, across the marsh at Standalone Point, and go along the strand to the foot of Bath Lodge where it would enter Mr Wynne's property.' The plan also envisaged that the railway would cross Drumcliff Bay on embankments which might provide the opportunity to reclaim the whole of the bay near Finod. Then, midway between Carney and Lissadell, there was to be a station, after which the line would: 'cross the road that leaves from near Carney on to Mr Francis Barber's farm.' This was a matter of some concern for Sir Henry, as Barber was by far his most important tenant. While it seems he did not actually voice concern about the prospect of smoking monsters coming so close to Lissadell House, 'the Company, anxious to meet the wishes of everyone, did not interfere with him at all.'

Anyway, this whole proposal was subsequently dropped in favour of Henry's original suggestion and plans then went ahead to run the new railway through Collooney and Manorhamilton to Enniskillen.

The Sligo Leitrim Northern Counties Railway was Incorporated by Act of Parliament in 1875 and the first section of line, that between Enniskillen and Belcoo, was opened to traffic four years later, after which work then proceeded through Manorhamilton – the company's headquarters – and Dromahair to Collooney from where, for five miles, S.L.N.C.R. trains continued on the existing tracks of the Midland Great Western Railway to Sligo.

Henry was appointed chairman of the company in 1882 and the new company did moderately well for a few years but was in serious financial difficulties by 1894 due to its indebtedness to the State, as a result of which it was advertised for sale by the Board of Works. Both the Great Northern and the Midland Great Western Companies expressed an interest in purchasing the company but Sir Henry strongly opposed any form of takeover. He drafted a 'Reconstruction Scheme' to re-organise the company, with the intention of developing its resources, and also to purchase outright the rolling stock which was then being leased. He even petitioned the Treasury – without success – to be allowed to take over the running of the recently built line from Claremorris to Coloney. The majority of the engines were 0.6.4. tank locomotives, a rather uncommon wheel arrangement, and two locomotives purchased around 1882 were named *Lissadell* and *Hazelwood* respectively, while another, purchased after his death, was named *Sir Henry*. Michael Hamilton, who had worked for the company, recollected in a personal account of the railway that, as a child, his favourite engine was the Sir Henry, 'because of its great size.'

The SLNCR locomotive, *Sir Henry*, purchased and named after him four years after he died. - (*photo. Neil Sprinks*)

A unique feature of this company was that its locomotives were never numbered, all being given names instead. Another feature, thought by Neil Sprinks to have been unique among British and Irish railways, was the fact that the doors of the company's passenger coaches 'were hung [hinged] on the right, with handles and locks on the left.' Sprinks also noted in his book about the S.L.N.C.R. that 'financial stringency led to longevity of equipment, and that there were remarkable anachronisms in rolling stock, signalling and workshop practices. But despite the shortage of money, there were many signs of ingenuity and enterprise…'

Despite the huge problems facing the company, it doggedly maintained its independence and, indeed, remained the last independent broad-gauge railway company in Britain or Ireland until its final closure. Sir Henry's re-organisation improved the company's financial position but profits were, at best, modest. For example, total receipts for 1896, one of the better years, amounted to £20,600 when profits stood at just over £4,400.

After Sir Henry died, his son Josslyn became chairman of the company, a position he continued to hold until 1931. Josslyn was then succeeded as chairman by Captain George Hewson, who told shareholders at the annual general meeting held in the following year:

> It was very largely owing to the way in which he [Sir Josslyn] had conducted himself at the helm, that the company had been able to avoid the storms that had afflicted the railways in general for the last few years. They had tried to persuade Sir Josslyn to stay with them but unfortunately his health could not stand it.

Neil Sprink's comment that the S.L.N.C.R. company was quite innovative, was certainly justified, for it was one of the first to experiment with rail-cars, initially fitting road buses with railway wheels and thereby cutting costs when dealing with light passenger traffic, later introducing specially built rail-cars. During Sir Henry's time, the company commenced operating a steamer service – which it was enabled to do under the Railways (Ireland) Act of 1896 – between Sligo and Belmullet. The *S.S. Tartar* was chartered for 'carrying Passengers, Goods and Live Stock and is intended to sail (weather permitting) without Pilot.' Calls were made at Rosses Point, Ballycastle and Belderrrig, 'but passengers joining or leaving the Steamer at any intermediate stopping place must arrange for small boats to put them aboard or take them ashore.'

The railway company struggled through the 1930s and found a brief respite during the 1940s when wartime petrol rationing curbed road competition, but encountered renewed difficulties thereafter.

A leading railway author, L.T.C. Rolt, wrote during 1952: 'I should doubt whether there is a more fascinating broad-gauge railway in the

British Isles than the main line of the S.L.N.C.R., which began operating in 1882 and has preserved a precious independence.' But not long after, the company was no more, and although it had been struggling in the face of declining traffic for many years, it was a decision made elsewhere that finally closed the line. The Northern Ireland government, in its determination to radically reduce the loss-making rail network, rendered the Sligo-Leitrim company's position hopeless by closing the Belfast to Enniskillen line in 1957, leaving the S.L.N.C.R. stranded with no northern outlet.

During its 75 years of operational life, the company was noted for its good management and its excellent staff relations – almost certainly influenced by the company's Gore-Booth connections. It continues to be remembered affectionately by local people, and one of two locomotives acquired only a few years before the closure (the last two steam locomotives commissioned for an Irish railway company) has been saved from the scrap heap for preservation.

* * *

The Times (London) sent a special correspondent to Ireland in 1881 to report on conditions generally after the recent famine and the subsequent land agitation. While he was in Sligo, he reported at some length on the work done by Sir Henry at Lissadell. The newspaper's description of the estate at Lissadell at this time bordered upon lyrical:

> [The house is] a beautiful and picturesque residence and deservedly worthy of its high prestige for antiquity [it was less than 50 years built] and beauty; in its lovely and secluded glens vegetation is matured with almost southern or Oriental vigour …. Beautiful ferns of the most rarest species spring up in the recesses of its … rockeries, unnumbered varieties of mosses and lichens fill its hollows, and make a peculiar ground shade out of the wealth of its wild primrose plants. Flowers of every hue and colour peep out amongst its shrubberies, even in the most isolated and retired corners, until the eye is surfeited with beauty, and the senses enthralled with the exhaled fragrance of odoriferous flowers, so profusely supplied by bounteous nature.

However, the same newspaper's descriptions of conditions for the tenants living outside the walls of Lissadell, four miles away at Ballyconnell, were anything but lyrical, the blame being put on the landlords there, notably 'Mr Gethin and Mrs Huddleston, both absentees, not known even by sight to their tenants.'

Although Henry had been re-elected an M.P., he continued to avoid any involvement in local politics, preferring to concentrate on his estate and his business interests. When a Unionist meeting was held in the Assembly Rooms in Sligo, in July 1895, and a member made a proposal suggesting Sir Henry's name as a candidate for the committee election, he declined to allow his name to go forward. Interviewed just after this about his views on Home Rule, he said he had never been able to see that it would benefit the country, and added that: 'There is no magic in Home Rule to suddenly change natural conditions. In the south and west we have no industries; the land is the only source of living.' He told the newspaper reporter:

> It is the absence of industries which creates poverty, and how will Home Rule cure this? No it is not Home Rule but time and education which are wanted. I notice that when the Irish go out to America, it is not to the land that they go, but to the cities, where they engage in industrial pursuits and are successful.

When, around the same time, the *Sligo Champion* chided Sir Henry for allegedly trying to influence the voting of some of his Ballymote tenants, inferring that conditions were not universally good throughout his estate, Canon James McDermott responded to the newspaper about these strictures:

> When, however, you imply that Sir Henry has ceased to be 'on excellent terms with his tenantry' I cannot, as parish priest, remain silent … in every corner of his Ballymote estate he is honoured and esteemed as few landlords are in Ireland in the present day…. Though Sir Henry's land is let a little, if at all, above the valuation, still he gave, during the past years, larger general reductions than any other landlord connected with the parish, while his contributions to the specially afflicted was simply magnificent.

A regular feature at Lissadell, inaugurated during Sir Robert's time, was the annual fête or 'Harvest Home' organised for the tenantry and employees. This usually took place in what was known as the Riding School, a large hall-like room used for exercising horses indoors, which was decorated with evergreens for the occasion. The *Sligo Independent* described the scene:

> Along the centres of the numerous tables were placed some monster roots – consisting of mangel, turnips and carrots. The Mangels averaging about 20lbs each, and the Swedes about 15lbs. these together with miniature ricks of Hay and bunches of excellent white Oats, showed off the tables to perfection in an agricultural point of view.

During the afternoon about 300 tenants and workers would sit down to a traditional dinner of beef, mutton and plum pudding, with Sir Henry and Lady Gore-Booth and other members of the family and their friends acting as helpers and 'paying every attention to their guests.'

The same newspaper reported on the 'Harvest Home' held in 1880:

When tea was served at 6 o'clock by Miss Hooper, Miss Anderson, Mrs Barber (housekeeper), Mrs Cosgrave, Lady Gore, Miss Gore, Master Gore, and Miss Constance, after which dancing commenced, led off by Mr Henry Miller, who took the part of master of ceremonies, and acted his part well. During the evening the amusement was varied by the singing of comic songs in which the Misses Siggins were conspicuous.... Supper came at 8 o'clock consisting of roast beef and beer.

At 11 o'clock, Sir Henry stood up and said the reason he did not give a harvest home last year was in consequence of the bad harvest, and consequently the depressed state of the country, but that next year, God willing, he would give the usual harvest home. He was responded to by three hearty cheers for himself, Lady Gore, Miss Gore, and all the Lissadell family, after which all separated in a most orderly manner, which speaks well for the people inasmuch as, though supplied during the day with an unlimited quantity of beer, there was not even a cross word spoken. It is very cheery in these days of Land Leaguing and Communist spouting to see a gentleman of Sir Henry's position and his high born lady placing themselves on a level and mixing with the people over whom Providence has placed them. Such condescension on their part gives pleasure to the people and creates confidence in all.

This happy rural prospect was certainly not the universal scene at this time. Instances of attacks on landlords' property and stock and, more seriously, on some of the landlords and their agents were becoming a cause for concern not only for the landlords but for large farmers too.

* * *

An article published in *Yachting World* in April 1896 described how Henry had, from his earliest childhood, developed a taste for shooting, fishing and hunting, but it was not until he left Eton College that he turned his attention to the sea, 'and acquired a small partly-decked boat, rigged as a yawl. Knocking about in Sligo Bay, with a boy for a crew, he gained his first experience of handling a boat.' Though the article did not refer to the fact, much of his early sailing had been with his elder brother, Robert, and the pair amused themselves, happily gaining confidence while sailing off the shore at Lissadell until, one fatal day, their boat overturned and Robert, the heir to the estate, was drowned and Henry was fortunate to escape with his life. This tragedy did not deter Henry from continuing to pursue his interest in sailing – indeed his interest in boating was probably further influenced by his cousin, the Earl of Dunraven and by his Wynne relations. More importantly, he was to be greatly impressed, in 1864, when at the age of 21 he was invited by the celebrated Arthur McMurrough-Kavanagh to join him in a fishing voyage in his private yacht.

One of the oldest families in Ireland, the McMurroughs claim an ancestry going back over 1,400 years. The saintly Moling, who became Bishop of Ferns, is claimed as an early member of the family, as were a number of the kings of Leinster, one of whom, Dermot, invited the Normans to Ireland in 1169 in order to help him in a dispute with the then High King of Ireland. Arthur McMurrough-Kavanagh was probably the most remarkable man that Sir Henry met during his entire life. He was born without arms and legs but overcame this incredible handicap, quickly learning to write and paint, and was already riding a pony at the age of four. He taught himself to shoot and fish and became an expert horseman. Encouraged by his mother who was determined that he should live life to the full, it seemed that nothing was impossible for him. He travelled widely – at first with his mother at the age of 15, to the Holy Land and the Middle East, and three years later he went with a tutor on an extraordinary tour commencing in Scandinavia, travelling through Russia and Persia as far as India. He became a keen yachtsman, sailing on ocean cruises in his private yacht, *Corsair*. In 1860, two years after he was made a member of the Royal Yacht Squadron, he purchased a new two-masted schooner, a craft of 150 tons. He named it *Eva*, after his famous ancestor who married Strongbow, or perhaps he called his boat after his daughter (or both), sailing in it to the Arctic Circle six years later.

Henry, as already noted, had originally met him through their mutual interest in shooting, but after purchasing his new schooner, Kavanagh invited Henry to join him on a fishing cruise to Norway. Henry found himself introduced to the delights of salmon fishing on the Pasvig River that formed the far northern boundary between Norway and Russia. This cruise, and the salmon fishing which accompanied it, had a most profound effect upon Henry. To his delight, the experience was repeated during the summer months of the following two years. So impressed was Henry by the quality of the fishing there that he decided to return to the same river, this time organising his own voyages to this region, becoming something of an arctic explorer and amateur scientist.

Eight years were to pass by before he finally arranged his own arctic voyage, when he set out for Norway accompanied by Thomas Kilgallon. There was an unfortunate initial setback to the adventure because, when they arrived at Hull, Henry discovered to his dismay that his carefully packed fishing rods had, somehow, got lost during the first leg of the journey. They proceeded, however, with a Captain Watson on his steamer *Tasso* and, three days later, arrived at Trondheim, in north Norway. From there they travelled further up the coast in a local steamer, the *Nordland*, which called at Bodø and Tromsø before sailing to Hammerfest, about 50 miles short of the North Cape, where Henry went ashore to try his luck salmon fishing and duck shooting. This fishing expedition was made possible by one of the other passengers, Sir William Smith, who lent Henry his own fishing gear to replace those lost or mislaid earlier. While ashore, Henry also managed to shoot his first polar bear and met King Oscar II of the then united kingdom of Norway and Sweden who asked the Irishman to show him how to handle a salmon rod. To commemorate their meeting, they had their photograph taken standing together.

Henry and Kilgallon then joined a Mr Power on board his ship, *Hyacinthe* and managed to shoot a seal from 120 yards. Six hundred miles to the north lay the lonely Spitzbergen (or Svalbard) archipelago, jointly owned by Norway and Russia, with its impressive but bleak range of snow-covered mountains rising to around 6,000 feet. Apart from a section of the western coast, which is accessible during the short arctic summer, the islands are surrounded by ice, and it was on that western shore that Sir Henry made his first real polar landing, spending several days hunting for deer before sailing back to Norway from where he returned home. The most memorable aspect of this trip for Sir Henry was that, despite having lost his fishing gear, he had managed to catch, with borrowed rods, no less than 879 lbs. of salmon.

These polar waters were explored initially, as might be expected, by Russians and Norwegians in search of new fishing grounds and for whaling purposes which later began to attract some other nationalities, notably the Dutch. Polar exploration effectively commenced later as a result of efforts to find a northern sea route to India and China – the famous Northwest Passage, north of Canada, and the less well-known Northeast Passage around Norway and Siberia. Neither of these routes had been traversed at the time of Henry's first polar voyage. The

Northeast Passage was not navigated until 1878, while the northwest route was only achieved in 1903. Henry's first arctic voyage took place in 1873 only a year after two of the earliest explorers of the Barents Sea (between Spitzbergen and Novaya Zemlya) – Payer and Weyprecht – had commenced their detailed exploration of the area. Five years after that, Nordenskjold began exploring the region, followed a decade later by Fridtjof Nansen, the famous Norwegian explorer and oceanographer, whose first arctic explorations, in 1888, were centred on Greenland, the same year that Sir Henry was sailing off that same coast. Like Sir Henry Gore-Booth, Nansen became interested in ice drifts and tested his theories near both Novaya Zemlya and Greenland between 1893 and 1895, though this was some 14 or more years after Sir Henry had been conducting similar observations. Robert Peary, the famous American explorer – whose subsequent expedition during 1908 was the first to reach the North Pole – commenced his arctic explorations with surveys of Greenland three years after Sir Henry's final voyage there.

Given all of this, it appears little short of incredible that Sir Henry was sailing in polar waters at the same time as – and even before – some of the most famous explorers of the region, and he was also studying the effects of drifting ice more than a decade before Nansen was more famously to do so. Henry's navigational skills and his general seamanship in relatively small boats were quite outstanding and also point to his physical fitness at the time, though there were indications that these hazardous voyages almost certainly damaged his health. The arctic islands of Novaya Zemlya (spelt in various ways) and Spitzbergen, which held such an attraction for Henry, had been first discovered during the sixteenth century, but Franz Josef Land, further north, was not discovered until 1872 (by the Austrians, Weyprecht and Payer, who named the archipelago after their emperor). They had stumbled upon the island group while engaged in searching for the Northeast Passage a mere seven years before Sir Henry landed there.[2]

In 1877, two years after Henry's first arctic voyage, again accompanied by Thomas Kilgallon, he sailed for Norway for the second time on the *Tasso*. As one of the local Sligo newspapers expressed it: 'Sir Henry, leaving the timid hare and the half domesticated pheasant

---

[2] Almost 122 years later, when a similar sized vessel sailed in arctic waters, its skipper was reported (*The Irish Times*, August 2000) as saying that he and his crew hoped to become the first to reach Franz Josef Land in such a small boat.

to less manly sportsmen, now and again betakes himself to high latitudes
where his quarry on land is the polar bear, and on the sea the arctic
whale.' He attempted to purchase his own ship when he reached
Trondheim but nothing came of it, so he joined the *Harald Hafagar*
and continued up the Norwegian coast for more salmon fishing which
resulted in a catch of more than 2,000 lbs., including a fine specimen
weighing 49lbs.

Thomas Kilgallon photographed in his old age, c.1925,
with Angus, Sir Henry's youngest grandson.

A year later saw Henry and Kilgallon once more on board the *Tasso*,
this time joined by an experienced arctic navigator, Captain Albert
Markham who, three years earlier, had sailed to latitude 83 degrees
20', which he claimed was the most northerly latitude so far reached, a
record which stood unbroken for 20 years. While Henry's main object
remained, as before, a 'sporting' voyage, the presence of Markham
ensured that it was also a voyage of discovery. Reaching Norway, they
transferred to the cutter *Isbjorn*, specially built to navigate in ice-bound
waters, the same vessel which the two Austrian explorers had used

when they discovered Franz Josef Land in 1872.

Sir Henry and Markham encountered ice on June 2 and sighted the snow-covered south-western cliffs of Novaya Zemlya a week later. Consisting of two very large, elongated islands stretching north of Siberia for almost 600 miles, Novaya Zemlya appeared on maps at the time showing details of its southern and western coast, while the eastern and northern sides were largely indicated by dotted lines, pending exploration. The island's northern coast, only partly explored, had been rounded for the first time by a Dutch expedition a year before. The *Isbjorn* headed for the narrow strait that separated the two islands, known as Matuschkin Scharr, where the party landed to shoot quantities of sea birds, catch fish and hunt reindeer in order to replenish the ship's larder. They erected a stone cairn, inscribing the name of their ship and the date on a piece of wood, and they also left directions where to find their written record, the details being placed in a sherry bottle for the benefit of a Dutch expedition led by Captain de Bruyne. Henry and Markham had arranged to leave the details of their own route as the Dutch were expected to arrive in the area shortly. Henry then made an unsuccessful attempt to continue eastwards through the strait, which would have led into the little known Kara Sea, described by David Roberts as 'almost perpetually ice-choked' and 'a graveyard for ships.' Blocked by ice, the party decided to go back to try sailing up the west coast instead, and they managed to reach a point 120 miles north of the ice-blocked strait.

Almost four weeks later, they returned to the strait of Matoschkin Scharr where the ice was now breaking up and the *Isbjorn* managed to navigate through to the Kara Sea, from where they attempted to sail up the as yet uncharted eastern side of Novaya Zemlya. Thwarted by more ice, they returned through the strait where they met Captain de Bruyne's Dutch expedition, and the two boats anchored alongside. The crews spent a pleasant evening together, exchanging not only topographical information but gifts of crockery and leather (the latter to repair boots) in exchange for victuals shot by Sir Henry's party.

Henry now had to decide what to do next, whether to follow the Dutch who were heading east towards Ice Haven, or to sail for Spitzbergen more than 800 miles to the northwest. He and Markham decided to do neither but, instead, to make one more attempt at sailing up the almost unknown eastern side of Novaya Zemlya. After encountering a severe storm which may have helped to break up the ice, they got through and reached the most northerly point of the island, and because it was the first British expedition to do so, they planted a Union flag to mark the occasion. However, as the headland had already been named Cape Zhedaniya by the Russians, they were deprived of the opportunity to call it Cape Markham or even Cape Gore-Booth. The party then continued in the direction of Ice Haven, where Henry conducted what he called a scientific examination of the edge of the ice. After running into more loose ice, the vessel was turned about at the insistence of the anxious Norwegian crew members, though Henry's grandson, Hugh, was to claim that the 'perfidious' crew did so while he was asleep below deck. Then, heading towards Franz Josef Land they met more ice, and when only 90 miles from their objective the *Isbjorn* had to be turned again for the journey back to Norway. Arriving there, Sir Henry got word that de Bruyne's Dutch expedition had landed on Franz Josef Land, confirming his view that he could have done likewise if he had not been impeded by an unduly nervous Norwegian crew. With winter approaching, it was now too late in the season to do anything about it except to plan his next voyage.

Before that took place, however, Sir Henry was invited to attend a meeting organised by the Royal Geographical Society in London at which his friend, Captain Markham, was due to speak about recent expeditions to the Barents Sea. Markham began his talk by announcing that Dr Nordenskjold, in the *Vega*, had a year earlier completed the first voyage from the Atlantic to the Pacific across the north of Siberia, the long sought-after Northeast Passage. He then gave an account of the voyage he had recently undertaken with Sir Henry Gore-Booth in the 40-ton Norwegian cutter, *Isbjorn*, chartered by Sir Henry. Markham related how they had navigated the Barents Sea and reached the coast of Novaya Zemlya, sailing northwards to a latitude of 78°24', describing how they had met 'many streams of pack ice, and these had thickened, so that they had to yield to the objections of the Norwegian crew and turn homeward.'

Captain Markham brought with him to the meeting 'his important collection of birds, insects, plants and rocks' assembled during the voyage. Lord Northbrook, who was present at the meeting, commented that Novaya Zemlya had been discovered by an Englishman, and he was glad 'that an Englishman was now contending with the Dutch in the field of arctic discovery.' Sir Henry received the congratulations of the Royal Geographical Society following this 1879 voyage:

> The results, as regards Novaya Zemlya are valuable, and those of your examination of the ice-line in the Barents Sea in September are more so. The

voyage forms one of a very necessary series of reconnaissances which are bringing together valuable information respecting what is now the best route northwards. In one respect it is the most important voyage of the series because you were in a very high latitude at a later period of the year than any other vessel.

Sir Henry and Captain Markham attended several more meetings of the Royal Geographical Society, and during one of Henry's London visits, while out walking, he met Benjamin Leigh Smith, a British polar explorer of some note. During this brief encounter, Smith casually remarked that he hoped Gore-Booth would come and look for him if he went missing during his proposed 1881 arctic voyage. This almost off-the-cuff remark, made during a chance meeting, was to have interesting consequences.

As it happened, Sir Henry stayed at home in 1881, but when the arctic 'season' ended in October, Leigh Smith failed to return from his voyage. Clement Markham, who became President of the Royal Geographical Society and was a cousin of Captain Markham who had sailed with Sir Henry in 1880, wrote to him at Lissadell to express his fear that 'Leigh Smith must have been caught [in the ice]. Without doubt somebody must go up to look after them next year.' There had been a number of instances where polar explorers, after their ships had been iced-up, had managed to survive the winter until help arrived in the following summer. So, hopes were reasonably high, provided that no catastrophe had occurred, that Leigh Smith and his party could be rescued as soon as the ice broke up.

Henry had made a number of unsuccessful attempts to purchase a suitable boat of his own for his arctic voyaging, but the news about Leigh Smith prompted him to renew his efforts. He travelled to London for a special meeting arranged by the Royal Geographical Society to organise a rescue bid, after which he searched several boatyards and found the boat he had been looking for, a 46-ton ketch under construction at Wyvenhoe, Essex. He instructed the builders to specially strengthen it against ice-crushing by means of stout cross-beams, and he also had steel plates installed to assist its passage through ice floes. When it was ready, he named it the *Kara* after the Siberian sea to the east of Novaya Zemlya, the limit of his arctic voyaging to date.

Writing about the *Kara*, Sir Henry described it 'as good a sea boat in really bad weather as I ever put foot into.' He was especially pleased that he had arranged to have it strengthened to withstand pressure from ice. One of his crew, a Norwegian, who had spent his life sailing in vessels of this class, told him 'there was no vessel in the trade that could compare with the *Kara* – her peculiar roundness and strength makes her jump up on the ice when a nip comes.' There was one drawback, however – it had to rely on wind-power, but although Sir Henry was 'fully aware of the superiority of steam in the navigation of ice … unfortunately he could not find a second-hand, or build a suitable steamer for the amount he was prepared to spend.'

Two months after the launch of the *Kara*, accompanied by Thomas Kilgallon and with an experienced whaler, Captain Bannerman, Sir Henry set out from the south of England for Novaya Zemlya, this time on a search and rescue mission. The poet, Yeats, was not impressed (and not too well informed either) when he wrote that Henry 'thinks nothing but the North Pole, where his first officer, to his great satisfaction, has recently lost himself and thereby made an expedition to rescue him desirable.' When Henry arrived at Tromsø in north Norway, several other boats were also gathering for the search for Leigh Smith and his crew. News reached them that the ice was unusually far south, and this spread a mood of depression among the would-be rescuers. Two boats, the *Kara* and the *Hope*, left Tromsø on July 4 and ran into a severe storm while approaching Novaya Zemlya, resulting in damage to the *Kara* when 'six feet of bulwarks were carried away, and three of the bulwark stanchions badly sprung by ice.' As a result, Henry's boat had to be towed to a sheltered bay by the *Hope*, where repairs were effected. The *Kara* and the *Hope*, later joined by the Dutch vessel *Willem Barents*, began a general search for the missing explorers along the western coast of Novaya Zemlya in the belief that if Leigh Smith had managed to survive the winter, this was the area he would have sought to reach. Even so, he might as easily be anywhere else in this inhospitable and still not fully explored region, and it was not unlikely that he and his party were all dead. The captain of the *Hope* left a message and some provisions close to Matuschkin Scharr in a cairn surmounted by a staff before retiring to the shelter of a nearby bay to await developments.

Nine months earlier, Leigh Smith's ship had sunk in less than two hours after being crushed by the ice. Although they had insufficient time to salvage all the food and equipment on board, the crew had managed to save 'about three hundredweight of biscuit, six barrels of four and some preserved vegetables.' A subsequent account published in the *Illustrated London News* recorded how they shot and ate a total of thirty-six bears and twenty-nine walrus which 'afforded a welcome addition to the food of the shipwrecked mariners.' When the ice began

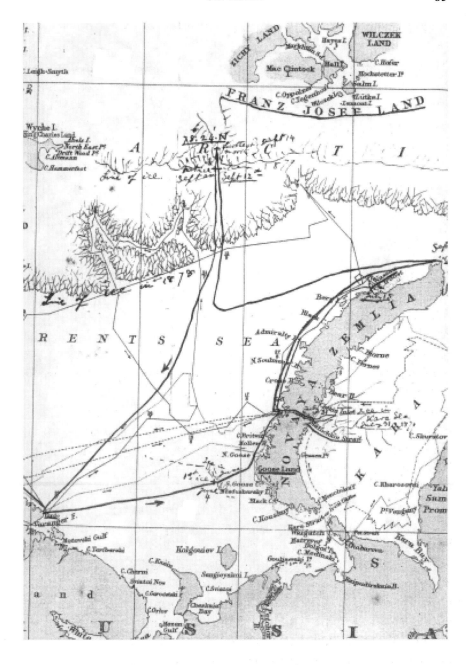

Map of the Barents and Kara Seas published by the Royal Geographical Society to indicate routes of pre-1879 arctic expeditions. On it, Sir Henry marked in thick black line the route of his own 1879 voyage indicating his failed attempt to sail up the east coast of Novaya Zemlya and his subsequent furthest north reached on September 14 – well beyond what was achievable a year earlier.

to break up, they dragged the ship's boats across the ice like sleds until they reached the edge, where the boats were launched and they then headed south for Novaya Zemlya, making a successful landfall close to Matoschkin Scharr. As the *Illustrated London News* reported: 'Here they saw the cairn and staff … left for their guidance … and indicating the spot where the *Hope* was then lying, only one mile distant, although she was hidden at the time by the point of land on which the cairn stood.' The climax of the tale is both near-miraculous and, at the same time, something of an anti-climax. Exhausted by their exertions, Leigh Smith and his crew slept soundly overnight, unaware that rescue was so near at hand (behind the nearest headland) until the next morning when they saw the approaching *Hope* and the *Willem Barents*.

Henry recorded on August 4 that the *Hope* sailed to meet the missing men and take them aboard, and that he and Leigh Smith were reunited the next day. Henry was amazed and delighted to find him 'looking older but quite well, in fact a great deal better than when I last saw him.' The reunion celebrations lasted into the early hours of the morning and although Sir Henry was invited to return to England with the *Hope* along with the rescued crew, he elected to return in the *Kara*. A souvenir in connection with this voyage, in the form of a photograph album containing many arctic scenes, was presented to Henry bearing the inscription: 'From B. Leigh Smith to Sir Henry Gore-Booth in grateful remembrance of assistance afforded to the crew of the *Eira* in the Polar Seas.'

Although he continued voyaging in arctic waters – on and off – for the next 15 years, most of these later trips were undertaken for purely sporting purposes and make for rather duller reading. He remained at Lissadell during 1883, but a year later sailed again in the *Kara*, which had undergone a refit after the adventures in 1882. This time he headed for Greenland waters, intent on whaling, for which purpose he had installed harpoon guns. Sir Henry had sent an article about whaling to the *Encyclopaedia of Sport* in which he wrote:

> By referring to Martin's *Voyage to Spitzbergen* (Hakluyt Society, 1855) ... it will be seen that formerly whales abounded along the ice at various points from Jan Mayen [Island] to Spitzbergen, and in the bays of the latter island; but even in Scoresby's time they had deserted many of their former haunts, and every year they retire for protection from their greatest enemy, man, further and further into the ice. He had, however, heard whalers assert that there are as many fish (sic) as ever, if you can only find them, and if the conditions of the ice will allow of their capture.

Hoping that whale numbers would be greater there, he headed for Jan

Mayen Island, about 400 miles north of Iceland, and described how the whales were pursued in what were little more than long rowing boats armed with a harpoon gun placed forward. When a whale was harpooned, its normal reaction was to dive, sometimes taking with it up to 600 fathoms of line. However, requiring air they had to resurface within half an hour or so, when further harpoons were used until the mammal died. Whales sometimes put up a violent struggle, and Sir Henry described an occasion when 'a Sperm Whale destroyed three small boats and injured the ship itself.' On another occasion a vessel named the *Essex* 'was actually sunk by a Sperm deliberately charging her twice.' Little was then known of the lifespan of whales, but Sir Henry later recorded an incident which occurred in 1894 when a whaler was operating in the Davis Strait between Greenland and Canada. The crew killed a whale out of which was cut a harpoon 'stamped with the name of the ship *Jean*, which had been sunk in 1861, 33 years earlier.' Sir Henry's 1884 whaling trip, which was reported in some detail in an article published in *Yachting World*, ended with a visit to both northern Greenland and Iceland on his way home.

* * *

Not surprisingly, Lady Gore-Booth, rearing her family of two sons and three daughters, was less enthusiastic about the wonders of the Arctic than her husband, and she managed, every so often, to persuade her husband to stay at home. Many years later, Henry's granddaughter, Aideen, related:

> When things used to get rather hectic here – and they did quite often in those days – he used to love to get away with his friends. My grandmother, Georgina, was very fond of him and hated him going away so she thought that if she got a lake made, perhaps he's stay at home and fish in it.

The artificial lake was constructed near the house, surrounded by willow trees, but it was hardly surprising that Henry found fishing in a pond no substitute for what he saw as the real thing.

While not over-enthusiastic about her husband's voyaging to the Arctic Ocean, she, too, could display a daring spirit. O'Rorke told the story of how Sir Henry's wife ordered her coachman to drive around the edge of the Derk at Knocklane. *Frazer's Handbook for Travellers*, described this feature as a place where:

at high incoming tides, particularly when impelled by the westerly winds, the sea rushes by various subterranean channels into the deep open basin, at a considerable distance from the shore, where the agitated waters foam to an extent which is often terrific [resulting in] a semi-circular chasm of seething waters, more frightful to look at than the crater of a volcano.

O'Rorke recorded that when Lady Gore-Booth's coachman showed reluctance to drive around by this formidable yawning chasm with its foaming waters, she 'drew a pistol and gave him the alternative of its contents or compliance with her wish. The coachman, thinking as well to have his quietus from water as from fire, screwed his courage to the sticking point and whipped up the horses.'

Henry and his wife were deeply devoted to one another and before setting out on his various long voyages, he always made careful legal provision for his wife and family. Prior to his 1882 expedition, he arranged for Articles of Agreement to be carefully prepared, nominating Webb to be responsible both as his Agent and Receiver on his own behalf, and he appointed his wife, 'Dame Georgina Mary Gore-Booth of Lissadell aforesaid to be my Attorney.' The Articles of Agreement also included a provision that John Ussher of Eaton Place in the County of Middlesex, 'be my true and lawful Attorney' should Lady Mary 'happen to depart this life during my absence.'

His wife had many interests of her own, one of which was her school of needlework, established in 1860 in one of the estate offices where the wives and daughters of the tenants were taught crochet work and embroidery. When they became skilled, they joined a workforce specialising in the production of 'ladies' and children's underclothing, children's frocks, robes, pinafores, etc. The school later introduced new lines including cushions, cuffs and collars, hand-knitted pullovers, as well as Donegal hand-woven and homespun tweeds. A printed catalogue and price list for chemises, camisoles, night gowns, smocks and other items was illustrated by Lady Gore-Booth herself. All the items sold were hand-made and prices seem to have been remarkably reasonable. Lady Mary was also a founder member of the Sligo Feis Cheoil, subsequently becoming president for life.[3] She was quite an accomplished amateur painter, having studied at the Byam Shaw Art

---

[3] Hubert Butler cited his own Aunt Harriet as one of the enlightened Anglo-Irish who had attempted to identify themselves with Ireland. She, too, organised the first Feis Cheoil in her area (Kilkenny), while he himself was later infamously expelled from the Kilkenny Archaeological Society which he had personally caused to be revived.

School in London, so it was hardly surprising that her eldest daughter was later to follow a similar route. After Henry died and her son Josslyn had taken over the running of the estate, she deliberately moved out of Lissadell House (with her granddaughter, Maeve Markievicz) to a house at Ballytivnan, and later to Ardeevin, because she was sure that her son would not marry unless left on his own.

The estate continued to thrive despite Henry's long absences, and Lissadell was described at this time by Sir William Stokes as 'this happy valley … a place of refuge for any bird, no nest is to be robbed, no bird killed within its bounds; so that you may see flocks of goldfinches of more than one hundred together …' Obviously, Stokes never saw the estate shooting record books.

* * *

For his next expedition, Henry fitted the *Kara* with a pair of new harpoon guns (at a cost of 36 guineas) and his first victim yielded eleven barrels of whale blubber with which they returned to Lerwick. He set out for more whaling north of Iceland, returning again to the Orkney Islands and down the east coast of Britain to leave the *Kara* once more in its Essex dockyard.

Two years after this voyage, in March 1884, a report was published in the (Dublin) *Daily Express* about an exhibition at the Royal Hibernian Academy at which the work of a number of painters had been mounted. Describing picture number 199, the newspaper's correspondent wrote that it was: 'an excellent portrait of an enthusiastic lover of Arctic exploration, and the action of the figure, negligently lounging against the arm of an old oak chair, cigarette in hand, is utterly free from the cut and dry effect of a conventional portrait.' This portrait of Sir Henry, whose head, the newspaper reported, was 'modelled with crisp decided touches, and tells with strength and vigour against the dusk background,' was almost certainly painted by Sarah Purser, who also painted Lady Mary and the sisters Constance and Eva at this time.

In 1888, Frank, William and Arthur James – possibly brothers – asked Sir Henry for information about Spitzbergen and Novaya Zemlya which they hoped to explore that year. Henry responded by joining them on the *Lancashire Witch* at Peterhead, near Aberdeen. With Frank and William and a group of passengers, they sailed for Trondheim in northern Norway where they were joined by Arthur James two days later. There was great excitement for several in the party, who had never been in the Arctic before, when ice was encountered for the first time during the voyage. A few days later, they reached the most northerly tip of Spitzbergen (the most northeasterly headland had just been named Cape Leigh Smith) but the ship had to return to Norway to land one of the passengers who had been taken ill. From there, the *Lancashire Witch* was sailed under Sir Henry's direction, to Novaya Zemlya, and through the Matoschkin Strait into the Kara Sea, largely free of ice problems because it was now the end of August – quite late in the year. They had not left Scotland until the end of July, and this was almost certainly the reason why the trip was not a very successful hunting and fishing expedition. On the other hand, the lateness in the season meant that much of the ice had retreated for the brief arctic summer, enabling the party to progress further into the Kara Sea. After the ship had been 'nipped' by ice, it was deemed prudent to return to Norway, before arriving back at Peterhead on October 20.

He described his next voyage in a letter addressed to 'My dear James,' probably William James with whom he had sailed in 1888:

> Our course was briefly this: We left Wyvenhoe [in Essex] early in April and had a very fast run down the channel to Tieraght Light [on one of the Blasket Islands] on the coast of Ireland…. Then all luck departed, nothing but light fair winds and heavy foul winds. We took the coast of Ireland on the chance of basking sharks, but the weather was so bad we could do nothing and finally sailed from Lissadell for the North on May 25.

Although only briefly mentioned in Henry's account, the arrival of the *Kara* when it anchored off Lissadell for two weeks, created quite a stir locally, and various members of the family, their friends, 'and all the county' went on board. On one of the evenings a dinner was arranged for the whole Gore-Booth family, after which members of the crew put on an entertainment of songs and dances. Constance, then 20 years old, wrote: 'We were much amused, notwithstanding Mama came on board to sit in judgement, which stiffened our marrow and wet our spirits.' Constance, already capable of demonstrating something of her determination to be independent, made a point of boarding her father's vessel several more times without her mother. She later described how, on one of these occasions, in quite stormy conditions, 'the crew [of the *Kara*] met us in their whaling boat and were much astonished by our Courage. Certainly we were nearly swamped. We came in from Raghly [harbour] to the ship and stayed on board til dinnertime.' After this local excitement, Henry resumed his voyage northwards and continued logging his description of the hunting trip which, however, was the most disappointing to date.

Henry and his crew on board his ketch, *Kara*, hunting for whales.

His next voyage was postponed because a visit to the West Indies and North America intervened. Once again, Sir Henry left no record of this extensive foreign tour, undertaken with Eva. It is likely that nothing at all would now be known of this event were it not for several mishaps on the rail journey through the Rocky Mountains, travelling east from Vancouver, which were the subject of reports in several local newspapers. This was almost at the end of their Canadian trip which had begun in Montreal on June 2, from where they travelled by boat from Winnipeg to see the Niagara Falls, after which they went by rail to Vancouver. Reports in the *Montreal Daily Witness* and the *Manitoba Free Press* referred to Sir Henry being 'with his daughter'[4] and that they intended to return to Ireland 'after extensive travelling through Jamaica, the Southern States and Canada.' The reports also mentioned that when the passengers were stranded at Ashcroft after a flood destroyed a railway bridge, provisions were very scarce as no rail traffic was getting through in either direction. One evening 'the passengers ... gave a special concert for the benefit of the sleeping-car

---

[4] Further details concerning this incident will be found in the chapter about Eva.

porters, under the patronage of Sir Henry Gore-Booth and Hon. G. A. Pearce, by the Transcontinental Troubadoura.'

* * *

In 1898, Henry sailed for what was to be his last arctic voyage, once again boarding the *Kara* in the south of England to try his luck once more in the Greenland seas. He crossed the Arctic Circle at the end of May and was off the coast of Jan Mayan Island by June 2, but the other details are sketchy and all the indications are that something was radically wrong. He was back off the Yorkshire coast by the end of July and the *Kara* was tied up at its Essex base by early August. This unusually early return not only hints that some of the old enthusiasm for these rigorous voyages was gone but that, more importantly, all was not well with his health.

The *Kara* drawn by Walter William May, R.I., who before embarking on a career as an artist, over-wintered on the Arctic ice three times as a member of one of the search expeditions for Sir John Franklin.

In the event, he never again sailed in his beloved and sturdy little vessel. Boating had been 'in his blood' from his schooldays, and sailing had been a greatly loved and life-long recreation. His decision to purchase a sailing vessel for his voyages to the Arctic no doubt reflected all this, but steam power had largely replaced sail because of its superior ability to cope with ice-fields. Who knows what extra sport or what discoveries he might have made had he chosen, albeit at greater expense, a steam powered vessel.

Yachting World described the *Kara* as 'a fine sea-boat, though rather slow in light weather owing to her somewhat heavy displacement. On two occasions in the ocean, with a very strong, hard wind aft, she logged 191 and 200 miles in the twenty-four hours.' Although still relatively new and maintained in good condition, her reliance on sail meant that already, at the time of Sir Henry's final voyage, there was no longer much demand for such vessels. After his death, Lady Gore-Booth asked their son Josslyn to dispose of the *Kara* and he made numerous fruitless attempts to do so before eventually selling it for £300 to Captain Petersen of the Faroe Islands. The *Kara* had cost £1,700.

After his 1898 Greenland voyage, Henry was advised by his doctor not to return to the cold arctic climates but to seek relief for his bronchial condition in warm, dry conditions. Taking this advice he travelled with Lady Gore-Booth to South Africa, but once again, like the rest of his visits abroad, no account survives about exactly where he went. His son, Josslyn, travelled to South Africa later in that same year, and some brief details of his outward trip are recorded in letters home, though none of them explain the reason for the voyage. The Boer War had just broken out so the most probable explanation seems to have been that Josslyn travelled out to accompany his mother and his ailing father home from the war zone.

Sir Henry and Lady Gore-Booth almost immediately made a further trip abroad – also undertaken for the sake of his condition – this time to Switzerland, when they travelled to the health resort of St Moritz. A local newspaper reported the arrival of 'Sir Henry Gore-Booth and family, accompanied by Dr McDowell, where they have taken up residence at the Kulm,' from which it seems likely that one or more of his daughters went with their parents. While there, he developed a very severe attack of influenza, and died quite unexpectedly. His granddaughter, Aideen, wrote many years later that his death resulted from an overdose of chloroform administered by a member of the clinic's staff, and that Lady Gore-Booth was with him when he died. Josslyn or rather, Sir Josslyn (for the title now became his), rushed from Sligo to his father's bedside but he had died before he could reach him.

Almost 100 newspapers and many periodicals throughout Ireland and Britain, printed fulsome tributes to Sir Henry. *The Irish Times*, after recording his death 'at St. Moretz (sic) in the Engadine,' described him as 'one of the finest specimens of Irish landlords ... a type of landed proprietor under which great things might have been possible for Ireland had others followed in his broad-minded and tolerant example.'

Because the family still owned property in Manchester and Salford, most of the local newspapers in the English midlands also recorded his death.

The *Times* highlighted the fact that he had served as a lieutenant in the Royal Munster Fusiliers. *Vanity Fair* mentioned that Sir Henry's death had taken place very suddenly 'in consequence of which his son, Josslyn, did not arrive in time to see his father alive.'

As was to be expected, the Sligo newspapers gave lengthy coverage to the news of his death, to his funeral, and to tributes to his memory. The *Sligo Independent* recorded that:

> In the Lissadell district where Sir Henry was personally known to almost everyone, the news created the most profound sorrow. There he was universally beloved for the many virtues which exalted his character He was large-hearted, generous, and genial.... His was an adventurous life but when at home in peaceful Lissadell, his most earnest endeavours were for the well being of his tenantry.... In every possible way he strove to improve the lot of the humble, and now that he has passed away to his forefathers, perhaps the best epitaph that can be inscribed over his remains is that the people loved him.

His widow, who survived him by 27 years, was a very strong personality and mirrored her husband's generosity and thoughtfulness towards others. She was a fearless and accomplished horsewoman, and besides assisting him in many of his acts of generosity and in his support for local endeavours, she was equally active in many matters in her own right.

When she died at the age of 84, after ailing for almost a year, many tributes were paid to her. One of the Sligo newspapers reported: 'Many will remember her unceasing efforts on behalf of refugee Belgians who were kept here during the early days of the Great War, and how she slaved, with her willing committee of helpers, to make their affliction less heavy.' Others recalled her kindness to the poor, her work establishing both a school of needlework – producing embroidery, crochet work and knitting – and the Sligo Feis Cheoil of which she was a founder member. The latter convened a special meeting for the purpose of expressing regret at the death of its late president. The Rev. Father O'Leary proposed a Resolution 'to give expression to their unfeigned regret at the great loss sustained,' adding that 'her term of office will long remain as a green and fragrant memory…. No one could be more assiduous than she in the dealings of the duties entrusted to her.' The Resolution was passed 'in silence, all members standing as a mark of respect.'

Sir Josslyn Gore-Booth, Sixth Baronet (1869–1944)

Sir Josslyn

'Forgotten by the country he loved'

Writing about what he termed 'distinguished Sligonians,' John McTernan commented that while Constance and Eva Gore-Booth are well remembered, 'rarely do we spare a thought for their equally remarkable but less famous brother, Josslyn.' It was a most happy chance that Josslyn was cast in a mould so very similar to that of his father and grandfather. Each built upon the work of his forebear, ensuring that the continuity of the improving work at Lissadell remained unbroken, so much so that well before Josslyn had reached middle age, the estate was one of the most progressive and one of the best-run anywhere in Ireland.

Josslyn Augustus Richard Gore-Booth, heir to the title as sixth baronet, was born in 1869, a year after his sister, Constance. Many years later, Josslyn's daughter, Aideen, wrote that her father, in sharp contrast to her Aunt Constance, was a very shy and sensitive person. When Josslyn was born, there was great rejoicing for the arrival of a son and heir. Bonfires were lit and a table was placed in the porch set with whiskey punch served to all that came. While still a baby, Josslyn had a narrow escape from a premature end when his nurse took him to the beach one sunny day, walking far out as it was low tide and, after sitting with the child for a time, she fell asleep. Captain Wynne's boat happened to pass by at a distance and the skipper noticed what looked like a heap on a sandbank, completely surrounded by the incoming tide. Turning his boat in the direction he then waded to the bank where he found both nurse and baby fast asleep, unaware of the danger, and brought them safely ashore.

Josslyn was sent to Eton College (which he was later to describe as a sink of iniquity, so much so that he was determined that he would never send any son of his there), after which he attended various tutors in London. Among the letters preserved among the Lissadell Papers, there is one addressed to his father in 1888 by Captain Walter James, a tutor whom Josslyn was then attending. He expressed his pleasure that Josslyn had been making 'very considerable progress indeed … [and] I think that of late he has improved very much in the subjects which he has taken up.' Around the same time Josslyn wrote to his father informing him that he now had a German tutor who charged 7s.6d. per hour.

Somewhat ambiguously, he added: 'which I think is a good deal.' Josslyn mentioned that he was concerned about having insufficient time to go to the gymnasium: 'I feel by my waistcoat I have expanded a good deal.' Whatever expansion there had been at this time, it did not last long, as is evident from almost every photograph taken of him throughout his life, showing him to have been very thin and distinctly frail in appearance – in fact, he never enjoyed robust good health.

Despite indifferent health, he felt it his duty to join the army, but because he suffered from poor eyesight, he had to apply three times before he was accepted into the Royal Munster Fusiliers, becoming a lieutenant. Following a very brief army career he went to Canada, working on a ranch near Winnipeg. He had been there for just one year when, 'after a dust up with the Fenians,' his father sent a message to him to come home immediately, which he did and, in his own words, 'regretted it ever after.' While in Canada, he gained ideas that he put into practice when his father sent him to work for a time in the family estate office in Manchester. And when, several years before Sir Henry died, Josslyn effectively took over the Lissadell estate, he introduced some of his Canadian ideas at Lissadell too.

While in their twenties, the three eldest of the family, Constance, Josslyn and Eva, were seen by some to share certain socialist ideals, though each was to develop their thinking in very different ways. Josslyn and Eva abhorred violence, while Constance did not. All three rebelled, though in very different ways. Roseangela Barone considered that Josslyn 'was a rebel only in the mildest sense' and she also saw in him 'the first symptom or stage of the uneasiness felt by the younger generation of the dominant class coming into full awareness of the Ireland in which they were placed.' William Butler Yeats wrote of the family that they were 'ever ready to take up new ideas and new things. The eldest brother is "theoretically" a Home Ruler, and practically some kind of humanitarian, much troubled by the responsibility of his wealth and almost painfully conscientious.' Quoting Yeats' comments in her book about the women of 1916, Elizabeth Coxhead made the point that the Gore-Booths 'were a united clan, and they stuck by Constance through all her troubles when, in the eyes of most of her clan she was irretrievably disgraced.'

During 1889, Josslyn sailed for South Africa in order to accompany his ailing father home. The Boer War had just broken out and was to claim the life of Douglas Gore-Booth, a second cousin, who died during the siege of Ladysmith. Before the end of the year, Josslyn's father was dead so that at the age of 31, Josslyn succeeded to the title, devoting the rest of his life to the development of the Lissadell estate and the welfare of the people both there and in the surrounding areas. He became an innovating farmer and a noted breeder of livestock. He took a special interest in cereal crops, and introduced a number of new varieties of potatoes, successfully competing with established growers in Scotland and elsewhere. He achieved remarkable successes in the field of horticulture, notably in the establishment of his garden nurseries and bulb farm.

Josslyn loved fishing and was a good shot, with or without his hollow cow. This latter was a decoy of his own invention, into which he could clamber and from which he was better able to shoot the wild geese on Lissadell's shore. T.A. Finnigan noted in his book about the area that the first Barnacle geese arrived in Lissadell in 1895, just four in number, whereas today the north side of Drumcliff Bay and the Lissadell estate between them have one of the largest mainland flocks of Barnacle geese in these islands. His many trophies, formerly displayed in the house, included some interesting stuffed species of birds and other wildlife, including a moose's head brought back from Canada.

Like his father and grandfather before him, he kept records of game killed both on the estate and elsewhere (including his year in Manitoba in 1892–3). Especially interesting is the Game Book covering the period 1887–95 in that, unlike those belonging to his father, it was published by Dublin printing firm, Browne and Nolan. It included a short Preface in which it was stated that: 'The habit of keeping a diary of the day's performance has now become so universal a practice amongst all true Sportsmen that it may appear superfluous to our stating a few attendant advantages.' These advantages, it continued, included arriving at conclusions about the increase or decrease of game on one's own estate and, in the case of rented shoots, the ability to decide whether the cost incurred was balanced by the game available. The Preface was amusingly signed: 'Wishing all, who may be like ourselves engaged in the pursuit of game, as good sport as we are at present enjoying, we have the honour to be, your most obedient servant, Magpie Weasel & Co.'

One is left to wonder, once again, how stocks of game managed to survive the regular onslaughts from the batteries of guns regularly ranged against them. Taking just a few figures more or less at random, Sir Josslyn and three friends managed to shoot 130 woodcock during a three-day period in January, 1892, and this was followed, a week later, by another three days of shooting during which 120 hares met their doom. Josslyn's

'Grand Total' for 1891–92 reads as follows: Hares 713, Rabbits 685, Grouse 77, Plover 120, Partridges 79, Pheasants 265, Woodcock 572, Snipe 766, Duck 25, Teal 6, Geese 9, Woodpigeon 74, Snipe 55: Total 3,606.

Lissadell had extensive, solidly built stone farm buildings, and store cattle formed an important part of the estate's livestock trade, with upwards of 300 new animals being regularly bought in to replace those sold. A similar number of sheep were grazed, many of which were sold with their lambs each spring. Dairy cattle were also kept, mostly Aberdeen Angus and Shorthorn, and Josslyn's carefully kept records ensured that only the best milk-producers were retained. Without this attention to detail and the keeping of precise records, it would have been very difficult to know which of the estate's various departments were running efficiently and making a profit. He was assisted in this work by his agent, J.P. Cooper who, though an accountant by profession was an excellent all-round manager as well. F.H. Purchas, a noted English horticulturist, went to see for himself the work then being undertaken at Lissadell:

> To Mr. Cooper's keen business instinct is due, in large measure, the admirable organisation that prevails, and the discovery of outlets for Lissadell's products. The account books are exhaustive yet perfectly simple, and when one remembers that there are over 900 open accounts with the public, and that every department is charged with its own separate costs and credited with its own receipts whether they be on account of the public or of one of the other estate departments, it will be easily realised that but for such simplicity, the work of book keeping alone would become intolerable.

Purchas described Sir Josslyn as 'highly respected throughout the country, and it is only the truth to say that, thankless as one has become accustomed to consider the Irish peasantry, Sir Josslyn has the good-will and the sincere benedictions of all his tenantry and poorer neighbours.'

An unidentified newspaper clipping retained among the family papers reported Sir Josslyn's engagement to Miss Mary L'Estrange Malone in 1906, noting that 'it gives great satisfaction to all concerned. Sir Josslyn having lived single for thirty-eight years, had almost come to be looked on as a confirmed bachelor.' The report added that: 'The bride elect is most attractive looking; her father, formerly Mr L'Estrange, took the additional name Malone on inheriting a property, and his sisters are married to Lord Muncaster and Lord Erroll.' Just a week before setting out for the wedding, Josslyn wrote to his fiancée detailing how he had been busy all the previous morning 'at the shirt factory.' He was also awaiting a deputation of employees from the Ballymote estate, and he was writing a speech for the shirt factory General Meeting 'to try and pacify irate shareholders.' In addition, he had to attend a meeting of the Sligo Leitrim Railway Company – all this during a period of three days. As a result of the unusual activity and the amount of packing, he noted that there were 'all kinds of rumours here that we are going to shut up the place and sack everybody! Am very glad we are going to America, it will give things time to quieten down … Goodbye till Sunday, Your loving Joss.'

Sir Josslyn and Lady Gore-Booth
photographed after their wedding in London, June 1907.

Josslyn and his bride-to-be were second cousins, their maternal grandmothers, Frances Charlotte and Henrietta Susan Savile Lumney of Rotherham, Yorkshire, being sisters, and their brother was the ninth earl of Scarborough. Josslyn's mother was born at Tickhill Castle, the Yorkshire property of the earl, while her father, the Rev. Saville Richard L'Estrange Malone, was a rector in Yorkshire and domestic chaplain to his uncle, Marcus Gervaise Beresford, Archbishop of Armagh. It was after Lord Muncaster's wife, Constance, that Josslyn's elder sister was named, and the particular spelling of the name Josslyn, which has continued down through the Gore-Booth family, also comes from the same Muncaster family of Ravenglass in Cumbria. Members of that family continued to act as trustees of the Lissadell estate until 1911.

Josslyn's marriage to Mary L'Estrange Malone took place in St Mary's Church, Bryanstown Square, London on June 12, 1907. The bride's dress was described as 'traditional, in white satin and Brussels lace.' The bridal party left for Wancote, Guildford, after the wedding and then proceeded to America from where, on their return to Lissadell they 'were welcomed by their delighted employees and tenantry, their arrival being celebrated by a magnificent display of fireworks and the lighting of huge bonfires.' A few days later, Sir Josslyn provided an entertainment for his employees and other guests when some 300 persons were served dinner in the Riding School close to the house, after which a sports day was held on the lawn. 'The football and tugs of war were greatly enjoyed by the spectators and ... at the conclusion of the sports, tea was provided for all, and dancing followed-on in the Riding School, Lady Gore-Booth leading off in the first dance with Mr Woods, a veteran retainer.'

Like his father and grandfather before him, Josslyn travelled abroad on a number of occasions but he, too, seems to have kept virtually no record of these journeys. Besides spending his honeymoon in the United States, he and Lady Gore-Booth went on a Mediterranean cruise in 1910, travelling on the *S.S. Dunotter Castle.*

Josslyn went on to manage the estate on scientific lines and, as already noted, carefully controlled every individual aspect of the business. At the same time he carried on many of the traditions originally established by his grandfather and subsequently pursued by his father. The estate continued to be intensively farmed and the most modern innovations of the time were adopted. Josslyn bred high quality livestock, including the fine Aberdeen Angus herd established by his father. Surplus stock was sold each year and in the catalogue for the 1941 sale it was claimed that 'the reputation of the Pedigree Calves is well known in every part of Ireland .... The Store stock from Lissadell enjoys a high reputation both at home and across the channel of being exceptionally sound good doers.'

When the Wyndham Land Bill was enacted in 1903, Sir Josslyn was one of the first proprietors to become involved in the scheme that encouraged landlords to allow their tenants to buy out their holdings. The money advanced by the Treasury was to be repaid over a period of just over 68 years, so that the Lissadell tenants who took up the scheme at the outset were not due to make their final payments until 1971. More than 1,000 tenants purchased between them some 28,000 acres of the original 32,000 acres that Josslyn had recently inherited, leaving the demesne surrounding the house as the principal block of remaining land. Far from being dismayed by this turn of events, Sir Josslyn then embarked on a quite remarkable series of enterprises to develop the full potential of the remainder of the estate. Within three years, he was employing over 200 people at Lissadell at an annual cost in salaries of £6,000. Crops were now being grown on a large scale, no doubt influenced by what he had seen while living in Canada. He concentrated on cereals and potatoes and he developed the estate's forestry business, planting large stands of trees, introducing a tree nursery and installing a saw mill.

During the year spent in Canada, Josslyn became convinced of the economic possibilities of growing timber on a large scale at Lissadell, and he had planted experimental plots of softwood trees in order to determine which species were likely to provide the best return in local conditions. He subsequently claimed that he was one of the first persons to recognise the particular suitability of Sitka Spruce, correctly forecasting that because Irish conditions were not unlike those which pertained along the Pacific coastline of North America from where this species originated, it would grow fast in this country. The success of its introduction was almost immediate, and it became the leading conifer for afforestation purposes, not only in Ireland, but also in large parts of Scotland and Wales. In more recent times, when the government policy of large-scale conifer planting began to be questioned, much of the criticism was directed at the Sitka Spruce[1]. Of the larger shrubs introduced, the rhododendrons had thrived so well that they grew to a prodigious height and the *Ponticum* species was already becoming almost a weed, requiring regular eradication. Many plants that were deemed less than hardy by specialist growers flourished luxuriantly in the mild micro-climate of Lissadell demesne.

The socialist tendencies seen by some not only in Constance and Eva, but also in Josslyn were possibly influenced by the scenes they had

---

[1] Nevertheless, in an article in *The Irish Times* in September 2000, Hugh Byrne, Minister of State with special responsibility for forestry, writing about the fact that trees are the lungs of the planet, went on to make the point that: 'The much maligned Sitka Spruce is the most efficient of these lungs.'

witnessed as small children when they observed their father and mother giving food and clothing to the hungry tenants during the 1879 famine. In Josslyn's case, the memory of that time instilled in him strong views about ownership and responsibility even before Lissadell became his responsibility. He had already recognised that he would be expected to emulate the paternalistic actions of his father and his grandfather, and he was determined that the estate would continue to thrive as it had in the past, not only for the benefit of the family but also for all those others whose livelihoods depended upon it.

Sir Josslyn and Lady Mary had eight children, four boys and four girls: Michael (1908), Hugh (1910), Bridget (1911), Brian (1912), Rosaleen (1914), Aideen (1916), Gabrielle (1918), and Angus (1920). One of the very few details surviving about the young family appears in an undated instruction written by their mother when Michael and Hugh were still very small, setting out a programme for their daily routine – probably for a new children's nurse:

> Breakfast 8 o'clock. Please fetch Michael and Hugh from the nursery to take them down to breakfast in the dining room. For breakfast they have about 3 tablespoons of porridge with milk and salt. Followed by eggs on alternate days, then, other days, fish or bacon and brown bread and butter, marmalade, golden syrup and honey, not jam or scones. They have milk to drink, but do not drink until the end of the meal. They say Grace before and after all meals.

The instruction went on to set down the children's routine in minute detail, including what the boys were to be given for other meals, and how lesson times were to be conducted. It even listed in precise detail when the windows of the various rooms used by the children were to be opened and shut.

* * *

When the Local Industry Committee was established in Sligo in 1901, Sir Josslyn immediately became an active member. Its object was to bring employment to Sligo, and among the suggestions made at the inaugural meeting was a call for the establishment of a woollen factory, or some similar industry. At its second meeting, the members were informed that negotiations were proceeding with 'a party' to set up a shirt factory, and this was successfully established in 1902. Three years later, it was employing between 60 and 70 women and a few men. By

1907, with receipts falling short of expenditure, the company was in serious difficulties and a decision to close it was tabled. Before taking this step, the members of the Industry Committee decided to approach Sir Josslyn (who was not present at the meeting), to see if he might help the business to carry on, which he did by taking over the running of the works himself. Commenting on this decision, the *Sligo Independent* wrote that Sir Josslyn, who already provided considerable employment at Lissadell, had 'now taken-on the shirt factory where the wages bill was about £1,000 a year, with plans to expand production.' The intervention prompted the *Sligo Times* to comment that 'Sir Josslyn's work for Sligo will never be forgotten.'

Almost two decades earlier, when Josslyn and his father heard about Sir Horace Plunkett's efforts to establish a co-operative movement in Ireland, they decided to become involved. Plunkett, having once condemned those of his own class who did nothing for the social betterment of their people, had decided to set a personal example by founding the co-operative movement in Ireland and encouraged others to support him. If Sir Horace sought natural allies in this kind of thinking, he needed to look no further than the Gore-Booths, especially Josslyn who became wholeheartedly involved in the movement at an early stage in its development. In her book about his sister, Eva, Gifford Lewis wrote:

> By the early 1890s, when Josslyn had been educating himself in socialism and co-operation, the movement in Ireland had steadied itself, lost many of its revolutionary overtones, and was in the process of being shown to be a workable system by Horace Plunkett and George Russell ... whose disciple Josslyn was.

Noting those Anglo-Irish 'who worked at the rediscovery of Ireland', she included Josslyn among those of their number who:

> were eager to reform and put their theories into practice. It is too quickly assumed,' she added, 'that reform in Ireland was a movement at grass-roots level, and that there was nothing but dead wood in the tree-tops; but reforming ideas were at large in a progressive section of the landlord class from early in the nineteenth century....

Plunkett was a son of Lord Dunsany, one of the largest land-owning families in Ireland, with estates in Dublin, Louth and Meath in addition to property in England. The family settled in Ireland in 1316 and played a distinguished role in public affairs down through the centuries. Like the Gore-Booths and many of the other Anglo-Irish families, they saw themselves as Irish and British at the same time. As Trevor West expressed it, while they 'valued their connection with the crown, they shared neither the myopic view of England as the source of all of Ireland's woes, nor the English disinclination to acknowledge Ireland's distinctive nationality.' Plunkett's first serious attempt to actually establish his co-operative idea was at Kilcooley, Co. Tipperary where his own sister had married into the wealthy Ponsonby family. It failed, partly because some of the local Roman Catholic clergy denounced it as a 'Protestant Plot,' and also because the local traders and shopkeepers feared the co-op movement would take business from them. Perhaps most discouraging of all, even the local farmers whom Plunkett sought to help tended to treat the whole idea with mistrust. As Professor J.C. Beckett expressed it, the movement 'was hampered from the beginning by the popular suspicion, encouraged by some Roman Catholic clergy and some politicians, that no good thing could come from a man who was at once a Protestant, a landlord and a Unionist.'

Plunkett established his first co-operative creamery in 1889 at Drumcollogher, Co. Limerick, and from this small beginning the movement began to spread across the country. Its motto was 'Ní neart go cur le cheile' – 'No strength without co-operation.'

The Drumcliff Co-operative Creamery opened a year later on 2 May 1896 when the first supply of the company's butter was, according to the *Sligo Independent*, 'placed on the market at one shilling a pound.' Within a very short space of time, Josslyn established three further co-operatives in the locality – the original one at Drumcliff, and the other three at Ballintrillick, Ballinfull and Kilasnet. In each of the four it soon became evident that virtually all the farmers in the respective districts had become members. After commending Josslyn for his work in establishing the Drumcliff Co-op, the *Champion* reported that:

> The hesitating became convinced, the wavering were made steady and a spontaneous request from over 500 persons to be placed on the Shareholders List crowned their efforts. It is gratifying to find a gentleman so young as Mr. Josslyn Gore-Booth, so vigorously exerting himself, to elevate and improve the condition of the Industrial Classes, but the fact is that the family have always identified themselves with every movement having for its object the amelioration of the labouring and industrious small farmers ....

Plunkett launched *The Irish Homestead* as the organ of the co-operative movement, appointing Father T.A. Finlay as its editor until, in 1905, George Russell (Æ) took over. Susan Mitchell, who later became involved in republican politics and got to know Josslyn through the co-operative societies, was appointed sub-editor, a post which opened the door for her into Dublin's literary society to which she aspired, having already begun to make a name for herself as a minor poet. As she became increasingly identified with republicanism, she wrote poetry and ballads in favour of Home Rule and against the British Empire, and it was this interest which led to her meet Constance, with whom she had much in common. Later when Constance was imprisoned, Susan Mitchell was one of her few visitors, looking after some of her personal affairs, and writing about her to Josslyn.

The hostile opposition to his movement may have made Plunkett consider that perhaps this reaction made his earlier strictures addressed to his fellow Unionists about not doing enough for the betterment of the people appear somewhat harsh and that the fault did not lie entirely at their feet. From the perspective of the Roman Catholic Church, the growth of the co-operatives was viewed with mixed feelings. The Catholic hierarchy, traditionally conservative, was uncomfortably positioned between the need to work with the British administration and, at the same time wishing to identify with its own overwhelmingly nationalist laity. It saw the advantages of agricultural co-operation and was aware that its ideals accorded broadly in line with what had been pronounced by Pope Leo XIII. As Liam Kennedy pointed out, while the clergy wanted to support any attempt to improve the economic prosperity of their people, they also feared that certain aspects of the new movement might produce results that could have adverse effects. They also had to take into account the hostility of most of the Nationalist M.Ps., as well as accusations that the whole thing was a landlord plot.

Catholic clergy were in a strong position to influence the success or otherwise of the local societies. They could stand aloof; or demonstrate outright hostility; or they could accept chairmanships and thus control the activities of individual societies, encouraging those aspects that were favourable for the farmers while stalling attempts that might harm the interests of the traders.

R.A. Anderson, the movement's secretary, had helped to pioneer agricultural co-operation, and wrote several times in glowing terms about Sir Josslyn. He called him a convinced and sincere co-operator who 'spared neither his excellent brains, his purse nor his efforts to make every society with which he was connected a worthy unit.' Lissadell House was frequently used for the meetings of the society, and Anderson recorded in his history of the organisation: 'I and others who made Lissadell their headquarters, will never forget the kindness of all the

Gore-Booth family, nor the fine, though unobtrusive part its head took in promoting the movement.'

Writing about Plunkett's vision for rural Ireland and the fact that he did not live to see his dream accomplished, Carla King commented that 'one has to answer that very few social reformers ever do. Yet, he had a profound effect, not only in Ireland, but on the social thinking of his day. His greatest obstacle was his failure to win over Irish nationalism, suspicious of his motivation.'[2] Plunkett's house, Kilteragh, in Foxrock, County Dublin, was described by Hubert Butler as a place that represented social endeavour and 'a meeting place for all those who were interested in their country.'[3] During 1923, while he was in America, it was blown up by anti-treaty forces. Though part of the house was severely damaged, much remained intact, and on the following day workmen erected beams to support the upper floors and to secure the house, but the republicans returned and set the damaged house on fire. Plunkett was distraught at the loss of the house, but even more so because of the destruction of all his detailed personal records, with the result that he could not, for two years, contemplate returning to Ireland. His subsequent visits were brief, and he died in England nine years later. Susan Mitchell – a committed republican and one of Constance's closest friends – was disgusted when she heard about the mindless destruction of Plunkett's home. She wrote that this was an 'ugly manifestation in the Irish character.... We are under no illusions now, our vanity is punctured, we have seen our ugly faces in the glass.'

* * *

When Josslyn succeeded to the title, he had also 'inherited' his father's faithful valet, Thomas Kilgallon, who continued to work at Lissadell for a further two decades. According to Valerie Pakenham, Kilgallon 'ruled the household,' an opinion that seems to have been borne out by the following story which, however, Kilgallon did not include when he wrote his own recollections about the family. The details have appeared instead in Mark Bence-Jones's book, *Twilight of the Ascendancy*, and concerned a visit to Lissadell, intended to last for three days, undertaken

---

[2] In a book about rural change in Ireland, edited by John Davis.
[3] Butler wrote in *Escape from the Anthill* that the Abbey Theatre and the *Irish Statesman* represented a 'bridge between literature and social endeavour, between Coole and Kilteragh'.

in 1913 by two young King-Harman brothers, Edward and Cecil, who, although related to the Gore-Booths, had not previously met Sir Josslyn. The incident as told personally to Bence-Jones by Leslie King-Harman, the younger of the two brothers, described how their visit started off on the wrong note. The pair not only arrived late but, on entering the mansion, the elder brother handed his coat to Sir Josslyn, mistaking him for the butler. Rather cross with the pair, Josslyn told them it was nearly dinner time, so they went directly up to their room to change, and after dinner, followed by a ball, they retired very late indeed to bed.

They had barely gone to sleep when Kilgallon woke them and said gruffly: 'You must get up, you've got to go.' 'Go?' the two brothers asked in sleepy astonishment, noticing that it was only just after six, 'We've been asked to stay for three days.' 'You've got to go, those are my orders.'

There was nothing for it but to get up and get dressed. At seven, without even a cup of tea, the two unfortunate young men were bundled into the carriage and driven into Sligo town to catch the eight o'clock train [to Boyle]... They felt very offended with the Gore-Booths, only to learn through a neighbour that the Gore-Booths were very offended with them. Eventually the mystery was cleared up: the Gore-Booths had indeed expected them to stay for three days, but the wretched Kilgallon had taken it into his head to get rid of them after barely a night.

* * *

Although the details are not known, Constance's finances had been, before the Easter Rising almost continually in a perilous state, even though she is known to have held shares during 1908 valued at £2,500. She had written several times to Eva about her financial situation, and wrote again in 1909 to say she 'was desperate for money.' Eva then wrote to Josslyn about this, saying she had tried to persuade Constance to write directly to him to request a loan 'but in a letter this morning she says she simply can't, that it is quite impossible she could ask you for such a thing.' Eva, like Constance, had also been living a somewhat Spartan life and she, too, was sometimes very short of money, but unlike her sister she continued to keep in touch with her brother though she rarely sought help. One known exception hints at a recent falling-out between them. It began: 'My dear Joss, in the days before you disliked me, you made me promise not to sell out [probably a reference to shares she had inherited] without telling you. You will not be surprised to hear I am forced to do so now.' The reference to Josslyn disliking her was almost certainly connected with the strained relationship that had arisen when both he and she found themselves in conflict over the administration of Constance's affairs. In any event, on this occasion, Josslyn responded a few days later by sending Eva £350 which she acknowledge in the most grateful terms:

> It is a wonderful help and such a blessing not to have to sell out for the time being. The future is an awful job. One hopes that living won't always cost the enormous amount that it does now. The weekly bills are more than 3 times what they were.... I am searching around to get some journalistic or writing work. If I could only earn two or three pounds a week it would be a great help.

Josslyn and Constance photographed together c.1895.
Their relationship deteriorated two decades later
after Constance disowned the family, which,
however, continued to care for her daughter.

A few weeks after the outbreak of the Great War in 1914, Sir Josslyn was reported in the local papers as having, at Ballymote, given 'a stirring appeal' for the local young men to join the forces, as he expressed it:

> That we may be free; fighting that we may be spared the horrors which have overtaken Belgium, Northern France, Poland and Serbia. And what of Ballymote? I had the honour of owning this town once, and now, by means of British credit, the ownership of this place is, I understand, being gradually vested in the occupiers. You have done with landlords. I was very sorry to lose you as tenants but … I expect you are glad to get rid of me as landlord. (A Voice, "No", and applause). You have won the land; you are winning the houses in the villages; you have won the trust of British Democracy. You know that in future – when the military party in Germany is broken – you come into your own. (Applause) … I, too, know something of the German idea of liberty, and I can assure you that, bad and all as the landlord was, Clanrickard himself was not a patch on what the Germans would be. No doubt I shall be told that Ballymote has done well, and perhaps it has, but it is a fact that there are still 7,225 recruitable men now left in Sligo ('Shame').… It is our duty to try to get them to realise that. Germany will not admit she is beaten until the last ounce has been thrown into the scale.

It was hardly surprising that Sir Josslyn decided to give his active support for the war effort, either by his encouragement of the recruitment campaign, or by the establishment of the munitions 'factory' which he was to set up later, or even by supplying fresh vegetables to vessels of the Royal Navy calling at Sligo. Like the majority of Protestants at the time, whatever their class, he regarded himself as an Irishman who supported the Union and felt it his duty to do whatever he could to 'defeat the Kaiser.' Lady Mary, sharing the same view, was actively engaged in local efforts to support a colony of Belgian refugees rendered homeless by the war, and temporarily settled in Sligo.

As an influential member of the Sligo Recruiting Committee, Josslyn wrote letters to the local schools and to the managers of the co-operatives and other businesses – including that of the Sligo-Leitrim railway company – suggesting that recruiting posters might be displayed in their premises. Dozens of letters were sent to him offering compliance with his requests, and there were also many letters from various organisations formed to support the recruitment campaign.

When Josslyn received a supply of booklets promoting recruitment to the 10th Battalion of the Royal Dublin Fusiliers, this may or may not have prompted the local regiment, the Connaught Rangers, to send their regimental band on a tour of the area to encourage recruitment to its own ranks. Over a period of ten days, performances were given, and speakers addressed the assembled crowds at Riverstown, Coolaney, Ballintogher, Easkey, Maugherow, Grange, Ballymote, Colooney, Tubbercurry, Strandhill and (on three separate dates) in Sligo town. A local newspaper recorded the scene at one of these recruitment meetings held at Lissadell:

> On the arrival of the fife and drum band from Boyle [Headquarters of the Connaught Rangers], where a recruitment meeting was held, they were immediately conveyed by motor to Lissadell House, being the guests of Sir Josslyn and Lady Gore-Booth for luncheon. Along the route, young ladies, waving the flags of different nations, greeted the passing cars with enthusiastic cheering, while a hearty welcome was also extended to them at the different villages.

As chairman of the Sligo Leitrim and Northern Counties Railway, Sir Josslyn had no difficulty in arranging the distribution of recruitment forms to the company's employees, accompanied by a printed covering letter:

> The case of each man will be considered separately with a view to rendering financial assistance to their dependants where necessary, and men when discharged from the Army or in a position to claim their discharge and desiring to re-enter the company's service, will, if physically fit, be found employment at the rate of Wages to which they would have been entitled if they had not enlisted. The services of every available man are required if we wish to preserve our independence as a Nation ....

In order to service the various machines used on the estate, Sir Josslyn had long since set up a very well equipped workshop complete with lathes, etc. After the outbreak of war, he offered the services of this department to the War Office and, as a result, he began the manufacture of selected parts for munitions. By 1916 he was sending regular supplies of shell bases and there is something mildly amusing about the concern, expressed in his letters of complaint to the station-master at Sligo, about the cost of carriage: 'The last two lots must have gone by Goods, as the freight was only 5s.1d.' He was comparing this amount with 9s.10d charged for his previous delivery, a difference which, he noted, 'appears to amount to one farthing (one quarter of an old penny) per base extra, which would render our work at this centre quite impossible. So we would be obliged if you would see that they are dispatched by goods train in future.'

His brother Mordaunt was working as an engineer for the famous engineering firm, Vickers, in Sheffield. He and Josslyn regularly exchanged letters concerning mechanical problems at Josslyn's workshops. Josslyn's workshops went on to experiment with the manufacture of complete shell cases and he was subsequently informed that an order 'for 7,000 weekly, of Division Plates for S.K. Shells was coming through, and other contracts would follow later.' During February 1917, Mordaunt suggested that Josslyn might consider developing his workshops and going into the manufacture of agricultural machinery after the war ended, listing some of the necessary equipment that would be required.

> You would probably need a good deal of plant to be at all independent, including an iron foundry and possibly a steam hammer…. You would probably need electric power. Would it be worth considering the possibility of a power station with a big reserve capable, say, of lighting Sligo? I can see I am letting one thing lead to another and am gradually turning Sligo into Sheffield!

Josslyn was beset by tooling problems, with the result that his correspondence with Woolwich Arsenal seemed to have been endless, and in view of the small scale of the undertaking at Lissadell, one wonders why the ministry considered it worth the trouble. His eventual output of 30 shells a month could have been fired off by a single artillery piece on the western front in a very short time.

The events that took place in Dublin during Easter Week, 1916 hardly impinged at the time on life around Sligo. The county's involvement appears to have been not much more than an arms seizure during the previous November, while at Lissadell the events would have seemed even more remote were it not for Constance's involvement. On Thursday April 27, Josslyn wrote in his diary without elaboration, the words 'Liberty Hall,' and followed the entry with: 'Maeve and Miss Clayton came to dinner.' Maeve was, of course, Constance's daughter who had been living permanently with her grandmother in Ardeevin, a house situated between Sligo and Rosses Point. However, at the end of the week Josslyn's entries were beginning to show some concern for his sister's safety, and on Sunday April 30 he wrote: 'Rebels surrendered. Boys drove, and I walked to church.' Monday, May 1 'No official news yet.' Tuesday May 2; 'In Wolseley [car] to Annaghmore to get O'Hara to write to Wimborne about Constance.' Charles O'Hara, living near Collooney, was the local M.P. and a friend of the family, whom Josslyn had asked to request the Lord Lieutenant to intervene on behalf of his sister awaiting trial.

A week later, on Monday May 8, Josslyn wrote: 'Sat. evg. paper –
Constance sentenced to death by court martial, commuted to penal
servitude for life by G.O.C.' Most accounts of her sentence simply
record the official reason – that it was commuted because she was a
woman – but Josslyn may have felt that his own efforts on her behalf
played at least some part in the final decision. Whether they did or not,
Constance was to tell him that she was very annoyed at what she saw
as her brother's interference in her personal affairs. The 'interference'
she had in mind came about when, after her sentence had been commuted,
Josslyn was informed that he was to be appointed as his sister's
administrator, though the actual appointment was delayed because the
Chief Secretary, whose signature was required, was out of the country.

While there is no record of his reaction to the news, he quickly found
that he had been given both an onerous and thankless job. For her part,
Constance wanted her sister Eva to look after her affairs, and had already
asked her to arrange the letting of her house, to put the contents into
store, and to arrange payments to the two women who had worked for
her. Unable to get instructions from Constance, and finding Eva reluctant
to tell him what Constance wanted done, Josslyn was put in a very difficult
position. The normally good relationship between Eva and her brother
became distinctly strained at this time because, although Josslyn was
officially in charge of Constance's affairs, Eva felt obliged to carry out
her sister's instructions rather than pass them on to Josslyn for
implementation.

While he had been awaiting the outcome of his sister's court martial,
Josslyn had contacted anyone and everyone whom he thought might be
able to influence the result. Although he totally disagreed with his sister's
revolutionary actions, he did everything in his power to intervene on her
behalf, making personal calls and writing letters to army officers and
officials at the highest level. Even after her sentence had been commuted,
he found himself drawn into making yet another intervention on her
behalf. This came about because of rumours that Constance had shot an
unarmed policeman during the first day of the rebellion. Though he could
not have known it, the matter was not raised at her court martial so it is
possible that Josslyn's concern was as much for the family name as for
his sister's reputation. Already determined to find out the truth of the
matter, it became more pressing when Eva wrote to him: 'Can you find
out exactly what happened at the court martial? I only heard half from
Con and we ought to know this to contradict the vile stories some
people are making.' He tried to ascertain details about the trial, writing

letters to army personnel, to the Chief Secretary and, eventually, to the War Office. The latter advised Josslyn to contact the Judge Advocates Court in London, as a result of which he was told that he could obtain a copy of the court martial transcript if he made a formal application, enclosing a letter from Constance indicating that she had no objection to the document being supplied to him. Constance wrote from Aylesbury Jail giving her permission (which in itself is interesting), but although this whole correspondence has been carefully retained among the family papers, there is no copy of the court martial transcript attached. Having gone to so much trouble to get this far, it seems unbelievable that Josslyn went no further with the matter.

Three months after the end of the Great War saw the beginning of the War of Independence. The Volunteers adopted guerrilla war tactics that were met by vicious retaliatory measures. Houses, large and small, were raided and set on fire, and some co-operative premises suffered a similar fate. Later, during the Civil War, things became even more dangerous for many people. In one of her prison letters to Eva at this time, Constance related a story that she had just heard:

> Did you know that they raided Joss? I heard a very funny account. He met them in the hall and let them look everywhere … telling them everything had been handed over to the police. They trotted round the house and found nothing and were very friendly. But when they had finished they just went straight to the garden and dug and found all they wanted! I would have loved to have seen his face!

Constance's version of this story differs somewhat from that given by Josslyn, who wrote that the IRA raided the house during the summer of 1920 while the family was at church. They found no guns but took his favourite gun case which he later found hidden in a gorse bush. It was all very well for Constance to have her little joke, but these were not amusing times, especially for landlords – not even for those like Josslyn. Some had been shot, others threatened, and alarming numbers of their houses were being torched under one pretext or another, and being a good landlord, as some discovered, was no protection when other agendas were circulating. Shortly after that raid, the IRA forced one of the maids at Lissadell to leave, accusing her of being an informer. Josslyn was soon to discover how vulnerable his own situation was when a group of his sister's anti-treaty colleagues kidnapped him. The incident could easily have had fatal consequences for him, despite the fact that he had been assured on several occasions that what he had done for Sligo would never be forgotten. That such assurances were meaningless as far as the IRA was concerned, was demonstrated in February 1922 by this incident, about which his son, Hugh, aged 12 at the time, later wrote a brief account:

> On the day my Father was kidnapped, Brian and I were playing in his study.... The hall door opened, my Father walked in ashen white, rattling the bunch of keys in his pocket, which he always did when he was disturbed or upset. Later we were told that he was working in his office that morning when masked men appeared, asked him to put his hands up, which he did. Several of their men were due to be hanged in Derry on the same day. My Father said [to them] might he go down to the house to tell his wife. They took him to a cottage on a side road near Grange, there he found Major Eccles, who had been pulled out of his sick bed and taken away. They spent the day there guarded by some men in uniform who were playing about with rifles outside. In the evening word came through that the prisoners had been reprieved and my Father was brought home.

It transpired later that this was just one of more than 80 kidnappings (some accounts claimed the figure to be around 200) then carried out by the IRA. This particular incident had been prompted by the arrest of eight armed IRA men travelling from Monaghan to Derry, who, when challenged, claimed that their mission was to attend a football match. In retaliation, the IRA rounded up a large number of prominent Protestants as hostages, including Sir Josslyn Gore-Booth, whose photograph was published in the *Daily Sketch* over a caption that referred to him as 'the brother of Countess Markievic.' After the British Government persuaded Sir James Craig to release 'the Monaghan footballers,' the IRA allowed their captives to return home.[4]

This was a very difficult time for those living in Big Houses. Lissadell escaped the torchers, unlike the fate that awaited Josslyn's cousin in County Cork. Bill Power described the King family's home at Mitchelstown as 'Ireland's greatest castle,' which was burnt down by Republicans because, he averred, they found it necessary 'to cover up the looting of priceless paintings, furniture and silver, [claiming] pathetically, they were denying a base to their Free State enemies.' Less serious, but intimidating anyway, was the fact that letters posted to the family at Lissadell during this period were often opened prior to

---

[4] According to local historian, Joe McGowan, Sir Josslyn and some others were taken hostage by the IRA specifically because three of their members were due to be hanged for the deaths of two Belfast prison wardens.

delivery and marked 'Censored by I.R.A' – just one of a series of relatively minor happenings pointing to the uneasy state of affairs generally.

Before the outbreak of the Great War, Josslyn had decided to sell the Ballymote Estate to the Congested Districts Board as part of his general retrenchment policy, but the negotiations dragged on for many years until, in 1921, he received a Preliminary Agreement from the Board. The C.D.B. proposed an offer for the lands concerned at Corran and Carbury 'at the price £3,474 Guaranteed Stock.' The sale was bedevilled by complications, one being a claim that Sir Josslyn was liable to pay commission because of the delay in the completion of the sale. Josslyn complained that the delay had been occasioned by factors outside his control, mentioning that the war 'was, of course, mostly responsible for it.' He expressed the hope that 'if the Conference between the Irish Party and the British Government is successful, the Irish Land Bill may come into operation speedily, in which case the sale might be closed in eighteen months.' The Bill was, in fact, enacted two years later, in 1923, and facilitated those tenants who had not already done so, to purchase their holdings from their landlords.

Sir Josslyn and Lady Mary in the garden at Lissadell

* * *

Most of Sir Josslyn's many enterprises proved remarkably successful, but none more so than his venture into the horticultural business not long after he succeeded to the estate. It took a great deal of patience on his part to create what became a very broadly based enterprise, comprising forestry, shrubs, herbaceous plants, alpines and bulbs, and he became especially innovative with the two latter categories. His bulb farm won for him many awards in both Britain and Ireland, and as early as 1904 he began exhibiting some of his narcissi in Dublin and Birmingham, and received awards of silver medals at both shows. In the following year, he was awarded the prized Royal Horticultural Society's silver medal for narcissi, and in 1907 he won the Royal Horticultural Society of Ireland Gold Medal.

Four years later, an advertisement in the 1911 Lissadell price list noted that there were then nine separate departments trading, providing between them labour 'for a very large number of hands, every one is being conducted on business lines, and gradually each is being made to pay its own way.' By 1914, the enterprise entailed the expenditure of over £5,000 per annum in wages for the bulb farm alone. Sir Josslyn described the work that he had been doing:

> During the past three or four years we have endeavoured to develop the natural resources of Lissadell for the purpose of giving employment and lending a hand in the revival of agriculture. Departments such as tillage, farming, forestry and sawmills are amongst others being developed, while early potato growing, started as an experiment in 1900 under the auspices of the Department of Agriculture, has been a great success, and an increasing area is every year being taken up by it.

His interest in potato-growing arose from the encouragement given by the Department of Agriculture which had become concerned about the importation of early varieties from Malta, Tenerife, France and the Channel Isles. Scottish producers along the Ayrshire coast had already entered this lucrative market, benefiting from that area's immunity to late frosts, and the Department considered that the even milder conditions enjoyed in west Cork and Kerry should provide growers there with an opportunity to do even better. The Lissadell estate enjoyed similar conditions and Sir Josslyn soon discovered that he could compete successfully with the Ayrshire farmers, even in the Glasgow markets to which the latter were much closer. A great deal of the successful work at Lissadell was due to its head gardener, Cooper, who wrote about the success of the Lissadell potatoes in 1907, mentioning the Glasgow experience:

Our growing each year since we started in 1903 has proved to us that Ninety-fold was our best all-round potato both for earliness and yield. For quality alone Duke of York beats it; while Epicure is a good cropper and is in demand in some districts…. Apart from the fact that our potatoes are of course much better known … we were able this year to sell our potatoes in Glasgow after Ayrshires had started. Last year, after Ayrshires had started, we would not get a potato into Glasgow.

The growing of potatoes was further developed in 1908 when the Lissadell Nurseries entered the competitive seed potato business following experiments conducted in Britain to see how Irish seed potatoes cropped in competition with potatoes from England and Scotland. It was the overwhelming evidence showing that Irish seed potatoes did best that persuaded Josslyn to compete in that market. His 1911 list claimed that 'the superiority of Irish-grown seed potatoes has been shown by the experiments conducted in different centres in England and is now well established. We are the growers of the best varieties, and shall be glad to send particulars on application.' A report sent by him to the Department of Agriculture stated that the growing of potatoes commenced at Lissadell in 1902 with just one acre, and this was more than doubled in 1903. It was further increased to between four and five acres during the ensuing three years, producing a crop with a yield of between £33 and £41 per acre.

The potato business prospered but even this accomplishment was dwarfed by his success in experiments with alpines and herbaceous plants, and narcissi bulbs. Within a few years, he had done sufficient work in his nursery business to produce his first price list of 78 herbaceous and alpine plants. This was a modest start, but no mean feat in such a short space of time, considering that plant propagation is a very slow process.

One of the first serious breeders of narcissi in Ireland was William Bailer Hartland of Cork who, in 1884, published *The Little Book of Daffodils* containing descriptions of over 100 cultivars, and is thought to have been the first list published devoted entirely to daffodils. Around the same period, F.W. Burbidge was pioneering daffodil hybridisation in conjunction with several Dutch breeders and he published *The Narcissus: its History and Culture* along with several other plant books. He had been a plant hunter in the East Indies before being appointed curator of Trinity College Botanic Gardens in Dublin in 1879, a post he held until his death in 1905. Among the other distinguished narcissi breeders in Ireland at that time were Miss Curry of Lismore, Co.

Waterford; John Poe of Co. Tipperary; Guy Wilson, in Co. Antrim; J. Richardson, Waterford, Sir Frederick Moore, in Co. Dublin and James Coey, who founded what was later to become the well-known Slieve Donard Nurseries in Co. Down. It seems likely that Sir Josslyn would have known all of these, and very probably others too, some of whom like himself, were also breeding other plants, but the majority were concentrating their efforts on the very wide range and the many different forms of narcissi already available.

Raising alpines and primulas proved to be the second most important speciality at Lissadell, and Sir Josslyn introduced a number of new cultivars. The latter included Aileen Aroon, Brian Boru, Red Hugh and Maeve, each of these names, intentionally, coincided with the names of members of the family. In fact, while he named a number of his plant introductions after his wife, daughters and sons, he also named some after friends, one of the latter being Sir Horace Plunkett. In a biography of Eva Gore-Booth and her friend Esther Roper, Gifford Lewis pointed out that 'Josslyn's choice of the name Red Hugh was highly significant.' She noted that 'naming one of his four sons after Red Hugh O'Donnell – the leader of the last great attempt to defeat the Elizabethan English in Ireland – demonstrated his nationalist sympathies and indeed his knowledge of Irish history.'

Winston Jones, one of Josslyn's neighbours, wrote that John Wynne, was 'a scientific observer of the Alpine flora of Benbulben', claiming to be the first to discover a number of rare plants there, but Josslyn, too, must have been aware of unusual alpine species growing wild in the Leitrim hills. A report in the *Journal of the Royal Irish Academy* in 1885 noted that *Arenaria viliata*, *Saxifraga nivalis*, and *Epilobium alsinifolium* had each been observed growing on the slopes of Ben Bulben and were unique in Ireland to that area. The *Dictionary of Gardening*, published by the Royal Horticultural Society described *Epilobium alsinifolium* as a plant found in the European mountains and arctic lowlands, but made no reference to Ireland. However, the Census Catalogue of the Flora of Ireland, compiled in 1987 by Mary Scannell and Donal Synnott, noted the presence of this rare plant (also known as Chickweed Willowherb) at nearby Glenade. A decade later, Webb, Parnell and Doogue confirmed, in their *Irish Flora*, that the plant continued to survive 'confined to one mountain cliff in Leitrim.' Other alpine plants found in these hills include species of *Carex*, *Draba*, *Dryas*, *Sedum* and *Thallactrum*, as well as the dwarf willow, *Salix Herbacea* and the mountain Juniper, *Juniperus Nana*.

Josslyn personally conducted the whole painstaking process of cross-fertilisation, choosing the plants to be hybridised, and patiently waiting to see the results. The uncertainty of the process held a special fascination for him and he was well aware that a single suitable bulb or plantlet might be the outcome of a hundred or more such experiments. On one occasion, while experimenting with narcissi, he produced one seed from over 200 hybridisations. His enterprise was getting into its stride when the horticulturist, F.H. Purchas, visited Lissadell, following which he commented in some detail upon what he observed, describing Sir Josslyn as a man who had:

> Thrown himself with all the energy of a strong and restless nature – with the energy of a man who is a glutton for work, who must be making records at sport, or trying his physical endurance, or doing anything but lounge – and it is certainly a pleasure to learn that such labour is not being thrown away, but that the estate and the people are benefiting, and that an example is being set for those whom such an example may concern....

> The horticulturist would need not an hour but a week in which to admire the plants and flowers that surround one. Even in mid-November begonias were still in bloom, and everywhere were patches of vivid colour. New Zealand flax, new spiraeas and poppies from far Tibet, beautiful veronicas with variegated leaves, rare Chatham Island forget-me-nots, St Brigid anemones – for which an enviable name is being earned – perennial flax, Killarney ferns, double Welsh poppies, Transvaal daisies and a thousand and one other plants grown in profusion, and show one at once the source from which is supplied the comprehensive varieties of alpine and herbaceous plants that fill the closely printed thirty-two page catalogue this year devoted to these alone.

The reference to St Brigid anemones, which was an Irish variety in the first place, was an allusion to Sir Josslyn's own strain which he offered in his first price list. They were described as a strain that was 'admitted by experts to be the finest yet seen, and the result of many years of careful selection.' Purchas described in some detail how Sir Josslyn selected the narcissi which he wished to cross, how the anthers – the part of the stamen containing the pollen – were cut out, after which the pollen from the selected cross was delicately applied to the stigma with brushes.

In their history of Irish gardening, Keith Lamb and Patrick Bowe commented on the evident success achieved at Lissadell. They described how the standard of cultivation of plants such as *Phyteuma comosum*, *Androsace*, *Saxifrages* and *Primula* 'would be the pride of many enthusiasts today, especially as the plants were grown in the open rock garden and not protected by pot culture in an alpine house.' In their view, Lissadell 'was, indeed, a great centre of horticultural activity in the opening decades of the twentieth century' but, as the authors also ruefully noted, 'it is sad to think that the conditions of to-day no longer favour the maintenance of such varied activities on a private estate.'

Price lists continued to be printed every year from 1905 onwards, the listings becoming both more extensive and more elaborate with each issue, notably with the inclusion of photographs of the nurseries and of individual plants. By 1908 the Lissadell price lists – they really deserved to be called catalogues – included over 300 alpines and an equally impressive number of herbaceous plants. The 1911 edition included a list of awards which Lissadell varieties of daffodils had gained to date: These comprised two Special Large Gold Medals issued by the Royal Horticultural Society of Ireland in Dublin; two further R.H.S. Gold Medals; and two medals won at Brecon and one at Shrewsbury. Also awarded were Silver Gilt Banksian Medals by the R.H.S. at both Birmingham and London. Silver Gilt medals were gained at Cardiff, Edinburgh, and Glamorgan, and a further 24 medals were won at various English and Irish shows.

New glasshouses were added in which daffodils, tomatoes and chrysanthemums were raised, each succeeding the other through the seasons. There were also ranges of forcing frames and potting sheds, and during most of this period the amount of ground used in the nursery business was gradually extended. By 1914, which was probably the peak year of the enterprise, the Lissadell Nursery was offering 1,350 alpines and just over 1,000 herbaceous plants, and Sir Josslyn had developed his horticultural business to a level hardly matched elsewhere in Ireland, the memory of which has since been all but forgotten.

The scale of his enterprise would have been sufficient to engage the capabilities of most men but in Sir Josslyn's case, his horticultural business was merely one estate department of eight. In addition to raising his own cultivars, Sir Josslyn kept in touch with developments elsewhere, obtaining bulbs from other breeders to add variety to his own. Purchas described how, in 1906, Sir Josslyn was impressed by a new *Narcissis poeticus* that had been produced by a breeder named Englehart. Called 'Acme', it was described at the time as perhaps the most beautiful of all his productions: 'The price is, however, a stiff one, viz. £15. 15s. per bulb. This is the highest priced bulb in the catalogue, though far from being the only one for which a heavy price has to be paid.'

Indeed, at this stage the Lissadell catalogue was offering 'Mrs R. Sydenham' at £10.10s per bulb, 'Dorothy Kingsmill' for £7.10s and 'Queen Maeve' for £3.3s., but other varieties were on offer at quite modest prices, some – such as 'Cynosure' – were available for 2s.9d. per hundred. Josslyn also built up a lucrative business in the sale of daffodil blooms, which were picked and boxed and sent by sea and rail to the London markets, competing successfully against the established growers of the Channel Islands and Scilly.

Josslyn pointing to the damage caused by the fire in the Estate Office, which the family was convinced had been started deliberately.

Sadly, most of the record books relating to the nursery business have been lost, probably in the disastrous 1941 fire in the Estate Office, but it is known that Josslyn was importing stock not only from Britain but also from France, Germany, the United States and Japan. He was justifiably proud of his achievements and, following one of his regular visits to the Botanic Gardens in Dublin he remarked that 'Lissadell is very much ahead of Glasnevin. There are very few plants either in flower or out of flower in the alpine garden which we have not.' His view appears to have been justified judging from an order placed during 1932 by J.W. Besant, the then Director of the National Botanic Gardens (the 'Royal' title had been replaced ten years earlier). This was for 30 different alpine species which his gardens did not then possess and all but two were promptly despatched from Lissadell. Josslyn was, however, envious of the system of labelling at Glasnevin, noting that 'all the plants were named with lead labels and stamped with bold type. As we have so much trouble keeping our plant names distinct, it might be worth trying the Glasnevin system in the Lower Garden.'

The decade between 1914 and 1924 threw up huge difficulties for all of Josslyn's enterprises, first because of the outbreak of the Great War and subsequently by the political unrest in Ireland. The need for the production of vegetables during the war had brought the bulb production almost to a standstill but this branch would have suffered a fatal setback anyway following the appearance, in 1915, of an eelworm infection which devastated the Lissadell Bulb Farm and the trade generally.

The combination of the war and the eelworm persuaded Sir Josslyn to cease activities at the bulb farm altogether and to consolidate his various other horticultural enterprises instead. He concentrated on the production of herbaceous and alpine plants, which he had already been growing with great success in the old Lower Garden. Visitors continued to be astounded by the range and quality of plants produced, one of whom, Henri Corrévon, a Swiss alpine plant expert, described what he saw at Lissadell as unforgettable. Corrévon noted in *The Gardener's Chronicle* that one particular alpine species, *Eritrichium namum* – a plant associated with high mountain ranges where it grows in rock crevices – grew happily at sea level at Lissadell. This striking plant of the borage family with its brilliant sky blue flowers and silvery cushion-like habit is often called 'King of the Alps.' It seemed to him that this *Eritrichium* and other high alpine species grew better at Lissadell than the Himalayan species, in contrast to his own gardens in Switzerland. He went on to describe the garden at Lissadell as presenting:

> an extremely beautiful and picturesque appearance, comprising as it does all the choicest of the alpine plants. I, for one, shall never forget so brilliant a picture. Here one may find the best of the rock plants, grouped together in colonies of ten, twenty, or even in some cases a hundred plants, looking as healthy and happy as in their own natural homes .... Here may also be seen the best primulas, geraniums, campanulas and saxifrages, together with plants from the far north and Arctic regions, all growing and flourishing in the mild, damp Sligo air. The rock garden is one of the largest I have seen, and is very well kept.

Josslyn must have been devastated when Cooper, his manager, decided to leave in 1922. Gabrielle, Josslyn's youngest daughter, later wrote that after 1920 'something of the spirit of the place and well-being had vanished.' She was alluding to the effect which the political upheavals were having on the estate although it seems that Cooper had his mind set on greater things anyway, and he went on to become a director of the Bank of England. However, there can be no gainsaying that the newly emerging Ireland was not to everyone's taste and many who thought so, including some of the Lissadell employees, simply left. Almost immediately after Cooper had gone, Joseph Sangster, the head gardener, also departed and later became one of the founder members of the well-known seed merchant firm, Thompson and Morgan. John Rogers came to Lissadell as manager after Cooper's resignation but he, too, departed little more than a year later.

The period prior to the Great War was a notable epoch for plant hunters – experienced botanists who travelled all over the world collecting specimens and seeds for new introductions at home – most of these men being sponsored by wealthy patrons or by the larger nursery firms. Sir Josslyn not only sponsored several such expeditions but also travelled abroad himself to the Alps, the Balkans, to the Pyrenees and the mountains of Bulgaria to engage in some personal plant hunting. His catalogue listed two dozen alpines described as having been collected by himself, more than half of which were saxifrages. Also listed were several herbaceous abelias originating from Josslyn's visit to the Balkans in 1910, and a related ramonda from the Pyrenees.

While it appears that Josslyn conformed to an unfortunate family tradition of not keeping a record of his travels abroad, an account of one of the plant expeditions sponsored by Sir Josslyn – to the Maritime Alps in 1912 – has survived among the Lissadell Papers. This was undertaken by H. McClanaghan, who worked for him at Lissadell, accompanied by C.F. Ball, who was Assistant Keeper at the Botanic Gardens in Dublin.

Despite the forced closure of the bulb farm in 1915, the nursery business continued until the economic consequences of the developing political situation gradually made more difficult the running of a business enterprise which depended upon peaceful and prosperous conditions. Sadly, of the more than 70 narcissi cultivars raised at Lissadell during the 21 years that Sir Josslyn marketed the bulbs, none appear to have survived, and it seems that of his primulas, only Red Hugh continues to be available from one or two specialist nurseries.

The Lissadell Estate suffered not only from the unsettled political situation but also from the ensuing 'Economic War.' The latter resulted from Eamon de Valera's decision in 1932 – after forming a government in coalition with the Labour Party – to discontinue the payment of annuities to the British Government. Britain retaliated by imposing crippling taxes on livestock and on livestock products exported to Britain, Ireland's only significant market at the time, and the country's vulnerable economy was disastrously weakened until the 'war' was settled six years later.

Against this background, Josslyn's various enterprises struggled to survive, and it is significant that the last full catalogue of plants was published in that same year. In it Josslyn commented that the previous year had been very bad for the nursery, adding that: 'We have decided to persevere with our annual list in the hope that things must mend sometime.' As Reeves Smith and Jupp commented 'Sadly this optimism for a brighter future was short-lived. The "Economic War" of 1932–38 did enormous damage to Lissadell as it did to the Irish economy generally.' They noted that six years later, 'the nursery continued to operate, though it is likely that the Lower Garden was gradually abandoned from this time.' Slim price lists continued to be issued until the nursery closed in 1955, but Josslyn's enterprise had effectively ended long before that when the many problems over which he had no control, and his own frailty as he entered his mid-seventies, made the continuing struggle so unequal. Today, there is almost no visible trace of the horticultural work undertaken by Sir Josslyn. Nature has taken over.

* * *

For Sir Josslyn, now in his mid-seventies, it was a serious cause for concern that his eldest son and heir, Michael, after being educated at Rugby School and at Cambridge University, developed a mental problem which was to render him incapable of taking over the running of the estate. Josslyn's Dublin solicitors advised early in 1943 that in the event of his own death, Michael, 'being unable to manage his own affairs, he would be taken in Wardship of the Court here.' A year later, Josslyn's accountants advised that a very considerable sum should be set aside to meet death duties and other costs, anticipating the time 'when eventually your successor takes over at Lissadell.' It was already clear that Michael, who was due to succeed, was quite incapable of doing so, and each of his three brothers had gone to serve with the British forces in the Second World War. Brian had joined the Royal

Navy, Angus was in the Irish Guards, and Hugh had enlisted in the Royal Irish Fusiliers. Hugh, the second eldest, who had trained as an estate manager was the obvious alternative choice to manage the estate, but his story, related in a subsequent chapter, was one more of the tales of sorrow that hung about Josslyn's life.

Afflicted by poor health and a series of personal tragedies, Josslyn also had to watch helplessly as the fortunes of his estate were being affected by events totally beyond his control. He took to his bed for most of his final year and died at Lissadell in March 1944, aged 75 years. Obviously there was a medical reason, but the catalogue of family misfortunes seems to have proved too much for him and it may well be at least partly true, as was said at the time, that he died of a broken heart.

His funeral took place on St Patrick's Day, 1944 in the little estate church built by his grandfather. The address was given by the Rt. Rev. Edward Hughes, Bishop of Kilmore, who described Sir Josslyn as a man of outstanding ability, energy, and character and spoke of Josslyn's great interest in and work for the Church of Ireland.

The astonishing success achieved at the Lissadell Estate during Sir Josslyn's time may have never been matched anywhere else in Ireland, but despite the downturn caused by the changed political and economic conditions, Sir Josslyn had continued to employ over 100 people even at the time of his death. That he achieved so much was all the more remarkable in view of the family problems which he and Lady Gore-Booth had to face, especially in their latter years. Sir Josslyn nominated his second son, Hugh, as heir to his free estate and continued to correspond with his solicitors in Dublin but he never completed the arrangements for re-writing his will. As a result, he died partly intestate with consequences that were to greatly complicate the lives of those who survived him. Like his father and his grandfather before him, Josslyn enjoyed few pursuits more than fishing and shooting. It will be recalled that his inventive mind dreamed up the idea of making a hollow cow into which he could clamber, and from which he could all the better aim his gun at some unsuspecting game bird or hare. As Esther Roper, life-long friend of his sister, Eva, observed:

> Yet, where his name survives, it is in the anecdotes of the kind that people love to dwell on concerning the eccentricities of the Anglo-Irish, and he still raises laughs by his invention of a hollow cow from which to shoot wild geese, and his successful pollination of a red primula called 'Red Hugh', as if his life was

spent alternatively on all fours in his garden with a pollinating brush, and lying in a hollow cow clutching a gun.

John C. McTernan, a local historian, expressed similar sentiments in different way:

> Outside the family circle one seldom hears mention of his name nowadays, and his memory is all but forgotten - not only by the people on whose behalf he laboured so zealously but also by the country he loved …. Some day, perhaps, the life and work of Sir Josslyn Gore-Booth will be accorded its rightful recognition and his name will find a niche on the pedestal alongside that of his now famous sisters.

An amusing pair of photographs of three Gore-Booth sisters and their friends. Eva, Mabel and Constance are second, third, and fourth from the right; their Scottish cousin, Joanna Arabella ('Jock'), is on the extreme left alongside Miss Noel, the family's greatly-loved governess at Lissadell.

Constance (right) photographed with her sister Mabel. Several biographies have mistaken Eva for her younger sister Mabel.

CONSTANCE

'This fascinating, incomprehensible rebel'

The Duke of Wellington – born in County Meath – claimed that the location of his birth did not make him an Irishman any more than being born in a stable would have made him a horse. Constance Georgine Gore-Booth, who was born in her father's town house close to Buckingham Palace in London on February 4, 1868, would also most surely have averred (certainly after she reached the age of 40) that her place of birth did not make her an Englishwoman. Her fortieth birthday was to be significant because until then she showed no particular interest in nationalism, so that more than two thirds of her life was spent as an Anglo-Irishwoman even if, during the latter decade of that period, she became an increasingly unconventional one.

Constance Georgine (whose second name is often misspelt even by some of her biographers) showed a strong, independent and defiant streak from an early age. Her father gave her a pony when she was four years old, and it was the duty of one of the family retainers to lead her out on her new steed to the lawn near the house. His instructions were to ensure that nothing more than a gentle trot was to be attempted, but as soon as she began to gain confidence, she started to dig her heels into the pony's flanks to encourage it to go faster. The unfortunate servant, anxious that the child should come to no harm while under his supervision, did his best to restrain the pony and its rider, and every session ended with him re-entering the riding school sweating profusely. So it went on until, inevitably, Constance got her own way and she broke free on her steed and, galloping furiously, disappeared among the plantations. She went on to make full use of Sir Robert's fine riding school, becoming, as many people have declared, one of the finest horsewomen ever seen in the west of Ireland. By the time she was 14 she had won her first race, already a fearless rider over fences and ditches – often on her own – riding for half a day to Raughley Point and beyond and even to the summit of Ben Bulben. She began to ride with the local hunt which met twice a week and became unusually proficient at driving a coach four-in-hand. Constance inherited more than her name from her County Leitrim born aunt, Lady Muncaster, who when she died in Cumberland in 1917; was described in the local newspaper, the *Whitehaven News*, as 'a skilful whip, she was equal to the feat of driving a four-in-hand and not seldom found enjoyment in the task.'

Sir Robert had died when she was eight, but it is probable that Constance heard at first hand about how the family, under his direction, had cared for the tenants during the Great Famine. When she was 12 years old, she certainly saw for herself images of distress which remained with her for many years as her father, Sir Henry, fed the tenants during the 1879 famine. Her father had made a point of insisting that his older children watched as he and their mother fed the starving people of the district in an improvised soup kitchen. Sir Henry also insisted that they should visit the tenants on the estate so that they, like him, got to know each tenant's family circumstances.

Despite this, some writers, for example Marian Broderick after writing about Constance's generosity towards the tenants, added: 'from whom, of course, she was supposed to keep her distance.' John C. McTernan, a local historian, was one who expressed the opposite view. He noted that one consequence of the children's visits to the tenants was that both Constance and Eva 'grew up in terms of intimacy and friendliness with the people of the surrounding countryside from whose lips they learned something of the legends and history of Ireland.' While many of the impressions gained at this time undoubtedly stayed with her, Constance was later to deny the paternalistic role played by her own family, renouncing and subsequently denouncing everything that it had stood for.

As she grew in her teenage years, her developing good looks were no disadvantage for a young woman who liked to be the centre of attention, though many years later her friend, Helena Moloney, wrote that 'the greatest defect in her character was her childish love of the limelight.' She and her sister, Eva – who was two years younger – were very close, and remained so throughout their lives. Eva was quieter, gentler and even more attractive than Constance, a view endorsed by W.B. Yeats in his often quoted lines:

> Two girls in silk kimonos, both
> Beautiful, one a gazelle.

Constance certainly never allowed her gender to prevent her doing anything. There was something of a tomboy streak in her, especially evident in some of her more daring feats or when she acted outrageously. A diary which Constance was keeping when she was only 14 years old gives a hint that she was already restless and unsure of what direction her life might take: 'What do I want? I don't know. Every thought has a contradiction to-night and I don't understand why.' Ten years later, while attending the Slade School of Art in London, she wrote: 'A whole London season older and not engaged or even wishing to be ...' During the years between these entries, Constance had grown into a beautiful young woman, attracting a host of male admirers. The opportunities for this to happen were almost limitless, between the soirées and entertainments at Lissadell and in the other Big Houses around it, not to mention the vice-regal balls in Dublin and the high society gatherings in London. One can only speculate why she kept her many admirers at arms' length. Was it simply, as has been claimed, that she was already disenchanted with her family's lifestyle, or was there more to it? She was later to criticise her family because: 'No one is interested in politics in our house.... Everyone accepted the status quo almost as if it were the will of God.'

She inherited various family traits. Behind her determined character, Constance could be extremely generous and kind, traits seen in her mother and, indeed, in her father. Her developing tendency towards socialism was shared with her sister Eva and, also – though much less obviously – with her brother Josslyn. Roseangela Barone, wrote a beautifully produced book in Italian about Eva, *La Quercia e l'Olivo*, which she also translated into English. In the English version she referred to Constance as 'impetuous, daring, unbiased and exuberant'. The term 'unbiased' seems curious until reference is made to the original Italian version where the word used is 'spericolata,' meaning reckless or foolhardy, indicating a very obvious mistranslation.

Constance went on to develop an interest in the stage, an interest that had its origins in the long winter evenings at Lissadell when the whole family – her parents, two brothers and two sisters, their grandmother, and an elderly aunt – indulged in private theatricals from time-to-time. On one such occasion two plays were performed, Constance taking the leading part in the second, playing the part of Lady Somerford, who 'attracted the amorous attentions of two gentlemen.' The *Sligo Champion* reported that:

Miss Gore-Booth certainly bore off the palm for the excellence of her acting. In the passionate scene where the Baronet demands that she shall assign to him her estate in default of giving him her hand, and when she refuses, her repudiation of the vile contract was, indeed, very fine. Miss Gore-Booth's representation of the loving and persecuted girl anxious to make any sacrifice consonant with honour for the man she loves, was an admirable one, and were it possible to imagine that she would ever tread the boards as a professional, as so many distinguished ladies have done, we would predict for her many historic triumphs.

Feeling she had inherited something of her mother's skill in painting, she became interested in this pursuit and began to sketch and paint, a pastime with which she began to seek to develop her own independent life. She took her studies seriously until other ideas began to intrude, a characteristic that was to become more evident later. These interests were to include several protest movements, notably the Suffragettes who were then campaigning for the right of women to vote. She was greatly influenced in this and in her interest in working for women's rights and for the poor by her younger sister, Eva, who settled in Manchester and later in London.

While all this was in the future, on the surface at least, life for Constance was very attractive indeed at this time, as she enjoyed not only these pursuits, but fishing, shooting and boating as well.

Constance sketching or painting a horse at Lissadell.

When she was 18, Constance went on a tour of Europe with her governess, with whom she especially enjoyed Italy, and spent six months in Florence where she took lessons in drawing. Queen Victoria's jubilee was celebrated in 1887 and, on St Patrick's Day, Constance was formally presented to the queen by one of her ladies in waiting, the Countess of Erroll who happened to be Constance's cousin. Constance wore an impressive white satin dress for the occasion, with a train three yards long and three white feathers in her hair. She then spent almost four months in London with her mother, enjoying the role of an aristocratic young lady about town, shopping and socialising.

A feature of the local hunting scene was the annual point-to-point meeting that marked the end of each season for the Sligo Harriers. First held in 1867, a year before Constance was born, the event was presided over by her grandfather until his death, and continued to be associated with the family for many years afterwards. In a report on one of the later meetings, the *Sligo Independent* recalled that the Gore-Booth connection with the event was being continued:

> … in the person of Miss Constance Gore-Booth. She arrived well mounted and in good hunting form and shed a bright ray of sunshine all round and as her grandfather had done in 1867. She entered into the spirit of the days' doings with a heartiness that made all feel comfortable. The young lady would blush if she overheard all the encomiums expressed by those who watched as she rode up seated on her palfrey [a saddle horse, especially for a lady] with an ease that would do credit to Diana herself. As she weighted out and mounted Paddy Connolly's Chance Shot, in his colours of yellow and black, she received a regular ovation. Her horsemanship was splendid. In the Diamond Plate she made the pace hot from the start and the gallant Major [Charles O'Hara] from Annaghmore found himself outrun by her very early on.

From 1889 to 1892, Constance lived for a time at Harcourt Terrace in Dublin, a quiet road close to the Grand Canal, where she enjoyed the buzz of the metropolis, often in the company of her mother. In her memoirs, *Seventy Years Young*, Pamela Hinkson recounted how Elizabeth, Countess of Fingall, remembered Constance during this period:

> I took Constance Gore-Booth to parties during the Zetland vice-royalty – her mother, Lady Gore-Booth, was a cousin of Lady Zetland. 'Con' was then a beautiful young girl and all the young men wanted to dance with her. She was lovely and gay in her youth at Lissadell, hunting and dancing, and she was the life and soul of any party…. She went with other young ladies of her class to parties at Dublin Castle, and sometimes I chaperoned her and stayed the night with her and her mother.

Having already gained a reputation for unorthodox behaviour, it is hardly surprising that stories about her, true or false, circulated widely. One of these claimed that she had, for a bet, stated that she could stop the city's traffic and did so by lying down in the street until removed by a policeman. Her regular appearances at Dublin Castle balls were a further source of stories: One such came from the pen of Lt. Colonel Cyril Foley, a former A.D.C. to the viceroy, who wrote about dancing with Constance at one of these events in *The Saturday Review* in September, 1893.

> At a luncheon party the day following one of these balls, I found myself at one of the many small tables…. A well-known gossip said to me "I saw you dancing last night with Miss Gore-Booth; how does she dance, and has she much to say for herself." My reply did not satisfy the inquisitive old woman. "Now, captain, tell me, would you prefer Miss Gore-Booth as a dancing partner or as a talking partner?" Annoyed by this inquisitive persistence, I said, "I should personally prefer her as a sleeping partner."

His remark was reported to the viceroy, and Foley was 'spoken to' about it. Foley added: 'I fancy [the viceroy] was really more amused than angry.' Another man attracted to Constance later became General Sir Alexander Godley whose family lived at Killegar, Co. Leitrim. He had joined the Royal Dublin Fusiliers and in his autobiography he wrote about what he termed the galaxy of beauty to be seen at the vice-regal balls in Dublin Castle. The Duchess of Leinster 'stood out among them all,' he wrote, and he then included Constance Gore-Booth in a list of 'the Irish girls [who] held their own.' Godley recalled a weekend spent at Lissadell where he met 'the most charming and most attractive eldest daughter of the house, with whom all the young men, myself included were madly in love,' and described how 'she made us throw our caps in the air for her to fire at with her revolver.' General Godley was, according to Tim Jeal, Lord Baden-Powell's biographer, 'a tall, good-humoured and exceptionally capable Anglo-Irishman who had served with distinction in Mashonaland.' 'B-P.' obviously had a high opinion of him, (he wrote the Preface to Godley's book), and appointing him Adjutant of the Protectorate Regiment and Commander of Mafeking's western defences during the Boer War. Godley's name was also mentioned by Thomas Pakenham in his book about the Boer War in which he described him in a manner which might have appealed rather more to Constance at that time as 'a polo-playing, pig-sticking, bushwhacking Irishman.'[1] Another possible suitor at this time, noted by Roseangela Barone, was Wilfred Ashley, whom she described as 'a young nobleman living in a nearby estate.' The Ashleys inherited Classiebawn and the Mullaghmore estate on the death of Lord Palmerston, and the property passed to the Mountbattens when Edwina Ashley married Lord Mountbatten.

In a diary Constance was keeping during 1892, a few brief entries give some hints that her convivial and varied lifestyle was less than fully satisfying. Aged 24 and still single, she wrote about looking for her 'real true love,' and kept notes about dinners and dances. One entry stated that she was 'writing rubbish because I have nothing to do to occupy my mind;' another said simply: 'Fooling around.' Perhaps more significantly, she also wrote: 'Women are made to adore, and sacrifice themselves, and I as a woman demand as a right that Nature should provide me with something to live for, something to die for.'

Constance and Eva travelled to Germany with their mother, the main object being to attend the annual Wagner Opera Festival at Bayreuth. They sat through three very long performances and went to see the composer's residence, Wahnfried, and his grave in the garden behind the house, and they also visited Liszt's tomb at the nearby Stadtfriedhof. No matter how hard her mother tried, however, Constance was showing obvious signs that she was becoming bored with and intolerant of her lifestyle. A diary entry gives a clear indication of what was uppermost in her mind at the time: 'If I could cut the family tie and have a life and interest of my own, I should want no other heaven.' For some time she had been trying to persuade her father and mother to allow her to go abroad to study art, the first hint of this developing interest since her visit to Florence six years earlier. For their part, her parents simply wanted Constance to be conventional and settle down with a suitable husband. She was old enough, of course, to make up her own mind, but she could do little unless her parents agreed to give her the necessary allowance. The more they tried to hold her

---

[1] However, while Constance was capable of acting outrageously, it may well have been the case that Alex Godley was more than a match for her in this respect. In his memoirs, he wrote about how he and his fellow junior officers stationed at the Curragh, would ambush an unwary sheep which: 'Once caught ... would be hurled through a window on top of some unfortunate who had gone to bed. The wreckage of his room by the maddened beast can well be imagined.' One might speculate endlessly what might have been the outcome had Constance agreed to marry him.

back, the more she resented it and them – a situation summed up in her diary entry: 'I see an opening daylight and freedom if I can only persevere and drudge and get my parsimonious family to pay.' Her father and mother continued to think differently, but her progress with her painting lessons at home may have encouraged her to press for the chance to go to London:

> Success and progress walled round by Family Pride, stinginess and conventionality. What is one to do? How am I to coerce them? How to break away? If I was sure of myself and knew I could succeed for sure, and make a name or, more to the point, money – I would bolt, live on a crust and do.

Her parent's attempts to dissuade their daughter from an occupation and lifestyle that was considered by them so unsuitable, created a dilemma for themselves as well as for Constance. While they may not have realised it at the time, they were actually driving her away from home and sowing the seeds that eventually caused her to turn her back completely on the family. Yet, despite all her bravado, it seems that some of it at least was an outer skin protecting an inner self-doubt, for she was haunted with the prospect of being ultimately unsuccessful and having to return defeated to Lissadell and forced to 'throw myself on the charity of one's family. A miserable failure is more than I can screw up my courage to face. So many people begin with great promise and greater hopes and end in nothing but failure.' Constance got her own way in the end and set off for London where her parents had arranged to place her in the famous Slade School of Art which, they must have hoped, was the nearest thing to a respectable art school. She studied under Alphonse Legros and with the Swedish Anna Nordgren, with whom she became very friendly, inviting her to stay at Lissadell where the two painted local scenes. Her two years in London were happy ones, enjoying society life away from the family, free to do as she wished when not busily improving her painting skills.

When she returned to Lissadell for Christmas, 1896, a meeting had been arranged to promote the Sligo branch of the Irish Women's Suffrage and Local Government Association at Drumcliff, and three of the Gore-Booth sisters, Constance, Eva and Mabel, took a prominent part in the proceedings. Held in Drumcliff National School, the *Sligo Champion* reported that there was a very large attendance, and as her first significant public occasion, the event was of some importance for Constance. It undoubtedly helped to shape her later life, giving her, as Liz Curtis expressed it, 'her first bite … of the apple for freedom' leading her to see, as Declan Kiberd noted, that Irishwomen were 'doubly enslaved' and had 'a double battle to fight.'

* * *

After nearly three years at the Slade, Constance felt an urge to move on to Paris, a notion that worried her father and mother even more than her earlier decision to go to London. Luck was on her side, however, because an aunt died and left her a small legacy so that, whether her parents willingly agreed or not, Constance was – for the present, anyway – financially independent. In Paris she attended classes at the Rodolphe Julian Academy (possibly influenced by the fact that Sarah Purser, her cousin, had attended there some years earlier) where she met Paul Henry and, more significantly, Casimir Markievicz. In his biography of Purser, John O'Grady wrote that Julian's was a place 'where the poor folk who went there were devoured,' and described the owner as a fat Provençal with 'a seductively mendacious manner.' While her modest legacy lasted, Constance enjoyed the new freedom of not having to worry about the cost of anything. When she was not studying she was able to go to the theatre and to restaurants, and sit in the pavement cafes with her artist friends, some of whom quickly discovered that Constance was hopelessly generous. One way or another, her money ran out and she had to appeal to her father for financial help, and when this was slow in coming she furiously accused him of trying to force her to return to Lissadell 'by starvation.' Defiantly, she boasted that she could 'live on two francs a day, and take her bath in a pannikin in the middle of the bare studio floor.'

A description of Constance during her Paris days, written by Violet Hunt, was published in *The Daily Mail* in 1916, just after the Easter Rising. Hunt and many of her friends had known Constance in Paris as 'Teuf-teuf,' after having first met her in a restaurant in Boulevard Montparnasse, the haunt of what she called 'the solemn, frock-coated rapins [art students] with their flowing black ties; dusky Poles, and Jewesses, and a few wide-eyed English.' The article continued:

> Suddenly, Camomille exclaimed, "Hooray! Here's my darling Teuf-teuf, now she'll tell you where to go in Paris." Teuf-teuf came up to our table like a winged Victory, walking in a flamboyant style that had every aspect of movement in it. She was a tall, thin slip of a girl, with tawny red-gold hair worn *a la Mérode* over her ears under her sailor hat. She had on a pink satin cotton blouse

very much open at the collar, from which a long white throat rose triumphantly. Her short-sightedness lent her face a peering, puzzled look, which was at variance with her perfect boyish frankness and camaraderie. She ordered an exiguous lunch and sat down. All the rapins looked at all the other rapins as if all the rapins were in love with her. I have heard that they were. One of them rose from his distant seat and offered her a light from his cigarette. When the handsome Byronic figure had gone back to his place she whispered to me: "I didn't introduce my friend. He is a genius, only very poor, and that makes him shy. He is a Polish Count. His name is Casimir Markievicz."

Some time just before this, Constance had met Stefan Krzywoszewski at a ball. He mistook her for an Englishwoman and thought she was about 20 years of age when, in fact, she was thirty-one. He described her as 'a living Rosetti or Burne-Jones' (as others also did), and subsequently introduced his Polish compatriot to her as Count Casimir Dunin de Markievicz. When doubts began to be expressed about his title, some claimed that in introducing Casimir to Constance as a count, his friend had done so in jest. Anyway, a friendship quickly followed and it soon became clear that the Irish Constance and the Polish Casimir – two strangers in a foreign land – shared a number of things in common. Both had come from landlord families and were members of minor aristocracy, and both were fond of the gay, bohemian lifestyle they had found in Paris. Each spoke fluent French and they shared a common interest in sketching and painting. He was tall and handsome, she was slim and attractive so that, certainly on the face of it, they appeared to be a good match for each other.

From Constance's point of view, Casimir's title must have been an added attraction, perhaps a crucial one because if she married him she would become a countess and she might also go on to achieve success as an artist, gaining long overdue respect from her own family. If she could never be Lady Gore-Booth of Lissadell, well, why not Countess Dunin de Markievicz of Denhofówka? After a year or so, the pair decided to become engaged and Constance wrote to tell Josslyn, who had just recently become head of the family following their father's death. The tone of her letter is almost unexpectedly tentative, as though the strongly independent, devil-may-care Constance was anxious at all costs to secure her family's approval. Although undated, it was probably written in February, 1900 and was addressed:

My dear Joss:
I am engaged to be married, and I hope you all won't mind because it's a foreigner, but I am awfully fond of him and he is not like a Frenchman, much

more like a fellow countryman. I love him very much and am very happy but I wish he was English because of you all, though I don't mind for myself, but I am so afraid of it being a barrier between me and you all, and make you think of me as an alien. He is an artist and very clever….

Shortly after this, a second letter from Constance set out some details about how she had met her fiancé. She told Josslyn that a Mrs Forbes Robertson ('she is a Pole') had introduced her to a great many of her compatriots 'and we have been great pals and comrades ever since.' Continuing, without mentioning Casimir Markievicz by name, Constance went on to relate, apparently without question, what Casimir had told her about himself. He had:

About £160 a year, that's all! I don't want him to settle any money on me. It's not necessary as I have my own. He is a widower and has a child who is with his [Casimir's] mother. He married very young and was most unhappy. His wife deceived him and there was a great scandal, her lover tried to kill her. They tell me he behaved wonderfully and was awfully good to her when she was deserted, ill and broken-hearted. She died of consumption a year ago. Being a Pole he has to have papers of identity and Passports. I have seen them but they are in Russian and I don't understand them …. He was educated to be a Barrister, but gave it up for Painting. He has great talent and has already gained a gold medal. I am telling you anything about him I can think of … If possible, we should like to be married the end of May as we both want to stay quietly in some place in the Country and paint big pictures…. Another thing, can you get me some official statement as to my family to send to his mother – they are very proud. I don't care a bit about money but would like to be sure I am "*noblesse*".

Earlier letters to Josslyn – usually when she was complaining about having so little money – could be quite abrasive, but this current correspondence was conducted in a different manner even though, as far as Constance was concerned, she must have felt annoyed at having to virtually plead her case. Her next letter gave Josslyn some further details, but like the earlier correspondence, she continued to refer to her fiancé as 'him' and 'he.' She added:

One thing I have not thoug… to say or you to ask and which is perhaps the most important of all, is his relationship with Russia. Thank goodness he hates politics and has never meddled in any plots or belonged to any political societies….

A further letter, written in response to Josslyn's suggestion that she should return to Lissadell on her own for a month so that the whole business could be sorted out, produced a forthright response:

I cannot agree to going home for a month without him. I have no intention and see no reason to leave here till he comes with me … I am quite pleased and willing to wait a bit and make everything as pleasant as I can, and have no objection to anybody making any enquiries they like, but I wish you to understand that I have quite made up my mind to marry him and nothing could stop me.

However, Josslyn continued to urge her to come back from Paris so that everything could be discussed in the family circle but Constance remained adamant that she would only return to Lissadell on condition that Casimir came with her. She demanded to know: 'What is your reason for wishing me to come alone?' Presumably Josslyn tried to explain the reason was that the family knew nothing about her fiancé's background and they were, consequently, concerned for her wellbeing. Perhaps this prompted Constance, in her next letter dated April 20, to refer to him by name for the first time, and volunteering the information that: 'It won't make any difference to Casi how I stand as to money.' She recognised that her brother's questioning was not simply personal but the result of family pressure – almost certainly mostly on the part of their mother: 'I don't envy you one bit at this moment, it must be a fairly dirty job looking into my affairs.'

It is clear from the ongoing correspondence from Constance that the family was both distinctly unhappy and deeply concerned. She was six years older than her fiancé. He was a Roman Catholic and Polish by nationality (although Poland had ceased to exist as an independent country so that he carried a Russian passport). He was a widower and the father of a young son, and there were rumours that he had a mistress, though these latter may have originated from his habit of boasting about amorous adventures.

Eventually, Constance told Josslyn her fiancé's full name including his claim to be a count, but this only fanned further doubts about Casimir whose title seemed, to her family, as difficult to verify as it was to pronounce. The many letters addressed to Josslyn by lawyers and from the Russian Embassy in London, give some indication of the lengths to which he went to enquire about Casimir's background; to ascertain the validity of his title; and also the likely standing of the intended marriage. The Russian ambassador replied that Casimir Markievicz was not entitled to designate himself 'Count,' stating that this title had never been native to Poland. One of the many points raised during this correspondence was that, having served in the Imperial Russian Guard, he was now a reservist and liable to be called for further military service, but there is no indication that any of these matters caused the slightest concern to Constance.

Josslyn's subsequent partly successful attempts to find out something about his sister's fiancé are well documented in the family papers, but it has taken almost a century since then for some of the interesting results of his enquiries to be made known. Details about the steps then taken only came to light following researches in the Tsarist archives in St Petersburg undertaken by Seamus Martin when Moscow correspondent of *The Irish Times*. In an article published in April 1994, he described how the British ambassador at St Petersburg contacted the Imperial Russian foreign minister who in turn requested the Russian ambassador in Paris to arrange for a member of the Okhrana, the secret police, to spy on Casimir Markievicz. As the ambassador expressed it:

> this person has won the trust of a relative of the Marquess of Salisbury [the British Prime Minister], who resides in Paris as an art student and, calling himself a nobleman and the son of a Count, is trying to persuade her to marry him.

A thorough investigation then followed, conducted by State Councillor Rachkovsky, which revealed that:

> Mr Casimir Dunin-Markievicz is said to have been born on March 15, 1871 [he was born in 1874] at Denfowka [Denhofówka], Russian Poland, son of Pierre Paul and Mrs. Marie Chrzaszczewska. Without right he takes the title of Count Dunin-Markievicz, in that Poland has never had a Count of that name.

Rachkovsky went further, doubting Casimir's right to prefix 'Dunin' to his name because it had royal origins, and he also confirmed some details about Casimir's first marriage to Jadwiga Splawa-Neyman. Rachkovsky discovered that she and their baby son, Stanislas, had joined Casimir in Paris in 1898 (he had been living alone there for two years), and after becoming pregnant again she returned to her relatives in the Ukraine during March 1899. She died from peritonitis (not consumption, as stated by Constance) shortly afterwards.

The Okhrana representative 'tailed' Casimir to his studio address in Paris, sending back comprehensive details about people with whom he had been studying. Details about some of his recently completed paintings were also noted, including a portrait 'of an Irishwoman who passes as his future wife who he is due to marry around next September.' Rachkovsky reported that: 'The couple have known each other for a long time already, she has been known in all the houses in which Mr

Markievicz has passed.' Rachkovsky's references to Casimir were invariably prefixed by the title 'Mr' and, after referring to Constance as 'Miss Gorbooth,' he described Casimir's lifestyle:

> He spends a lot of money [living among] young people of both sexes of eccentric appearance and disposition [and] since the death of his wife he indulges in all pleasures which take up every instant of his time. Apart from this stormy life, there is nothing with which to reproach him.

The validity of Casimir's title was to be questioned again 16 years later, after the Easter Rising, when police enquiries were made in order to establish Constance's true nationality. This drew a response from the Polish Consul that 'there was no such man as Count Markievicz' but he knew 'a man called Danui Markievicx, a play writer living in Warsaw [who] before the European war was a Russian.' This detail appears in Dr Barton's book about the 1916 court martial records, to which he added that when Casimir was traced, 'he refused to give details of his marriage abroad and his Polish nationality could not be established.' Five years after this, when she was about to travel to the United States on a fundraising mission, Constance applied for a Polish passport. When completing the form, she did so without using the title 'Countess', and she also omitted the word 'Count' in connection with her husband's name. Yet, on the same application form, she wrote her father's name as 'Henry William Gore Booth, (Bart)' and her mother's as 'Lady Gore Booth.' It may seem curious that when completing this form, Constance was not only unsure whether her wedding had taken place in 1899 or 1900, but she also subtracted two years from her actual age!

In the most recent biography about Constance, Joe McGowan quoted the claim that she 'refused to travel on a British passport and, ironically, applied for and was given a Polish passport.' However, among papers lodged in the National Archive there is a letter from the Chief Secretary's Office at Dublin Castle in which a Mr W. Doolin stated that: 'This lady, having lost her original British nationality by marriage with a Polish subject, cannot be granted a British passport.'

How Casimir's status has been viewed in Poland is also interesting. For example, in the respected Polish publication, *Polski słownik biograficzny,* (Polish Biographical Dictionary), the entry for Kazimierz Markiewicz describes him as the son of a landowner (*ziemianin*), with the added detail that the Markiewicz family 'used [the Polish word is '*używali*'] the title count.' Another Polish publication, *O heraldyce i 'heraldycznym' snobismie,* (Heraldry and Heraldic Snobbery), by Szymon Konarski, included the name Markievicz in a list of some 120 Polish 'pseudo-counts,' i.e., those who improperly claimed the title particularly when living or travelling in Western Europe. Also in Poland, just after the fall of Communism in Europe – a decision was made to name a state primary school in Warsaw in honour of Constance. It was given the title *Szkola Podstawowa 335 im* (in the name of) *Konstancji Markiewicz,* without ascribing to her the title 'Countess.' Also significant is the fact that when notices announcing Casimir's death were published in the Warsaw newspapers, no mention was made of him having been a count.

While no *conclusive* evidence had, up to that point, been produced to prove the matter either way, all of the foregoing – especially when taken together – appears to make the point that Casimir was not a count. Added to all this, it may seem strange that Casimir's son Stanislas, who lived a financially precarious life drifting from one unsatisfactory job to another, made no claim to inherit his father's alleged title. This begs the question, why not? After all, a title could have 'opened doors' for him. The explanation for this, it seems, lay in a sealed letter written by him which he gave to John McCann before emigrating to America. McCann, a journalist, playwright and a member of Fianna Fáil, was instructed not to open the letter until after Stanislas had died. As Donal Nevin has written in his forthcoming biography of James Connolly (which he has kindly allowed the author to see), McCann subsequently wrote a magazine article about Constance in which he quoted the contents of the letter. It read: 'Dear John, My father was *not* a Count – Yours – Staskow.'

The disputed question about Casimir's title also had some bearing on the more general question of his family's actual status – a matter of no small importance to Constance when she decided to marry him. In one of her letters to Josslyn, she wrote: 'Of course I am a very poor marriage for him.... He is a hereditary nobleman [which means] the son of a count whose family has been on a certain property for seven generations.' Marcus Wheeler, Professor Emeritus of Slavonic Studies at Queen's University, Belfast, wrote an article in 1998 for the Polish publication, *Tygiel Kultury,* in which he questioned whether or not 'the boot was on the other foot' in that the Gore-Booths were, arguably, at least the equal of the Markieviczs. In translation, part of this article read:

> In geographical and social terms there were many similarities between the
> Gore-Booth estate at Lissadell and the Markievicz estate at Żywotówka
> in the Ukraine; and, although before their marriage Constance seems to have
> been apprehensive as to how she would be regarded by Casi's family ... the
> simple fact appears to be that Casimir Markievicz was not a count, but that he
> was a member of what in Poland is called the szlachta. This term is variously
> translated 'gentry' or 'nobility,' and was usually, though not necessarily,
> associated with landed property. It appears that, at the end of the 18th century,
> approximately 20% of the free inhabitants of Poland ... fell into this category,
> which may explain why the more ambitious or snobbish were inclined to lay
> claim to an additional title.'

Citing *Encyclopedia staropolska* (Encyclopedia of Old Poland),
Professor Wheeler added that, in medieval Poland, the title was
sometimes 'simply adopted by persons who judged themselves
meritorious.' However, it should be stated that there is no doubt that
the Dunin-Markievicz family comes from old Polish gentry stock that
can be traced back to the late fourteenth century. The family was
originally of Lithuanian extraction when what is now known as the
Ukraine had been part of the Grand Duchy of Lithuania, which in turn
was a component of Rzeczpospolita – a union between Poland and
Lithuania that originated with the Jagiellonian Dynasty some six
centuries ago. Professor Norman Davies of Oxford University, who
has written much about this whole region, describes the middle-rank
nobility (szlachta średnia) to which the Dunin-Markievicz family
belonged as equivalent to what the French called the 'petite noblesse.'
This latter designation is especially interesting when seen in the context
of Constance seeking (just after her engagement), as she expressed it in
a letter to her brother, 'some official statement [because] I would like
to be sure I am noblesse.'

Concerning the validity of Casimir's title, the views of Dr Michel
Kostecki are especially interesting because he is related to the Dunin-
Markievicz family through his mother. Asked by the author, he
responded:

> One cannot be absolutely certain one way or another, though no other members
> of the Markievicz family seem to have used the title, [and] several authoritative
> publications – Polish, French and Russian – listing the Markievicz family among
> noble families also do not indicate any title.

Dr Kostecki also takes the view that it was not unusual for Polish
noblemen:

who had substantial means and an appropriate lifestyle [to use] the title of Count and Baron as titre de courtoisie, and when some of these families went to other countries they were often addressed as Counts and Barons, and in certain cases even given official recognition of their titles.

While concluding that 'the probability that Casimir Markievicz acquired the title of Count during his lifetime is not very high,' Dr Kostecki is understandably anxious, looking at the question from the family viewpoint, that too much emphasis should not be placed on this matter. Indeed, it should be said that this is also not unimportant when seen from an Irish perspective, especially for all those who regard Constance as one of the icons of the Irish republican movement. The notion of questioning her right to the title 'Countess' could well be judged to be nothing less than an underhand attempt to take away from her status.[2] Yet, in truth, it appears that the title was of little importance to her other than at the time when she was about to get married. Subsequently, she seems to have placed little if any store on the title, almost invariably neglecting to use it and seeming to prefer to be known, instead, simply as 'Madame.'

Some of the views expressed by Constance at this time were to become totally at variance to those held by her just a decade later and, as Professor Wheeler has noted, indicate something of 'her emotional but undiscriminating way of thinking.' That her understanding of Polish history (resulting from her visit to Casimir's home after her marriage) was very limited is shown by her assertion that the Polish people there and the Irish shared the fate of subjection to foreign rule. 'This perception,' as Professor Wheeler pointed out, 'ignored the fact that in the kresy – the Polish-Ukrainian borderlands where the Markievicz family lived – Polish landowners were the masters while the peasant underclass were not Poles but Ukrainians.' Moreover, as he perceptively noted:

> the seeds of future misunderstanding between Constance and her husband may have been sown as early as this: she went on to see comrades and allies in the revolutionary fighters against Tsarism – while Casi and his son saw them as the destroyers of their family home.

---

[2] If the Poles placed little store by aristocratic titles, their neighbours in the Hapsburg Empire certainly had little regard for what they saw as minor ones. An interesting example of this concerned the Archduke Franz Ferdinand who was assassinated at Sarajevo in 1914. When he married Sophie Chotek von Chotkova und Wognin – a daughter of one of the ancient noble families of Bohemia – he was criticised for having married beneath his station. In the eyes of the Court in Vienna, she was 'merely a countess.'

This latter point was a reference to the fact that the Markievicz home was virtually destroyed by the Bolsheviks in 1919, a distant parallel of the destruction of many Big Houses in Ireland, demonstrating the extent to which Constance and her husband were to find themselves politically on opposite sides.

Even though very few details about Casimir's background were known to Constance's family at the time, the family had little option but agree to the marriage. Their remaining concern was that it should be valid both in the United Kingdom and in Imperial Russia, and that the wedding would take place in an Anglican Church. She settled the latter point herself, telling Josslyn: 'I have been considering the marriage question for some time and I am quite determined to be married in a Protestant Church. The idea of a Catholic marriage is merely to please Casi's mother.' Constance thought it unlikely that the Catholic authorities would consent to 'mixed' marriages 'unless you promise them the children.' She had sought advice and had been told that in order to make 'mixed and foreign marriages' legal, she must be married 'either before a Registrar or in an Established Church.' She saw herself faced with, as she expressed it, 'a choice of two evils: 1. Marriage recognised by Rome with Popish Babies or 2. Marriage not recognised by Rome and one's Babies one's own. I choose the latter.'

Casimir did not hold strong personal views either way, only regretting for his mother's sake that the marriage was not to be conducted according to the rites of the Roman Catholic Church.

So at last the wedding date and venue were fixed and the combination of Sir Henry's death earlier in the year and the less than wholehearted family approval resulted in the wedding being a relatively low-key affair with only 50 guests. It took place in September in Marylebone Anglican Parish Church, London where the service was conducted by the Rev. F.S. Le Fanu, who had been rector at Lissadell some time earlier. The bride, who was given away by Josslyn, wore a white satin dress with a three-foot long train of Brussels lace, and a tulle veil. She carried myrtle and orange blossoms, and she had four bridesmaids, her sisters Eva and Mabel wearing violet dresses, and two friends were in green. Casimir wore a smart dark tunic with a gold braided collar and cuffs, white trousers, and a tricorn hat. In an attempt to cover any of the anticipated complications, the marriage was additionally solemnised in a registry office and in a ceremony conducted in the Russian embassy in London, but suggestions that everything might be copperfastened by adding a Roman Catholic wedding service were turned down by Constance herself.

After the wedding, the couple travelled to the Ukraine, staying at Casimir's family estate, riding and hunting whenever the snow or muddy conditions resulting from the early onset of winter permitted. Constance met her new mother-in-law as well as her four-year-old stepson, Stanislas, known in the family as 'Staskow.' They remained in the Ukraine throughout the winter, and Constance said afterwards that she had never been so cold in her life. When the couple returned to Ireland in the spring of 1901, Constance told a friend that she pitied the poor peasants who were living in conditions worse than she had ever witnessed at home, and she did not see – in contrast to Poland – that Ireland suffered from any political grievances.

Casimir Markievicz.
Constance's decision to marry him was a cause of great concern to the family because so little was known about him.

They arrived together at Lissadell for the first time in May, and despite certain nagging reservations about his background, including his earlier marriage and his limited financial means, the family could see that he was pleasant and witty, and mixed easily and well in company. It seems that Constance saw security in her old home, for she was now pregnant and she decided to stay there for the birth of their baby, a daughter whom they christened Maeve (Constance occasionally spelt the name Meave and Maev). The couple continued to live at Lissadell for about a year before returning to Paris, leaving Maeve with her grandmother. They rented a studio from Boleslaw Szanowski, who painted a portrait of Constance which is now in the Dublin Municipal Gallery of Modern Art, and they visited the Ukraine in 1902 and again the following year. After that they settled in Dublin in St Mary's, Frankfort Avenue – a present from her mother – in the Victorian redbrick suburb of Rathgar. Following their second visit to the Ukraine, Constance and Casimir brought young Stanislas back to Ireland with them and the boy liked his stepmother, initially at least, and he adored Lissadell, where Lady Gore-Booth treated him with great affection while continuing to look after young Maeve. In a letter to Sarah Purser, George Russell wrote of:

> the Gore-Booth girl who married the Polish Count with the unspellable name; is going to settle in Dublin about summer time, and as they are both clever it would help to create an Art atmosphere. We might get material for a revolt, a new Irish Art Club. I feel some desperate schism or earthquaking revolution is required to wake up Dublin in Art matters.

The Markievicz's played a prominent role in developing the Dublin Arts Club but no one, not even Constance herself, then foresaw the very different kind of revolt or 'earthquaking revolution' which she was to join a decade later. Constance and Casimir quickly settled down to their new life in the city, which at the time had a remarkably strong cultural and artistic tradition, and where they contentedly led a lifestyle probably only a few degrees less bohemian than that experienced in Paris. Constance was very much at home in this *milieu*, mixing with artists, poets, writers and intellectuals, going to the theatre, and continuing to attend social functions and balls at the Castle and the viceregal lodge.

Besides painting, Casimir shared her interest in writing and staging plays but several writers commented less than favourably on Constance's acting. Hogan and Kilroy's volume about the Abbey Theatre quoted a *Freeman's Journal* review of the staging of Casimir's play 'The Dilettante' in 1908. Referring to Constance as 'Miss Constance Gore' it pulled no punches, stating that she had 'a congenial part as Althea. She looked it, and acted with spirit, though a little restraint here and there would have been better. She carried her infatuation beyond the bounds of probability, and some of the laughter in the wrong place was pardonable.' Her voice was considered too 'posh' and too shrill even by some of her best friends. After Constance's death, Hanna Sheehy Skeffington, recalled that when both of them were 'on the run,' Constance once disguised herself as a feeble old lady, but 'she was always recognisable by her voice, so she had to be dumb as well.'

One of their near neighbours in Rathgar was George Russell with whom both Casimir and Constance combined to stage an exhibition of their paintings, and it was two years later that the trio, along with Yeats and some others, established the Dublin United Arts Club. Both Constance and Casimir exhibited their work at various venues in the city, at one of which, in 1904, she showed 76 works while he exhibited 84. It was Casimir's idea to invite George Russell to exhibit with them, a proposal he agreed to rather reluctantly. According to Henry Summerfield in his biography, Russell was greatly encouraged by the public response to his work, so much so that he continued to exhibit with the Markieviczs until 1909. She had been renting a cottage at Balally (from the Fitzsimmons family at nearby Moreen), not far from the Dublin Mountains, where the pair sometimes painted. They began to study art again with P.L. Dickenson, who rated both of them as painters of considerable merit, but thought that they 'could have been first rate had they worked.' Anne Haverty noted that they both had private incomes 'and while they were far from well off, there was insufficient pressure on them to have a real commitment to their painting.'

* * *

Although Constance seemed happy to move in this social and artistic circle for a few years, her restless spirit soon sought some new outlet, initially through helping the underprivileged. It can hardly be doubted that she was influenced in this by her favourite sister, Eva, who was already working in England both on behalf of the poor and for women's rights generally. Conditions in the slums of Dublin were appalling, and wages for those who could get employment were extremely low. Later, during the 1913 general strike (or lockout), Constance became involved in running food kitchens set up to relieve the intense hardship suffered by the poor. Parallel with this situation, but separate at the outset, was the simmering political situation in connection with the Home Rule movement, and when the leaders of the main workers' organisations,

James Larkin and James Connolly, formed a self-defence Irish Citizens' Army, a potent merger followed.

Somewhere in all of this, Constance found herself attracted to the cause of Irish nationalism, led on by a whole series of what appear to have been coincidental events. Most versions of the story of how it all began accord with what Henry Boylan wrote about Constance's interest in Republicanism being 'first aroused by back numbers of *The Peasant* and *Sinn Féin* left behind by a previous tenant [at Balally Cottage], Padraig Colum.' Whatever way it all began, she found herself led to a cause that she hoped would also interest Casimir. His country's history was even more awful than that of Ireland, having ceased to exist on the political map after being occupied by Austria, Prussia and Russia but – as Constance had earlier noted herself – Casimir was not at all interested in politics. He watched his wife's initial struggles to identify herself with her new-found cause with wry amusement, following, as Nancy Cardozo wrote, Maud Gonne's footsteps 'from Castle society to militant nationalism.'

It was at this time that George Russell introduced her to the leader of Sinn Féin, Arthur Griffith, but the latter distrusted her motives, not only because she could have been a spy but, perhaps worse, 'a bored socialite.' For her part, Constance took an instant dislike to him, causing her to write later: 'Mr Griffith was very discouraging to me and very cautious. I first thought that he merely considered me a sentimental fool; later on I realised that he had jumped to the conclusion that I was an agent of the enemy.' According to Margaret Ward, Constance joined Sinn Féin not because she had strong convictions about its policies but because it admitted women into its ranks. If Constance disliked Griffith, then Yeats (whom William Trevor credited with influencing Constance 'with his nationalism') was beginning to feel much the same way about her. Roy Foster quoted from a note written by the poet to a friend in 1908 in which he mentioned that he had met Madame and had 'argued with that steam whistle for an hour.'

If she lost a few friends, she also gained others, and her meeting with Bulmer Hobson, was to prove highly significant. Hobson was a member of the Irish Republican Brotherhood and edited the organisation's periodical. Crucially, he had organised a nationalist youth movement in Belfast. One introduction led to another, the next being to Helena Moloney, a member of Inghinidhe na hÉireann, a movement founded by Maud Gonne in 1900 as a woman's political organisation with strong feminist leanings. Margaret Ward wrote that Constance was to recall years later that this organisation was 'always in favour of the most extreme action possible.' Constance accepted Moloney's invitation to attend its next meeting, and she arrived there direct from a function at Dublin Castle wearing evening dress and a velvet cloak. Not surprisingly, this, along with her upper-class accent, caused many of the members to suspect that she really was a spy. Whatever about their first impressions, Constance soon convinced them that she wished to work with them. Her first serious involvement came about when the organisation decided to publish a monthly penny newsletter, *Bean na hÉireann*, for which she designed the title page, depicting a peasant woman against a background of a round tower and a rising sun. Strongly influenced by Eva, Constance continued to be interested in the movement to secure voting rights for women. She spoke at a number of meetings organised by the Irish Women's Franchise League, although she described it as 'a very vague organisation' which had, she thought, 'a British stamp on it.' She also became increasingly attracted to James Connolly and identified herself with his socialist ideals, eventually coming to admire him over and beyond all the others in the republican movement.

Constance and Casimir spent Christmas 1908 at Lissadell. The rest of the family had come to like 'Casi' and even at this stage may have found him easier to get on with than Constance. Their marriage was already in trouble, mainly due to Constance's absorption in politics, which Casimir continued to watch with detached amusement, making light of his wife's activities and once describing her as 'my floating land mine.' His drinking and his alleged womanising probably did not help matters. She often jokingly said to her friends: 'I don't know why Casimir ever married me' until, one day, Casimir retorted: 'He didn't.' There may be some truth in the suggestion, made by several writers, that the union between Constance and Casimir was more like a friendship than a marriage, and that it might have been better for both parties had it so remained. The inevitable break-up, when it came, seems to have been quite amicable, and Casimir disappeared for long periods to Paris and to his homeland. He had little choice in the matter because, as Constance distanced herself from 'Castle' society, Casimer's commissions for portraits – virtually his only source of income – dried up. Meanwhile Constance put her marriage, her daughter, her stepson and the Gore-Booth family – excepting Eva – behind her (she never visited Lissadell again) and became totally absorbed in her new-found political interests.

A year after Bulmer Hobson sponsored her as a new member of Sinn Féin, she became involved in the formation of Fianna Éireann, or 'The National Boy Scouts.' Constance claimed that the idea of forming a separatist scout movement was hers, not Bulmer Hobson's, although Hobson had, in fact, not only started a similar organisation for boys in Belfast seven years earlier but had actually named it 'Fianna Éireann.' Constance wrote about the establishment of the Fianna in *Nodlaig na bhFianna*:

> It was some time in March 1909 that I read an account in *The Irish Times* of 800 little Irish boys, being paraded in brigades and sections before the Lord Lieutenant. Somehow, the idea of these Irish lads haunted me.... Nothing could be sadder than seeing these boys saluting the flag which flew in triumph over every defeat this nation has known.... The idea came to me of starting an organisation for boys. An organisation that would weld the youth of Ireland together to work and fight for Ireland.

However, even if credit for the original idea is due to Hobson, there can be no doubt that the organisation formed in Dublin was specifically hers, helped by her friend, Helena Moloney and, indeed, by Hobson. While based on the model devised by Lord Baden-Powell, her Fianna boys were trained to be more like soldier cadets unlike Hobson's original Fianna which, according to Moloney, 'did not have a military character.' Constance used both a hall she rented in Camden Street, as well as her cottage at Balally for the organisation's exercises.

Hobson lent Constance a book describing an experiment, conducted by an enlightened County Clare landlord, John Scott Vandeleur, for the tenants on his Ralahine estate near Newmarket-on-Fergus in the 1820s. The project proved to be a precursor of the co-operative movement which it pre-dated by over 60 years. She was characteristically enthusiastic about the notion of reviving this experimental co-operative idea with her Fianna boys, no doubt conscious of how successful her brother had been in this field along with Horace Plunkett. Wasting no time, she rented Belcamp Park, and moved into what was then an old, isolated house near Raheny, north of Dublin which, with its farm buildings and walled gardens, was in poor condition. She described it as 'a big house, but we got it very cheap and the garden is in very good order and ought to pay.' During this period, she appears to have been on reasonably friendly terms with Josslyn, and she wrote to him offering a painting, 'one of the best I have ever done of Dublin seen through a sunny mist.' In return he sent his sister 60 roses to furnish the garden at

Belcamp. Her experiment was a hopeless failure because, as Seán O'Faoláin wrote in his biography:

> Impatient to succeed, she took no account of the evident disadvantages. She moved there to create her own model co-operative, but the project was an utter disaster, made worse when Casimir returned from Poland to find that the comfortable family home in the south city suburbs had been replaced by a barrack of a house sitting in the middle of eight bleak acres.

Anne Haverty made it sound even worse: 'However brave and noble … the boys were urban warriors who knew nothing of country ways, and they wandered among the fields and boreens of the locality leaving a trail of havoc in their wake.' After the Belcamp debacle, Constance moved to Surrey House in Rathmines, which became her home from 1911 until 1916, but Casimir did not wait for this happen, going back once more to Europe. He was not to return to Dublin for another 13 years. The marriage was now effectively ended.

Writing about Surrey House, Sydney Gifford recollected that 'you never knew when you entered whether you were going to walk into a rehearsal for a play, a piece of real life drama, a political discussion, or a placid domestic scene. Madame, with an hour or so to spare, might be upstairs painting somebody's portrait, or bent over a piece of embroidery.' Recalling this period many years later, Hanna Sheehy Skeffington described how Constance, who lived quite near her, would:

> come flashing in to invite one to an impromptu party; to meet Eva, her sister – pacifist, feminist, poet; [or] to talk to Liam Mellows…. Again, rushing in to cheer and wish one luck when, in 1912, a group of us broke government windows in Dublin Castle, the Custom House, the GPO, in protest against the omission of Votes for Irish Women in the then Home Rule Bill.

Throughout this period, most of her time was taken up with Fianna activities and she decided to take the boys on their first camping experience near Glencullen, not far from her Balally cottage. After arriving at the campsite, she was so intent on preparing tea, reading poetry, sketching and other activities that she left it until dark before deciding to pitch the tents. In the circumstances – and considering it probable that none of them had ever erected a tent before – this latter exercise proved very difficult. The ensuing confusion was made worse because, according to her account: 'Candles were the only important thing we had forgotten.' She accompanied the boys to Mass on Sunday morning, after which a thunderstorm struck and, because she had not taken the precaution, on sloping ground, of digging shallow trenches, the contents of the tents were soaked by the rain running through them. Her account of the camp described several other mishaps which, she decided, should be recorded in her narrative so that subsequent members of the Fianna 'would know something of it.' Summing up the camping experience she wrote: 'It convinced me finally that a boys' organisation could be made a success in Ireland, but I saw that the English loose system of organisation by sections and patrols would not work here. It would have to be run on the line of a Boys Republic and an army….'

In fact, what she termed the 'loose' system, was actually known in Scouting circles as the patrol system, which played a significant part in Baden-Powell's movement becoming by far the largest youth organisation the world has ever known, and a membership in Ireland that eventually rose to more than 60,000. Her conclusion that such a system would not work for the organisation founded by her was undoubtedly correct as it was based rather more on the lines of military cadets. Outwardly, though, Fianna Éireann appeared to be very similar to the scout organisation because the uniform was almost identical. Indeed, it was thought amusing in Fianna circles that their boys should ambush scouts going to their meetings in order to steal their broad-brimmed hats so that, as Padraic Colvin wrote: 'innumerable quantities of Baden-Powell trophies were won in honourable combat on the streets of Dublin.'

Despite the shaky beginnings of the Fianna, not helped by Sinn Féin's initial distancing itself from it, her organisation went on to play a significant role in the 1916 Rising. It has been said, perhaps harshly, that apart from her exertions among Dublin's poor, her work with Fianna Éireann represented the sole successful venture of her life. It was, perhaps, the only single endeavour to hold her interest and attention for any appreciable length of time – from 1909 until shortly before her death 18 years later. Its contribution to the Republican cause was a body of young men well trained in the use of guns, some of whom ranked among the most prominent participants of the 1916 Rising.

The Women Worker's Union was founded in 1911 by James Larkin whose sister, Delia, wrote down details about its inaugural meeting which Maria Luddy has quoted in her book about women in Ireland. Constance, who was asked to speak to the meeting, told her audience how glad she was to have been asked:

by Mr. Larkin to come here and address you. Without organisation you can do nothing, and the purpose of this meeting is to form you into fighters. As you are all aware, women have at present no vote, but a union such as has now been formed will not alone enable you to obtain better wages, but will also be a great means of helping you to get votes and thus make men of you all. (Cheers and laughter)

During that same year, along with Helena Moloney, she burnt a Union Jack during an open-air meeting and denounced those members of the corporation who had recently accepted honours with all the contempt, as James H. Murphy wrote, 'of an aristocrat toward those in trade.'

In 1913, a tram strike was followed by a general lockout which the employers hoped would break the growing power of the Transport and General Workers Union. Arnold Wright, an Englishman, described the situation from the perspective of the authorities:

> There were features in the struggle which differentiated it in a marked and alarming way from any previous industrial uprising in Irish history, or indeed in the history of the United Kingdom. The striker, by a vicious process of reasoning, became a revolutionary invested with the revolutionary's powers of mischief … which cut at the very roots of social order.

A warrant was issued for the arrest of James Larkin, the strikers' leader, who hid at Surrey House where Constance helped him to adopt a disguise which enabled him to walk unrecognised (initially) through the crowds assembled at the Imperial Hotel in Sackville Street. Larkin had planned to speak from an open window of the hotel, but before he could do so police baton-charged the crowd and arrested him. When Constance tried to accompany him she received a blow to the face from a policeman's baton and she later claimed that they had used their batons 'like shillelaghs.' The 1913 lockout lasted for six months and resulted in great hardship for the families of the strikers and it was reckoned that some 50,000 people in the city were starving. Constance, along with Helena Moloney, Helen Laird, Hanna Sheehy Skeffington and Larkin's sister, Delia, began organising a food kitchen at Liberty Hall, begging food from friends and pleading with others to help in running the relief work. Even her comfortable home in Rathmines was open house to many of the people involved with her at the time.

According to Frank Robbins, it was the custom of the newly formed Citizen Army when out marching to sing patriotic songs like 'Sinn Féin Ambháin' and 'The Peeler and the Goat.' After the war broke out in 1914:

We also sang The Germans are winning the War, me Boys, composed by Madam Markievicz. It was not what you would call a song at all. It was doggerel. Madam Markiewicz also wrote the song Armed for the Battle. The music was not original, it was the air of a revolutionary Polish song.

While Constance fell out with Griffith, Hobson and McNeill, she also struck up some very cordial friendships, notably among the women republicans and with James Connolly, to whom she had been introduced by Larkin, and with whom she found she had much in common. Connolly lived with her for a period in her Rathgar home, and although he paid ten shillings a week for his board and keep, this did not prevent some detractors from speculating that there was more to it than friendship. A poem which she later wrote about Connolly's death may have fuelled this speculation, the first two lines of which read:

> You died for your country my Hero – love
> In the first grey dawn of Spring …

Of course, it is all too easy – especially in retrospect – to smear a person's reputation by innuendo. The nearest she ever seems to have got to commenting on their relationship was when she contributed an article for *The Nation* in March 1927, where she described her first meeting with Connolly 16 years earlier:

> When he began to organise the Irish Citizen Army, he brought me along, teaching me, as he got to know me, as a comrade, giving me any work that I could do, and quite ignoring the conventional attitude towards the work of women. This was his attitude towards the work of women in general.

Following the outbreak of the Great War, while her brother Josslyn was busy arranging the erection of recruitment posters in Sligo, she was equally busy tearing down similar posters in Dublin. Alexander Godley, one of her erstwhile suitors, who by this time had become a general, deeply regretted the fact that Redmond's request for a separate Irish army was turned down along with his own alternative idea of forming three distinctively Irish divisions based on Belfast, Cork and Dublin. This was despite the fact that, as Tom Johnston has pointed out, his uncle, John Robert Godley, was Under Secretary of State for War at the time.

Constance took part in a parade (the authorities called it a 'manoeuvre') in central Dublin which came to be mentioned during the enquiry held after the Easter Rising. The Chief Commander of the Dublin Metropolitan Police, Colonel Edgeworth Johnstone, when asked to comment on a report that a mimic attack had been made on Dublin Castle in October 1915, replied: 'No such thing took place; it is a fairy tale.' What actually happened, he said, was that: 'On the night of October 16, a large portion of the Sinn Féin Army marched by Ship Street, close to the Castle.' Superintendent Dunne reported: 'It is a serious state of affairs to have the peace of the city endangered by a gang of roughs with rifles and bayonets at large at that time of night, with a female like the Countess Markievicz in charge.'

Constance was experiencing serious financial difficulties at this time, and successfully approached Josslyn several times for money blaming her problems on having to look after Staskow. Frank Robbins, in his history of the Citizen Army, quoted her comment about her financial situation during the months prior to the Rising: 'I have already overdrawn my bank account for my next quarter's allowance to the extent of £45, and if this bally revolution doesn't take place, I don't know how I'm going to live.' The 'bally revolution' was to commence less than six months later when Patrick Pearse, its leader, called for a 'blood sacrifice' to awaken Irish nationalism.

* * *

The plan for the Rising in Dublin envisaged the occupation of a series of important, strategic buildings, coupled with a general uprising throughout the country, but a series of mishaps resulted in the event going off, as Professor Joe Lee expressed it, 'at half cock.' Crucially, when Eoin MacNeill heard that the Royal Navy had intercepted the expected German arms shipment, he attempted to cancel the arrangements. While it did go ahead, the resulting confusion meant that the number of insurgents taking part was drastically reduced and, with the event virtually confined to Dublin, the task of the military dealing with it was greatly simplified.

Constance Markievicz drove from her home to the city in her car to take part in the Rising, collecting and distributing first-aid equipment before parking it at St Stephen's Green opposite the United Services Club. She was dressed in a green outfit, complete with a hat adorned with black or dark green feathers which, according to Brian Behan, was based on 'the uniform of the Boers when they fought the British in South Africa.' Sheila Pim – quoted by León Ó Broin – recalled: 'Someone had seen her on St. Stephen's Green, a cigarette in her mouth and a pistol in each hand.' Constance's appearance was colourfully described by Elizabeth Bowen as being 'in the uniform of a colonel of the volunteers' but she was probably correct in her assumption that Constance's arrival 'supplied the first touch of drama.' Incidentally, Foy and Barton claimed that Constance had arrived wearing 'a slouch hat with ostrich feathers' when, to judge from various photographs taken at the time, the feathers looked very much more like those of a cockerel. When she brought first-aid supplies to Michael Mallin, Commandant of the St Stephen's Green garrison, he promptly appointed her as his deputy.

At the outbreak of the Great War, Constance had expressed the view that Ireland could benefit from a prolonged conflict, hoping it would end with a German victory. Given her thinking, it is not difficult to see her taking charge of trench digging in the park – an idea hastily conceived, ill thought-out and, as it proved, untenable. Originally the plan had been to secure both the square of St Stephen's Green and all the prominent buildings around it, including not only the Royal College of Surgeons but also the most strategic building of all, the massive Shelbourne Hotel. The fact that no attempt was made to seize the latter was hardly 'a critical and surprising blunder,' as stated in their book about the rebellion by Foy and Barton. Rather, it was deemed an impossible target given the reduced garrison numbers available to Mallin who, having served in the British army, had some idea of what was militarily possible and what was not. In this connection, it is interesting that several writers appear to have held the view that Constance Markievicz rather than Michael Mallin had been in charge of operations at St Stephen's Green. Elizabeth Bowen, for example, wrote that Constance 'should have occupied the buildings at the four corners instead of deploying her men in [St Stephen's] Green itself.'

The British began occupying several buildings including the Shelbourne Hotel where, that night, they installed a machine gun on the roof from which they commenced firing next day at the insurgents below. Elizabeth Bowen described how 'its overhead rattling fire made the chandeliers tremble' but its effect upon the insurgents in the open trenches below was a great deal more serious. They had no option but to withdraw into the College of Surgeons' building and to some of the other houses on that side of the square. Situated mid-way along one side of the park, the college was by no means an ideal strong-point as it allowed only limited opportunities for sniping, though its solid construction afforded the defenders secure shelter, which may have been a factor in its garrison being one of the last to surrender.

Diana Norman related the curious (if not improbable) story that Constance organised an arrangement whereby 'for humanitarian reasons' a flag was to be hoisted at noon to bring about a temporary truce, 'stopping the firing just long enough for a hotel employee to nip across into the park and feed the ducks.'

The end came on the following Saturday April 29, at 3.45 p.m., when Pearse and Connolly along with their G.P.O. garrison surrendered. A British officer drove Elizabeth Farrell, a member of Cumann na mBan who had been with Pearse, to the College of Surgeons. Farrell's own account, quoted in Roger McHugh's book on the Rising, mentioned that when they entered by a side door she saw Countess Markievicz and gave her Pearse's order for surrender, which Connolly had specially countersigned. Constance was very much surprised because she had understood the Rising had been nationwide and that reinforcements were on their way to the city. Some of the garrison did not want to give up, but when Constance saw Connolly's signature, she told Mallin she completely trusted Connolly, and they agreed to the surrender.

A police constable who was a witness at the subsequent court martial of Mallin, said that he was present 'at the College of Surgeons when Mallin and the Countess Markievicz came out of a side door of the college. The prisoner [Mallin] was carrying a white flag but was unarmed, but the Countess was armed.' Captain (later Major) de Courcy Wheeler, to whom the garrison surrendered, was distantly related by marriage to the Gore-Booth family, and he subsequently gave evidence against her at her court martial. When the men were lined up to be marched to Dublin Castle, de Courcy Wheeler offered to drive Constance in his car but she insisted on marching with the others with, as Max Caulfield wrote, 'all the pride and dignity of a lady of the Big House.' Escorted by soldiers of the Staffordshire Regiment, the crowds who were watching were mostly hostile, with shouts of 'Shoot the traitors' as they were marched away to await their fate. In her own words: 'We marched to the Castle and then to Richmond Barracks, given biscuits and a cup of tea, then to Kilmainham [Jail]. Solitary confinement at once.' *The Irish Times* reported that when she surrendered, Constance Markievicz 'was still wearing top boots, breeches, service tunic, and a hat with feathers.' The report added that 'she shook hands with her officers' and then handed over her revolver – after kissing it – along with a quantity of ammunition, 'which on examination was found to include military and also round-nosed (expanding) bullets.'

Expanding (or 'exploding') bullets, which caused horrendous injuries, had been outlawed by the Geneva War Convention. The allegation that the insurgents used this ammunition was raised by a senior officer of the Royal Irish Constabulary at the subsequent Commission of Enquiry, when Inspector Price stated that: 'the ammunition used by the rebels in the fighting was of a terrible character. These were flat-nosed bullets, split bullets and, in the [General] Post Office reverse bullets were found.' When Pearse became aware that ammunition supplied to the insurgents had included 'explosive' bullets, he noted in writing that these were 'against the rules of civilised war and ... therefore, we are not serving [them] out to the men.'

The Irish Times, which was the only newspaper in the city that managed to keep publishing throughout most of Easter Week, reported that:

> Structurally the College suffered little damage, but some of the paintings in the boardroom have been irretrievably ruined. The life-sized portrait of Queen Victoria, which was painted by the late S. Catterson Smith, R.H.A., and placed in the college in 1887 in commemoration of Her Majesty's Jubilee, was cut out of the frame and torn into fragments.

Constance, (who had been presented to the queen as a debutante in that same jubilee year), would have been aware of the amount of work involved in painting full-length portraits and might, in other circumstances, have acted to prevent the painting's destruction.[3]

According to official statistics, Constance was one of 3,226 prisoners (77 were women), taken to the Richmond Barracks in the immediate aftermath of the Rising in Dublin. Of that total, 183 were tried by court martial, of whom 15 were executed, and 1,939 were interned. The official list of casualties lumped civilians and insurgents together (because it was sometimes impossible to accurately identify which were which), giving a total of 180 killed and 614 injured.

---

[3] Coincidentally, another (earlier) full-length portrait of Queen Victoria painted by the same artist which had hung in Dublin's Mansion House, was one of a number of paintings taken down on the instructions of Mrs Tom Clarke when she became Lord Mayor of Dublin in 1939. Three and a half decades later, Homan Potterton – who was to become Director of the National Gallery of Ireland in 1980 – wrote an article for *The Irish Times* about missing paintings. In it he posed the question: 'Where now, for instance is the portrait of Queen Victoria ... listed once as being in the Mansion House, Dublin?' It was, in fact, still there in the basement, from where it was subsequently rescued, in poor condition and minus its frame, from where it has since been sent to the Hugh Lane Gallery for conservation.

Unofficial figures suggested that 64 insurgents died and almost twice that number of civilians were killed. Military casualties were stated to be 103 killed and 357 wounded. Police casualties numbered 15 killed (three being members of the D.M.P.) and 26 wounded. Nine Orders were awarded to members of the military, the most senior recipient being Lt. Col. Joseph Aloysius Byrne, a Catholic officer of the Inniskilling Fusiliers from Derry. In addition, eleven Military Medals were awarded and 34 men were Mentioned in Despatches.

Michael Mallin and Constance Markievicz after their surrender – photo © National Museum of Ireland.

The severity of the sentences and the number of executions carried out resulted from the fact that martial law had been declared. However, Robert Kee took the view that Maxwell, the commanding officer, 'was being lenient in shooting only fifteen rebels,' adding that 'where Irish nationalism was concerned, nothing could be safely judged only by the light of reason.' Not unexpectedly, accounts of the Rising seem to have overlooked Sir John Maxwell's military background to seek possible reasons for acting as he did. The fact that he was one of the senior officers during the disastrous Gallipoli campaign may have coloured his view about the numbers of men whose death sentences he was to confirm. The failed invasion at Gallipoli involved very heavy casualties, including the deaths of more than 2,000 Irishmen serving with the 10th Irish Division, and ended with a forced withdrawal at the end of December 1915, only a few months before the Easter Rising. Major-General Sir John Maxwell was sent almost directly to Dublin to direct the British Army operations there. He issued the following statement on May 11:

> In view of the gravity of the rebellion and its connections with German intrigue and propaganda, and in view of the great loss of life and destruction of property resulting therefrom, the General Officer Commanding-in-Chief has found it imperative to inflict the most severe sentences on the known organisers of this detestable rising and on those commanders who took an active part in the actual fighting which occurred....

For him, the heavy military losses he had so recently witnessed in Turkey must have made the rebellion in Dublin seem a relatively minor affair. However, another part of the equation was the fact the government had placed all the decision-making at this time in the hands of the military whose senior officers, including Maxwell, would not have taken into account the possible political ramifications resulting from 15 executions. However, Asquith, the prime minister, having been warned of the possible consequences, travelled to Dublin to discuss the matter with Maxwell and it may be significant that the last two executions took place on the following morning.

The events of 1916 have been heavily romanticised and, as with all wars great and small, Easter Week saw episodes of gallantry and self-sacrifice, but there were ugly and mean incidents too. One of the latter concerned the very first victim of the rebellion, Constable James O'Brien of the Dublin Metropolitan Police, a force whose members were unarmed. Standing at the entrance to the Upper Castle yard, he was shot dead in cold blood by an insurgent leader, Sean Connolly, the first casualty of the Rising. Connolly was, in turn, shot by a sniper's bullet later the same day, and Dr Kathleen Lynn, a great friend of Constance, rushed to his assistance in a vain attempt to save his life. Another early victim was also a member of the same unarmed force, Constable Lahiffe, shot at St Stephen's Green. Some sources placed the responsibility for his death on Constance. Max Caulfield's account of the rebellion claims that she 'took aim with her Mauser rifle-pistol. As she fired, two men beside her also shot. Lahiffe slumped to the ground, hit by three bullets.' 'I shot him!' shouted the Countess delightedly. 'I shot him.' Brian Barton, in his book about the court martial records, wrote that in speeches made after her release from prison she 'had claimed with pride to have fired the second shot.' The fact that she had been seen firing her pistol at an army officer standing at a nearby window around the same time seemed to lend some credence to the allegations, but responsibility for the killing was never established, nor was there any attempt to formally charge her with it.

Even so, Josslyn was sufficiently concerned about the allegations to approach various influential people in an effort to ascertain the truth. Father Sherwin, at the Catholic University Church at St Stephen's Green, sent a letter to Josslyn to assure him that 'it was not your sister who fired the shot. She has given me leave to state that this is a fact.' Josslyn wrote to one of his sister's nationalist friends, Susan Mitchell, who sent Josslyn a note quoting Mrs Rudmose Browne (wife of a Trinity College professor whose son had been sent to St Enda's school, run by Patrick Pearse). Mrs Brown told him that Constance assured her that 'she had never shot a policeman and she was not near the Castle when that much talked of policeman was shot.'

Obviously there was some confusion here, for no allegation had been made against Constance about the constable stationed at the Castle gate. But even leaving that aside, the claim made by Constance that she had not been in the vicinity of the Castle at the time is contradicted by her own account of what she had been doing immediately prior to the Rising. In it she described how, before to going to St Stephen's Green, she had been distributing first aid equipment along with Dr Kathleen Lynn. They reached the City Hall, she wrote: 'Just at the very moment that Commandant Sean Connolly and his little troop of men swung around the corner and he raised his gun and shot the policeman who barred his way.' Risteárd Ó Glaisne referred to this incident in his book about Irish protestants, where he quoted Dermod O'Brien's disapproval of what he regarded as his sister's (Nellie O'Brien's) involvement in extreme republicanism: 'It is women like Con Markievicz and Dora [French] and Nellie who have led on young men like Sean Connolly to take other people's lives and lose their own.'

By a strange coincidence, Casimir (from whom Constance had heard nothing for five years) wrote at this time to tell her he had been seriously injured in combat on the Carpathian front, from where he had been evacuated to a hospital in Kiev. So, while Constance had been hoping for a German victory in Europe, her husband as well as her stepson were fighting against the Germans. Indeed, while the Rising was taking place in Dublin, the Germans and Austrians had pushed the Russian forces out of most of what had been Russian Poland, occupying huge tracts of territory surrounding Casimir's home. Casimir had made his decision to join the Imperial Russian forces in the knowledge that the Tsar had promised the Poles fighting alongside the Russians that their country would be granted autonomy after the war. Perhaps it may be too fanciful to describe this gesture as some kind of mirror image of what Redmond had hoped to gain from Britain in 1914. For their part, as Norman Davies noted, the Germans permitted the celebration of Poland's National Day on May 3, 1916, the day before Constance faced her court martial. In any event, the fact that both her husband and stepson were fighting both in defence of their family estate and to defeat Germany, was just one of the many curious contradictions of what she once called her 'hurry-scurry' life.

After the leaders of the rebellion had surrendered, it was announced that they would be brought before Field General Courts Martial and that the public would be told the results of their trial when sentences had been confirmed. No time was lost in organising the trials of the main leaders of the Rising, the first being held three days after the surrender when Thomas Clarke, Patrick Pearse and Thomas McDonagh were sentenced to death. A wardress passed the news to Constance that night and she heard bursts of gunfire early next morning. Later that day, May 4, she was brought out of her cell to attend her own court martial in Richmond Barracks to face charges of taking part 'in an armed rebellion ... waging war against His Majesty the King ... and causing disaffection among the civilian population of His Majesty.'

Among those who gave evidence at her court martial was the army officer – Dr C. de Burgh Daly, who had been fired at by Constance. He described how he had stood beside a window of the University Club overlooking St Stephen's Green and had seen Constance Markievicz 'dressed in a man's uniform, green with a brown belt, and feathers in her hat.... About one o'clock she leant up against the Eglinton monument and took a deliberate pot shot at me in one of the open windows of the University Club. I was ... in uniform, and the distance was about 50-60 yards. She could not tell I was a doctor but, I suspect, considered I was a combative officer as I had ribbons on ....' Daly added that he had no knowledge of her killing anyone, but he was certain that 'she was ready to kill policemen and combatant officers or men.' He also said that that she 'mixed up kindness and killing in accordance with her convictions on the rebellion and how to conduct it. I bear her no ill-will, and hope one of these days she may use her talents for the real benefit of our country.' In her own account of the shooting incident, Constance recollected that she saw Daly 'retire in time, and saw the bullet strike the top of the window, just where his head had been.' The court martial found Constance Markieviez guilty of the charges. She was sentenced to death by being shot, but with a recommendation, confirmed on May 6, that it would be commuted to penal servitude for life 'solely and only' as the official document stated, 'on account of her sex.'

Seán O'Faoláin, whom Fintan O'Toole saw as 'the chief dissident in nationalist Ireland,' was the first to write her biography. He admitted in his account that 'how she received her sentence we do not know.' Her subsequent biographers appear to have relied on an account written by Constance herself which drew a picture of a defiant woman who was not intimidated by the all-male military tribunal, or even by its likely consequences. One of her biographers, Jacqueline Van Voris, quoted Constance's description of Brigadier General Blackader (President of the Court Martial), as 'a fuzzy little officer with his teeth hanging out to dry' and included her assertion that she had given 'the fuzzy little officer beans, and defied him to shoot me.' Another biographer, Elizabeth Coxhead claimed that Constance received her sentence 'radiantly,' though her source for this detail is unclear. In their book about the rebellion, Foy and Barton noted 'her considerable capacity for embroidering her own exploits,' a trait that may or may not account for the totally different version of events recorded by William Wylie, who acted as prosecutor at her trial.

Wylie painted a picture of Markievicz's demeanour during the court martial so at variance with what Constance wrote as to make the two versions irreconcilable. Indeed his version of the event leaves him open to the charge of simply being totally hostile. In his more recent book about the aftermath of the Rising, Brian Barton questioned what he called Wylie's 'wilful and scurrilous evidence.' Whatever about that, it is worth looking at Wylie's record during the course of a number of the trials, especially as he was the only other individual known to have written a first-hand account of these proceedings, subsequently published in León Ó Broin's biography. W.E. Wylie, who was pursuing a legal career and was already a King's Counsel when he joined the British Army in 1915, was surprised when he was told that he had been appointed one of the prosecuting counsel for the courts-martial of the insurgent leaders. He seems to have taken quite an independent view of the subsequent proceedings, being openly critical of the haste at which the trials were held, and their secrecy. Wylie also disapproved of the fact that some of the main leaders were denied the opportunity of calling witnesses, and he sought, without success, that all the defendants should be provided with a defending counsel.

He was prosecuting counsel at the trials of, among others, Patrick Pearse, Thomas McDonagh, Éamon Ceannt, Thomas Clarke, and Constance Markievicz, each court martial being held before three army officers – none of whom were required to have legal experience – and a prosecuting counsel. Wylie wrote of Patrick Pearse that he 'looked a decent chap,' and he thought that Thomas McDonagh was a 'poet, a dreamer and an idealist.' He recalled that McDonagh declined to make a statement when invited to do so, and took the view that his execution was unnecessary. His described Thomas Clarke as 'perfectly calm and brave, a kindly man,' and wrote that Ceannt was not only brave but was 'the most dignified of any of the accused.' In contrast to these and similar views about some of the others on trial, Wylie's comments about Constance were devastatingly critical, commencing with his remark that 'the one which did not impress me and the court in the same way was Constance Markievicz.'

According to his version of what happened, her reputation had caused some of the military to think she might cause trouble at her court martial, and that she might even attempt to throw things at the presiding officers. Wylie wrote that this prompted the president of the court, General Blackader, to pointedly remove his revolver from its holster and place it on a table beside him as she was being escorted into the room set aside for the purpose. Wylie felt that the General need not have troubled because, as he wrote, 'she crumpled up completely,' crying 'I'm only a woman and you cannot shoot a woman, you must not shoot a woman.' Wylie contrasted her behaviour with the fact that 'she had been preaching to a lot of silly [Fianna] boys "death and glory, die for your country," etc., and yet she was literally crawling. I won't say any more, it revolts me.' He did not believe her written version in which she claimed that she suffered remorse when her death sentence was commuted because she had wished to be allowed to die with her comrades. As far as he was concerned, her demeanour during the trial was 'craven' and 'a repellent and undignified spectacle.'

Which version is to be believed? Was Wylie's account a 'wilful and scurrilous distortion,' possibly reflecting a 'deep-rooted sexual prejudice and rank misogyny on his part' as asserted by Dr Barton in his account of the court martial proceedings? That Wylie seems to have been a person with an independent mind appears to be borne out by several factors including the fact that Eoin McNeill (as quoted in Michael Tierney's biography) thought that, although sentenced to penal servitude for life, he had found Wylie 'fair.' Furthermore, even though Wylie was a law officer who had been appointed by the British government, he was asked by representatives of the Dáil in September 1922 to arrange secret conversations to see if a truce could be arranged. It may also be significant that when the newly independent State was established, he was appointed a judge of the High Court, a position he held for 12 years, and after a distinguished legal career he went on to become, for many years, president of the Royal Dublin Society.

Besides the accounts written by Constance and by Wylie, there existed a third version of the trial – the official papers and report of her Court Martial, but for some unknown reason these were not released into the public domain until 2002, almost four decades after those of the executed leaders. Many would hold the view that the latter documents would have been adjudged more sensitive than those concerning a person whose sentence had been reprieved. There was some expectation that these newly released papers might, once and for all, indicate which of the two already available accounts of Constance's trial were to be believed. The official papers record that she made a statement to the court: 'I went out to fight for Ireland's freedom and it doesn't matter what happens to me. I did what I thought was right and I stand by it.'

This was in the anecdotal tradition of a number of Irish treason trials, explaining her motivation and the reason why she took up arms, and while this does not appear to represent a craven response, it would hardly – by itself – settle the matter one way or another. However, perhaps crucially, the documents confirm that Constance made this statement at her court martial, clearing up some doubt that it may have been said (or even written) by her prior to the actual trial. The confusion may have arisen because it is known that she also attended a preliminary hearing. Some details about the latter were mentioned by the late Thomas P. O'Neill, Professor Emeritus, UCG, when writing to *The*

Irish Times in July 1993, following the publication of Anne Haverty's biography. He referred to this hearing which was conducted by the deputy judge advocate-general, Sir Alfred Buckmill, during which Constance had made a separate statement after being asked if she had anything to say. Quoting Buckmill, Professor O'Neill wrote that she stated: 'We dreamed of an Irish Republic and thought we had a fighting chance.' Buckmill's account continued: 'Then for a few moments she broke down and sobbed. It was a natural reaction to stress and disappointment.' O'Neill made clear his own criticisms of Wylie's recollections especially because, as he expressed it: 'To wring tears from a woman's eyes is no credit to any gentleman.' Historians and others may continue to argue about how Constance deported herself during her trial but Casimir's reaction to it all was typically casual because even at this stage he did not take his wife's revolutionary activities very seriously. Referring to her reprieve; he simply quipped that if her sentence had not been commuted, 'half of Debrett's would have been thrown into mourning.'

Before the announcement of the reprieve, both Josslyn and Eva had made strenuous efforts to have the sentence commuted and Josslyn had sought to obtain a transcript of her trial. In addition to contacting Major Charles O'Hara of Annaghmore, a Sligo M.P. with considerable influence, asking him to intercede with the Lord Lieutenant, he also wrote to others who might be in a position to help, including Casimir.

Constance was left alone in her cell awaiting her fate. She was unaware that her commandant, Michael Mallin, had made some extraordinary statements at his own court martial, implying that the responsibility for the actions of the insurgents at St Stephen's Green was not his but that of 'the Countess of Markievicz [who] ordered me to take command of the men as I had been so long associated with them. I felt I could not leave them and from that time I joined the early rebellion.' This claim was plainly untrue, as were several other assertions made by Mallin, including his avowal that he had given explicit orders 'to make no offensive movement.' His prepared statement seems to have been a desperate attempt to save his own life – even at the risk of further endangering that of Constance whom he had personally, and on his own initiative, appointed his second-in-command. Yet, as already mentioned, it is not unusual to find accounts of the events at St Stephen's Green crediting Constance rather than Michael Mallin with being in command there. Lady Fingall, who was friendly with the Gore-Booths, recalled in her memoirs, that Constance was 'dressed in a green uniform [and was] commanding the rebels in the College of Surgeons.' And, as recently as February 2001, Blánaid Quilligan, writing in *The Irish Times*, seemed to be under the same impression when she wrote that the college 'was temporarily employed as a battleground for Countess Markievicz and her forces during the 1916 Easter Rising.'

Still not knowing her fate, Constance heard more bursts of rifle-fire on the following morning, and that evening, a soldier unlocked her cell door and offered her a cigarette. As the two sat smoking, he gave her the names of those already executed. In the morning, another soldier arrived, a young officer, who formally read out the sentence of the court. The verdict was 'Guilty. Death by being shot. The Court recommended the prisoner to mercy solely and only on account of her sex.' She was subsequently moved to Mountjoy Prison, and a few days later heard that her closest and most admired friend, James Connolly, had been shot.

* * *

Her family background, her accent and her manner of speech (she pronounced Ireland 'Aaahland') had made it difficult for Constance to be accepted into some of the branches of republicanism. However, by dint of determination, hard work and not a little bravery she had proven her credentials, though she seems to have felt that there was one further obstacle to a full acceptance. During Easter Week, alongside over one hundred men and a dozen or so women, she witnessed, each evening, almost all the others kneeling to recite the Rosary. Standing outside this circle, she seems to have concluded that the one remaining factor affecting her relationship with her republican friends was her religion, and she wrote later stating that it was at that time that she decided to convert to Catholicism. As Jacqueline Van Voris expressed it in her biography of Constance: 'Joining the Church was one way Madam identified herself more completely with the cause of Ireland,' while another biographer, Joe McGowan, made the sweeping comment that 'Con felt it was not right to belong to a church that represented the rich rather than the poorer people.'

After deciding to convert, Constance asked the Roman Catholic chaplain in the prison, Father McMahon, to give her the necessary instruction but made it clear that she was not concerned about the finer points of dogma. Her attitude puzzled him greatly and he told her friend, Hanna Sheehy Skeffington, that while Constance had expressed a wish to become a Catholic, she would pay no attention to him when he tried to explain transubstantiation and other dogmas. Constance told him he was not to trouble trying to explain such things to her as she 'already believed all the Church teaches,' and then dismayed him further by venturing the opinion that 'Lucifer was a good rebel.' No wonder he viewed her as 'an enigma.' So, not for the first or last time, she had made up her mind to do something and she simply wanted to get on with it, becoming a somewhat unorthodox Catholic, favouring a workers' republic, and sympathetic to bolshevism and communism.

Apart from the fact that changing one's faith was often regarded as tantamount to betraying one's community, a negative consequence of her 'conforming' (to use a term more commonly used about changing religious affiliation in earlier times), was that she thereby advanced the view – quite widely held at the time – that Protestants were not really Irish and were therefore unlikely to be found supporting the nationalist cause. The facts prove this to be nonsense, because Protestants were among the ranks of some of the most prominent nationalist leaders of their time. While a few continue to be revered, many others – less well known – have been forgotten, including half a dozen or more who would have been personally known to Constance. Only two women were given commissions during the Rising, both of whom were Protestants, which suggests that if Constance felt her religion was some kind of problem, the leaders of the rebellion did not. One was, of course, Constance, who had already been appointed a Staff Lieutenant, and the second was her friend, Dr Kathleen Lynn, a daughter of a Mayo rector who was appointed a Captain. The latter was also Chief Medical Officer in the Citizen Army during Easter Week and was later, as someone expressed it, 'imprisoned for bandaging Sinn Féiners.'

Another friend of Constance who was deeply involved in republicanism was Susan Mitchell – a cousin of the Gore-Booths – who claimed that her family had 'been Protestants since Luther, and probably long before!' She was a member of Cumann Gaedhalach na hEaglaise (the Irish Guild of the Church) which, besides its aims to promote the use of Irish in the Church of Ireland, also supported Irish ideals generally. Mitchell was one of the few persons to be permitted to visit Constance during her first prison incarceration and, as Hilary

Pyle wrote, she became recognised 'as a figurehead of non-political nationalism in the Church of Ireland.'

Constance, sketched by 'Doss'

Markievicz and Mitchell had known each other well since the time they had been members of the circle of artists that also included Casimir, George Russell and others exhibiting paintings in Dublin. Moving in or very near this circle was another now largely forgotten name, Nelly O'Brien (Neilí ní Bhriain). She and Constance had much in common, not least their very strong nationalistic feelings although each had come from Protestant Anglo-Irish stock. Both women were to attend a rally held in Dublin in April 1918 to protest over the moves to introduce conscription in Ireland. This meeting was presided over by Constance Markievicz and as Hilary Pyle wrote: 'Nelly O'Brien of Cumann Gaedhalach na hEaglaise [was] heading the Protestant protest against conscription alongside Roman Catholic opponents of the Bill.' Charlotte Despard, Dora French and William Partridge were further Protestant republicans whom Constance knew well – the latter went on to become vice-chairman of the Irish Citizen Army Council and actually served with her and Michael Mallin in the College of Surgeons garrison. George Anderson of Colga House, a Sligo Republican and a Protestant member of Sinn Féin, who went on to become Captain in the Volunteers, was almost certainly personally known to Constance.

Although the list does not stop there, one further name worth adding is that of Dorothy Stopford, through whose aunt Sir Roger Casement initially made contact with the republican movement. Stopford, along with her sister, her aunt, and her cousin, Elsie Henry, were all 'in the thick of things,' but Dorothy's case is especially interesting. Like Constance, she came from an Anglo-Irish Protestant family, a background that may well have contributed to the almost 'gung-ho' attitude they both shared which perhaps makes it easy to see the similarities in the attitudes and language of these two women. Like Constance, Dorothy Stopford loved to dress up, though the latter preferred riding breeches and an eyeglass rather than a military-style uniform complete with an eye-catching hat and a cigarette.

Stopford, however, saw no reason to turn her back on her family and former friends, but neither did she see any reason to convert to Catholicism, because, as León Ó Broin wrote of her, 'she enjoyed her religion.' On one occasion she made it clear that she continued to be on good terms 'with all the gentry and Protestants, they are very nice and broadminded' – a view which Constance would most certainly not have shared. Stopford recalled how, one day, she went to a Mothers' Union meeting in the local rectory, where 'we had prayers and sang hymns … I met all the ladies of the parish. Next minute I am out … with the IRA.' The two women shared the same, almost breathless enthusiasm for an adventurous lifestyle. Both were, certainly at first, objects of some curiosity and suspicion as far as their Catholic republican comrades were concerned, but Stopford never saw her membership of the Church of Ireland as an anomaly. 'I sternly refuse all efforts to be converted and say I prefer to go to Hell. Then [her comrades] all exclaim that they know it's wrong, that they can't believe I will go to Hell. We have great sport.'

As soon as Eva heard of the court martial reprieve, she applied for and was granted permission to visit her sister, travelling from London with her life-long friend, Esther Roper. On arrival at the prison they were joined by Susan Mitchell. Eva found the visit extremely frustrating: 'Nobody who has not gone through the ordinary prison visit can realise how unsatisfactory it is, nor what a strain it is, to fling one's conversation across a passage with a wardress in it, to a head appearing at a window opposite.' Knowing that Michael Mallin had been one of the leaders executed (but knowing nothing of his statement about her at his court martial), Constance asked Eva to find his widow who was expecting the birth of their child, to see what could be done for her. She also asked her sister to seek out several other women whom she wished to help.

While Constance publicly denounced her well-connected family, their reaction and the general reaction of their friends to her predicament was, almost without exception, remarkably sympathetic and lacking in bitterness. One of Constance's Hounslow relatives (through her maternal grandmother) wrote from Belvoir Castle, Grantham: 'My dear Connie, you are a dear naughty child to get into this trouble your mother has announced to me this morning. I do not like your not being well....' Eva received a letter in a similar vein from Sir John Leslie of Castle Leslie, County Monaghan, written from the Royal Inniskilling Fusiliers' Barracks, Enniskillen where he was serving. He hoped his earlier letter to Constance (which has not survived) had given her 'a ray of pleasure' and added:

> It is dreadful to think of the charming high-spirited girl I used to know being a prisoner.... Perhaps they will find her some kind of work that might suit her clever, artistic fingers. An enormous Army doctor was in here yesterday who described being captured by Constance in person, who deprived him of his belt and allowed him to look after the wounded Sinn Féiners. Her pistol was enormous; he was terrified of it going off. I don't know what the dear child would say if she knew that I was commanding the garrison here, defending bridges and controlling the district. Shall we ever have peace and quiet?

Less than a week after her visit to Mountjoy Prison, Eva received a letter from her sister, the first permitted by the prison authorities, in which Constance gave extraordinarily detailed directions about closing her home and placing furniture and belongings in store. Addressing Eva as 'Dearest Old Darling' she wrote: 'It was such a Heaven-sent joy seeing you, it was a new life, a resurrection, though I knew all the time you would try to see me, even though I'd been fighting and you hate it all so, and think killing is so wrong ...'

Eva had made her disapproval clear to her sister more than once and also admonished Constance for her sometimes jokey, light-hearted attitude, which was probably Constance's way of coping with some of her difficulties. For all that, Eva continued to be supportive of her sister to the end of her life, and although she suffered from indifferent health, she paid regular visits to Constance during her various subsequent prison incarcerations.

In her letter, Constance asked Eva to thank both Esther Roper, and Susan Mitchell for visiting her – 'You are three dears and you brought sunshine to me, and I long to hug you all!' Her home had just been raided by the police, but she wrote that all her valuables were with a friend. She was concerned about the cost of storing furniture and her pictures and books, but wanted 'nothing thrown away.' Constance apologised to her sister for 'giving such a lot of worries and bothers,' and despite the long list of things to be done, she added, 'I feel, too, as if I hadn't remembered half.' After commenting that 'it's very economical living here,' she added that she was 'half glad I'm not treated as a political prisoner as I should feel so greatly tempted to eat, smoke [she was a heavy smoker] and dress at my own expense. In the meantime I live free ....' Curiously, although she was writing to her favourite sister, she signed the letter, 'CdM.'

Eva and her friends went to check out her home, and discovered it had not only been subjected to a police search but vandals had subsequently also entered and everything was in a mess. While it was not clear what, if anything, had been removed by the police, it was obvious that the other unwelcome visitors had made off with many of Constance's belongings, everything from saucepans to paintings.

When Constance heard she was being transferred to Aylesbury Prison in Buckinghamshire, she derived some consolation from the fact that it brought her closer to Eva, now living in London. She wrote that she was going to be:

> Quite amiable – am not going to hunger strike, as I am advised by my comrades not to. It would suit the government very well to let me die quietly. I want to work for the Army, that's all. I look forward to seeing you the whole time. Put on your prettiest hat when you come! Give Esther my best love. My family must be quite amusing about my latest crimes!

Her family had no reason to be 'amusing' about her situation. Josslyn had, not for the first time, made strenuous efforts on her behalf for which he got no thanks. As far as Constance was concerned, his well-meaning efforts to secure a reprieve were no more welcome than his attempts, 16 or more years earlier, to ascertain whether or not her relationship with Casimir would make for a sensible marriage. One of the reasons why she was now so icy in her dealings with her brother was because he, rather than Eva, had just been formally appointed administrator of her affairs, which involved making a decision about what was to happen to her home and its contents. Eva was her trustee and, as Constance wrote, was 'therefore the most natural person to look after things … I suppose it's because she's a woman!' So, while Eva was already trying to sort out her sister's personal affairs, Josslyn was now given the official responsibility of dealing with them, notably the sale of Constance's home.

Josslyn found this latter task, because of the disruption resulting from the Great War and the recent rebellion, extremely difficult. This is reflected not only in the files of correspondence to and from the solicitors involved, but also in the strongly worded letters from Constance, putting all the blame for complications and the delays on him, no doubt reflecting her general resentment and frustration. One of the persons interested in purchasing the house was Harry Clarke, described in one of the solicitor's letters sent to Josslyn as an 'artist of North Frederick' [Street], just then embarking on a career as a noted stained glass artist.

In another letter, Constance requested her sister to 'ask Joss to give Maeve £1 to buy an Easter egg,' but less conventionally, she sometimes communicated with Eva by experimenting with what she called 'mystical experiences.' These involved the two sisters concentrating their thinking about each other and, though they were far apart, they claimed to find solace in being able to be in touch with one another in this way. Eva wrote a poem about these experiences, one verse of which reads:

> The peaceful night that round me flows
> Breaks through your iron prison doors,
> Free through the world your spirit goes,
> Forbidden hands are clasping yours.

In July 1917, Prime Minister Lloyd George called for a convention to discuss Home Rule and although Sinn Féin refused to participate, it was followed by a general amnesty for all involved in the rebellion. As a result, Eva collected her sister, bringing bright clothes to cheer her so that: 'Constance, herself again, thin but beautiful, in a blue dress instead of that twice too large, left the prison for ever' although, as it transpired, forever did not last very long. She stayed at her sister's

London home for a few days, until Helena Moloney and Maire Perolz had travelled to London to accompany her back to Dublin. Anxious to be back 'in the swing of things,' Constance travelled to Ennis and gave a passionate speech in support of Éamon de Valera who was canvassing for the vacant West Clare seat. The result of the subsequent election, an overwhelming victory for de Valera, marked a turning point for the Republicans.

When Sinn Féin held its annual convention in the autumn of 1917, a strong sense of unity was evident, strikingly emphasised when Arthur Griffith and Count Plunkett stood down as candidates for the presidency so that Éamon de Valera could be appointed unanimously. Almost the only voice of dissent at the meeting was that of Constance Markievicz who, although all the other prominent leaders had decided to give him their support, vociferously opposed the election of Eoin MacNeill as a member of the party's executive. She never forgave MacNeill, even if others had, for his attempts to stop the Rising. Life was once again a whirlwind of activity for Constance, not only because of her involvement with Sinn Féin – she was now on its executive – but she continued her connections with many other organisations too. These included Cumann na mBan, the Irish Citizen Army, the Irish Republican Prisoners Dependent Fund, the James Connolly Labour College and, of course, her own Fianna Éireann.

Growing more and more powerful, Sinn Féin awaited the opportunity which it anticipated would present itself during a general election, and the British Government handed it an unexpected present when, in April 1918, Lloyd George introduced a Bill to empower conscription in Ireland. Losses on the western front had been appalling and the Prime Minister saw this move having two advantages – first that of tapping the so-far 'under-used' manpower in Ireland and, second, hoping thereby to reduce Sinn Féin's capacity to cause further trouble. His Chief Secretary in Ireland was one of many who saw the dangers posed by the scheme, but Lloyd George pressed ahead and the Bill was enacted a week later, although the entire Irish Parliamentary Party voted against it. Éamon de Valera prepared a strong statement setting out his case for opposing conscription in which he referred to those Irishmen who had already died fighting on England's side:

> England attracted to her armies some of the flower of our manhood…. Their bones lie today buried beneath the soil of Flanders, or beneath the waves of Suvla Bay, or bleaching on the slopes of Gallipoli, or on the sands of Egypt or

Arabia, and Mesopotamia, or wherever the battle line extends from Dunkirk to the Persian gulf. Mons, Ypres, will be monuments to their unselfish heroism....

His references to some of the terrible battles of the war were quite perceptive and his description of those Irishmen involved as unselfish heroes was probably the closest he ever came to acknowledging the part played by up to a quarter of a million Irishmen serving voluntarily in what he himself termed the 'Irish Expeditionary Force.' He went on to add that:

the land they loved dearest on earth ... and the land they fondly hoped their sacrifice might assist to freedom, still lies at the feet of the age-long enemy .... Is it not right, then, to refuse ... to give up the sons ... she can ill afford? What Ireland is to give, Ireland alone must determine.

A month later, on the pretext of a 'German Plot' – the existence of which Constance vigorously denied in a letter to her sister – over 70 prominent members of Sinn Féin were arrested and she was apprehended, along with her dog 'Poppet,' while returning to her home in Rathmines. According to *The Times*, she, 'accompanied by a large brown spaniel dog' and 45 male prisoners were taken in a warship to Holyhead from where the men were marched to a rest camp: Constance, along with her spaniel, was taken to serve her prison sentence, but a short time later, the dog was freed and brought under escort to Eva's house. Like the others, Constance was not a prisoner but an internee, and consequently was not permitted to have visitors, but when Maud Gonne MacBride and Mrs Tom Clarke also arrived at Holloway a few days later, visiting mattered rather less as the three were permitted the right of association.

In her autobiography, Mrs Clarke described how the three women lost weight and 'Madam Markievicz became a nuisance to me over it; she fussed, which I hate, so I told her one day if she wanted an occupation to look elsewhere.' Clarke claimed that while she continued to press for better food and conditions, Constance was concerned about 'giving trouble', because she feared that she might be transferred to another prison too far away from Eva. Mrs Clarke, who seems to have disliked Constance, also related that on one occasion there was a dispute as to which of the three had the highest social status.

Madam Markievicz claimed that she was far above Madam MacBride; she belonged to the inner circle of the vice-regal set, while Madam MacBride was only on the fringe of it ... Madam Markievicz took pains to make me aware of the social gulf between us; it didn't worry me.

Still at Holloway, Constance was chosen by Sinn Féin as one of its 73 candidates at the election which was held a month after the end of the Great War, the first to be held after suffrage had been extended to women over 30 years of age. Neither Constance nor anyone else in Sinn Féin saw it as a disadvantage that more than half of the party's candidates were in jail. Indeed, as she expressed it, 'my present address alone will make an excellent electoral address.'

The campaign run on behalf of Constance had the backing of the Irish Women's Franchise League, though it is obvious that she would easily have won the seat anyway. The result of the election as a whole was an overwhelming victory for Sinn Féin, which gained over two-thirds of the Irish seats. However, because Sinn Féin had adopted a policy of abstention, Constance Markievicz, the first woman elected to any European parliament did not take her seat, attending the new Dáil Éireann instead when she was released from internment.

Eva had been a member of the suffrage movement for many years in Britain and had worked hard in the hope of securing a number of the English seats in that same election. There was considerable disappointment in the suffrage movement, not only because none of its candidates headed the poll but when Constance – their remaining hope – was elected and then spurned her seat at Westminster, their disappointment was all the greater because they saw it as a lost opportunity. As the suffragette publication, *The Vote*, commented: 'The irony of politics decided that the only woman elected to the British House of Commons should be Constance Georgine, Countess Markievicz who, in accordance with the Sinn Féin tactics of her party, never took the seat she won as M.P.' Could she have taken her seat at Westminster anyway? The *Irish Independent* at the time quoted a statement made by the Home Office making the point that it had no record of Casimir Markievicz having become a naturalised British subject, and consequently 'Madam Markievicz would therefore be ineligible to sit in parliament.'

Despite the suffrage setback that had come as such a blow to Eva, when Constance was released from Holloway in March she received a warm welcome from her long-suffering and ever accommodating sister with whom Constance stayed for a while in her London home. When she returned to Dublin, Constance found herself appointed Minister for

Labour in Éamon de Valera's cabinet, having been appointed in her absence at the first meeting of the Dáil on January 22, 1919. De Valera had written to ask if she would accept the post, to which Constance replied in a note comprising just ten words: 'I can give you all my time for Ireland's work.' Mrs Kathleen Clarke, widow of the executed leader, told a different story – claiming that Constance had threatened to resign and join the Labour Party if she was refused the appointment. If she and Constance shared a common political outlook, they obviously cared little for each other's company. Writing to her sister before her own release, Constance told Eva that Kathleen Clarke had just been freed: 'Of course I miss K. very much, but for the first time in my life I was thankful to see the back of a dear friend.'

Writing about this period, Francis Costello thought that her presence as Minister was largely symbolic, possibly because Constance was, for much of the time, 'on the run.' Her term of office was short-lived for, when de Valera restructured his cabinet he removed Constance from the Executive, a move seen by some as a foretaste of his subsequent policy concerning the position of women in public life. Declan Kiberd wrote of the politics of the new State 'which would deny the manly woman epitomised by Constance Markievicz and Maud Gonne, opting instead for de Valera's maidens at the rural crossroads, themselves a pastoral figment of the late-Victorian imagination.' In the meantime, however, delighted with her appointment, Constance wrote to her sister on note-paper headed 'Dáil Éireann, Department of Labour, Mansion House, Dublin:' 'Dearest Old Darling, It is so heavenly to be out again and to be able to shut and open doors.… It is almost worth being locked up for the great joy release brings. It is so funny, suddenly, to be a Government and supposed to be respectable! One has to laugh.'

After speaking at a meeting in Newmarket, County Clare, Constance was apprehended and charged with having made a seditious speech and she found herself in prison once again, this time in Cork. After Constance had been freed in October, she addressed a meeting organised by the Socialist Party to commemorate the anniversary of the Bolshevik Revolution, reflecting something of her interest in a workers' republic. In this respect, Roy Foster has suggested that romantic Celticism (he referred to Standish O'Grady's unlikely assumption that ancient Ireland had pioneered Communism) may have been an influential factor, but her tendency to become enthusiastic about ideas before she seriously considered their implications renders it difficult to be sure of the depth of her interest in Bolshevism, Communism, Leninism and/or Marxism.

As a disciple of James Connolly, she certainly favoured one or more of these 'isms', and at least one writer drew a comparison between her and the Polish-born Róża Luksemburg who, as Rosa Luxemburg, became the co-founder of the German Communist Party. Griffith and O'Grady expounded the view that: 'holding on to the fusion between republicanism and socialism [she] resurrected the ghost of Connolly in opposition to the treaty.'

In her volume on Irish Catholicism, Mary Kenny wrote about the reaction of the Catholic Bishop of Ross, Dr Denis Kelly, in 1919 when he heard that Sinn Féin elements in Dáil Éireann had spoken supportively about Bolshevism. He noted that several speakers 'held up to admiration what was going on at the present moment in Russia and Hungary.' Bishop Kelly said that he had 'been aware that Countess Markievicz had called for support for the Bolsheviks previously, and [at the time he] hadn't minded her wild ideas, but now he found that these wild ideas were held by respectable men.' Mary Kenny added, in parenthesis, 'Eccentric females could be safely ignored, but not sensible men.'

During that same year, Constance stayed for a time in the home of the first leader of the Labour Party in Dáil Éireann, Thomas Johnson. In his biography of Johnson, J. Anthony Gaughan recounted some details of a meeting of the Socialist Party of Ireland held to mark the second anniversary of the Bolshevik Revolution. He quoted Markievicz who had 'praised the educational work being done by the Bolsheviks and expressed the view that an educated working class in Ireland was essential.'

Just before Christmas, the police raided nearly 200 houses, including the home of Constance Markievicz, but luckily for her she was away at the time. As she told her sister: 'It's awfully funny being on the run … I fly round the town on my bike for exercise, and it is too funny seeing the expression on the policemen's faces when they see me whiz by.' Nine days after attending one of the Dáil sessions, she was once again arrested and taken to Mountjoy Prison. and Michael Hopkinson referred to this incident in his book about the last period of British rule at Dublin Castle. Based on the journal kept by a senior civil servant, Sturgis, who – though having no formal title – was in effect the joint assistant Under Secretary. He wrote that Madam Markievicz was, 'a thorn in the side of Sinn Féin, so it may have been a pity to take her away from them.'

The opportunity presented by her arrest was taken to charge Constance – somewhat belatedly – for her part in founding Fianna

Éireann, and she was sentenced to two years' imprisonment. In prison she spent some of her time studying Irish but found it difficult without a tutor. Already fluent in Latin, Italian and French, she was obviously familiar with a failing common in language books compiled to help beginners:

> I wish I knew why grammarians always search the world (or dictionaries) for the words you want least in a language and give them to you to learn and leave out the ones that you want every day. I can talk about hawks and flails, scythes, rye and barley, magicians, kings and fairies; but I couldn't find out how to ask for an extra blanket or a clean plate or a fork....

Meanwhile, the murderous guerrilla war continued until a truce was sought and signed, but a political solution had yet to be agreed. After many months of negotiations, an agreement was signed in December 1921 involving a treaty which, given the complex political situation, fell short of most people's expectations but one which the Irish delegates in London considered to be the best that they could obtain at that time. It was to prove disastrously divisive at many levels, including personal. George Russell, with whom Constance had been so friendly, declared himself in favour of the Treaty terms, which, according to his own memoirs, caused her to remark: 'George, you are an idiot.'

* * *

Constance, having cut herself off from her family at Lissadell, continued to have little contact even with her mother who continued to bring up Maeve who was by then a young woman. Constance did write from Mountjoy, but without access to her mother's correspondence (virtually all letters sent to Constance were either lost or were later destroyed by her daughter), it is sometimes difficult to understand the context of some of her remarks. On one occasion she told her mother that she very much admired 'Cecil.' This was a reference to her uncle, Cecil L'Estrange Malone who, after a distinguished career during the war (he took part in the famous Cuxhaven raid, the first occasion when torpedoes were launched from aircraft), he became a communist and was imprisoned for treason. Constance wrote of him: 'Truly, he is a wonderful man. I must say how much I admire his self-sacrifice. It is quite heroic when you think of the career that he has renounced for his principles.' This was little short of a deliberate taunt, for Constance would have been well aware that the rest of the family looked askance at what they would have perceived as the very strange activities of their mother's brother.

She was released in July 1921, and subsequently joined in the acrimonious Dáil debate about the Treaty, the terms of which – notably in relation to the oath of allegiance to the Crown – were so vigorously opposed by de Valera's group that it was to split Sinn Féin into two factions. Constance spoke vehemently 'as a disciple of James Connolly' against the Treaty terms which she claimed were vague, condemning in particular the oath. She also opposed Arthur Griffith's proposed guarantee to southern Unionists, whom she called a privileged class, that they would have representation in both chambers of the new State parliament. She could see no good reason why 'a privileged member of classes established here by British rule' were to be given 'a say'.[4]

Constance insisted that she should have been on the delegation that had gone to London 'because she knew the English mind' – a suggestion that begs the question, what might have been the result?

> By that black drop of English blood in me [a reference to her English-born mother], I know the English – that's the truth. I say it is because of that black drop in me that I know the English personally better than the people who went over with the delegation.

She mocked Michael Collins who, with Griffith, had been part of the team that had negotiated the terms of the Treaty, and she repeated an unlikely rumour that had been circulating in Dublin, that he hoped to marry Princess Mary in order to ensure that he was made Governor of the new State. She told Collins that he had been 'befogged' when he had met the British Prime Minister; and she called one deputy 'an old woman' and accused the pro-Treaty deputies of being 'jugglers and twisters.'

On January 7, 1922, 64 deputies voted for the Treaty and 57 voted against it. Two days later de Valera resigned as President. When the vote to appoint Arthur Griffith in his place was being taken, de Valera walked out of the Dáil along with his anti-Treaty followers. Sinn Féin was now irrevocably split in two and, coincidence or not, most of the

---

[4] According to Terence de Vere White, her own party leader had – before the Treaty was signed – given Griffith his consent to assure Lord Midleton 'that they, the Southern Unionists, would be represented, and their interests safeguarded, by a Second Chamber in the Legislature.'

women deputies including Constance were, along with Erskine Childers, in de Valera's faction, which was promptly labelled by a Dublin wit, 'the women and Childers party.' The days of debating overflowed into bitter recrimination and name-calling, described by Roy Foster in his book about Irish and English connections as 'exchanges redolent with ironies, and expressing a tangled history of Irish-English interactions and borrowings of identity.'

Childers was accused of having been an English spy, while Constance Markievicz saw no irony in asserting that Griffith was 'a Welsh name.' She was, in turn, the butt of a taunt from Deputy O'Keeffe who, reminding her of her origins, told her that 'an O'Keeffe will never yield to a Gore-Booth.' Collins judged de Valera's action in walking out to be one of contempt for the sovereign assembly authorised by the Irish people and shouted after the departing deputies, 'Deserters all! We will now call on the Irish people to rally to us. Deserters all!' Michael Ceannt called back: 'Up the Republic' and Collins responded: 'Deserters all to the Irish nation in her hour of need. We will all stand by her.' This drew the response from Constance: 'Oath breakers and cowards,' prompting Collins to make the pointed retort: 'Foreigners, Americans, English.' Constance had the last word: 'Lloyd Georgeites,' she shouted as she left the chamber, never to return.

In his biography of Cearbhall Ó Dálaigh, Risteárd Ó Glaisne described in some detail the dilemma facing Éamon de Valera and his party following their walk-out, noting that some time later, he was to declare that 'no decent Republican will ever enter that Dáil' (because of the requirement under the terms of the Treaty making entry conditional on signing the oath to the British sovereign), and that shortly afterwards he was to add that those who took the oath 'who did not mean to keep it were nothing more or less than perjurers.' He appeared to copperfasten his view a year later when he pledged that so long as his party's T.D.s 'were representatives of the people they would never take an oath to a foreign king.'

By the time Constance returned from a six-week fundraising tour in America, the simmering row over the Treaty had already ignited into a very ugly civil war, and this relatively brief period must rank as one of the worst and most bitter periods in Ireland's sad history. Constance, asleep in the early hours of one morning, woke up when she heard the sound of loud explosions coming from the city centre and guessed that the Four Courts was under attack. She dashed into town and joined with a section of the anti-Treaty forces occupying much of one side of

Upper O'Connell Street where, after the surrender of the Four Courts garrison, most of the subsequent fighting in the city ensued. It was all over in the city in a few days, and Constance managed to make her way to a friend's house. The grim struggle eventually ended when de Valera ordered his forces to 'dump arms' but the bitterness endured for decades afterwards.

After the poet and playwright Padraic Colum married in 1913, he and Mary went to America. As a result of the outbreak of the First World War, Mary, who had been involved in Cumann na mBan, missed the uprising and did not return to Dublin until the middle of the Civil War. Along with Constance, Yeats, Lady Gregory, George Russell and the rest, she had joined the city's literary and dramatic circles, but she now found – as Casimir was to discover a few years later – that Dublin was no longer the city of a decade or two earlier. 'The atmosphere was very changed from my student days when poetry and a sort of mystic romance filled the air.'

Describing a meeting at Russell's house, she wrote:

> The strangest, and at the same time the most familiar sight of all was Constance Markievicz, sitting in her usual place on the couch in the corner.... There she sat, she who had fought side-by-side with men in the insurrection of 1916, had been condemned to death, had her death sentence commuted to imprisonment, and had recently been released.

Colum, who reflected upon how Yeats had admired Constance as the daughter of a great landowner, Sir Henry Gore-Booth, added:

> But now she sat there, she whom I remembered as a beautiful woman, only second in beauty to Maud Gonne, was haggard and old, dressed in ancient demoded clothes; the outline of her face was the same, but the expression was different; the familiar eyes that blinked at me from behind glasses were bereft of the old fire and eagerness; she gave me her limp hand and barely spoke to me.... What she had fought for had not really come into being.

Mary Colum, who had known Constance 'in her vibrant maturity,' recalled being told by her; 'I am not interested in men, for I have had my pick of too many men.' Although she compared her to an extinct volcano, Colum did not intend this as a criticism, for she admired much of what Constance had done.

In November 1923, Constance was once again in prison, having been arrested canvassing for signatures on a petition for the release of republican prisoners. She was taken to the North Dublin Union, converted into a temporary internment camp, where accommodation consisted of large dormitories 'haunted by ghosts of broken-hearted paupers.' She went on hunger strike ('I only did three days'), because she felt she had been arrested simply for spite. She was released on Christmas Eve after four weeks' detention. 1924 saw her busy again with Cumann na mBan and the Fianna. Military training was still on her agenda, and she told the women that disarmament had got them nowhere so it was necessary to plan to fight again. In the next breath she was telling a friend: 'Don't talk to me about politics, tell me how to get bread for the children ... politics ought to be nothing more or less than the organisation of food, clothes and housing.' Perhaps it was this remark that prompted O'Faoláin to write that 1924 was for Constance 'the end of the heroic life of a revolutionary ... all the adventure was gone.'

Casimir Markievicz, following a visit to London, took the opportunity to travel to Dublin during the summer. He found Constance still as active as ever, although she had visibly aged. He had looked forward to meeting his old literary, artistic and theatre friends but found the city had changed. It now seemed cheerless and lacking in the old vivacity he had recalled with affection. Soon he was gone, back to Poland again, to return just once more in three years time, but his brief visit seems to have had at least two effects upon Constance – a re-awakening of her old interests with the stage and with her painting. She began to spend entire days sketching and painting in the Dublin mountains, and she also started exhibiting again. Commenting upon one of these events (where 41 of her pictures on display had been painted in Holloway Jail), *The Irish Times* reported that her paintings were: 'sufficiently well expressed to suggest that the painter missed her vocation.'

Outwardly, she continued to be cheerful and enthusiastic but now, aged 57, she looked even older than that, worn out by the years that had alternated between prison terms and, when free, her almost ceaseless activity. Even though she wholeheartedly agreed with the Sinn Féin abstention policy that precluded its elected members from taking their seats in the Dáil, she must have found the political situation very frustrating. When the new Fianna Fáil party was publicly launched in April 1925, she presided at the meeting, having resigned her membership of Cumann na mBan because, according to Margaret Ward, membership of both organisations contravened the constitution of the latter. Constance wrote a strange letter to Eva in December 1925. It began, as usual, 'Dearest Old Darling:'

> The tragedy of Christ's life to me is far greater than it was during the few terrible last hours of suffering. For every church and every sect is but an organisation of thoughtless and well-meaning people trained in thought and controlled by juntas of priests and clergy who are used to doing all the things that Christ would most have disliked. And yet I don't know how this can be avoided, for without organisation Christ would be quite forgotten, and all organisation seems in the end to go the same road, and if it does not go in for graft and power it just fizzles out…. Everything here is very dull. The main thing is the appalling poverty that meets one everywhere ….

This was followed by another strange letter, this time explaining something of her political views at this time to her sister:

> I wonder what you think of us all? I sometimes think that people get rather mad when they go in for politics. The latest has made me laugh since it began. Dev., I say like a wise man, has announced that he will go into the Free State Parliament if there is no oath and this has caused an unholy row. I myself have always said that the oath made it absolutely impossible for an honourable person who was a Republican to go in, and that if it were removed it would then be a question of policy, with no principle involved, whether we went in or stayed out … Dev. thinks the moment has come to start out attacking the oath and demanding its removal. Maev[e] blew-in on her way to Sligo and commandeered the car. Is there any chance of your coming over this year at all? It is such an age since I saw you and that beastly channel and the long journey costs such a lot and I never have any time or money anyhow.

While Constance and Eva remained close friends all their lives, it is difficult to avoid the conclusion that whereas Eva had given selfless and practical support to her sister – especially during Constance's darkest periods – Constance did not seem to go out of her way to reciprocate. Eva never enjoyed good health, yet she travelled many times over 'the beastly channel' to be at her sister's side. And although she, too, lived a hand-to-mouth financial existence, it did not prevent her from ungrudgingly undertaking 'the long journey [that] costs such a lot.' But whether her sister knew it or not, Eva was now seriously ill, and shortly afterwards Esther Roper sent a telegram to Constance to inform her of Eva's death. The news dumbfounded Constance who replied immediately by letter:

> Everything seemed to go from under me, I simply can't realise it. There was no one ever like her. She was something wonderful and beautiful, and so simple

and thought so little of herself. I don't think she ever knew how much she was to me. Her gentleness prevented me from getting very callous in a War ….

If Eva never knew how much she had really meant to Constance this may well have resulted from Constance's apparent difficulty in communicating her own innate feelings – even to those closest to her. Although she enjoyed Casimir's company, she had seemed unable to relate to him intimately, and even though in these latter years she was seeing a little more of her daughter Maeve (now in her mid-twenties) than at any time in the past, their relationship was more like that of two friends rather than mother and daughter. Now, despite all Eva had done for her, Constance – so often guided by her emotions – decided not to attend her sister's funeral, explaining that she would not be going: 'because I simply could not face it. I want to keep my last memory of her so happy and peaceful, and nothing but love and beauty and peace.'

Some of Constance's biographers seem to have been anxious to avoid mentioning anything that might detract from the 'Joan of Arc' image. Perhaps reflecting this, Jacqueline Van Voris quoted from the above letter but omitted the sentence 'I don't think she ever knew how much she was to me' and also the paragraph indicating that Constance would not be attending the funeral. Two months after Eva's funeral, Constance did make the journey to London and visited Eva's grave, staying with Esther Roper, from where she wrote to her aunt, Mrs L'Estrange:

> I feel very sad leaving this house probably for the last time. Every corner of it speaks of Eva and her lovely spirit of peace and love is here just the same as ever. And Esther, too, who is her spiritual sister, I hate leaving. And the more one knows of her the more one loves her, and I feel so glad Eva and she were together, and so thankful that her love was with Eva to her end.

She continued to find it impossible to visit Lissadell, but realising that her mother was unwell Constance wrote a curious letter to Josslyn in January 1927, hoping that she 'wasn't suffering too much.' She expressed concern that her mother 'had never asked me there [to her house, Ardeevin] since. I never bothered, as I didn't particularly want to go. I was so busy always.' Lady Gore-Booth died just a few weeks later, and some of the references made in the newspaper obituaries about her life might have been written about her eldest daughter. These included the fact that Lady Mary had been a fearless horsewoman, had done so much for the poor, and had gone to an art school in London as a young woman. But the gulf between daughter and mother – in death as in life – was so great that Constance simply could not bring herself to attend her mother's funeral. This was a very lonely time for Constance, and the story is told about how one of her friends called unexpectedly to see her in Dublin and found her staring out the window with tears running down her cheeks.

The weather was exceptionally harsh that winter and matters were made worse by a grave shortage of coal. Constance collected bags of turf which she brought into the city in her car, some of it from the Dublin Mountains, and some which had been sent to her by an old friend, Albinia Broderick, Lord Midleton's sister and a member of Cumann na mBan. Though now in her late fifties, she thought nothing of hauling heavy bags of fuel up flights of stairs in the back-street tenement houses where many of the poorest people in Dublin lived. They were to remember Constance both as the most thoughtful person they had even known and as the best-hearted person who ever lived. As Van Voris recorded, her kindness and help on behalf of the poor 'in this last winter of her life is remembered in countless stories,' In his poem dedicated to her after she died, Cecil Day Lewis wrote 'All the poor of Dublin rose to lament her, / A nest is made, an eagle flown.'

The fact that she retained her seat in the 1926 elections must have brought her some satisfaction, but her party, recently re-named 'Fianna Fáil', failed to secure an election majority.

A year later, while attending a party meeting, one of the members noticed that she looked unwell and a few days later Josslyn was informed that his sister had been taken to hospital in Dublin and he promptly sent roses to her. His brother Mordaunt, in London, wrote to say: 'I don't know if you have heard that Constance is in the Thomas Dunne [Sir Patrick Dun's] Hospital in Dublin with appendicitis. I gather she has been operated on and is in a poorish way.' A telegram arrived at Lissadell on the following day from Dorothy Macardle: 'Countess Markievicz had second operation to-day. Condition critical. Please write her daughter to come Dunne's Hospital, Dublin.' Josslyn additionally received a postcard sent by the Matron of the hospital: 'Patient keeps much the same as yesterday. She had a fair amount of sleep last night and expressed a wish for some more roses. I said I would let you know.' He had also received a letter from his sister Mabel, married to Charles Foster and living near Falmouth, to say that Esther Roper had written to her 'on the day that they broadcast for Maeve. It sounded so desperate when they sent an S.O.S.'

Although she was seriously ill, Constance insisted that she wanted to be in a general ward 'with the poor.' No aspect of her life has been so underrated as her work for the underprivileged, doubtless because it went largely unrecorded. Her decision to be taken to a public ward was a final symbolic gesture aimed at the poor of Dublin, though Coxhead's description of Sir Patrick Dun's as 'a slum hospital' was something of an unnecessary exaggeration. Maeve did manage to get from England to her mother's bedside as did Esther Roper, whom Constance told, 'Eva has been by my side ever since I came here.' Unexpectedly, Casimir also arrived at the hospital from distant Warsaw, along with Stanislas, her stepson. She showed her visitors the roses that Josslyn had sent to her and valiantly tried to appear cheerful. Two days later, Casimir was informed that she had suddenly taken a turn for the worse and he rushed back to the hospital. He stayed with Constance until she died in the early hours of the following morning, July 15, 1927. He sent a telegram to Josslyn: 'Constance passed away peacefully this morning 1 a.m. Markievicz.'

A notice of Casimir's death as published in a Warsaw newspaper described him as an author, artist, painter and [commercial and legal] adviser to the American Consulate General, but made no reference to his having been a count which, in the circumstances, would have been very unusual. An unknown hand has altered Casimir's age as stated in the notice.

Controversial in life, Constance also proved controversial in death. Such was the political bitterness at the time, that when preparations were being made to arrange a lying-in-state, neither the City Hall nor the Mansion House was made available. Instead, her coffin was taken to the Rotunda from where, on July 17, the funeral procession left for Glasnevin cemetery. In the leading coaches were Count Markievicz and his son Stanislas, and Sir Josslyn and Lady Mary Gore-Booth; in the other coaches were Éamon de Valera, Dr Kathleen Lynn, Art O'Connor, and Sean T. O'Kelly, Madam Gonne McBride, Mrs Charlotte Despard, Mary McSwiney, along with many of her other friends. Six bands followed, along with representatives of all the organisations with which Constance had been associated, including contingents of the Citizen Army, the 1916 Club and Fianna Éireann. A large number of members of the Workers' Union of Ireland paraded behind a red banner which bore an inscription in Russian, but perhaps the sight that would have pleased her most, could she have witnessed it, was the huge turnout of the poor people lining the streets of Dublin.

At Glasnevin cemetery, soldiers and detectives were already in place on the orders of a government that had feared that some unseemly demonstration – or worse – might take place. However the formalities were then halted by an extraordinary occurrence as reported in *The Irish Times*:

> There was an interval of about an hour while the crowd stood around the plot waiting for the coffin to be borne to the graveside. There was some disappointment among the waiting throng when the Rev. J. Fitzgibbon, the chaplain of the cemetery, announced that the burial would not take place in the plot until the following morning, and that the coffin had already been placed in a vault in the O'Connell Circle, but the vault had already been closed, and the chief mourners were taking their departure.

After the coffin had been placed in the vault de Valera delivered the oration, reported as follows in the same newspaper:

> Madam Markievicz is gone from us. Madam, the friend of the toiler, the lover of the poor. Ease and station she put aside and took the hard way of service with the weak and the down-trodden.

> Sacrifice, misunderstanding and scorn lay on the road she adopted, but she trod it unflinchingly. She now lies at rest with her fellow champions of the right – mourned by the people whose liberties she fought for, blessed by the loving prayers of the poor she tried so hard to befriend.

> They would know her only as a soldier of Ireland, but we knew her as a colleague

and comrade. We know the friendliness, the great woman's heart of her, the great Irish soul of her, and we know the loss we have suffered will not be repaired. It is sadly we take our leave but we pray High Heaven that all she longed and worked for may one day be achieved.

Many of the accounts of Constance Markieviecz's life quote these words from de Valera's oration but without including some of the very perceptive observations which he then added. For instance, after stating that: 'a troubled, tempestuous, picturesque career is at an end' he then continued:

> She had developed, changed and achieved greatness through the turmoil of her country's history. In the pages of fiction, there is nothing more strangely bizarre or more incoherently contradictory than this wonderful outcrop of Irish landlordism and Dublin Castle, this brilliant, fascinating, incomprehensible rebel; once the protégé of royalty and vice-royalty, anon the darling of the slums, and always alert, intense, vivacious, consumed with the fires of a burning devotion to whatever cause happened to capture her restless and enthusiastic, intellectual personality…. Class and station she put aside and took the hard way of service with the weak and down-trodden....

Under the headline 'Burial of Madam Markievicz,' *The Irish Times* reported the delayed funeral on the following day:

> In the presence of a small gathering of mourners, many of whom were women and girls, the burial of the body of Madame Markievicz took place in the Republican Plot in Glasnevin Cemetery at 9.30 o'clock yesterday morning.... The vault in the old O'Connell Circle where the coffin had lain since Sunday evening was opened on the arrival of Count Markievicz (husband) and his son, Mr. de Valera, and Fianna Fáil and Republican deputies. Five boys of the Fianna Eireann headed the procession from the vault to the Republican Plot. A green uniform, which had been worn by Madam Markievicz in St. Stephen's Green during the 1916 rebellion, was lowered into the grave with the coffin. Prayers for the dead were recited by the Rev. J. Fitzgibbon, C.C., Cemetery Chaplain and two other priests.

Josslyn and the family received scores of letters of condolence, representing, between them, the contrasting views about Constance's life. There were formal letters from such public bodies as the Sligo Corporation, Leitrim County Council, Roscommon County Board of Health, the Dublin Industrial Board and even the Pennsylvania Women's Press Association. Most of those who had worked closely with her and who sent letters of condolence to Lissadell were, of course, quite unknown to the family, as were the many ordinary people who simply wanted to express their own deep feelings about Constance. Her old friend, Helena Moloney, mentioned in her letter that shortly before she had died, Constance had broken her arm:

> cranking the car, which was like a small boy's toy to her … it was a very old car – a bargain from some Army stores. I always thought it was too heavy for her, but she had a childish pride in her own strength and her truly splendid energy.… She dismissed it [her injury] with a laugh and said it was nothing at all and didn't hurt. She was like that all the time, overdoing it in mental and physical work. Miss Coughlan – her landlady here – looked after her very well … I think after all, she has been very lucky in the time and manner of her death, although to her friends and comrades her loss is irreparable.

The above mentioned Frances Coughlan wrote to Josslyn, apparently in reply to a letter of thanks sent to her by him: 'It is gratifying that Madam's relations appreciate the efforts of my family to make things as bright and easy as possible for her – as it was no effort really. We all loved her heartily and sincerely and I believe she knew it.' Another woman who knew her, Agnes Murphy, wrote to the family from London:

> Pardon the intrusion of a stranger who feels impelled to write to you of the unique place your sister held in the hearts of Irish people .... When shall we look for her like again? Ireland is indeed bereaved by the loss of this rare spirit.

Mary Colum described Constance as 'a fighting Irishwoman, a woman of high aristocratic courage who was afraid of nothing – that, at least, the aristocratic training at its best can give, moral and physical fearlessness – but how rarely at its best!' T. Ryle Dwyer put it another way, writing that:

> instead of being ridiculed for her sometimes outlandish behaviour, writers have admired her because she was so independent and high spirited. She lived a spirited life, unafraid of any danger, and oblivious of the fact that many people thought it, to put it mildly, distinctly odd.

There were also scores of letters from relations and friends of the family, many of whom regretted the direction which Constance's life had taken, and while the thoughts expressed were sad, there was a remarkable absence of bitterness in most of them. Even the few that hinted at criticism were tinged with regret too, like the one sent by Janette L'Estrange, who wrote from Kent to say: 'Today I see poor Con's restless and unhappy life has ended. May her evil deeds be forgiven for the many kind ones she has done.' Lady Westmacott wrote:

I am so sorry to read of poor Constance's death, but I remember distinctly our happy times in the Montparnasse quarter. I hope you will forgive me writing in your sorrow – but my thoughts carried me back to the old days in Paris – before poor C. began her troubles.'

And from Enniskillen, came the following from Harry Wynne: 'I think I know how you feel about Con's death. As you know, I knew her in the old days. She was one of the very best, and we were all very fond of her. I like to think of her as I knew her then.'

Lady Fingall, in her letter, recalled Constance as 'the lovely girl who had delighted parties at Adare and at the Castle.'

Dublin witnessed two exceptionally large funerals at this time, those of Constance Markievicz and of Kevin O'Higgins, a government minister who was shot dead in cold blood by members of the IRA as he walked to Mass. Fifty-five years later, Conor Cruise O'Brien was to write rather unkindly: 'At the latter were the massed ranks of respectability, at the other the rabble.' But perhaps the Latin tag – *Interdum vulgus recte videt*[5] – got it right.

In his blockbuster history of Britain and Ireland, Norman Davies rather strangely called her 'a radical English aristocrat.' In her biography, Elizabeth Coxhead described Constance as 'a splendid, generous, strong-hearted creature [but] remembered for the wrong reasons in the wrong way,' and regarded 'with a curious ambivalence, accused of undue fanaticism and bitterness, blamed for much that was not her fault.' Foy and Barton wrote: 'Beneath her aristocratic hauteur, her undoubted theatricality, and her considerable capacity for embroidering her own exploits, she possessed courage and flair, and certainly craved military action.' F.S.L. Lyons viewed her as 'an eclectic, even by the standards of her class; she overflowed from domesticity into public affairs,' while the *Oxford Companion to Irish History* described her as 'one of the most romanticised political figures of the early twentieth century.'

The life of 'the Rebel Countess' tended to attract extreme views, then and since; she was viewed either as Ireland's Joan of Arc or half-mad. Given such extreme points of view, is it possible to be absolutely fair to Constance Markievicz's memory, and is it possible to reconcile such opposing views about her? For most people the answer must be 'no,' for it would require someone like Dubslav von Stechlin, a character in one of Theodor Fontane's novels, to assert such a definite

---

[5] Sometimes the rabble sees what is just.

opinion and then to add: 'And if I had said the opposite, it would be equally true.'

It may be an exaggeration to assert that she wrecked the lives of her husband, her daughter and her stepson, but each of their lives were blighted in one way or another. In Casimir's case, he was able to joke about it, but the two children she had abandoned were extremely bitter about her. Young Stanislas accused her of breaking up the family, while Maeve averred that, at the age of 20, she did not know what her mother looked like. Certainly it is difficult to comprehend the casual way in which she not only abandoned her own baby daughter, but left her to be reared in the very environment which she so publicly and so often condemned. And when uttering these condemnations she never once exempted those of that class – not even her father and her brother – who had made a significant contribution in their own area.

As with the rest of us, much of her character was already in her genes and several of her most notable traits came directly from her mother who, especially when young, was an attractive, unorthodox and very determined woman. Josslyn, while inheriting some of the same genes, was quite different from Constance, being quiet and shy, characteristics that tended to conceal his remarkable success in raising the family estate to an extraordinary peak of performance. A significant measure of this success stemmed from his ability, inherited from his father, to plan meticulously, a trait that eluded Constance completely. She certainly inherited at least one other of Sir Henry's great strengths, his seemingly inexhaustible energy, about which George Russell once wrote that she 'was gifted with energy which would never let her be still.'

Writing about Alice Stopford Green, a daughter of a Church of Ireland archdeacon, Roy Foster might almost have had Constance in mind when he noted that 'she may be seen as a representative of those Ascendancy Irish whose insecurity drove them to extremes of identification.' Though several writers have described Constance as the 'Joan of Arc of Ireland,' this appellation more properly belonged to Maud Gonne. Even so, it underlines the fact that these two women had so much in common. Foster thought that both Maud Gonne and Constance Markievicz exemplified 'a sort of *trahison des debutantes* which gave Gonne a conviction and base [to a] restless and insecure spirit.' Both had been good-looking 'upper class rebels' who had sought out nationalists but were initially met with some suspicion. It is equally true to state that – like Gonne – Constance had a 'capacity to inspire devotion and a deep belief in self-sacrifice [which] would create for her a unique place in Irish public life.' Her work for the poor in Dublin's slums is difficult to quantify, perhaps because those who benefited were unlikely to be able to leave behind them any significant record of her activities. However, the impressive representation of those voiceless people along the streets of the city during her funeral was mute testimony in itself. During her last years, she spent almost recklessly on these activities what remained of her dwindling resources, neglecting both herself and her health.

She gave her all in the cause of Republicanism and paid heavily for her endeavours, serving a whole series of prison sentences and spending several long periods 'on the run.' The word 'sacrifice' features strongly in the annals of the Rising and is used almost invariably in references to the executed leaders. Writing about the events at St Stephen's Green in 1916, Elizabeth Bowen suggested that: 'With those who died for this country, on the gallows, in battle, or by the bullets of execution squads, must be counted those who died of broken hearts.' Constance Markievicz did not die before a firing squad, but is it altogether too fanciful to make the point (even if many may not agree) that she and some others may have made an even greater sacrifice than those leaders who died?

A young Constance (right), photographed c.1884, with Mordaunt, Eva, and Mabel. Josslyn is in the background.

The sacrifice made by Constance, and the sacrifice endured by the widows and children of those who were shot, continued for so much longer. Michael Mallin's widow, for example, was expecting the birth of their baby when he was executed, and was left to cope alone for the rest of her life. Patrick Pearse was dead four days after his surrender, and he died with his ideals and his hopes for Ireland intact. It was Mary Colum who wrote that, unlike Yeats, Patrick Pearse 'did not live long enough to be disillusioned with mankind.' Constance survived for 11 more years, living a life of self-sacrifice and relative poverty. She lived on to witness partition and the country's descent into a terrible civil war which was, in turn, followed by her party's exclusion – if that is the correct term – not only from government but also from the Dáil itself. In a sense, but only in this particular sense, did she not, indeed, sacrifice more than Pearse? In his poem, Easter 1916, W.B. Yeats mentioned McDonagh, MacBride, Connolly and Pearse by name, though not Markievicz, but he might have had her in mind too when he composed the lines: 'Too long a sacrifice / Can make a stone of the heart.'

Yeats, who had been besotted with the young Constance and Eva, the two attractive sisters at Lissadell, wrote bitter verses about Constance in her later life, and about what he saw as the downfall of a beautiful and courageous woman:

> That woman's days were spent
> In ignorant goodwill,
> Her nights of argument
> Until her voice grew shrill.
> What voice more sweet than hers
> When, young and beautiful,
> She rode to harriers.

These lines were penned despite the fact that several writers, including William Trevor, credited Yeats with influencing Constance with 'his nationalism'. Trevor might have been writing about her rather than about Lady Gregory when he made the comment that it was common among spirited women of the time to demand 'more of life than hunting and housekeeping.'

Just five years after her death, the first of more than a half a dozen biographies was published and in it, Sean O'Faoláin's frank opinions caused quite a stir. J.M. Hone, reviewing the book for *The Spectator*, considered that her work with Fianna Éireann 'was her one personal contribution to extremism but, as her biographer admits, little of her work in any field of organisation survives, even as a memory.' He went on to state as his view that:

> She accomplished no task of either intellectual or practical importance …. Restless and excitable, quite devoid of fear, a lover of adventure and of the limelight, un-subdued to the conditions of her sex – and to the social conventions, she might – born in any other country of a similar aristocratic parentage – have given herself up equally to the cultivation, in the form of extreme action, of humanitarian and socialist ideals. But in no country but Ireland could she have come to cut a serious figure in revolutionary politics.

Postage stamp issued to commeroate the centenary of Constance Markievicz's birth.

Reviewing the same biography for *The Irish Times*, Cathal O'Shannon wrote:

> To readers to whom Madame was a political idol, this book will be a provocation; to those who did not share her ideas or her dreams, it may well be a delight; to the multitude who are interested only in her name, it will supply material for no small amusement.

O'Shannon accused O'Faoláin of basing his account of her connection with the Citizen Army on Sean O'Casey's book which, he claimed, was 'incomplete.' O'Faoláin subsequently made a response in defence of his book in the same newspaper, stating that he had presented Constance Markievicz:

> as a woman who was a fool and a heroine, as a woman who drove down bravely from the remote heights of the big houses to the very popular Irish aspirations, as a woman who did so because she had fine instincts, a big heart and a warm

human sympathy…. When Nationalistic symbolism subsided after the civil war, she began then, and only then, to think hard – as hard as she could think, poor muddled soul – but she died before she could think her way out of the jungle of her dreams – a sad figure, because her life was never rounded in the end.'

In the Preface to the 1967 re-print of his biography, Sean O'Faoláin noted that a second biography of Constance Markievicz had just been published – written by Anne Marreco. He welcomed this development saying that 'two points of view are better than one … for, whatever else one may think of Con Markievicz – even when we have given full weight to all her fancies, and follies, and fanaticism … we may all agree that she was one of the most gallant creatures …' The publication of Marreco's biography almost coincided with another, written by Jacqueline Van Voris and both were reviewed together by Benedict Kiely for *The Irish Times*. He sympathised with Constance's parents in their concern over their daughter's determination to study art in Paris, viewing it as almost chilling that she 'could have fitted-in with some of the lymphatic women interested in art that drift lonely as clouds through some of Moore's shorter fiction and autobiographical books.' And, after returning to Dublin:

> her marriage had not been an absolute success and she had not succeeded either as an actress or a painter…. Did she dread … the prospect of admitting failure before the family? The truth would seem to be simply that she was a generous impulsive girl, that she cared for the poor … and that in the Dublin of the early twentieth century it was damnably obvious that the poor needed somebody to care for them.

* * *

A memorial to Constance Markievicz, in the form of a limestone bust portraying her in her Fianna uniform, was unveiled by Éamon de Valera in St Stephen's Green, Dublin, in July 1932. In his oration he said that:

> To many she was simply a strange figure, following a path of her own, and not accustomed paths…. She was not content to see misery about her without striving to remedy it…. That is why she took her place there among the men in Easter Week, 1916. The glamour that followed 1916 did not take her away from the poor. She stood with the poor and with the poor she died, and it was the poor, mainly, who followed her to the grave.

As noted by Sighle Bhreathnach-Lynch in a chapter contributed to Lawrence W. McBride's book, *Irish Images and Icons*, the original memorial, carved by Albert Power, was partly damaged by vandals in 1945 and more seriously so two years later. A replacement bust, the work of Seamus Murphy, R.H.A., was subsequently erected on the same site. Seventy-six years after her death, a 20-foot bronze memorial to her memory was erected at Rathcormac, a few miles from Lissadell. It was unveiled by Seamus Brennan, Minister for Transport, who described Constance as 'a remarkable woman, and one of the outstanding social and historical figures in our history.'

George Russell, who encouraged Eva's early ventures into poetry, penned verses described by Mary Colum as 'that lovely lament for all lost dreams, for all unrealised desire.' It could almost have been an epitaph for Constance:

> Be not so desolate
> Because thy dreams have flown,
> And the hall of the heart is empty
> And silent as stone …
>
> Thy gentlest dreams, thy failures,
> Even those that were
> Born and lost in a heartbeat,
> Shall meet thee there.
> They are become immortal
> In shining air …

—Eva Gore-Booth (1871–1925)

EVA

'Even worms shall have wings'

Eva Selina Gore-Booth was born in 1870, two years after Constance and a year after Josslyn. The three elder children of Sir Henry and Lady Georgina Gore-Booth grew up very much aware of the other Ireland that lay outside the estate walls at Lissadell. Like her elder sister and brother, Eva clearly recalled – although she was only nine at the time – the scenes during the famine winter of 1879-80. All three were profoundly affected by the memories of starving tenants coming to Lissadell House for food and clothing – scenes that their parents wanted their children to remember. Constance and Eva were educated by several governesses – notably Miss Noel, who taught them Latin, Greek, French and German, and instilled in them an interest in art and literature. The two girls were very pretty and Eva, who was sometimes a sickly child and given to daydreaming, had a wistful look which tended to enhance her appearance. When describing Emmeline, one of the characters in her novel, *To the North*, Elizabeth Bowen might almost have been writing about Eva Gore-Booth, characterising her as angelic, ethereal, not quite of this world, spiritual – and short-sighted too. Recalling Eva as a child, Miss Noel was to write:

> That wonderful part of the West of Ireland, with all its legends and history which she adored, must have formed her mind more than anything. How her writings bring back memories of the days spent by the Atlantic, and the happy times when we tramped about wild places.... Of course, her pre-conscious mind was storing up so much more than we dreamed ... [She was] a very fair and fragile child, most unselfish and gentle, with the general look of a Burne-Jones or Botticelli angel. As she was two years younger than Constance and always so delicate, she had been, I think, rather in the background and a little lonely mentally, but music was a great joy to her. The symbolic side of religion had just then a great charm for her, and always of course the mystical side of everything appealed most. Though her sight was always poor, she was an absolutely fearless rider.

Fearless horsewomen in the Gore-Booth family were two a penny it seems. When the two sisters grew older, she rode with Constance to a Land League meeting at Boyle, more than 30 miles away, where they openly declared that they were on the side of the people and against class privilege. Eva immersed herself in folk history, reading the legends about Queen Maeve, whose reputed tomb is visible from Lissadell; and about the tales of the Sidhe, the entrance to whose kingdom was said to have been on the side of Ben Bulben. She knew the stories about Diarmuid and Gráinne, and how the former was killed by a boar near that same summit, and how the two lovers were buried together down-slope in Gleniff.

Later, as she became interested in spiritual matters, she read about the Irish saints including Columcille who founded the monastic settlement at nearby Drumcliff. Esther Roper, who came to know Eva better than anyone else, wrote that she was 'possessed by a passionate adoration of beauty in all its forms' and was absorbed by what she was to later call 'inner things.' Among examples cited is the story told about how Eva once walked for days with sharp stones in her shoes without apparently noticing them at all, while she herself once said that she would sometimes ride for a whole morning and, on her return, not know where she had been. It is not difficult to see here the seeds of her interest in mysticism and spiritualism that were to become evident in her later writings in both poetry and prose. One of Eva's Manchester friends, Margaret Wroe, recalled their first meeting:

> The first time I remember seeing Eva Gore-Booth ... she was reading as she walked, holding the book close up to her eyes, for she was very near sighted .... She always left the world of incident for the world of thought whenever she had the least excuse ... She always gave me the impression that she was struggling to understand and explain to herself her own inner life, which she came to believe was not a matter of earth life, but of many, and through her own experience to find a key to the problems of the world....

Once, when very young she was discovered taking off her coat to give to a child by the roadside, and nothing could persuade her that this was wrong. She also recalled how Eva, as she grew into a beautiful young woman, began reading widely, especially English and German literature. There are some vague hints that there may have been some lack of feeling between Eva and her mother – perhaps due to a parental difficulty in coping with a dreamy daughter. On the other hand, she had found consolation in the company of her adored grandmother, with whom she discussed both mystical and religious feelings, later describing her thinking at this time (in the third person) as follows:

> She had realised clearly and practically the fact of death ... a sense of ... some life in the world beyond the senses ... [and] she put it into clumsy words that

half shocked herself. Now I understand it all, and it's delightful to die, and wonderful to think of anybody being dead.

Eva and Constance spent long days together, the latter already interested in painting and sketching, while Eva read aloud 'poetry, philosophy, history – indeed any book of interest that she could find.' In her book *Poems of Eva Gore-Booth*, published in 1929, Esther Roper wrote in the introduction that Eva 'grew up on terms of sympathy and friendship with the peasants. Her father prided himself that, however bad the relationship between landlords and tenants elsewhere, at Lissadell at any rate there was never any trouble.'

Though younger than Constance, there can be little doubt that, as Eva grew older, she came to have a greater influence on her sister than vice-versa, and it is interesting to note that one writer described Eva as 'the other rebel sister.' Her rebelliousness, however, took an altogether different form from that adopted by Constance, for while it is certainly true that she shared her older sister's sense of nationalism, as a committed pacifist she was to disagree strongly with Constance's involvement in the use of force.

Esther Roper regretted that there was so very little on the record about her friend's childhood, but it is thanks to Miss Noel that most of what is now known about her early years has been recorded. Miss Noel, with whom Eva continued to have a very friendly relationship over many years, recalled that when Constance was taken to London by her mother for her 'coming out,' she stayed with Eva for several months. When it came to Eva's turn to be a debutante, Miss Noel remembered that, unlike Constance: 'Society of the fashionable kind did not, I think, ever appeal much to her, though she loved congenial people and much enjoyed the great concerts, Handel Festivals, etc.' Esther Roper was of the opinion that the young Eva was 'haunted by the suffering of the world, and had a curious feeling of responsibility for its inequalities and injustices.' The Dutch-born writer and journalist, Kees van Hoek, described her as 'a great patriotic descendant of an old planter's family.' He related how, when visiting an inmate at the Sligo Infirmary, Eva asked an old lady to tell her something of her youth. As the woman told her tale of the bad old times, one of the nurses tried to intervene, but Eva insisted on hearing the full story because 'I like to realise what we have to make good.'

She clearly recalled the kindness shown by both her father and mother to the tenants, and she must also have known something of what her grandparents had done for the starving people during the Great Famine.

Even so, her growing understanding of Irish history gradually led her to a disenchantment with her own society. Perhaps something of this was expressed in her poem 'The Land to a landlord:'

> You hug to your soul a handful of dust
> and you think the round world your saved trust …
> The bracken waves and the foxgloves flame
> and none of them ever heard your name …
> Near and dear is the curlew's cry,
> you are the stranger passing by …

The poet Yeats became infatuated with the young Eva – and with Constance too – but he felt inhibited by his own sense that, as Roy Foster wrote, 'the lifestyle at Lissadell was at a level to which Yeats's family did not aspire.' Consequently, 'his own social as well as his personal inhibitions … kept him at a certain distance from the Gore-Booths.' Despite this, Foster added, the poet breached this gap 'through the power of art' and also because of what Yeats saw as 'the Gore-Booth enthusiasm for the *avant garde.*' Perhaps his infatuation with Eva and Constance came to nothing simply because neither Constance nor Eva was seriously interested in marriage, but he organised seances for the sisters and, more importantly, began to give helpful critical advice to Eva concerning her efforts at composing verse.

Sir Henry went on an extensive tour of the West Indies, the United States and Canada during 1894, accompanied by Eva. When returning eastwards from Vancouver by rail through the Rocky Mountains, their train was delayed for several days because some bridges had been washed away during flooding, as mentioned in an earlier chapter. After several days of waiting for the bridges to be repaired, she became tired of admiring the striking scenery through the window of a railway carriage. She decided to see some of it at closer quarters and left the train to better enjoy the views, notwithstanding that warnings had been given to passengers to stay in the train because there were bears about. She followed a track through the forest, bringing with her a book and a packed lunch. After several hours of exhilarating walking through the sweet-smelling conifers, enjoying the beautiful trees, flowers, butterflies and scenery, she became aware that someone was following her, and saw that it was a tramp. As she quickened her pace, so did he, so she decided to jump into the undergrowth in the hope that he would pass her by. Instead, she soon saw the tramp's face peering at her through the bushes and was surprised when he asked her if she knew where she was. She had no idea, but as he seemed friendly she offered to share her lunch with him. As they sat eating, he told her that she was the first person he had spoken to for several months. When they finished eating he led her back to the stranded train where she discovered that some of the men had set out looking for her, fearing that she might make a fatal encounter with a bear. She survived, unlike any record of what her father had to say about the incident.

A year after this, Eva and Constance accompanied their mother on a visit to the annual Wagner Festival at Bayreuth, and while in Bavaria they travelled further south to Oberammergau where they attended a performance of the famous passion play staged there every 10 years. Eva was back in Europe soon after this for health reasons, threatened with consumption. When she arrived in Venice, she was given the alarming news that she was seriously ill and was advised to stay for the winter in the Mediterranean climate.

Constance and Eva, the famous portrait by Sarah Purser
(*Reproduced by kind permission of Michael Purser*)

While still recuperating, she strolled around a beautiful garden at Bordeghera, near San Remo, overlooking the Ligurian Gulf in northern Italy where she met Esther Roper, a young Englishwoman, a chance meeting that was to have a profound effect on the lives of both women. Esther and Eva quickly found that they had much in common besides poor health. They spent a delightful period in Italy and began a friendship which was to last for more than 30 years. Eva recalled that fateful encounter in verse:

> Was it not strange that by the tideless sea
> The jar and hurry of our lives should cease,
> That under olive boughs we found our peace
> And all the world's great song in Italy?

Both had been staying in a house, Casa Corragio, built about 15 years earlier by George MacDonald, a philosopher and evangelical preacher. He kept an open door for the local villagers, for friends, and for unknown guests including those who wished to recover their health. It was for this latter reason that the two women stayed there and, as Eva wrote later: 'Each was attracted to the other, and we became friends and companions for life.' Roseangela Barone likened the fateful meeting to 'the acorn buried in the earth ... ready to turn into an oak.' Eva's lines on the same theme ran:

> The acorn is a common thing and small,
> Child of the sun, and plaything of the wind,
> You think it is of no account at all,
> Yet at its heart great forces crash and grind.

Barone was one of a number of people who saw Eva as a Botticelli-like figure, comparing her to Constance, 'a Rosetti-like figure, exuberant, racy, bewitching.' She noted that the contrast between the two sisters 'sharpened as the years went by, due to the different paths chosen by the two sisters,' but despite this, as she wrote, they remained 'indissolubly tied to each other.'

Fascinated by Esther's account of her work in England for underprivileged women, Eva returned to Lissadell determined to work alongside her new companion. Less than a year later she joined her friend in Manchester, and set about her new goal of campaigning for women's rights in an area where, coincidentally, her own family had strong connections. The fact that there were many Booth relations in the area may well have been a factor in avoiding an outright confrontation with her parents over leaving Lissadell. Nevertheless, they were dismayed when she decided to leave home in 1897, and found it hard to credit that she chose Manchester with its frequent fogs and its smoke-laden air as her new home. Through the Booth connections, Sir Henry continued to have the gift of the living (that is, he could appoint the rector) of the Sacred Trinity Church, Salford in Greater Manchester, and he had appointed his own uncle, the Reverend Henry Francis Gore-Booth to the post two years earlier. Thousands of Eva's great-uncle's parishioners were extremely poor and his work among them very probably made a deep impression on her.

The illness that had brought Eva and Esther together in Italy turned out not to be consumption after all, but Eva continued to suffer from poor health. While she probably hid her real feelings from her parents, she sometimes yearned for the clean, fresh air of Lissadell and for all the places in that neighbourhood she loved so much.

Esther, a committed suffragist, was convinced that Lancashire was the natural home of the women's movement and must have convinced Eva that this was so, claiming that the women there 'are among the most skilled and talented of the country's workers.'

Although Eva often gave the impression that her mind was on ethereal matters, she was, nevertheless, a very practical person. She continued to busy herself writing, especially poetry, and she published her first book of verse later that same year. She sent a copy to Yeats who wrote to her saying 'I think it is full of poetic feeling and has great promise.' He was especially impressed by her poem 'Weariness,' regarding it as 'really most imaginative and is, I think, in the mood in which you are yourself. The last four lines are really magical.' Those four lines read:

> The stars are what the flowers seem,
> And where the sea of thoughts is deep,
> The moonlight glitters like a dream,
> On weary waters gone to sleep.

Yeats's letter of advice and encouragement ran to five pages. His amorous interest had long since been switched to Olivia Shakespeare (whom one of his sisters described as 'Willy's latest admiration, very pretty, young and nice') and who, the poet thought, bore a resemblance to Eva Gore-Booth. Eva, for her part, greatly respected Yeats and invariably sent him a copy of her latest work for appraisal. On this occasion he advised her to: 'Try always to express and to symbolise an emotion, as you have done in there [the four last lines] remembering that description, thought, and fancy, and all the rest can only be used in poetry as a means to this end, and never as an end.' He went on to say of her verses:

> The defect of your work is that your thought, as apart from your feeling, is still too slight, too pretty, too phantastical … I, in fact, agree with what Russell said in his review of your book in the [Daily] Express, except that I think that your power is wholly lyrical, that you would do well with lyrics made out of the old Celtic legends and memories, but not with Celtic stories.

George Russell had written to compliment her on the volume, adding:

> I am sure you have it in you to do still better work. You do not suggest an unexhausted fountain. I think if you lived here [in Ireland] among people who are thinking like you and trying to express the same life, you would find the companionship good for your work, and pleasant as well. I know you feel bound to your work in Manchester, but if ever there was a place which needs a champion of women it is Ireland.

If Russell wanted her to return to Ireland, it was Yeats who first put the idea of going to England into her head. Later, he was greatly disappointed when he realised that her new-found interests in feminism and women's trade unions were occupying her mind to the detriment, as he saw it, of her poetry. Writing to an American publisher (in a letter quoted by Alan Denison in his book of collected letters written by George Russell), A.E. thought:

> She really is of the order of poets. She is the daughter of Sir Henry Gore-Booth, and has chosen to desert the most beautiful home in Ireland to work among the factory girls in Manchester. A tall slim defiant girl with enough ideas to stock half a dozen poetesses but too defiant of her technique at present to do the perfect things she might.

Reviewing her first book, *The Irish Times* predicted that it would 'some day be sought and prized by the collector of first editions.' While the reviewer went on praise some of the poems, he thought that others were 'hardly robust enough to bear transplanting into a permanent position; they suggest an over-potted seedling which, as gardeners know, will mysteriously dwindle, peak and pine, in its too spacious abode.' The anonymous reviewer considered that 'Miss Gore-Booth shows that her ear for rhythm and rhyme is fine and true, though in metre her weakest point seems to be an occasional tendency to intersperse her Heroics with Alexandrines and Octosyllabics.'

Perhaps because Eva anticipated some less than enthusiastic reviews, she inserted the following adaptation from Lessing on the first page of her book:

If, Reader, for these poems you should lack
All sense of gratitude, all words of praise,
At least you might be thankful for the lays
that I kept back.

Russell's suggestion that she should have considered returning to Ireland to concentrate on Celtic themes is interesting, raising the question whether Eva might, in that event, have gone on to become not a minor but a major poet. He correctly guessed, however, that her friendship with Esther Roper and her commitment to working for various women's causes in Manchester were too strong to allow her to leave England. The heart of industrial England may have been a world away from Lissadell, but this proved no insuperable barrier for Eva who could, in a flight of imagination, be there in an instant.

At Clitheroe through the sunset hour
My soul was far away,
I saw Ben Bulben's rose and fire
Shining afar o'er Sligo Bay.

Her close relationship with Esther may have raised a few eyebrows, even if the two women showed no self-consciousness about their feelings towards one another. Certainly Gifford Lewis, their biographer – who considered this aspect of their lives in some depth – concluded that there was nothing physical in their friendship, and the late Fennor Brockway, who worked for a time with the two women, told Gifford Lewis, that relationships such as theirs in the suffrage movement were not unusual and no one thought anything of it. In his view, there was simply nothing suggestive of passion in it and it is clear that they respected each other's privacy. Martin Pugh, a biographer of the Pankhursts, made the point that women at that time, with limited financial means and who wanted to live independent lives, found their situation fraught with difficulties which they overcame by living together, thus sharing not only experiences but expenses too. Pugh added: 'Sex was not a particularly important element in lives that were filled with a full range of interests, political causes and friendships.'

Only a small minority of men supported the campaign for women's rights but it is also the case that the movement lacked universal support among women. Eva may not have been anti-male, though it is clear that she could equate men with pomp, power and pride, and saw women in a very different light, as depicted in her poem 'Women's Rights:'

> Oh, whatever men may say
> Ours is the wide and open way.
> Oh, whatever men may dream
> We have the blue air and the stream.
> Men have got their towers and walls
> We have cliffs and waterfalls…
> Men have got their pomp and pride –
> All the green world is on our side.

The male-dominated churches may not have been helpful either. Fintan O'Toole has written about Bishop Edward O'Dwyer, who in his 1912 Lenten pastoral stated that the question of votes for women had hitherto been 'merely academic' and had simply provoked 'a smile of amusement rather than serious consideration.' He felt sure that most women would regard the idea that they should have the vote 'as an absurdity' and be glad that Catholic reverence for women had 'restricted the activities of woman's life to the peace and quiet of her home. She was made by God too frail, too delicate, too good, to mix with the rough ways of men in the world.' O'Toole's comment was that 'on the streets, however, the women of the Franchise League were perfectly capable of mixing with the world.'

According to Ben Levitas, when the Women's Social and Political Union was founded by Emmeline Pankhurst in 1903, Hanna Sheehy Skeffington, was inspired to establish the Irish Women's Franchise League with the help of Margaret Cousins, forming a franchise movement 'with a distinctly militant strain of Irish feminism.' Sheehy Skeffington's involvement was also mentioned by Carmel Quinlan, who noted that she first became aware of the work of another prominent worker for the cause, Anna Haslam, 'through Esther Roper – Eva Gore-Booth's friend.' Anna Haslam and her husband Thomas, a Quaker couple, were seen as examples of those who were deeply involved in the Irish suffrage movement but despite the fact that they worked diligently for the cause, their place in recorded Irish history 'has been minor to the point of invisibility.'

Quinlan blamed this state of affairs on the fact that the work of such women in that era 'has been dominated by the nationalist agenda and by the women of Inghinidhe na hÉireann and Cumann na mBan [so that]

Anna Haslam cannot hope to compete with Maud Gonne McBride or Countess Markievicz as a national icon.' Eva and Esther not only supported the franchise movements but also the women trade unionists in their campaigns to obtain decent wages for the thousands of poorly paid female mill-workers. Eva went further by encouraging women to raise their perception of themselves, and she organised evening classes for this purpose.

This idea later blossomed into what was called the University Settlement in the slums of Manchester, based on the model established in one of the poorest areas of London as a memorial to the historian, Arnold Toynbee who had worked there. The University Settlement in the Round House at Ancoats Hall in Manchester attracted university men and women who wanted to give practical help to working class people. Converted from a chapel built in 1821, only the round outer walls of the old building were serviceable. As noted by Eva, she found herself almost totally absorbed in the re-building project, becoming one of what some people called 'the Toynbee Cranks'. She personally organised literature and music classes for the women, introducing them to the works of writers like Shakespeare, Shelley, and Emerson and, given the underprivileged background of most of the women, she was surprised and encouraged by the response. Two decades after these classes were discontinued, she received a letter of appreciation from a Helen Atkinson:

> It had been quite a pleasure to me ... to recall the old days when I attended your Sunday morning reading classes at Ancoats. Two of the things that I have found the lack of in London – the reading classes in the morning of a Sunday, and the musical afternoons at the [Round] Hall.

Eva also formed a dramatic society for the women, which was also recalled in nostalgic terms many years later by another of its former members, Louisa Smith:

> We called ourselves the Elizabethan Society.... We were very raw material but keen on acting; she showed such patience and love that we would do anything to please her and she got the best out of us .... We thought she was a being from another world. I don't think I exaggerate when I say we say we worshipped her, but she never knew it. She was so utterly selfless.... She took us on picnics, and they seemed to be different picnics from any I had ever been to, so jolly and free, no restraint about them.... She was very frail and delicate herself, but full of pluck and determination ... and, withal, so sweet and gentle that one could not help loving her.

Besides these activities, she found time to become involved as the representative for the Women's Trade Union Council on the Technical Institution Committee of Manchester City Council and she joined in a campaign to prevent the exclusion of girls from scholarships at the Municipal School of Technology.

The circle in which Eva moved was distinctly unorthodox, and although she and all the others involved in the various schemes insisted that progress to achieve all their aims had to be achieved by peaceful means, many outsiders looked upon them as unfeminine and disruptive. Mrs Sarah Dickenson, with whom Eva shared the secretaryship of the Manchester and Salford Women's T.U.C. in 1900, later wrote that her first impression of Eva was that she had a 'charming and interesting personality.' As she got to know Eva better, she found:

> all the beautiful traits in her character. The friendly way that she treated all the women trade unionists endeared herself to them. If she was approached for advice or help, she never failed. She is remembered by thousands of working women for her untiring efforts to improve their industrial conditions, for awakening and educating their sense of political freedom, and for social intercourse.

When the women's labour movement established its own newspaper, *The Women's Labour News*, Eva became its editor, and she outlined the aims of the publication in its first issue:

> To light a few street lamps here and there in the darkest ways, to let us at all events see one another's faces and recognise our comrades and work together with strong, organised and enlightened effort for the uplifting of those who suffer most under the present political and industrial system.

Time and again, Eva found herself called upon to speak on behalf of women workers and the suffrage movement so that addressing audiences, large and small, represented no problem to her. One of the most important of these occasions occurred in 1906 when she was chosen to join a deputation which was confident that it could finally persuade Sir Henry Campbell-Bannerman, the Liberal Prime Minister, to grant the vote to women. Gifford Lewis's biography of Eva and her friend Esther Roper records Eva's contribution, one of nearly a dozen made on that occasion, in which after explaining her own involvement, she went on:

> What we want to put before you is this. The number of women who are engaged at this time in producing the wealth of this country is double the population of Ireland. This is a very large number. These women are all labouring under gross

disability and disadvantage of an absolute want of political power. Every day we live, this becomes a grave disadvantage because industrial questions are becoming political questions which are being fought out in Parliament. The vast number of women workers have their point of view … but these interests are not considered and the whole effect of their crushing exclusion is to react on the question of their wages. We feel … that our industrial status is being brought down. It results from the fact that we have no political power. That is the lesson that the working women of Lancashire have learned, and that is the thought they want to bring before you to consider … that they cannot wait.

Eva's delegation had set out with high hopes, but returned from the meeting with the Prime Minister bitterly disappointed. Some of the members blamed the lack of any positive response on Mrs Pankhurst's high-profile acts of violence. The split down the middle in the franchise movement over whether or not constitutional methods alone would produce the desired results, echoed a similar dilemma for Irish politics a decade later. As Lewis expressed it: 'While Eva had been toiling in committee rooms and arguing, arguing, arguing, Constance was teaching her Irish boy scouts to shoot, and was preparing to serve in an armed uprising against the Crown.'

Mrs Emmeline Pankhurst, born in Manchester of parents who had already been advancing the cause of women's franchise, founded the Women's Franchise League in 1889 and was one of the founders of the powerful Woman's Social and Political Union. Two of her daughters, Christabel and Sylvia, were also deeply involved in the movement, one faction of which later became increasingly militant, its members setting fire to letter boxes, damaging golf courses and breaking windows in public buildings. Eva totally disapproved such violence and, while Pankhurst's group claimed a membership of nearly 10,000 at the turn of the century, Esther Roper, Eva Gore-Booth and their non-militant followers were able to muster three times that number of signatures in favour of their campaign in 1901.

It was in that year that Eva and Esther first met Mrs Pankhurst's twenty-year-old daughter, Christabel, who was so captivated by the two women that she joined in their activities, including a poetry course organised by Eva. June Purvis, who commented that spinsters were the backbone of the women's movement, also credited Eva and Esther with promoting Christabel's initial training in suffrage activism. Sylvia Pankhurst wrote that her mother 'was intensely jealous of her daughter's new friendship' and she described Eva as 'a minor poet of some distinction.'

In his biography of the family, Martin Pugh wrote that Esther and Eva were 'two remarkable and talented women [who] were to be so influential in Christabel Pankhurst's personal and political development.' She even joined them for a holiday in Italy, but when the campaign to obtain voting rights for women appeared to be getting nowhere, she began to adopt some of her mother's violent methods and the friendship ended. Not long after this, however, Christabel and a fellow suffragist interrupted an election meeting at which Winston Churchill was one of the speakers, as a result of which police ejected the two women from the hall. Christabel spat at one of the officers, a technical assault that earned the pair a brief imprisonment. Eva and Esther, despite their abhorrence of any form of militancy, met the two women on their release and presented them with flowers. However, the extinction of a blossoming friendship between Eva and Christabel caused some to suggest that a poem written by Eva at this time alluded to this parting of the ways:

> The Lamp has gone out of your eyes,
> The ashes are cold in your heart,
> Yet you smile indifference – wise,
> Thought I depart, though I depart.

During 1903, Esther and Eva formed a new organisation, the Lancashire and Cheshire and Other Worker's Committee, which had 'womanhood suffrage' as its principle object. This new body, as Ina Zweinige-Bargielowskia noted: 'signalled that the demands of the [earlier] National Union appeared too narrow to many working class women who found increasingly uncertain … support for women's suffrage within the labour and socialist movement.' Another writer, Bertha Mason, described the work being done by Eva Gore-Booth and her friends as being:

Chiefly responsible for the wonderful revival of interest in the question of the enfranchisement of women…. There can be no doubt that … this [work] made a deep impression on Parliament, and caused many who had hitherto treated the agitation as an 'impractical fad' and 'the fantastic crochet' of a few rich and well-to-do women, to enquire seriously into the why and wherefore of the movement.

* * *

Eva published her second book, *Unseen Kings*, in 1904, a volume that included a play about the death of Cuchulainn, along with a collection of poetry which had been previously published in various periodicals. George Russell considered that Eva's verse output 'had increased greatly in power and there is a continuous swing or ecstasy in the sound.' He wrote to Eva, congratulating her on a play which, he thought, 'would do admirably for the Red Branch Cycle performances we hope to have in the autumn here.' His intention was to have 'Unseen Kings' performed along with Douglas Hyde's 'The Tinker and the Fairy,' and with Yeats' 'Kathleen ni Houlihan.' However, it was rejected by the Abbey Theatre and was eventually staged by Casimir Markievicz in 1911 – the only one of her five verse plays to be performed.

Later in the same year she published *The One and the Many*, a further collection of verse which included her best known work, 'The Little Waves of Breffni,' the latter written during a brief holiday at Lissadell. It was widely praised at the time, and when the book was reviewed in *The Manchester Guardian*, the Breffni poem was seen as 'one of the most beautiful things that any writer bar none in the new Irish movement has produced.' Kathleen Tynan thought that it 'will go singing in the human heart so long as the heart answers to poetry.' George Russell told Eva that its lines demonstrated that she had, as he expressed it, 'slipped into it at last – the Celtic manner.... It ought to be natural for you to do so – a West of Ireland woman and County Sligo at that.' More than 30 years later, after Esther Roper published *The Selected Poems of Eva Gore-Booth*, *The Manchester Guardian*, noting the little poem's inclusion described it then as 'a tiny lyric ... which is the extent of most people's knowledge of her, and is, of course, a beautiful incantation, and admitted her at once to the Celtic heritage....'

1905 saw the publication of *The Three Resurrections and The Triumph of Maeve* – a further collection of poems and a play. 'The Triumph of Maeve' related the Celtic story of Queen Maeve's daughter Fionavar who was the warrior queen's great joy in life. After returning from battle, Fionavar began reflecting upon the scenes of death and pain she had witnessed, and suddenly fell dead in front of her mother, crying bitterly, 'Is this the triumph of Maeve?' Her death fulfilled a prophesy that she would die in battle – not of wounds but of pity for the men slaughtered. Fionavar's death instantly changed her mother's attitude, causing the warrior queen to abandon fighting and to give up her kingdom in order to find her own soul.

To Constance.

Outcast from joy and beauty, child of broken
                              hopes forlorn
Lost to the magic mountains and parted from
                         all flowers
Robbed of the Harvest Moon that shines on far off
                         fields of corn
Bereft of raindrops on green leaves, bright
                    wrecks of fallen showers

Nay not outcast whilst through your soul a
                         sudden rapture thrills
And all your dreams are shaken by the salt
                              Atlantic wind
The gods descend at twilight from the
                              magic hearted hills
And there are swords and primroses in the
                    country of your mind.

Your is that inner Ireland beyond green fields
                              or brown
                    Where waves break
                         dawn-enchanted on the
                         haunted Rosses shore
                    And clouds above Ben
                    Bulben fling their
                    coloured shadows down
                    Whilst little Rivers
                         shine and sink in
                              wet sands
                              at Crushmor.

Christmas card sent by Eva to her sister in prison,
in which she sketched Constance's image.

Eva re-published part of the work a decade later, in 1916, in an edition illustrated by Constance who was then serving a prison sentence in Aylesbury Jail. When Eva sent her a copy of the book, Constance commented: 'I love the book. It's a real joy.' She then added: 'They put the rose in the triangle on its side, didn't I put it upright?' Drawing attention to a printer's error, she made no comment on the theme of the play – forsaking violence. Reviewing this, the 1916 edition, *The New York Times* noted that there was 'something ironical about the fact that the illustrations in the pages of this most passionately pacific work should be made by so convinced and practical a direct actionist as Constance Markievicz.' George Russell told Eva that he liked it and asked: 'Do you not think you are drawing upon something ancestral in your emotions when you write in Irish themes? This is one of the most perfect poems I have read of yours.'

Eva's next work, *The Egyptian Pillar*, published in 1906, included her poem about Glencar Waterfall which, after Breffni, includes what are perhaps her best known lines, and this was followed a year later by *The Sorrowful Princess*. Besides her books, she was also contributing to various publications in Britain and Ireland, including *The Savoy*, *The Nineteenth Century*, *The Yellow Book*, *The New Ireland Review* and *The Irish Homestead*.

1912 saw the publication of *The Agate Lamp*, yet another collection of poems, including some based on paintings she had seen in Italy, drawing praise from George Russell who thought her poetry breathed 'the same eager adventure of the mind that inspires all Eva Gore-Booth's work.' Helen Nicholl, whom she came to know at this time, described Eva as 'a bright undaunted personality, someone who almost seemed to float in like a frail flower petal, but full of fun and sunshine, pleased with the smallest thing, adoring colours, constantly sketching us and delighting in our freedom ....'

Eva, whose poor health had caused her to meet Esther Roper in the first place, continued to suffer from bronchial problems in smoky Manchester and, in 1913, her health took a turn for the worse. The pair decided to move to London, hoping that the atmospheric conditions in the metropolis would be better than in the industrial midlands. They resumed campaigning for various women's causes and when the Great War commenced a year later their strong belief in pacifism led them into involvement with several new movements – including those founded to help conscientious objectors. They also supported the campaign opposing recruitment which involved, among other things, tearing down posters. Constance was doing the same in Dublin, though her motives were rather different, and while the two sisters were thus engaged, Josslyn – as already mentioned – was busily arranging the erection of recruitment posters around Sligo. Unlike Constance, Eva continued to keep in touch with Josslyn, and in some of her letters she thanked her brother for gifts of a pheasant or a grouse, or for plants and bulbs for the garden of the house she shared with Esther. Sometimes there were references in these letters to her financial difficulties and on at least one occasion she appealed to him for money to tide her over some particular difficulty.

A few months before the planned rebellion, Constance wrote a breezy letter to her sister, giving no hint of what was to come:

> Old Darling, For God's sake send a line and let us know you're all right …. Why don't you come over [to Dublin]? Get out of London anyhow, as you can't be doing any suffrage work at present. Here everything seems so quiet and peaceful. Except for money troubles one has nothing much to worry one. Best love, Darling – yrs. Con.

W.B. Yeats also wrote to Eva at this time, one sentence of which seems to have anticipated a phrase forming in his mind which differed only slightly from what was to emerge later as one of his best known lines: 'Your sister and yourself, two beautiful figures among the great trees of Lissadell, are among the dear memories of my youth.'

The 1916 Rising took most people by surprise and few more so than Eva Gore-Booth. Despite the close relationship between the two sisters and their regular and intimate correspondence, it seems that Constance gave no hint to Eva about the planned event or of her own intended involvement in it. No doubt it was essential that the preparations for the rebellion went ahead in great secrecy, but there is evidence that Constance was less than open – no doubt with good reason – with her sister even concerning some of what she had been doing during the previous seven or eight years.

Eva was, however, well aware of her sister's work among the Dublin poor – especially during the 1913 lockout, and she also knew of Constance's involvement with the trade unions and of her friendship with and admiration for James Connolly. Eva regarded Francis Sheehy Skeffington, a confirmed pacifist, as a kindred spirit and she had a great sympathy for the nationalist cause, though she continued to hope, like him, that it would follow a non-violent course.

It seems that the first news to reach Eva about Constance after

Easter Week concerned her impending court-martial. Certainly, Josslyn contacted Eva at this stage, as he did with many other people in a desperate bid to have the expected sentence commuted or, as Esther Roper wrote: 'to prevent the taking of vengeance.' Eva immediately wrote dozens of letters to people in England who might have had some influence – not only to intervene on behalf of her sister, but also to save the lives of the other leaders, though the time to organise anything was pathetically short. As soon as she heard that Constance had been reprieved she again lobbied influential friends, this time to try to get permission to visit her in prison, and she wrote a poem commemorating those who had been executed.

> No man shall deck their resting place with flowers;
> Behind a prison wall they stood to die,
> Yet in those tragic flowerless graves of ours
> Buried the broken dreams of Ireland lie.

Eva's reaction to Constance's predicament was totally characteristic; she literally dropped everything in order to hasten to her sister's side as soon as she had secured permission for a prison visit. She travelled from London with Esther and, joined by Susan Mitchell, they arrived at Mountjoy Jail only five days after Constance had been told of her reprieve. Eva wrote to ask Josslyn: 'Can you find out exactly what happened at the court-martial? I only heard half from Constance and we ought to know this to contradict the vile stories some people are inventing.' She subsequently described how they had to speak to Constance across a corridor while she stood facing them behind her cell door, watched by a wardress. The experience moved Eva to take up another cause, for the betterment of conditions for people in prison.

As already noted in the previous chapter, when Eva heard that Josslyn was going to be appointed administrator of Constance's affairs after her sentence had been commuted to life imprisonment, she was almost as annoyed about the matter as her sister. Neither of the women could understand why Eva should not have been nominated to look after Constance's personal affairs, with which she was much more familiar than Josslyn. In a letter to her brother, Eva made her views quite clear, pointing out that she had already been given detailed instructions by Constance about her business affairs including what she wanted done about her house and its contents. From the correspondence which ensued, it is obvious that Josslyn did not relish the task given him, especially when Eva pointedly made matters difficult for him by refusing, certainly at first, to pass her sister's instructions to him. She informed him that she could not give him the information he sought until he showed that Constance had agreed to this. For his part, Josslyn tried to explain that, because Constance was allowed only one letter each month, it seemed pointless to him to waste that rare opportunity in order to get information from Constance that he could so easily obtain from Eva. Letters between them got more and more convoluted and tetchy, forcing Josslyn to comment rather mildly: 'Things seem to be getting muddled.'

And so they were. Eva wanted to get on with clearing out her sister's plundered house which, following a search by police, had been broken into by vandals. She blamed the police for ransacking the house and for removing some of the contents, including paintings, though it seems more probable that most of the missing items (including plants from the garden and saucepans from the kitchen) were stolen by intruders who knew the house was unoccupied. Eva had to return to London, and wanted to give the keys of her sister's house to Susan Mitchell, as instructed by Constance, although she ended up giving them to Josslyn. He was being pressurised in turn by a solicitor seeking instructions about letting the house, as he had several potential clients including the stained glass artist, Harry Clarke. The solicitor seemed to have little idea of Josslyn's dilemma when he suggested that 'the only person who might question any decisions made would be your sister, Madam Markievicz … but under the circumstances, is she not likely to agree to everything you do for her?' Meanwhile, Susan Mitchell wrote to Josslyn to ask for the keys of the house so that she and Mrs Russell (A.E.'s wife) could sort out Constance's belongings 'and see to the packing and storing of furniture and paintings … and leaving it ready for the house agent.'

Eva identified with two people who had played different roles in the events leading to 1916 – Francis Sheehy Skeffington, as already mentioned, and Sir Roger Casement, both of whom she likened to Christ. Sheehy Skeffington was one of about 130 non-combatants killed in Dublin during the Easter Rising, but the circumstances of his death ensured that his name continued to be well remembered long after all the others had been forgotten. When he was returning home to Rathmines on the second day of the rebellion, there was sporadic sniper fire between British soldiers and the insurgents, based in and around Jacob's biscuit factory. He was arrested by two soldiers who brought him to Portobello Barracks for questioning, and two more men, Thomas Dickson and Patrick McIntyre, were shortly afterwards brought to the same guard room. Asked if he was 'a Sinn Feiner,' Sheehy Skeffington replied that while he was in sympathy with the movement he was not in favour of militarism. All three men were detained overnight, and on the following morning, an officer, Captain J.C. Bowen Colthurst, entered the guardroom and informed the Sergeant of the Guard: 'I am taking these prisoners out of the guardroom and I am going to shoot them, as I think it is the right thing to do.' Another officer present reported to the adjutant what he had heard but before any intervention could be organised, Captain Colthurst had already brought the three prisoners outside along with a firing party and, on his orders, the men were placed before a wall and shot dead.

Returning to the guardroom, Colthurst told the adjutant what he had done, explaining that he had just recently lost a brother in the war and that he was as good an Irishman as the men he had shot. Colthurst was subsequently tried by court martial and found guilty of the murder of the three prisoners, and was also found to be insane at the time and 'ordered to be detained in a criminal lunatic asylum during His Majesty's pleasure.'

Hannah Sheehy Skeffington corresponded occasionally with Constance and Eva as well as with Esther. All three women were heartbroken for Hannah over the circumstances of her husband's murder, whose only actions in the rebellion were his attempts to prevent looting. Eva must have approved of his earlier selfless act in resigning as Registrar of the Royal University, protesting over its refusal to recognise women graduates. On hearing of the death of Francis Sheehy Skeffington, she wrote:

> No green and poisonous wreath shall shade
> His brow, who dealt no death in any strife,
> Crown him with olive who was not afraid
> To join the desolate unarmed ranks of life …

Hannah wrote to Esther Roper years later, after Eva's death: 'She was such a rare fine spirit and she seemed to suffer acutely any wrong or injustice to others. I shall never forget her in those days after 1916, when she came over to see us in our desolation and to comfort us all she could.'

The story of Eva's other hero, Roger Casement, is too well known to require more than a brief repetition here. As it turned out, his involvement in the Rising was peripheral but, having landed in Kerry from a German submarine after organising an arms shipment, he was caught and taken to London where he was charged with high treason. When Eva was asked by his cousin, Gertrude Parry, if she would attend Casement's trial, Eva replied, 'I don't think I could bear to look on him thus. It would seem like going to stare at his misfortune.' When pressed further, she agreed to go, and attended Bow Street Police Court each day and Eva noted that despite his recent ordeal he presented a well-groomed and distinguished appearance. On the first day, Casement saw her sitting in the gallery, and when their eyes met he smiled and she smiled back. He wrote that evening to his cousin, Gertrude: 'Give my love to Eva, I thought her looking very tired to-day.' Gertrude visited him in prison and recalled that on several occasions he asked 'What does Eva say?' or 'What is Eva doing?' She commented: 'Always he spoke of her thus, simply by her Christian name.' On another occasion Gertrude remarked rather touchingly that she noticed something else – 'A mutual attraction. A little half affair.'

Casement's trial involved two other persons, one of whom, Robert Monteith, is sometimes recalled but the second, Private Daniel Bailey, who had landed in Kerry with Casement, has long been forgotten. Often overlooked, too, is the fact that the case made against Sir Roger did not rest solely upon his attempt to import arms from Germany; but included the charge that he tried to 'seduce' Irishmen who had been taken prisoners of war while serving in the British Army, to join a specially formed German Irish Brigade.

Private Bailey was tried during the same hearing because he had 'defected to the enemy,' and he gave evidence that he was among more than 2,000 Irish soldiers who had been transferred to a special prisoner of war camp near Limburg in December, 1914. He told the court that they were better treated and received better rations than before, and he recounted how, shortly afterwards, Casement came to the camp to address the men on four occasions, encouraging them to join the planned Irish Brigade to fight for Ireland. Each man was offered £10, a special green uniform, and a promise that should Germany lose the war they would be given free passage to America, but most of the soldiers gave him a hostile reception each time he visited the camp. It was Bailey's opinion that out of 2,500 prisoners, 52 men had opted to join Casement's brigade. Constance, then serving her sentence in Aylesbury jail, had been one of the vocal supporters of the idea to encourage Irish soldiers to defect.

Eva continued to attend the court, as witness after witness contributed to the steady build-up of evidence. Her admiration for Sir Roger

Casement must have been enhanced at the outset when, aware that Bailey had been a railway porter and was unlikely to have sufficient financial means to defend himself, Casement had told the court that he was prepared to pay for his defence.

Eva personally knew C.P. Scott, the well-known editor of *The Manchester Guardian*, and pleaded with him to organise press support for Sir Roger, and she also approached Lord Carew, the Foreign Minister, who drew the attention of the Cabinet to claims that Casement attempted to stop the Rising. In support of this intervention Carew laid before the other members an unpublished appeal on behalf of Sir Roger that had been prepared by Eva Gore-Booth. Indeed, as Jeffrey Dudgeon wrote in his volume about Casement, Eva also attempted to persuade U.S. President Taft 'to sign a petition to gain a reprieve … by getting across the fact that his intention after landing in April [1916] had been to stop the Easter Rising.' In his book about the emerging independent Ireland, Eoin Neeson speculated that 'the theory that [Casement] came from Germany to "stop" the Rising may have originated with Eva Gore-Booth … who wrote a letter during Casement's trial making this allegation – presumably in an attempt to moderate the case against him.

Obviously she wrote more than one such letter, but it was all in vain when faced with mounting evidence along with accusations of homosexuality that weighed hopelessly against him. The case ended with the Lord Chief Justice placing the traditional black cap on his head as he passed sentence of death by hanging, after which Casement paused for a moment to smile to his friends in the court before being led away. An appeal was heard a month later and *The Irish Times* reported that Casement was looking very weary with the long strain, 'but throughout the day he smiled to a lady who sat near him and who evidently did all she could by responsive smiles to cheer him.' The appeal did not succeed, and several further interventions were made in vain including an audience with King George V, which Esther Roper attended, but they were informed that the King's Right had been vested in his ministers, rendering him powerless to act. He was later to direct that Casement be stripped of his knighthood, awarded in 1906. The court entered a *nolle prosequi* in the case of Private Bailey, who was then released.

When permission was sought to have Casement's body handed over for private burial, the request was refused, prompting Eva to write the lines about the unmarked, quicklime grave where his remains lay for more than half a century before being finally brought back to Ireland.

> No cairn-shaped mound on a high windy hill
> With Irish earth the hero's heart enfolds
> But a burning grave at Pentonville
> The broken heart of Ireland holds.

Eva was deeply affected by Casement's death, in whose memory she additionally penned the following lines:

> The rulers of the earth, savage and blind,
> Have dug Gethsemane for all mankind,
> For their honour and their glory and their pride
> In every age the heroes of all nations died.
> Thus Joan of Arc and Socrates were slain
> By the world's bane,
> Jesus Christ a thousand years ago
> They served so,
> And Roger Casement, just the other day,
> Went the same way.

Not surprisingly, Eva and Esther found yet one more movement to join at this time, the League for the Abolition of Capital Punishment. As the Great War dragged on to its bloody conclusion, the two women, as committed pacifists, found themselves attending the trials of numerous conscientious objectors. Two years later, Eva wrote an article for the *Catholic Bulletin*, in which she summed up her feelings for Roger Casement. 'It might be said of him that while many have died for their countries and for great causes in all ages, no man has ever, in the annals of history, done more than he did by the manner of his dying to exalt and glorify the country of his love.'

When Eva and Esther returned to London following their visit to Constance in Mountjoy Prison in Dublin, they had been unable to discover what charges had been made against her at the court martial, nor could they discover which prison Constance was to be transferred to in England. This was to lead to an extraordinary happening a week or so later. Back in London, Esther had a premonition that if she went to Euston Station she would meet Constance. Despite her scepticism, Eva accompanied Esther to meet the Holyhead train where they found:

> a strange little procession … First a brown cocker spaniel, well known in Dublin as "the Poppet," then a couple of soldiers with rifles, then Eva and Constance together, smiling and talking. Lastly an officer with drawn sword, looking very agitated.

Though he did not know it, the officer had good reason to be agitated, because his prisoner had just slipped a folded sheet of paper into her sister's hand. It was a document containing the names of the three officers who had sat in judgement at Constance's court martial, the charges made against her, and the verdict – in fact most of the information that Eva and Josslyn had been trying for some time to obtain.

The movement of prisoners was never announced in advance by the authorities so this chance meeting in a busy London railway station is difficult to rationalise if the telepathic explanation claimed by Esther is not believable. The two sisters had, from time to time, been practising telepathy and found they could communicate with one another even when several hundred miles apart, and they continued with these mystical sessions – especially during the various prison terms served by Constance. Some versions of this story wrongly attribute the strange premonition to Eva rather than to Esther who, for her part, later denied that she was psychic and, indeed, recorded that this was the only occasion during her lifetime that she had such an experience.

Esther Roper, like Eva, had been horrified by the experience of visiting Constance in Mountjoy but continued to accompany Eva whenever the latter succeeded in getting permission to visit her sister at Aylesbury and at Holloway. Esther had no particular interest in or knowledge of Irish politics until her friendship with Eva convinced her there was a strong case in favour of Irish nationalism, and she shared Eva's concern for Constance. Esther wrote:

> I ask myself how in Heaven's name shutting out the sun, the wind and the sight of the trees could make a rebel loyal or a thief honest … I marvel at the patience and courage with which a fiery soul like Constance's went through the ordeal and learned from life before the end, as she did, the lesson of love and pity.

They continued to see Constance as often as the prison authorities permitted, travelling the 80-mile round-trip to Aylesbury by rail, and Eva made a Christmas card for Constance in which she inscribed the following verse:

> Yours is that inner Ireland beyond green fields or brown,
> Where waves break down enchanted on the haunted Rosses shore,
> And clouds above Ben Bulben fling their coloured shadows down,
> Whilst little rivers shine and sink in wet sands of Crushmor.

Their prison visits continued until December 1917 when a general amnesty was declared and all the Republican prisoners were returned to Ireland. Eva's prose play, 'The Sword of Justice' was published in

1918, and in the same year she published her small volume of verse entitled *Broken Glory* containing a number of poems relating to 1916, including 'The Age of Gold,' which reflected her pacifist views:

> When Jacob's Ladder reached the skies,
> And the earth shone like other stars,
> And men were not called great and wise,
> Nor had they fashioned prison bars,
> And tigers had not learned to slay –
> I slept alone in the dark wood,
> And when the sun rose every day
> I saw why God called his work good.

Also included were laments for Roger Casement and Francis Sheehy Skeffington, as well as several poems she had written for Constance in prison, one of which was composed for her birthday in February, 1917:

> What has time to do with thee,
> Who has found the victor's way
> To be rich in poverty,
> Without sunshine to be gay,
> To be free in a prison cell?
> Now on that undreamed judgement day,
> When on the old world's scrap heap flung
> Powers and empires pass away,
> Radiant and unconquerable
> Thou shalt be young.

A month after the end of the Great War, a general election was held which brought a landslide victory to Sinn Féin, many of whose candidates – like Constance – were in prison. The suffrage movement in England saw the election as an opportunity to secure seats for its own candidates but, in the event, not one of the Womens' Rights candidates – not even their leader Mrs Pankhurst – was elected. When news spread that Constance had won a seat in Dublin, the movement's initial pride and joy quickly evaporated when it became known that as a Sinn Féin candidate she would not be taking her seat at Westminster. Eva had worked hard on behalf of the English candidates, and having supported Constance during her darkest prison days, she found her sister's abstentionist policy very frustrating.

In an article written for the *Daily Mirror*, Eva expressed regret that no women M.P.s had 'materialised' except:

in the rather shadowy form of an Irish woman, the result of whose political connection is her present address in Holloway Gaol, and who has no intention of hanging up her hat on the special peg reserved for her at Westminster, even if she were free to claim it. I need not say how profoundly I regret this result of the first woman's election …. We Suffragettes, would have welcomed the advent of women M.P.s as a guarantee that Parliament would cease its age-long habit of putting a blind eye to the telescope as soon as a question involving women's special interests is concerned.

Perhaps it is only fair to mention that it is unlikely that many people had cast their votes for Constance Markieviez because of her earlier support for the pre-suffrage movement, or even because she was a woman. In a book about her own family, Maud Wynne made the comment on the special peg reserved for Constance at Westminster that 'with true British phlegm and regard for order and tradition, her name was inscribed over the peg in the member's vestibule for her top hat and overcoat, and funnily enough was side by side with that of the then Sir Edward Carson.'

Eva published *The Inner Life of a Child* during this turbulent period, describing it as 'very intimately connected' with the inner life of her own childhood at Lissadell where, as she described it, there was:

a little wood that had once held a garden, and was now so isolated from the world that it was called by us children St. Helena. A great many snowdrops grew among the hemlock roots, and here and there the formal lines of white in the tangled grass pointed out the place where once there had been flower beds. The little ruined summerhouse was covered with ivy…. It was here that a child came alone, bewildered and appalled by the sudden thrill of the first touch of the world's mystery.

She was describing the old garden that had lain alongside the original house at Lissadell, abandoned some four decades earlier, traces of which are still to be seen close to the sea shore. At the end of the book she wrote that, growing older: 'The time comes when we want to renew our experiences of the inner life to patch up our quarrel with the Unseen, to win back for ourselves a place in the Communion of Saints.'

* * *

By 1919, Eva and Esther felt physically and mentally drained by all that had been happening and went on a tour of Europe to recuperate. Much of their time was spent in their beloved Italy where they found great happiness, especially in the Ligurian countryside where they had first met. On a visit to Rome, they stayed with Gavan Duffy. Then representing Dáil Éireann there, who arranged a papal audience. Eva had thoughtfully bought rosary beads for Constance, and brought them to the Vatican where the Pope not only acceded to Eva's request to bless the beads for her sister then in prison, but surprised many present when they continued to talk at length in Italian.

From there the two women went north to Lake Como, to the Italian Alps, and up through the steep Maloja Pass into Switzerland, where they stayed in what is still a quiet resort, Sils Maria. Situated between two small lakes, the Silser See and Silvaplana in the Upper Engadine and not far from St Moritz (where Eva's father had died two decades earlier), they walked among the alpine meadows admiring the wild flowers and the snow-capped peaks. Eva's romantic love of nature is evident in a letter written at the time to a family friend, Clare Annesley:

> We are having a lovely time with your Brother Sun and your little Sisters the Alpine flowers and your beloved little Brothers the bright orange butterflies, but we're not at all sorry to miss your Mother the Thunderstorm and your sister the Lightning.... This place is wonderful – such meadows – we have been reduced to getting a little book about the flowers – Brother Fly is entirely absent and this place is alive with Sister Water – such torrents.

From the same resort, Eva wrote to another friend, T. P. Conwil-Evans, whom she invariably addressed as 'T. P.'

> Our world is bounded by Maloja on the one side and St. Moritz on the other... here the cows eat flowers instead of dry grass so, of course, they are better than English ones and get over Foot and Mouth disease quite easily.

After re-crossing the border into Italy, she wrote in a similar vein to another friend, Margaret Wroe, from an upland village, Santa Maria Maggiori, having travelled there through Locarno and the beautiful Centovalli region:

> It's a heavenly place, a lovely broad valley full of wild flowers and delightful walks near Domodossola,... It's lovely to be right out of England and far from Tottenham Court Road, and heavenly to sit in a wood and write for most of the time....

It was during this happy period that she wrote many of the poems subsequently published in *The Shepherd of Eternity* which was not, however, published until 1925. At the same time she also began working on her *Study of Christ*, which occupied much of her time until it was published in that same year. *The Manchester Guardian* critic hailed her work on *The Shepherd of Eternity*, calling her 'one of the most sensitively clear, yet intellectually sure exponents of the mystic faith among modern poets ...' The following lines are from this work – the last to be published during her lifetime:

> Every fountain to the skies
> Clear and foam-less shall arise;
> There are bright wings for all things,
> Even worms shall have wings;
> The Living Waters, ascending
> Rainbow coloured, shining, blending
> With the everlasting Light,
> Transfigure the world's night;
> This is the song the Shepherd sang,
> with many runs and shakes and trills,
> The Shepherd of Eternity,
> piping o'er cypress-shaded hills.

Back in England, Eva wrote to her friend T.P. Conwil-Evans again to advise her that she just received a prison letter from Constance:

> all over-printed with regulations about not using slang and being respectable, and keeping up with your respectable friends. Anyway she sent you a long message which I give you before I forget. I was to say how glad she was to hear from you, and "tell Mr Evans [T.P.'s husband] not only do I remember him for himself, but I remember him for Debussy to whom he introduced me. How I'd love to hear some more, I've never heard any since."

Eva published a volume during 1923 comprising what might be termed her late Christian poems, entitled *A Psychological and Poetical approach to the Study of the Fourth Gospel*, a title which was hardly likely to catch the imagination of a general audience. For most people, her convoluted thinking, touching on psychology, philosophy, and astrology, was much too difficult to follow. She started to take a deeper interest in religion, studying Gnosticism, exploring Pantheism and reading works relating to Theosophy and the Rosicrucians as a method of gaining a greater knowledge of God by means of contemplation or direct communion.

She also began to study the Greek New Testament, concentrating on St John's Gospel, viewing it as an eye-witness account of the life of Christ written by his favourite disciple whose account differed in certain respects from the other three Gospels. Suspecting that certain passages had not been accurately translated, she visited the British Museum in order to check the early Greek manuscripts there and translated this fourth Gospel herself directly from the Greek. She hoped to try to comprehend some of the symbolism used by Christ in his teaching, and was especially intrigued by Christ's remark to his mother: 'Woman, what have I to do with you?' She felt that if the translators, who were almost certainly men, had mistranslated the original, then this could have had an enormous influence in the exclusion of women from celebrating the Eucharist and from preaching. She commented:

> Perhaps few besides women will appreciate the importance of the fact that women were not mothers and sisters to Christ, that he cared nothing for physical qualities and relationships. Women were to him simply human beings embarked, like all others, on the divine adventure of life ....

In her poem, 'Sacrifice,' four short lines neatly reflect something of her perceptive religious thinking during these later years:

> If Jesus Christ had not been crucified,
> God's mercy would have passed this sad world by.
> 'Our deed is then most greatly justified,'
> Pilate and Caiaphas might well reply …

She began to consider ideas about the importance of life over and beyond sex, writing that:

> If one first stipulates that the word "it" shall mean the very essence of real life and no idea of lifelessness, the easiest way of avoiding gender difficulty seems to be to give up the "he's" and "she's" and stick to the neuter.

The Inner Kingdom, her next work, was described – after her death – by the *Theosophical Review* as a little book:

> worth its weight in gold. It is amazing that a book of so small a compass can reach out to the farthest end of things. These five essays are Eva Gore-Booth's last gift to her fellow men – they were completed just before she was stricken with a fatal illness – and are a distilled essence of a lifetime's thought.

It was just two years after their memorable continental holiday that Eva was told she had cancer, and by Christmas 1925 she was seriously ill. She and Esther decided not to tell relations and friends for as long as possible. Confined to her Hampstead home, she read widely and continued to study biblical texts, while Esther arranged for friends to come to read aloud or play music for Eva.

As her condition worsened, Esther's brother, Reginald, came to live with the two women, taking turns with his sister to nurse Eva. Sometimes when feeling better, she would sit in the garden and one day, when doing this, Eva re-appeared in the house and told Esther:

> You know I have always been afraid of death and I could not get away from the fear of it. Then, quite suddenly, I heard the words: 'I will come to you,' slowly and clearly, just like that. Then came the words: 'I have promised, remember,' very distinctly. It was overwhelming. There was a radiance all round and I was filled with an extraordinary feeling of joy, the greatest I have ever known. Remember, remember, I shall never be afraid of death again.

There were brief respites, during one of which Eva wrote what is thought to have been her last poem:

> Suddenly, everywhere,
> Clouds and waves are one,
> The storm has cleared the air,
> The sea holds the sun
> And the blue sky -
> There is no under, no above,
> All is light, all is love -
> Is it like this when you die?

A few weeks before she died, Richard Michael Fox, a historian, visited Eva and part of the conversation turned on Italy, then taken over by the Fascists. Asked why the people had not opposed this autocracy, Eva replied that nothing in the world was worth fighting for, 'because fighting marred everything.'

During the final few days, she was tended day and night by Esther and her brother, both taking it in turns to be at her bedside until she died on June 30, 1926. She had entered 'the secret door, the door in the air' – her own description of death. Her funeral took place three days later in the nearby Hampstead Parish Church and she was buried in the adjoining churchyard. During the funeral service, the words of Psalm 23, The Lord is my shepherd, were sung, as were the hymns, 'Holy, holy, holy, Lord God Almighty,' and 'Jesu, lover of my soul.' Two verses from her poem 'The Deliverance' were printed on the funeral service sheet:

> I would build a form of my fierce desire,
> My feet shall be free of the grass and its groves,
> Strong with the secret of Love and Fire,
> Standing with Christ on the glimmering grave.
> For the rainbow's light, and the wild bird's wings,
> And the waves have pierced through an age-long sleep,
> With a broken song at the heart of things …
> No more shall I wander, and wander, and weep.

One of Eva's friends, Evelyn Underhill, wrote an obituary for *The Times* which was published about a week after the funeral, in which Eva was described as 'one of the most distinguished Christian poets of our time [and] a true mystic.' Eva's work for the poor and for women's rights was also recalled but without any reference to her involvement in the suffragette movement. Underhill wrote that Eva Gore-Booth:

> will be chiefly remembered as a mystical poet [whose verse] placed her among those of that small group of poets who have not only sought, but have found the Hidden Beauty where the river finds the sea.

The obituary then summed up Eva's life:

> Her enthusiasm for the things of the spirit, far from rendering her aloof from human interests, overflowed and found expression in social and political work, in passionate appreciation of beauty, as well as in the beautiful poems which reveal the deep sources of her life.

In her will, Eva left her entire estate and effects to Esther Roper, who used some of the money to commission a stained glass window in her memory from An Túr Gloine (Tower of Glass) Studio, founded in Dublin by Sarah Purser. It was installed two years later in the Round House at Ancoats, Manchester, where Eva had conducted her special classes for women several decades earlier. A depiction of Eva's face, copied from a photograph taken when she was a child, was incorporated in one of the figures included in the design. Manchester City Council demolished the building during the 1980s and it seems likely that the memorial window simply disappeared along with the building's rubble. Despite exhaustive enquiries by the author and by others, its actual fate continues to remain a mystery.

Her younger brother, Mordaunt, who lived in London at the time, attended the funeral and afterwards wrote to their mother suggesting that the family might erect a plain Celtic cross over her grave. He informed his mother that Esther Roper was 'quite broken up,' adding that she and her brother 'have been quite admirable all through. The suddenness of it really made it worse for them, but for Eva it was better.' He had not heard from Constance, but Maeve told him she was unable to attend the funeral 'owing to her leg, but sent flowers.'

Eva's grave at Hampstead, London.
Her younger brother, Mordaunt, suggested
that a Celtic cross should mark her grave.
(*photo, courtesy of Gifford Lewis*)

The headstone was duly erected, bearing Eva's name, and the dates of her birth and death. A space was left below the inscription for the addition, in due course, of Esther's name and details, and these were inscribed eleven years later. An obituary published in *The Manchester Guardian*, read in part:

The death after a short illness of Eva Gore-Booth takes from us one of the most distinguished Christian poets of our time… The career of Miss Gore-Booth, whose fragile physique only enhanced the vivid inward life which was radiated by her whole personality, was a complete answer to those who regard the mystic as a person who remains aloof from the interests, struggles and sorrows of practical life.… She loved the poor and was especially concerned to uphold the rights of working women and improve their economic position.…

She hated war, cruelty, greed, injustice, not merely for their own sakes, but because they conflicted with that eternal mercy and love which she felt to be the greatest of all realities.

The Irish Times recorded that by her death:

Ireland loses a charming poet and essayist whose work held no mean place in the Anglo-Irish literary movement of the new century.… Some of her lyrics have appeared again and again in modern anthologies, and promise to hold an undying place in Irish literature. The Little Waves of Breffni, perhaps is the best known of these, and admirably represents the wistful air and racy Irish imagery, which were … often recurring in her work.

George Russell wrote about Eva's life in *The Living Torch*, first published in 1937 and reprinted in an edition edited by Monk Gibbon in 1970. The following extracts seem to sum up her spirit:

When I look back along the aisles of memory, I can conjure up the image of Eva Gore-Booth as I saw her a quarter of a century ago, like a star half hidden in a mist, a fragile yet gallant figure breaking out in sudden transcendentalisms from cloudy, luminous silences, a little breathless, always in pursuit of the spirit, just as her sister Constance was a little breathless in pursuit of her national ideals.…

She would not have sung so often about Beauty, but would have made much more beautiful songs. Yet, in spite of this imperfect craft, we feel respect for the poet because the nature is so steadfastly set on noble things, and here is no insincerity. It is proof of this that she was not content to be the spiritual dreamer but must try to change her world. We get some revelation of this woman, ardent for reform, whose good heart compelled her to social service, to build up trade unions, to work for the poor.

She had ideas and intuitions to overflowing, as many as any poet in her time … but she had a most radiant, iridescent personality, and one clings to the memory of that flashing spirit while rarely remembering its utterances.

On hearing the news, Constance wrote to Esther Roper to say that she would not be attending her sister's funeral. Later she wrote, perhaps regretting her earlier decision, to say she would consider going to see her sister's grave. She told Esther that Eva's gentleness had 'prevented me getting very brutal and one does get very callous in a War. I once held out and stopped a man being shot because of her ....' She also wrote to say: 'I'd love some personal relics of her ... my things were all destroyed so often.' Esther seems to have responded by suggesting that Constance might like to have a cross which she had found among Eva's possessions, prompting the reply: 'I should love the cross, our Granny left it to her. She loved it so much when we were girls together.' In a will, drafted when Constance was ten years old and when Eva was eight, their grandmother had written: 'To Eva Selina Gore-Booth, my diamond Maltese Cross, [and] miniature of her Aunt Selina Hill....'

Constance suggested to Esther that she should consider printing Eva's unpublished work, of which there was a considerable body:

> The one thing we can do to honour her is to make her work known, and to help her to immortality here in this world through the ideals she lived for.... Her human presence was so beautiful and wonderful but with her the spirit dominated every bit of her, and her body was the human instrument it shone through. It is so hard to put things like this down in a way that anyone can understand.

When Dorothy Macardle heard that Esther had decided to publish a selection of Eva's poetry in a single volume and had arranged to do so with the publishers, Longmans, she suggested: 'Advertise with the *Irish Press*, that's where you will get your sales. I hope you will get a leader page article as well.' Macardle's advice to use de Valera's newspaper rather than *The Irish Times* or the *Irish Independent* may have been at least partly motivated by the fact that she had worked for a time for the *Irish Press*. Besides, it was not for nothing that Professor Joe Lee described her as the 'hagiographer royal to the Republic.' Asked by Roper for help in writing about the events that followed the Civil War, Macardle replied:

> The whole proceeding is a long, involved story, difficult to summarise.... Could you not say simply that in the election of 1922, during which the terms of the Collins–de Valera pact were broken by Michael Collins, she [Constance] lost her seat. I know no book that tells the story except my own unfinished one.

Roper might have been better advised to seek guidance from a less partial source.

The World's Pilgrim, written by Eva during her last 12 years, would have remained unpublished had it not been for Esther Roper. The reviewer in *Times Literary Supplement* thought that: 'In her prose, perhaps, more than in her poetry, she exemplified the saying which she gives here to Pheidias, that: 'Real force is a quality of truth, and any other kind of force is merely violence.' *Poetry Review* described it as 'an unusual book [in which the dialogue was described as] conspicuous for its sympathetic handling, its beauty of diction, and vigour of thought,' and added that: 'The author's sympathies are clearly with those who break away from the traditional convention in art as well as in thought.'

After Roper had published *The Selected Poems* in 1933, Francis Stuart reviewed it for the *Irish Press*:

> It would not be fair to judge Miss Eva Gore-Booth's work by the standard of great poetry. One does not, in any case, feel that poetry was for her more than, one can say, a side-line, a refuge of secret, tender, whimsical moods from the stress of more practical things like politics and philosophy.

A critic in the *Quarterly Review* described Eva as 'the lamented Irish poetess, whom we have on occasions dared to rank not very far below the tenderest and sternest of all poetesses – that unconscious Calvinist, Christina Rosetti herself.'

Just a few years after her death, only four of her books of prose were still in print: *The Sword of Justice*, *The Inner Kingdom*, *The World's Pilgrim* and *A Psychological and Poetic Approach* ... – perhaps reflecting the perception that her non-poetic writing never achieved real success. And a few more years later, almost all of her published books were already out of print, the exceptions included *The Shepherd of Eternity* and *The House of Three Windows*. Her literary output was considered in the *Dictionary of Irish Literature*, edited by Robert Hogan:

> In her quiet but useful and busy life she found time to write enough poems and verse dramas to fill 650 pages when they were posthumously collected.... She is a more considerable poet than many of her contemporaries in Ireland, but she never managed to break out of the poetic conventions of her youth. If she seldom was inept, she really never was memorable.

It is difficult to avoid the conclusion that even her poetry has now been largely forgotten. Most of the selections of twentieth century verse published in recent years have failed to include any of her compositions – not even 'The Little Waves of Breffni,' which *The Manchester Guardian* had described as that which is 'the extent of most people's knowledge of her.' Perhaps there are the beginnings of a revival of interest in her writing, and even in her persona, as somewhat hopefully expressed by authors Kit and Cyril Ó Céirin: 'Although long overshadowed by Constance, Eva Gore-Booth is now being recognised for her social and feminist work and, ironically, for her pacifism.'

* * *

Scores of letters expressing sympathy were sent to Lissadell by people who were quite unknown to the family. Among the many touching tributes was one written – not by an eminent writer in some literary publication – but by one of the 'working women' for whom Eva had organised literary classes in Manchester 20 or 30 years earlier. On learning of Eva's death she expressed her grief:

> We were a class of sixteen girls. I think we were all machinists and we were rough. Miss Gore-Booth used to teach us Shakespeare and how to act.… If any of us were feeling seedy or worried about business or home she showed such understanding sympathy that we came away feeling we had a real friend.… Miss Gore-Booth was always sympathetic with the downtrodden and worked and lectured might and main interviewing members of parliament on their behalf till conditions were mended.

> She was very frail and delicate herself, but full of pluck and determination and would stand up for people she knew to be unjustly treated even though the world was against them, and withal so sweet and gentle that one could not help loving her, and as the years went by she seemed to grow more sweet.

> In her passing she has left a great gap.

Anyone interested in learning more about Eva's life should consider reading Gifford Lewis's biography of the two friends. Describing the last weeks of Eva's life as she lay seriously ill, she quotes Esther Roper's account:

> Death came suddenly after two days of illness.… [She] suddenly said to me: 'This is death.' 'Yes it is', I said, 'but you told me you would never be afraid of it again.' 'Oh, no,' she replied, 'I am not afraid, pray that it comes quickly.' At the end she looked up with that exquisite smile that always lighted up her face when she saw one she loved, then closed her eyes and was at peace.

The brothers, Brian (top) and Hugh Gore-Booth.

BRIAN AND HUGH

Quis separabit?

Sir Josslyn and Lady Mary Gore-Booth had four sons and four daughters, and Josslyn must have felt satisfied that, having four possible male heirs, the future of the family line was assured for at least one more generation. However, as someone once said, 'the only thing you can be sure of in this life is that you can be sure of nothing,' and this proved to be the case for the Gore-Booths of Lissadell.

As already mentioned, Michael, the eldest son began as a young man to develop symptoms of mental instability which were to render him incapable of running the family estate. Hugh, the second eldest, whose story is told in the latter half of this chapter, went to England to study estate management, a move seen as Sir Josslyn's determination that if Michael was unfit to take over the estate, then Hugh would be trained to do so. Both of the other two brothers also went to England, Angus to attend university, while Brian went to train in a naval college as an officer in the Royal Navy. It is unclear why Brian chose this career, especially as there was no naval tradition in the family though, of course, his grandfather Henry had been a outstanding sailor.

Brian Gore-Booth was born on 23 December 1912, so he was less than four years old when his Aunt Constance was taking part in the Easter Rising, and 10 when the Irish Free State was established. After attending Mourne Grange School in County Down, Brian went to the Royal Naval College at Dartmouth in 1928, with the result that his school and college years and all of his subsequent working life were spent either in the United Kingdom or in its service. While he occasionally wrote in quite affectionate terms about Ireland, it is hardly surprising, that he became something of an Anglophile.

After two years at the naval college, Brian was sent with three other cadets to Devonport Naval Dockyard where he joined his first ship, the cruiser, *HMS Norfolk*, on May 12, 1930, finding it in dry dock having a propeller repaired. The early months of his service were relatively humdrum as he got used both to his new surroundings and to the daily routine on board ship. Included in this routine, and a part of his training as a junior officer, it was Brian's duty to make regular entries in a heavily bound naval journal or logbook. Inside the front cover of this tome there were printed instructions indicating that regular entries were to be written up 'during the whole of a Midshipman's sea time,' the objective of which was 'to train Midshipmen in the power of observation, the power of expression, and the habit of orderliness.'

The instructions required young officers to record in their own language, observations about all matters of interest or importance in the work carried on at their stations, in the fleet and in their own ship. Midshipmen were required to insert their own drawings of ship's equipment, or anything of relevance, including maps and charts. Brian's neat sketches and his detailed maps were exceptionally good. He had to submit his journal each week to his Captain, or to an officer deputising for him, who would write occasional comments in the margins and initial the most recent entry. On the completion of their training, midshipmen were required to produce their journals – Brian completed two – 'at the examination in Seamanship for the rank of Lieutenant.'

At the end of August, Brian and others from the *Norfolk* temporarily joined *HMS Vivid* for 'gunnery' training – not as might be expected, naval gunnery but the use of rifles, bayonets, and even cutlasses, 'all good fun,' as he commented. After that, the *Norfolk* left its base with the other ships of the Home Fleet, bound for the naval base at Invergordon in the far northeast of Scotland, a place that was to become famous, or infamous, in Royal Naval annals a year later. Brian saw the liner *Mauritania* passing close by to starboard 'going at about 20 knots, she looked a most striking sight.' The ships' officer who regularly checked Brian's log book inserted an exclamation mark after spotting Brian's entry in which he stated that the *Norfolk* had passed the 'Isle of White.' However, this was no lazy 'cruise' along the south and east coast of England, as Brian discovered; because the naval authorities had arranged a whole series of incidents simulating wartime activities with mock submarine and seaplane attacks, and during the latter *HMS Norfolk* was deemed to have been sunk.

When the fleet arrived at Invergordon, Brian listed the ships as they approached the naval base – they included a number of the most famous British naval vessels of the day – the battleships *Nelson*, *Rodney*, *Warspite*, *Barham*, and *Malaya*; the battle cruisers *Renown* and *Repulse*; followed by the cruisers *Hawkins*, *York*, and *Tiger*. This impressive fleet was subsequently engaged in further manoeuvres off the Scottish coast, mainly firing the big guns at practice targets, but whenever the *Norfolk* was back at the Invergordon base, Brian and a few fellow junior officers availed of shore leave to go swimming, fishing or shooting. Brian also managed to spend a weekend – the first of many – with his Leven cousins living nearby at Nairn.

Almost two months later, at the end of October, the fleet set sail 'for the south and civilisation,' leaving Invergordon and the nearby mountains which were covered in snow – and after sailing in very stormy conditions all the ships of the squadron returned to Portland. These early months were typical of many to follow, with periods spent moored in naval dockyards interspersed with brief forays and some longer ones for gunnery, torpedo and other practices. During the 1930 cruise (September-November), *HMS Norfolk* encountered very rough weather several times but Brian made no reference to how the rough seas affected him personally. In fact he was often sea-sick, but probably deliberately omitted mentioning this in his naval journal, where his only comment about weather conditions at this time was a description of how destroyers ploughed into the huge waves which, at times submerged the entire forward half of these relatively small vessels.

The *Norfolk* returned to her home base at Devonport early in December 1930, where Brian and most of the crew went on extended leave until the new year. In January, the squadron sailed west to embark on its winter cruise, and after the *Norfolk* passed The Lizard Rock with its lighthouse at a distance of six miles, Brian recorded that it was 'the last land we shall see until we reach the Barbadoes.' During that night, a flotilla of destroyers lay in wait for a mock attack against the squadron, but 'only star shells were fired.' On most days during his first Atlantic crossing, Brian and the rest of the crew were engaged in regular exercises, despite continuing rough weather until one day conditions became so extreme that the exercises had to be abandoned.

Two weeks after leaving England, *HMS Norfolk* arrived at Bridgetown, Barbados and that evening Brian, along with most of the crew, went ashore where 'the bathing is simply marvellous and the water the warmest that I have ever encountered.' Back on board, most of the crew engaged in washing down the ship after which it was repainted because 'while coming across the Atlantic a lot of paint seems to have peeled off and our sides are an awful sight.' When the *Norfolk* departed from Bridgetown, it was 'amid the lamentations of most of the white populace of Barbadoes' as it headed for St Lucia, the second largest of the Windward Islands.

After a few more days, the *Norfolk* headed for Dominica, then one of the Leeward group of islands but which became part of the Windward Islands archipelago in 1940. The *Norfolk* then called at Anguilla to participate in a ceremony of naming the 'Norfolk Pier' in the port. Fifty-five members of the crew took part and the ship was open to the public for the rest of the day. Four hours after sailing from there, Brian's ship arrived at St Kitts where the newly commissioned *HMS Scarborough*, already docked there, attracted his attention. He attended a party at Government House in the afternoon and in the evening he drove to Brimstone Hill – 'one of the many Gibraltars of the West Indies,' and visited the fort built by Sir Thomas Warner in 1640.

Along with the other Royal Navy vessels now in the area, including the *Nelson*, *Rodney*, *Hawkins*, *York*, *Adventure* and the *Dorsetshire*, *HMS Norfolk* sailed for Gibraltar early in March, calling at Madeira. After a major naval exercise involving ships of the Atlantic Fleet as well as those of the Mediterranean Fleet, an impressive convoy converged on Gibraltar on March 18.

The *Dorsetshire* left the squadron for England with Rear Admiral Best on board, who was leaving the squadron. It was he who, up to this point, had regularly marked and made comments on Brian's logbook. Rear Admiral Astley Rushton took his place as the new squadron commander who, unlike Best, declined to underline spelling mistakes and contented himself by initialling the log book every few weeks. The squadron left Gibraltar for Devonport and Brian saw England again for the first time in over three months.

After leave and an official visit to the *Norfolk* by members of the Norfolk Regiment, the cruiser embarked with the rest of the squadron for Invergordon, the squadron sailing in line ahead. At the end of May, the Second Cruiser Squadron 'weighed' and sailed out into the North Sea to Scapa Flow naval base, before proceeding towards Denmark, rounding its northern coast to enter the Baltic Sea, docking at Liepaya, in Latvia in advance of celebrations for Latvian Independence Day. The other visiting naval vessels arrived on the following day. Brian was impressed by the appearance of the French and German warships which were 'of the most modern design, especially the [cruiser] *Königsberg* which had three triple six-inch turrets.' In particular, he noted that the pair of after-gun turrets, instead of being situated half-way along the after deck, were sited as close to the stern as practicable, thus maximising the capacity of the stern guns to fire forward. The Royal Navy was to regret its failure to be as observant about this point as was young Lieutenant Gore-Booth when its ships set out to tackle the incredibly well-designed *Bismarck* and *Prinz Eugen* during World War II.

The British warships then sailed for Stockholm, the approaches to which, with its reputed 24,000 islands, greatly impressed Brian. During the squadron's stay, the Swedes celebrated Midsummer's Day, a general holiday. During the first of three days, the *Norfolk* was opened to the public, and over 3,000 visitors availed of the opportunity to tour the ship. A team representing the vessel went to a nearby sports ground and played a team from HMS *Devonshire* in a game of Rugby Football. During the game, an explanatory commentary in Swedish was broadcast over loudspeakers for the benefit of the bewildered attendance.

Brian sailed in a small cutter for six miles to one of the islands of the Skärgården in the Stockholm Archipelago where he found 'a most perfect little cove' for swimming and sunbathing, and he then went riding in the Augården, 'a sort of old park in the northern suburbs of the town.' One evening the ship's crew entertained what he called the local British 'colony' to an 'At Home' before the squadron left for the German naval base at Kiel. The *Norfolk* moored alongside a number of German warships – the cruiser *Königsberg* (which Brian had admired at Liepaya) and the battleships *Hessen* and *Schleswig Holstein*. Little did anyone then know that nine years later, among the opening shots fired in World War Two would be those fired from the gun turrets of the latter vessel aimed at a Polish fort. Of even greater significance, as far as Brian was to be concerned during the coming conflict, Kiel was also the main submarine operations centre, and much of the old city was to be blasted during bombing raids designed to curb the lethal activities of this most effective arm of the German navy.

Brian went by train with a group of British sailors to visit the Deutsche Marineschule at Flensburg where midshipmen of the German navy had been trained since 1911. Brian thought it was modelled on the Royal Naval College at Dartmouth and was impressed by the facilities which he saw there, describing them in unusual detail, and he also enjoyed sailing with the German sailors to 'a *café dansant* at Gluxburg' [Glucksburg]. *HMS Norfolk* travelled through the Kiel Canal with Ober-Leutnant Godt on board as liaison officer, and it is quite possible that this was the Eberhardt Godt who, a decade later acted as Admiral Dönitz's Chief of Staff directing the entire deadly German submarine fleet, becoming a Rear Admiral before the end of the Second World War.

* * *

The British squadron returned to Invergordon accompanied by two destroyer flotillas, all of them participating in mock war-manoeuvres on the way. Back at this base, Brian and a few colleagues went ashore for some shooting, managing to bag a few rabbits after which he wrote: 'In the evening, coming off in a liberty boat, there seemed to be a certain amount of unrest among the sailors, owing to the general reductions in naval pays.' This was the first hint noted in his log book that there was naval unrest, a simmering disquiet that was to erupt into what subsequently became known as the Invergordon Mutiny.

Brian photographed in naval uniform

Early in the 1930s, most of the developed world was experiencing severe economic problems, difficulties that forced the British government to put in train a series spending cutbacks. The Chancellor of the Exchequer announced in Parliament a number of tax increases along with cuts both in benefits and in the salaries of various categories of government employees – and some of these cuts were of the order of 25 per cent. The armed services were included under the general scheme, and the decisions concerning the navy were relayed to the first Lord of the Admiralty, Sir Austen Chamberlain, and it subsequently transpired that the most severe naval cuts were to be applied to the lowest paid ranks. Rumours, commonly referred to as 'buzz' among naval personnel, concerning all of this had already been circulating among the naval personnel when the Atlantic Fleet sailed from its home port to assemble at Invergordon for autumn exercises in the North Sea. The fleet arrived at the Cromarty Firth on Friday September 11, without receiving any definite information about the impending pay cuts.

The details of these pay reductions had been forwarded to Rear Admiral Tomkinson on board *HMS Hood* who, crucially, put the information to one side for future distribution to the fleet. When the men went ashore at Invergordon, they discovered that some of the details of the pay cuts had been published in the newspapers, confirming their worst fears about reductions in service pay. Fears quickly turned into anger, not only in view of the severity of the cuts, but because of the manner in which the news had leaked out. Groups of men stood sullenly discussing the information on the quays, in recreation rooms, and in the canteens. Many of the sailors were worried because the reductions were to take effect in less than a month, long before they were likely to get leave, so making it impossible for them to discuss the situation with their families.

The next day, Sunday, unusually large numbers of men went ashore for church services after which they bought and read the Sunday newspapers which carried further details about the government's economic measures. Groups of men engaged in informal meetings and one of the men from the *Norfolk*, Len Wincott, addressed a large meeting and called on the men to return to their ships and commence strike action. A football match, already arranged, provided the men with an opportunity to hold a general meeting ashore, and some 700 assembled in the sports ground. They decided to adopt 'passive resistance' and planned to prevent the fleet from putting to sea until their case had been properly heard. Returning to their ships singing popular songs, all appeared set for a confrontation with the officers. Once aboard, further leave was cancelled, and while the men performed normal duties they continued in their determination to prevent the fleet from sailing for the autumn exercises due to commence on the following day. Brian recorded in his journal that 'there was a lot of unrest owing to the libertymen coming off the shore tonight because today the reductions in pay of naval ratings was promulgated.'

All shore communications were then cut off but this did not prevent the men from shouting messages from ship to ship and singing loudly on deck far into the night, sounds that some of the older people still living at the base recall.

Many observers, both at the time and since, blamed the Admiralty for the unrest because it had been so tardy in informing the men of the government's decisions. Brian's low-key references to the whole affair probably reflected his own position as a junior officer and also the fact that his journal entries were carefully read each week by a senior officer. Although *HMS Rodney* was generally regarded as having the fleet's most radical crew, Leonard Wincott from the *Norfolk* was the single most prominent ringleader. One of the ship's officers requested him to present a written statement of grievances which, as Dr Marinell Ash wrote in her history of the Cromarty Firth, 'was hardly a manifesto:'

> We, the loyal subjects of H.M. the King do hereby present my Lord Commissioners of the Admiralty, our representations to implore them to amend the drastic cuts in pay that have been inflicted on the lower deck.... The men are quite willing to accept a cut which they, the men, consider in reason.

A copy of this document was smuggled to the *Daily Herald* which labelled the incident 'a mutiny,' even though the men's actions fell far short of making their officers walk the plank. Brian recorded that:

> A[t] 06.30, when we turned out for P.T., we found that owing to the reductions in pay, the men of the *Dorsetshire* had commenced a campaign of possible resistance. During the Breakfast all the other ships in the harbour joined them in refusing to do their duty as a demonstration to show that they thought that the fact that the A.B.s [Able Seamen's] pay was cut a shilling a day was unreasonable, and in some cases, men could be heard to state that they would be better off on the dole.

> In the *Norfolk*, all was normal until 08.30 when the lower deck was cleared and everybody mustered aft. The Captain then gave a speech in which he summed up the situation, but stated that he hoped that the men of the *Norfolk* would continue to do their duty in the normal way, as all that was possible was being done to investigate cases of hardship caused by the reductions in pay. The ship's company was then dismissed and both Watches were sounded off.

> But only a few able seamen 'fell in' with the P.O.s (Petty Officers) and the leading hands. The remainder slouched furtively forrard – on strike.

During the day, there was cheering from the entire fleet in the base which, as Brian wrote 'signified that all ships in the port were of one mind, and their men were on strike.' The demonstration continued on the following day when the cheers of the sailors echoed to and from the ships anchored in line along the Cromarty Firth. Rear-Admiral Astley Rushton boarded the *Norfolk* to speak to the men but after he left, they refused to act on orders. Later the captain summoned another meeting, though only a small number of men attended. He told them that the Atlantic Fleet was now leaving for its home port where all cases of hardship would be properly investigated. This seemed sufficient to persuade the men present to prepare the *Norfolk* for sea and she sailed that evening with the rest of the Second Cruiser Squadron, heading for Plymouth without further incident. The most serious consequence of the whole affair was that it added to Britain's already serious financial position, precipitating a run on gold reserves. Eighteen million pounds was withdrawn during a period of two or three days, an unprecedented amount at the time, and the value of sterling against the dollar plummeted, eventually forcing Britain off the gold standard. Brian described the whole business as:

> one of the blackest days in the annals of the British Navy. Even although the Captain told the men that its effect would be far reaching when realised by other countries, especially at a time of national crisis … when everything possible to increase the country's credit was required, it made no difference. They still continued with their selfish demonstration and foolish cheering.

The 'mutiny' achieved limited success, forcing the Admiralty to review and reduce the pay cuts and, in the longer term, to improve conditions for the men and minimise class distinctions on board the ships. No officers were taken hostage – or even threatened – and accusations that the incident was pre-planned or was a Communist plot were obviously incorrect. Outside the environs of Invergordon, the whole thing was quickly forgotten, but for the people of the little town, the unscheduled early departure of the fleet and its 14,000 men after only five days instead of the usual two months represented a serious loss of income for the entire area. It also raised fears that the Admiralty might contemplate closing down the naval base altogether but if the authorities seriously considered this option at that time, the gathering political storm clouds over Europe ensured that the base, strategically close to Germany, was not abandoned – at least, not then.

* * *

Back in Plymouth, Brian witnessed the launch of a new 6,000 ton cruiser, *HMS Leander*, (which was actually constructed for the Royal New Zealand Navy), noting in his journal that it had an incredible maximum speed of 42 knots. He was mistaken in this for, like *HMS Furious*, it had a designed speed of 32.5 knots. However, Brian's log book entry was not questioned or corrected by the ship's officer who seemed to pay more attention to the spelling of words like 'manoeuvres.'

His second winter cruise commenced in stormy January weather as the squadron headed once again for the West Indies, covering much the same ground as his earlier one, calling first at St Kitts, and then at Nevis. The cruise continued to Barbados and Trinidad, and the squadron then returned to Devonport and Brian went on leave on St Patrick's Day.

Brian was among a handful of the *Norfolk's* crew transferred to the aircraft-carrier, *HMS Furious*, for two week's of 'air training.' It took Brian some time 'and several scalp gashes' to get used to the reduced headroom on the carrier, but he enjoyed the open space of the flight deck which he found to be 'just perfect for a game of hockey.' He was taken up in one of the carrier's planes, and while he did not like flying, his only comment on this occasion was: 'In formation flying, all pilots keep their eyes glued on the leader who signals all manoeuvres such as turns with his hands.'

After sailing to the north-east Scottish coast, the *Furious* anchored off Dornoch, a short distance from Invergordon, in full view of Dunrobin Castle, the palatial seat of the Dukes of Sutherland. Perhaps Brian was aware that these had been ruthless landlords who, a century earlier, had conducted mass evictions that put similar efforts on the part of some of the Irish landlords in the second league. Those on board should have been able to see the seventy-foot high memorial to the first Duke of Sutherland on Ben Bhraggie, high above the castle, erected at a cost of almost £15,000 – approximately the sum of one year's rental from the entire Sutherland estate. John Prebble, who has written a number of books about Scotland, was told by a local man that most of the money was raised by contributions from the tenantry and that 'all who could raise a shilling gave it, and those who could not awaited in terror for the consequences of their default.' Sea manoeuvres continued for several days off the Dornoch coast before the squadron entered the Firth to anchor once again at Invergordon – their first visit eight months after the so-called mutiny. Brian's log book for the next day records that: 'During the forenoon there was a plotting exercise,' perhaps an unfortunate term to use in the circumstances. This short summer cruise was confined to home waters, taking in Scapa Flow, the Isle of Lewis and Arran, after which the squadron returned to Devonport.

Brian was transferred to *HMS Royal Sovereign* in November 1932 just before the vessel sailed for Malta, calling briefly at Gibraltar. Almost two months later, the newly commissioned destroyer, *HMS Defender*, arrived and Brian was one of two crewmen transferred to this very much smaller vessel which, however, he declared to be 'most comfortable.' He liked the spirit of co-operation between officers and men on board which he thought was a special feature to be found in smaller ships, 'rather than that of aggression so often found in bigger ships' – a comment which, with the benefit of hindsight, was to prove significant. Brian wrote that he enjoyed his destroyer experiences and hoped that 'it may fall to my lot to become a destroyer officer in the future,' another remark to prove significant later.

Brian's neat sketches were a feature of his log book. This
drawing was titled 'French Crabbers at Scilly, June 1932'.

Throughout the previous five years, there had been no indication, either in letters sent to his family or in his log book, that Brian was unhappy in the navy, but from the middle of 1935 onwards it became increasingly clear that this was so. It is known that he was prone to sea-sickness, but despite this he had several times stated a preference for smaller ships, and had very recently expressed the hope that he would, one day, become an officer on a destroyer. It may have been no coincidence that the first hints that he was thinking of giving up his naval career came in letters to his father after he had transferred to the battleship, *HMS Royal Sovereign*. At 25,700 tons, this was by far the largest vessel he had ever sailed in, more than twice the displacement of his first vessel, *HMS Norfolk*, a cruiser of just under 10,000 tons, and more than 20 times heavier than the destroyer, *HMS Defender*, which displaced a mere 1,175 tons.

Brian had written to his sister, Bridget, mentioning that 'Lord Mountbatten … has started to teach me to play polo which is the only thing I look forward to at the week-ends.' After similar hints, this further indication that he was unhappy in the navy was followed by a letter to his parents making it clear that he thoroughly disliked the *Royal Sovereign*:

> I have struck a bloody awful ship, which is a greater jar after the old *Norfolk* …
> I am simply counting the days till I get back to England and nice people who
> have got nothing to do with the Navy. Even the women know as much about
> the ships as one does oneself out here.

Perhaps because he was conscious that the family might misinterpret this latter remark, he added: 'They are all dreadful, so you need have no fear.'

During April 1936, Brian wrote home on *HMS Sturdy* notepaper, indicating a further change of ship. The vessel was at the time docked at Plymouth, possibly for a re-fit, as he and the ship's captain were the only crew members on board. In this letter, he apologised to his father for making him unhappy.

> I really must leave the Navy. I know jobs are damned hard to get, but I think I
> could get one. Everyone advises me that if I am going to leave, I had better
> leave while I am still young. You see I simply don't fit. I hate the sea, and my
> only happiness is when I get ashore.

His letter continued in this vein for five pages, ending with Brian's deep regret that he had failed his father.

* * *

So, against his fathers' wishes, Brian left the Royal Navy in the summer of 1936 after which there is a gap of several months during which no information about him is available. Yet, by the end of that year, he had set up business in London as a literary agent even though there is no apparent indication prior to this that he had any ambition – let alone any experience – to work in this field. His company bore his own name, 'Brian Gore-Booth & Co.,' and was described in promotional material as 'Literary, Lecture and Broadcasting Agents.'

> This firm aims at offering to authors a very comprehensive service for the disposal of their work and the expansion of their existing markets, enquiries from new authors are welcomed and the firm is receiving a demand particularly for new fiction writers which it is quite unable to meet. Editorial commissions of all kinds can be obtained for clients, and ideas for articles and factual books by authoritative writers are particularly sought.

The company claimed to be in a position to place articles, books, etc., 'both at home and throughout the English speaking world, and would negotiate translation rights abroad where it was represented at the time in Stockholm, Paris and New York. Claims were also made that the firm had a thorough knowledge of the film market and maintained close contact with the B.B.C. Despite his own total lack of previous experience, and allowing that his firm ran into financial difficulties several times, Brian seems to have run his new business with at least a modest degree of success. In his offices at Chancery Lane in London's W.C.2 postal district, he employed a small staff, and two names were to crop up frequently over the next three years or so, those of Alan Fraser, who was manager, and John Davie. It seems reasonable to speculate that that these two men already had some knowledge of the trade. Brian's secretary was a Miss Kenyon who, with Davie, were appointed by Brian to be his executors a few years later.

There were some very difficult periods when business was distinctly bad, but he and his loyal staff managed to weather these storms. Whatever Brian lacked in actual experience seems to have been offset by his pleasant outgoing personality – as a member of the family expressed it, 'he had a way with people.' While the fact that he was a good mixer brought him into contact with a very wide circle of friends and possible business acquaintances, it seems more than likely that both Davie and Fraser, with previous experience in the business, were a stronger factor in the comparative success achieved in a short time. Even so, writing about Brian's achievements, the art editor of *The Sphere* described his agency firm as a 'brilliant piece of work for so young a man' (he was 26 at the time). Bernard Strachy wrote in *The Author* that 'no client had a more shrewd, helpful and guiding counsellor, and no friend had a more loyal, courageous and stimulating intimate.'

Davie and Fraser very probably took the initiative in the decision to branch into various aspects of lecturing. If one were to judge by the names of those commissioned to take part as speakers in one of the lecture series organised by the company, this venture seems to have been quite successful. Among the list of names were those of some of the acknowledged leaders in their various fields at the time, including Peter Scott, the well known naturalist and son of the polar explorer; Denzil Batchelor, author, broadcaster and journalist, who had just returned from Spain where he had been a war correspondent; C.B. Fry, one of England's most renowned all-round athletes who had a special interest in promoting sport among young people; and Ludwig Koch, who pioneered the recording of bird song, originating what were called 'Song Books,' a combination of text, photographs and gramophone recordings.

During 1937, Brian's second year as a literary agent, a book was published for which, according to Dr Malcolmson, Brian had acted as the author's literary agent. In fact, it had more than an agent's interest for him because it was entitled *The Mutiny at Invergordon*, and was written by Kenneth Edwards, Lt. Cmdr., R.N., Ret'd., a copy of which was found among Brian's effects after he died.

Brian is known to have written at least one article for a London newspaper, the *Morning Post* – as it happens it was critical of de Valera's attempts at the time to curb the capacity of the second chamber to obstruct legislation prepared by his government. Clearly Brian's political views were coloured in the first place by his schooling in Northern Ireland and his college days in England. Among those who, like Brian, attended Mourne Grange school in County Down at that period was the future Canon Cosslett Quin, a well-read Church of Ireland rector who, as Cosslett Ó Cuinn, became a fluent Irish speaker. Risteárd Ó Glaisne, in his biography (in Irish) of Quin recollected being told by him that he had been sent to what he called 'a very pro-British establishment' by his fervently Unionist father, and some of Quin's recollections of the school are quoted in the book:

> Unless I am wrong, the father of one of the boys whom I knew when he was there, Price, was head of the Intelligence Section in Dublin Castle. There were two Gore-Booths there, and I remember another boy saying to me about one of them, "Don't tell anyone but his aunt is that dreadful Countess Markievicz."

It appears that Brian aspired to become a writer in addition to his career in the agency business but little has survived to show that he succeeded. Among the Lissadell Papers there is a tantalising hint in a clipping taken from an unidentified and undated newspaper (possibly the *Belfast Telegraph*) about what might have happened, in which the writer suggested that Brian Gore-Booth had what amounted to an option to write an important biography:

> Not more than twelve people in all Ulster know a secret about Lord Craigavon which I may now tell. Many people tried to persuade him to allow an official biography to be written, but time and again he refused. Brian Gore-Booth came nearest, but that was a few years ago and Craigavon said the time was not right.

Though he frequently told his parents how his literary business was faring, Brian hardly ever went into details about the work involved. One of the very few such references, made in a letter to his father, concerned Sir Charles Harrington 'whom you remember, was so kind to me at Gibraltar, has asked us to make the arrangements for the publication of his memoirs.' Brian then added: 'This may prove to be quite profitable.'

Brian was gregarious by nature, mixing easily in company. Perhaps, the restricted opportunities for socialising during his naval service had been one of a number of factors that made him decide to leave. Certainly, once he established his new business in London, he spent much of his spare time during evenings and at weekends mixing with friends and with his many relations scattered around different parts of Britain. He often went shooting, fishing or sailing, and during one weekend with friends at Bath he managed to bag 160 pheasants – 'all great fliers off high hillside coverts.' On another occasion, in Wiltshire, he went flying, after which he made the comment that nothing would ever make him an airman. He also entertained liberally at his own apartment. In a letter to his mother he mentioned that his brother, Angus, had 'turned up … looking very fit, en route for the Old Radlean dinner,' adding that 'Hugh turned up yesterday after Smithfield [Agricultural] Show.' Shortly after this, he met Angus again, 'en route to his examiner.' Brian thought that if his youngest brother was interested, he might be able to assist him to get a job 'on a newspaper or with a publisher.'

Brian decided to mount an exhibition stand for his company at the National Book Fair, and claimed that his was the first agency to do so. Though he described the idea as 'a long shot,' he later wrote that 'some good new clients' were attracted, and he had also secured the serial rights 'for the latest Edward's book.' With the onset of a new year, he told his father that he had decided he had too often in the past allowed himself:

> to be swayed by trivial matters, and this year I am going to try, D.V., to keep the main objective in view. Last year I lost much valuable time going out too often

and fooling about. This year I must try to control events more and be more sensible, spend less money, and waste less time.

Lord Dunally, a friend of both Brian and Hugh, wrote a description of Brian's office:

Brian had his own room, a bright, tidy little place with well ordered shelves packed with correspondence, files and reference books. Brian was justifiably very proud of it. When I came in he was almost always on the telephone, speaking slowly, very precisely and to the point. His top hat lay on his desk and he told me that this was kept specially for difficult interviews and truculent customers.

I remember the life and bustle of the office, its orderliness and obvious industry. But far more I remember the extremely happy atmosphere. The undertaking was not only adventurous, it was an adventure. The crew of the ship, metaphorically speaking, were like the followers of Drake and Grenville – they were partners rather than paid servants, with their share and vital interest in success. Brian, though, was an ideal employer. He liked the people who worked with him and knew them.

There was real colour, too, about the enterprise. Brian dealt with colourful people, men and women who had something to tell their fellow beings – novelists, historians, short story writers, journalist and lecturers. Brian's mental diet was not the saw dust of bank balances and stock market ledgers – it was the bone and blood of human personalities whom he had to study, understand, and capitalise in print. He did not, like the banker, happen to make acquaintances while earning his living. It was precisely in order to earn a living that he got to know people and to know them really well…. He reached the ideal position of combining business with pleasure, and succeeding in both.

While his sister Aideen wrote that 'his brief career as a literary agent met with success and he achieved much in a short time,' it is difficult to make any precise assessment of the success or otherwise of Brian's agency business. After less than four years in the business, the clouds of war were already gathering across Europe, so that the full potential of his undertaking was never realised. It is clear that it went through periods of crisis – which, on one occasion, caused him to ask his father for a loan 'as the bill for the rent and light are due here and I cannot meet them without your assistance.' Expressing how wretched he felt about the matter, he promised to start the return payments straight away. He was, he said, cutting down on his expenditure. Yet, almost in the same breath, he added that he had attended a most stylish ball at Holland House where, unfortunately, there were so many guests that he 'never caught sight of the Queen but I saw the King very close up more than once.' In that same letter he wrote that he had also attended a ball given by the Duchess of Grafton. He had also attended the marriage of a family friend, Robert Phillimore, and had seen his mother's wedding present there. He wrote to his parents to tell them he was coming home to Lissadell for a short break at Easter. 'At last I believe the war clouds are beginning to disperse. Although one hardly dares to hope so, I believe the chances of peace are now greater than they have been for a very long time.'

Brian sketched the Royal Yacht during the annual review at Weymouth, 1932.

Brian wrote this letter just after the *Anschluss*, Hitler's invasion of Austria, in March 1938. His hopes for peace were soon to be put under renewed strain when, six months later, Hitler demanded that Czechoslovakia cede its German-speaking territories, known as the Sudetenland. It was only after Britain and France decided not to oppose the take-over – the so-called Munich Agreement – that the threat of immediate war was averted. After this appeasement of Hitler, Brian wrote: 'Once again we can settle down to a short period of uneasy peace.' He was right to use the words 'a short period' because, six months later, German troops stormed into the rest of Czechoslovakia and once again no nation was prepared to intervene. The only questions were – what country was next on Hitler's acquisition list, and for how much longer would the rest of the world do nothing to stop him. As a naval reservist, Brian knew that if Britain became embroiled in a war with Germany, he would be called up for service. He wrote letters to his parents almost every week and most of them at this period included some reference to the uneasy political situation in Europe.

After Germany had taken control of the remainder of Czechoslovakia, Brian wrote about the major implications that Hitler's expansionist moves were likely to have for the rest of Europe, and concluded that it was very disheartening 'that such confidence as was created by [the] Munich [Agreement] is now blown to the four winds.' 'Sooner or later,' he wrote, 'we shall have to face up to Hitler, and I do not think it can be delayed much longer,' words written just six months before his prophesy came true. If he was worried about the thought of having to re-enter the navy, this was not expressed. Instead, he wrote to his father to voice his concern about the implications that any enforced absence would have for his business. He told his father that the worsening political situation:

> puts one's little efforts at earning a living, etc., in a particularly futile light, as probably the world in which Literary Agents exist will not exist many months more. However, one can but do one's best and should one be called to fight it will be in the sure knowledge that anything is preferable to domination. Perhaps they may yet find a solution which will not involve bloodshed, but I fear it may already be too late. Do not laugh at what I have to say. At Lissadell you ought to be storing essential things which will keep, and which may become difficult to obtain in time of war. You ought to remember, too, that you may be able to provide a refuge for friends and relations who may be forced to leave their homes here. It could be better to think about these things now so that we as a family will not fail in our duty to the community if the worst comes. Plans for emergency are being made in all the country houses here and I feel sure you should take heed of these possibilities.

Brian ended his letter on a further gloomy note: 'Business, once again, has been brought almost to a standstill.' Yet, in his next letter, his worries about the agency enterprise had, for unexplained reasons, evaporated: 'The business,' he wrote, 'continues to sweep on in a wave of new prosperity.' Encouraged by this and despite the uneasy state of Europe, Brian was determined to expand the business abroad, and to this end his partner (probably A.G. Fraser) was about to embark on a tour of the leading publishing centres on the continent. He hoped to realise his dream that the enterprise might become 'the leading firm of Literary Agents' and thus 'establish my own financial position sufficiently securely for me to develop new fields.' Shortly after this, Brian wrote of his disappointment that his application for financial assistance for the project from the British Council had been turned down.

Many of Brian's regular letters to his parents ended, 'My love to you all and God Bless you and keep you.' Occasionally they included other references that hinted at his religious feelings, as in the following paragraph:

Given the strength to pursue some end, I sometimes feel that you can achieve almost anything in this world, D.V. It is but a question of harnessing a sort of divine force against which nothing can stand. Sometimes I have had it for a very short time and achieved marvellous results while it lasted. Unfortunately, then come periods of pessimism and depression when one seems to plunge downhill to depths as extreme as the heights you were on before.

Behind his cheerful exterior there was this more sombre side to Brian's character, as illustrated by a comment made in one of his letters sent to Lissadell after a spell of visits to the dentist: 'Teeth are, I suppose, but milestones to the grave, and going to the dentist is just one of the many futile efforts which we make to arrest a natural progress towards eternity!' Early in August 1939, Brian instructed his solicitors on what was to be done 'should circumstances arise under which the business continued without my assistance.' He posted a copy to his father, telling him that he had just cancelled his planned holiday in Portugal because he thought it best to be prepared for 'any eventuality.' He speculated that 'if Hitler makes any move against Poland over Danzig, the balloon will go up' which was precisely what happened, for World War II began when the German battleship, *Schleswig Holstein*, shelled a Polish fort near Danzig. Hitler may have gambled that Britain and France would do nothing, as had happened in the case of Austria and Czechoslovakia, but this time both countries felt a stand had to be taken, not least because they felt bound by existing treaties between the two nations and Poland.

Just over a week before the outbreak of the war, Brian wrote to his firm's solicitor giving instructions which he wished them to file 'in case there is a war and I am called up for service before I am able to make more detailed arrangements with you.' He instructed that in the event of hostilities, Mr A.G. Fraser 'will be in sole charge of this office, and empowered to act on behalf of my partner and myself in all matters which may arise.' Little is known about Fraser, but he seems to have been an older person (perhaps not liable for conscription) and may have been a steadying influence in the running of Brian's company. Brian detailed the current arrangements whereby he received 'fifty-five per cent of all monies available for distribution between us, and my capital holding in the business is £500.' He outlined again what he wished to be done 'should circumstance ever arise under which the business continued without my active assistance,' in which event he now wished his interest to be taken over by his youngest brother, Angus Gore-Booth.

The Germans quickly overran western Poland, whose troops made a gallant but futile attempt at defending their country on three fronts (Germany, Czechoslovakia and East Prussia), until the Russians attacked them on a fourth front from the east, and Brian expected almost daily to hear news of his expected call-up. He found it difficult to concentrate on his work because of the continuing uncertainty and because he found it necessary to make so many contingency plans to ensure that the business of the firm continued smoothly.

* * *

Just one month after the beginning of the war, Brian wrote home to say he had received a letter from the Admiralty advising that he was being transferred from the naval reserve to the regular navy, and confirming that he would retain his old rank and seniority. Remembering that his old naval cap was somewhere in his bedroom at Lissadell he asked the family to post it to him. He was aware that it might be difficult to find because 'Hugh borrowed it last time I was home for Raghley Regatta.' By mid-October, he had obtained his uniform but still awaited news, not only of his call-up but also whether the navy would decide to send him to sea or, as he thought possible, that he might be appointed to a posting ashore. In view of his outburst in 1936 – 'I hate the sea,' this may well have been wishful thinking on his part.

The long wait ended a few weeks later when Brian received instructions from the Admiralty to report for service, and he joined the destroyer, *HMS Exmouth*. Whatever his thoughts about the situation as a whole, he must have been pleased that he was posted to a small vessel. Apart from his expressed frustration at having to leave his business just when it seemed to be succeeding, nothing is known about his thinking at this time other than he felt he was simply doing his duty. This was partly due to the fact that Brian was unable to communicate to his family what he was doing in the navy. Censorship was strict about references to military matters, and his family, too, had to be circumspect about what they wrote in letters to him, as all letters sent abroad were carefully scrutinised by Irish censors too.

One of Brian's cousins, Rosamund Leven, who lived at Glenferne House, near Nairn in northeastern Scotland – not very far from the Invergordon naval base – wrote to Lady Gore-Booth during November to tell her that Brian had been staying with the family. 'I told him to come if he ever got leave in Scottish waters ... he was pretty well played out when he arrived. He has had a pretty hard time of it but seems very well ... and so happy just doing anything. We are all very fond of him.' By some coincidence, a friend of the family, Minnie Clarke, who lived in Armagh, wrote on the same day: 'I hope you still have good news of him. I am always thinking of him and praying for him. The poor sailors are having a hard time.'

The sailors were, indeed, having a hard time. While the first six months of the conflict came to be known as 'the phoney war,' as huge masses of armies faced each other without engaging in serious fighting, the picture at sea was totally different. The Germans sent an unambiguous signal to Britain and France on the very first day of the war when the liner *Athenia*, carrying British children and American citizens away from the war zone, was sunk off the northwest coast of Ireland despite the fact that three years earlier Germany signed up to what was known as the London Protocol which denounced submarine war on merchant shipping. Thereafter, German U-boats continued to target lone merchant ships with deadly efficiency, forcing their opponents to organise their shipping into convoys escorted by naval vessels, and it was escort duties to which the *Exmouth* was assigned throughout this period.

Convoys, for obvious reasons, moved at the speed of the slowest ship, so the task of the escorts was boring and often frustrating. The convoy route from the Thames to the Firth of Forth and onwards around the north of Scotland seems to have been the regular beat of Brian's vessel – which was probably then based at Invergordon – judging from the fact that he visited his cousins near Nairn several times during the late autumn and early winter of 1939. This route was particularly vulnerable, not only from submarine attacks but also from enemy aircraft and, subsequently, from mines as well. It was also a period of especially bad weather, with frequent violent storms. Life on board destroyers and corvettes was hardly comfortable at the best of times, as these small vessels were tossed about in the mountainous seas like corks, but despite the discomfort most sailors almost looked forward to such weather because it made it virtually impossible for submarine commanders to attack shipping. However, the weather made no difference to the effectiveness of mines which, off England's east coast, were having such a deadly effect that during one period in November, sea traffic was halted altogether. During the first six months of the war, some 100 ships, naval vessels and merchantmen alike, were sunk by mines. Although the British did not know it at the time, the entire German submarine fleet had already been deployed at sea at least a week before Britain and France had declared war, and it was submarine warfare that ultimately did the greatest damage to shipping.

Most people who remember some of the events of the Second World War probably recall something of the appalling shipping losses wreaked by the U-boat campaign – running to millions of tons. Less well known, however, is the price paid by Germany. Peter Padfield, in his definitive account of submarine warfare in World War Two, pointed out that of some 1,162 U-boats built, the Germans lost almost 800. The submarine arm of the German navy comprised some 40,500 officers and men, of which over 30,000 were killed and more that 5,000 were taken prisoner after being rescued from their sunken craft, a higher proportion of losses suffered than any other branch of their armed forces.

Brian wrote to his brother, Hugh, in November telling him that his ship was a destroyer, and practically always at sea. 'At first it was a pretty savage change of life and I was very sea-sick, but now I am settling down and feel already as if I had never been out of the Service at all, rather than a gap of five years since I was last at sea.' He commented that he was 'among an exceptionally nice bunch of brother officers, and it makes a great difference to know that everything we do is vitally necessary to the welfare of the country.' He wondered if Hugh might get home for Christmas, adding that his own chances 'are very remote.' He wished to be remembered to Angus and mentioned that he was getting weekly letters from Miss Kenyon, his secretary at the Agency office. She kept him informed about developments in the literary business, prompting Brian to comment: 'I hope they will keep things until our return.' In a letter sent to his family which he penned on Christmas Day he wrote:

It is Christmas Day and I am at sea – a wonderful day with marvellous lights in the sky at dawn, and one of the most beautiful sunsets I have ever seen. I suppose to everyone engaged in war, today seems rather a mockery – to talk of peace and good-will towards all men when one is engaged on a mission of destruction. But still the old spirit, the best of Christmas spirit, has done us all good. For a few hours frayed nerves have been put aside and differences of rank forgotten. We have faced the threshold of the coming year and gazed on the dreary road ahead together hoping that our next Christmas will be spent in happier circumstances…. It has really been a happy day within the narrow limits of this tiny ship. The first lieutenant dressed as Father Christmas – we visited the sailors to give them a share in the goodies you and others had sent us. Everyone forgot their cares and faces looked less strained than normal. Now it is evening and we are bound for home. Our captain has been awarded the D.S.O.

[Distinguished Service Order] for our part in recent operations. I can tell you nothing more.

Because of censorship, most of Brian's other letters at this time were necessarily rather uninteresting. Just after the New Year he wrote in a letter to his mother: 'The Nazis show signs of being increasingly tiresome, which is rather a bore for anyone who appears to so utterly lack the heroic spirit as I do.' In another letter, he wrote hopefully:

> Perhaps there will be a break in the clouds soon. I do feel we are fighting not only for victory but to exterminate all sorts of Evil Things. This experience brings home the true nature of Christian Religion and if one had never been through it one might never have found its inner meanings – that roots of happiness lie in service for others and forgetfulness of self, and self sacrifice …. I know some ancient truths I never knew before. I have tasted the strength of leaving oneself in other hands in times of great adversity.

His destroyer continued to be involved in escorting convoys of merchant ships off the east coast of Britain, and soon afterwards his convoy was being shadowed by a German submarine watching for a favourable moment to attack. Exactly what happened will never be known, being one of many similar incidents during the long years of World War II, but on Tuesday, January 23 1940 a telegram from the Admiralty arrived at Lissadell: 'Admiralty deeply regret to inform you that your son, Sub-Lieut. Brian Gore-Booth is believed to have been on board *H.M.S. Exmouth* and is therefore regarded as missing presumed dead.'

On the same date the Admiralty issued the following communiqué: 'The Secretary of the Admiralty regrets to announce that H.M.S. Destroyer, *Exmouth* (Captain, R.S. Benson), has been sunk by mine or torpedo and it is feared that there are no survivors.'

The *Exmouth* was the fifth British destroyer to be sunk during the first five months of the war, and the first from which there were no survivors. A month later, the Admiralty drafted a standard letter for next-of-kin who wished to enquire about the loss of the *Exmouth*, though there is no evidence that Brian's family did so. It stated that the destroyer 'was lost with all hands in position 58° 18′ N., 02° 25′ W, in the Outer Moray Firth.' It gave the known details, including the fact that the *Exmouth* had been ordered to hunt for a U-boat known to be in the area, but at 0535 it was torpedoed, as it later transpired, by U 22, commanded by Kapitänleutnant Karl Heinrich Jenisch, who sank a Danish merchant ship in the same convoy shortly afterwards.

Confirmation of the sinking came from the *SS Cyprian Prince* which had been astern of the *Exmouth*, whose captain heard two loud explosions, initially thought by him to have been caused by depth charges dropped in an attack on the unseen submarine. When *HMS Exmouth* failed to respond to calls for her position, several aircraft and minesweepers, as well as two lifeboats searched the area but, as the Ministry of Defence recorded, 'only a lifebuoy from the *Exmouth* and some floating debris were sighted.'

Part of Brian's letter, in which he wrote about having 'tasted the strength of leaving oneself in other hands at times of great adversity' was later quoted by the Rev. J.R. Wesley Roddie at a service in University Road Church, Belfast, when he described Brian's words as 'a confession of faith, beautiful, sincere and self-revealing.'

On the day before the Admiralty telegram arrived at Lissadell, Brian's mother posted a letter to him saying that she had just sent him a parcel containing a cake 'cooked from a recipe of Nannie's sister-in-law.' The letter was later returned to Lissadell undelivered, and stamped 'Return to Sender – Admiralty Instruction.'

Six days after the *Exmouth* went down, *The Irish Times* reported that 15 bodies from the vessel had been washed ashore on the northeast coast of Scotland and had been buried together with military honours. The report noted that 11 of the victims had been identified and three more bodies were washed ashore on the day of the funeral. From this it appears that none of the bodies of the other 172 men on board were ever located and presumably went to the bottom of the sea with the ship. There is no written record of the family's reactions to the news – their devastation can only be imagined. Brian had celebrated his twenty-eighth birthday just one month earlier, and his death resulted in a very large number of letters of condolence being sent to the family. That *The Irish Times* should have reported the loss of the *Exmouth* was no coincidence. Its editor, R.M. Smyllie, hailed from Sligo and personally knew several members of the family. In a letter to Sir Josslyn he expressed his sympathy: 'I knew Brian very well, and one could not know him without liking him. I had a letter from him on the day before he went to sea and he seemed to be looking forward to his service.'

There were scores of other letters expressing similar sentiments, including one from Sub-Lieutenant Robert Phillimore, whose wedding Brian had attended three years earlier, who told Angus that his own ship and the *Exmouth* 'were screening with the same convoy when, sadly, the *Exmouth* 'was sunk by a U-Boat.' Four months later, a letter written by Sam Lombard Hobson on *HMS Whitshed* notepaper arrived in Sir Josslyn's post.

> Perhaps I can give you a piece of interesting information about the Exmouth. I gather little or nothing was known about her fate. In February I had the fortune to sink my second U-Boat. Out of this we got 41 German prisoners. On one of the prisoners I got a notebook showing various details of where the U-boat had been and what it had been doing. It was badly spoiled by the sea water and I sent it to the Adrmiralty where they managed to find the information that this submarine had sunk a destroyer at about the time and place of the Exmouth's whereabouts ... I think it is obvious that she was torpedoed and as she sank her depth charges must have gone off and killed everybody instantly.

Commenting on the vulnerability of small destroyers in his *History of the Second World War*, Sir Winston Churchill referred to the sinking of *HMS Exmouth*: 'These unarmoured vessels with nearly two hundred men on board became, as *Grenville* and *Exmouth* have shown, a prize and a target for a U-boat in themselves .... It is unsound to place so large a human stake in an unarmoured, highly vulnerable vessel ....'

Lord Mountbatten, a former destroyer captain, told the author William Pattinson in an interview that most naval men had a preference to serve on destroyers because they had a small enough complement 'for the Captain to know everybody by sight and by name,' a view that had been shared by Brian. Mountbatten felt that destroyers were 'by far the most glamorous of all the types of warship' and that sailing in these small ships 'was the most exciting way to serve because ... destroyers were out in the fray the whole time.' Significantly, he added, 'I suppose more people were killed in destroyers pro rata than any other form of naval warfare.'

After the news about Brian reached the family, they were especially concerned for two of their other sons serving far from the family circle in its time of crisis. Hugh was a lieutenant with the Royal Irish Fusiliers, then stationed in Kent, and Angus was serving elsewhere in England with the Irish Guards. Hugh was grateful for his parents' concern and was, in turn, anxious for his father and mother who had to bear the news 'coming as it does on top of Michael's nervous disturbance.' In the same letter Hugh wrote:

> Poor Brian always prayed that he might have the courage to face the War when it came, as for some years past he inevitably realised it would. For a man of slight physique whose horror of war was a constant apparition, nothing could surpass the heroism of his example – everything pales into insignificance beside the noble unselfishness with which he gave himself for service ....

There is a sense of irony in the fact that when Brian's death was reported in the British newspapers, his name was almost invariably linked with that of his Aunt Constance before any mention was made about his grieving parents. The headline in the report published in the *London Evening Standard* on January 26 was typical: 'Countess's Nephew Lost in the *Exmouth*.' The *Standard's* report read: 'A nephew of the Countess Markieviecz, the first woman to be elected to the House of Commons, was among the officers who lost their lives in the sinking of the destroyer *Exmouth*....' There was a different, if more expected emphasis in the *Times Literary Supplement* where the headline was: 'Literary Agent Killed' and this report described him as 'well read and interested in political and social conditions.' The Dublin *Evening Mail* reported that 188 men had lost their lives on the *Exmouth* and 'the list included many Irish names.' *The Irish Times* quoted from a letter written by Brian just after he had been posted to the *Exmouth* (presumably the same one mentioned by Smyllie in his letter to the family): 'I am among an exceptionally nice bunch of fellow officers and it makes a difference to know that everything that we are doing is vitally necessary to the welfare of the country.'

* * *

During the time that Brian had been running his agency business in London, he rented an apartment in Lower Sloane Street and had a housekeeper, invariably referred to as 'Miss Leahy,' who looked after both the flat and Brian. While he often entertained his many friends there, little is known about his home life at that time as he tended not to detail such matters in his letters to the family apart from references to visits from relations. A rare reference to Miss Leahy (who hailed from Cork) occurred in a letter in which he mentioned he had recently been unwell 'with a chill on the liver,' but he had fully recovered 'thanks to the excellent ministrations of Miss Leahy.' In another letter he asked his mother in a post-script, 'Could Leahy be accommodated at Lissadell if necessary?' They both got on well together and sometimes, when he had guests to dinner, Brian would jokingly apologise about the meal being late, 'explaining' that Miss Leahy 'had been on the bottle' a short time earlier. For her part, she took this kind of banter in good heart.

A picture of this aspect of his short life and of Miss Leahy comes through strongly in a series of letters which Elizabeth Leahy sent to

Brian's mother after his death. In the first of these, she wrote to Lady Gore-Booth to express her regret at the news about Brian and it is clear that she genuinely shared in the family's devastation. While sorting Brian's belongings at the flat, she was unable to account for some items because:

> Dear Mr. Brian took some of the linen to sea with him, also a mahogany box which use[d] to stand on the chest of drawers in the bedroom, also the little bottles which fitted inside the box with silver tops on. It is sad to write this …. I did not think a fortnight ago to-day there was going to be such grief in store for us … I feel now I have not only lost an employer but a friend as well. He was very young and most considerate for his years. I went down to the front door when he was going away, and before he got into the car he said to me, if they gave him a [shore] job in Harwich he would take a flat up there and send for me to look after him. I told him I would go, but it was not to be.

Later she wrote again, enclosing a list of the contents of Brian's flat. From the manner in which she wrote down the details it is clear that she was a well-organised, methodical woman who was engaged in carefully and sympathetically tidying up Brian's London domestic affairs. In her letter she thanked his mother for sending her a copy of the *Sligo Champion* in which there was a report about Brian. She told Lady Gore-Booth that 'the letters Mr Brian wrote were very beautiful and he seemed happy.' and she mentioned that Mr Franklin, who worked in Brian's agency, had told her that he had dinner with him at Christmas on board the *Exmouth*. She continued to write at regular intervals for more than a year, reporting on how she was sorting out various matters at the flat and, later responding to various requests from Lady Mary.

With one of her letters she enclosed a small notebook bearing the title 'Sayings of Brian to his Housekeeper, Elizabeth Leahy:' Examples included: 'I could tell at once when I put the key in the door that you were in the flat. It looked so nice with the flowers about the place, it was just like coming home, I did miss you when you were away.' Another entry read: 'I wonder which of us will go first. If I go first, I will tell St. Peter he must not let you into Heaven; you are to come down below to look after me.'

Elizabeth Leahy always addressed Brian's mother as 'My Lady' and signed her letters 'Yours very respectfully,' and she referred to the younger members of the family as 'Mr Brian,' 'Mr Hugh,' 'Miss Bridget,' etc. During this period, Lady Mary sent parcels to her of butter and eggs which were very scarce in Britain and sometimes sent flowers as well. In one of her letters, Miss Leahy told Lady Gore-

Booth that 'yesterday, Sunday, while at Mass, through the Service, Mr Brian seemed to be near, and I know I am not to see him. I am proud to have worked for him; One don't meet people like him every day to work for.' Brian's mother told Elizabeth Leahy that she intended to travel to London 'with the two young ladies' – probably Aideen and Gabrielle – presumably to complete Brian's affairs. It was hardly surprising, given all of this, that Lady Gore-Booth offered Elizabeth Leahy a job at Lissadell which, however, was declined. Instead, she expressed the hope that after the war she might be spared 'to visit Ireland again, though for now all the laughter and merriment is gone from this flat.'

One week before news came through that *HMS Exmouth* had been sunk, Angus had written to Hugh about 'goings on' at Lissadell and ended it with the words: 'Well, I must stop and write to Brian who appears to be finding the strain of it all. I should not care to be thrown into the sea this weather.' Eight days later, Angus wrote to Hugh again: 'It is terribly sad about Brian; when I got the wire [telegram] at first I could not comprehend, but after a little while the full force of sorrow came upon me and I wept.' Sir Josslyn wrote to Hugh on the same day, still awaiting further details but feeling that 'there can be but little hope …. It will be a cruel blow to you, you were so much together …. We are only among many suffering and we would think of others too. May God bless you, your affec. Father.' Thomas Kilgallon, Sir Henry's old valet, by then retired, was living with his daughter in Sligo. He travelled to Lissadell by taxi and stayed for several days to keep company with Sir Josslyn, who of course, he remembered as a boy and young man. Writing to Hugh about this, Gabrielle thought 'it was very nice of him to come, he said to us that we were just like his own children. He has made such a difference to Daddy, he sat with him and talked with him nearly all day.'

Bridget wrote to her brother, Hugh, stating that she would remember Brian for his bravery because:

> He simply dreaded and abhorred the very idea or thought of war, and yet when the call came, he went without a murmur. To a person of his temperament the whole thing must have meant absolute hell …. You have no idea how kind and considerate people have been. All sorts of very unexpected people have sent wires and letters of sympathy…. I think everyone here feels it very much, Brian was so popular with everyone. I think they feel they have lost someone belonging to themselves.

While the family was still grieving over Brian's death, Stanislas Markieviecz wrote to Sir Josslyn. Known in the family as 'Staskow,' Constance's stepson had been, like her daughter, Maeve, left largely to fend for himself. Now in his forties, he had lived a miserable life, existing on mere scraps of jobs and was perpetually short of money. Without at least this minimal amount of information his letter at such a sensitive time could be seen to be totally lacking in tact. He wrote to suggest to Sir Josslyn that he hoped he could be considered suitable to take Brian's place as a partner in the agency business:

> I do need a start in life, Joss, and I've had a dreadful time of it. I'm sure your poor old Brian would have wished you to do this for me to commemorate his memory. You know that I have had less chance than Maeve and any of the others of my generation. It has been War and Revolution, and whole periods of unemployment since I left here [Ireland] in 1915, little more than a schoolboy.

He detailed his parlous financial situation and pleaded that if it were not possible for him to join the agency business, perhaps Josslyn would consider paying the cost of his fare to Paris 'and a few pounds for expenses.' In that event he hoped to join the Polish Army-in-exile, and he wrote that he was prepared to risk death on duty rather than continue living in Dublin on £100 a year 'which is living death.' The letter continued: 'I know perfectly well that you wish to assume no responsibility in respect of me; my claim is only moral; you were all fond of my father, and it was Con, really that broke our lives up …' He apologised for 'making this approach at a time of distress' and ended his plea for help: 'If it wasn't killing me, I would not trouble to forego all my pride … but needs must.' Across the top of Staskow's letter, Josslyn wrote four words: 'Thanked for previous letter.'

There was a suggestion, possibly originating with his sister, Bridget, that the story of Brian's life should be published. The difficulty was that neither he nor any member of the family had thought to write down the details of his young life so that the family, as well as some of his many friends, would have to be asked to pool their knowledge of him. Sir Josslyn wrote to various relations and friends with this idea in mind, hoping that it would be possible to produce 'some form of memoir of Brian, not on the lines of a conventional biography but more a picture or portrait of him and of the many sides of his character, his work and activities.' Frank Clements, who had worked with Brian in the agency business, when approached made some suggestions after making the comment that 'a life so short held more of promise than achievement.'

He thought that: 'A portrait, if properly completed, might well have an interest and significance beyond the circles who knew him.' Clements reckoned that the success of the enterprise would depend largely upon the response from persons 'providing a picture of the Brian they knew, illustrated with anecdotes … to show not only what he was doing, but what he thought and planned and dreamed of, perhaps above all what he valued.' However, nothing, came of these plans.

Among the Lissadell papers there is an unsigned ten-page tribute to Brian, thought by the family to have been written by Lord Dunally with whose family in County Tipperary Brian had been friendly. The journalist, Terence Prittie, (as he was before he succeeded to the title) shared a flat with Brian in London for about two years, and what was written in this tribute was almost certainly Dunally's response to Sir Josslyn's hopes of publishing a book about his recently deceased son.

> I first met Brian in 1933. He came on a visit to my home [at Kilboy] in County Tipperary without knowing myself or any of our family … Brian, only a year older than me in fact, was very much more mature mentally…. In 1935 and 1936 I began to piece together some of the mosaic of Brian's life … I began to appreciate the amazing range and vigour of his interests. I met his friends – and there are people who say that you get to know a man by knowing his friends. I liked them. I visited his home, and he himself told me more about it. Last of all, I began to learn something of his life and a little of the naval career, which he had left [in 1936] so rightly but so regretfully….

Brian and Terence Prittie met again while travelling from Dublin to Liverpool – both heading for London, and when Brian subsequently telephoned him, Prittie agreed to share the flat in Sloane Street. After observing that it was not necessary to write it 'entirely in a spirit of sober reflection,' Prittie's tribute continued:

> I should miss some of my most pleasant memories of Brian if I forgot his gaiety and love of bright lights, music and the clatter of happy company, the abandon with which he threw himself into merriment and the natural poise and overflow of charm which enabled him to find genuine pleasure in society.

> Nobody's life is unmixed joy, and Brian, I know only too well, had his dark hours like the rest of us. He had, to an alarming degree, the sense of doom in our Anglo-Irish race. Fortunately, such moments of sadness, if only too real, were comparatively rare. My pictures of Brian are nearly always the very reverse of sombre.

John Drummond, one of the authors for whom Brian had acted as agent, paid tribute to him in the preface to his book, *The Bride wore Black*: 'I must express my gratitude to Brian Gore-Booth who encouraged me to take liberties with Shakespeare's perfect English. Unfortunately, he will never read this book, as he has already given his life in this war for the ideals we all feel but cannot express.'

* * *

Brian's elder brother, Michael Savile Gore-Booth, was the first-born child of Sir Josslyn and Lady Mary Gore-Booth and as the eldest son was destined to become the seventh baronet after his father's death. Born in 1908, he was educated in England, first at Rugby School after which he went to Trinity College, Cambridge. Around that time, Michael had begun to show signs of absentmindedness, followed later by more worrying symptoms developing into a mental condition, already mentioned, which precluded the possibility that he could ever take over the running of the family estate. It was as a consequence of this that Sir Josslyn decided that his second son, Hugh, should be trained to take his brother's place.

So Hugh, who was two years younger than Michael and two years older than Brian, after attending Mourne Grange School in County Down was sent to Oxford University to study at the School of Rural Economy. He gained a B.A. degree in Agriculture, and later an M.A. degree, also in Agriculture, and he appears to have been a good student, being described by the Sibthorpian Professor of that school (Plant Science) as 'easily the best student of his year and passed the final examination with distinction.' He went on to become a Fellow of the Land Estates Society and was later elected a Qualified Associate of the Society, passing that body's professional examination a year later in 1932.

Hugh loved fishing, and while he was working at various Scottish and Welsh estates to gain practical experience, he was introduced to some of the finest rivers in Britain. Later when abroad on holidays and subsequently when on active service, he availed of every opportunity not only to fish but also to indulge in two of his other favourite outdoor occupations, botany and ornithology, and many of the letters which he sent home during the latter period included references to these pastimes. Hugh wrote articles for angling magazines, including *The Fishing Gazette*, about some of the rivers near Lissadell, including the Erne, Bunduff and the Bundrowse. Hugh's interest as an angler went back to the time when, as a small boy, he often accompanied his father on fishing expeditions, especially to the River Erne.

After completing his training at Oxford, he was offered a position on a farm in southern Sweden where, for a fee of 200 kronor a month, he was to be taught up-to-date Swedish farming methods, but he decided instead to go to the Ty-Uchaf Estate at Llanover, Wales. He was already quite an expert salmon and trout angler when he commenced working there, and the fact that a fine salmon fishing river, the Usk, ran through the estate may have been a factor in his taking employment there. As part of his duties, he organised lettings and often accompanied groups of visiting anglers to the best pools, keeping detailed records of both his own and their catches. When he left, as sub-agent, the owner of the estate, Major Herbert, wrote to Hugh thanking him for all he had done there, expressing regret that it had not been possible to appoint him head agent – possibly the reason for him leaving. In a subsequent letter, Herbert wrote to tell Hugh of the estate's many successes at the recent Royal Show for which, as he wrote, 'you are largely responsible.' Hugh then moved to Scotland, working for a time on a large farm owned by Jock Jardine in Dumfriesshire. Five years after he left Oxford, he returned to the university as a staff member, having been appointed lecturer in estate management at a commencing salary of £250 per annum, with board and lodging included.

In 1934, Hugh set out on what seems to have been his first holiday abroad, the main purpose of which, not surprisingly, was to fish for salmon and trout. His destination was Lapland, and this suggests that it was also something of a personal pilgrimage to one of the arctic areas which his grandfather, Sir Henry, had visited for the same purpose 70 years earlier. During the eight-day outward journey, he met an ex-Indian army colonel who told Hugh that he was 'a friend of the Sligo's [at Westport House] and had fished at Delphi, Kylemore and on the Erriff River.'

Hugh finally arrived at Linahanaki, describing it as 'the only Arctic port which is Finnish property.' This was the case pre-1945, but Finland was forced to cede its narrow corridor outlet to the Arctic, then wedged between northern Norway and Russia, to the Soviet Union when the latter claimed this territory during World War Two. As far as the Soviets were concerned, this was no more than re-incorporating some lost territory, for in Henry's time, the Pasvig corridor – along with the rest of Finland – formed part of Imperial Russia.

Hugh was greatly impressed by the extensive forests, the innumerable lakes, the tundra and the people of what he termed 'the last European wilderness.' He spent most of the holiday in the region of Boris Gleb where he fished the River Pasvig which then formed the border between

Norway and Finland. Most of the inhabitants were Saami, and Hugh wrote that conditions there 'cannot have altered in any notable respect from the days of my grandfather.'

When Sir Henry first visited the region, he had sailed as a guest of Arthur McMurrough Kavanagh and he returned subsequently on an expedition organised by himself where as Hugh noted, he fished the Pasvig 'with the most amazing results.' Hugh found only modest success there, partly because the water levels were very low but also because the Norwegians were netting salmon commercially at the river's estuary. After being told that log-rafting, Canadian-style, was also damaging the fishing, he forecast that the area would be completely spoilt for anglers and holidaymakers in a few year's time. He could not have foreseen that less than a decade later, many of the largely nomad Saami people – who had followed their reindeer herds for centuries – would be killed when caught up in the fighting between the German and Russian armies during World War II.

While staying at Boris Gleb, Hugh decided to find out if any of the older inhabitants remembered his grandfather. It was here that Sir Henry had met the king of Norway and Sweden, and this was also the locality where his valet Kilgallon had shot the bear that had attacked Sir Henry. Hugh asked a ghillie to suggest someone in the area who might have some recollections of his grandfather, but his enquiry 'drew a blank.' Hugh thought that 'the Irish and Scotch ghillies could learn a thing or two here. The Lapps think nothing of negotiating their cockleshell boats down a rapid equivalent to below the Grassard on the River Erne.' He also commented that the people of the region bore 'a strong resemblance to the Irish in deportment, and possibly humour.' Continuing his search for someone who might have remembered his grandfather, he was advised to cross to the Norwegian side of the Pasvig, where at the village of Elvenes, he went to an inn and visited a Mr Klerk, who told him:

> I was only a little boy when your Grandfather used to visit these parts and rent the Pasvig fishing from my father. But I can remember your Grandfather and in the morning after he had been fishing, he fetched a wheelbarrow or a cart for the fish that he had caught, and I have seen as many as a dozen great salmon lying below in the fish house at Elvenes.

He broke off this conversation and left the room briefly, returning to show Hugh 'a photograph of my Grandfather, with Tommy Kilgallen and the dog Lassie and a stuffed bear, evidently staged [photographed] on one of the Lawns at Lissadell.' Klerk continued: 'Yes, your

Grandfather would wade the shores of the river for many hours at a time for he did not care so much for harling [a Scottish term meaning trolling for fish] from the boats, and he would catch a great many large salmon.' Klerk also remembered the incident when Sir Henry met the king at a nearby pool, and how Henry had given him a demonstration how to catch large fish. He told Hugh:

> Your Grandfather instructed His Majesty how to kill a salmon. It was the pool under the Foss [waterfall] that the King killed a salmon and this pool, in recognition, has borne the title ever since of the 'King's Pool.' It was from a high rock beside the Foss that your Grandfather hooked the salmon and handed the rod to the King, and after the fish was played your Grandfather gaffed him. The King and his courtiers then retired to lunch up river, your grandfather also accompanying the party.

When Hugh asked Klerk about the location of a place known as Grense Jakobselv, or Jacob's Elv (where Kilgallon had shot the bear), he responded by pointing across to the Finnish side of the river in a northeasterly direction and said: 'It was there that your Grandfather was accustomed to go in pursuit of the bears and many's the miles he walked while hunting that country, even the Lapps were not fit to stay the pace and length of his travel.' After showing Hugh some photographs of his own hunting trophies, Hugh thanked Klerk and then went to see the King's Pool for himself. He recorded that he saw the high rock from which Sir Henry hooked the fish before handing the rod 'to King Oscar IX' [he later corrected this to Oscar the Second]. Hugh reckoned that the total cost of his own 1934 holiday, including travel and accommodation, was not more than £32.

Hugh went on a second fishing holiday to Swedish Lapland during 1935, flying from Croydon, near London, to Copenhagen and on to Stockholm, and from the latter he travelled by overnight train to Arvidsjaur. Hugh admitted, in a letter to his father, that he had been nervous on the long flight – his first experience of commercial air travel. On his arrival he was struck by the beauty of the forests, carpeted with heather, blueberries and moss growing among the scattered grey boulders.

Angling was again the main purpose of the holiday, and he found an abundance of lakes and rivers, many of them yielding quantities of grayling, a salmon-like fish common in northern Europe. However, he found the fishing rather disappointing and the local Lapps blamed this on an exceptionally mild winter, followed by unusually low water levels. In 1936, Hugh went on yet another fishing holiday, this time to Iceland where he rented a cottage, and six months later he wrote an article for *Game and Gun* magazine, describing his experiences there, mentioning that Irish monks had settled in Iceland long before the Norwegians.

During the autumn of the following year, Hugh travelled to the Aran Islands, hoping to see for himself the relatively primitive farming methods there and also to further a new-found interest in the Irish language which he had not previously had an opportunity to study. His sister, Aideen, was to claim that he became a fluent Irish speaker, and while this was certainly an exaggeration, there is no doubt that he began to take an interest in the language during his early and mid-twenties. It must have been a remarkable stroke of good luck for him that during the sea crossing he met an enthusiastic and fluent Gaelic speaker, none other than Máirtín Ó Direáin, who was born on Inishmore and continued to live there. Risteárd Ó Glaisne, who published over 20 books in Irish, held the view that Ó Direáin was one of the best poets writing in the language. Ó Direáin took an immediate interest in and liking for Hugh who then spent several weeks with him on Inishmore. With Máirtín's ready help, Hugh practised what he had already learned from a textbook he had been using and which Ó Direáin later recalled, had the title *Clocha Scáil*, written by Sean Ó Dálaigh, who wrote under the pseudonym 'Common Noun.' Helped by his friend, Hugh extended his vocabulary and, using the Irish names, he described in a notebook the various kinds of seaweed which the islanders harvested, naming each one in Irish: '*Corlach, Feamuinn Dubh, Feamuinn Dearg, Slata Mara, Carraigín, Duileasg, Sleabhcán,* and *Creannach.*'

Six months after Hugh's sojourn on the islands he wrote an article about Aran which was published by *The Farmer and Stock-Breeder* magazine. As might be expected, it concentrated on the farming methods employed by the islanders including the use of seaweed as manure which was spread both on grass and on arable land. He commented that 'the general tendency for a stranger is to underestimate the agricultural value of the land; first impressions are, however misleading.'

It was after this experience that Hugh drove to Oxford where he gained an M.A. degree. He then spent the following four weeks touring the north of England and Scotland, calling on various friends and a few relations on the way. Most of this long trip was undertaken in appalling wintry weather, in an old Hillman car that regularly refused to start.

Undeterred by frost, snow, ice and an unreliable vehicle, he drove over high moors and several mountain passes, stopping overnight either in cheap boarding houses or with friends or relations. Returning south through Glasgow, he made a diversion to Helensburgh to visit Joanna Arabella Gore-Booth. Known to the family as 'Jock,' she was a daughter of Sir Robert's brother, Henry, and was 93 years of age when visited by Hugh in 1937. He described how, when he called to her house, Mary McDonald, a pleasant Highland servant conducted him to the drawing room:

> where Jock Gore-Both sat before the fire in a little armchair, a shawl and a blanket over her head and her feet resting on a stool. She looked round when I entered and recognised me ... Jock will be 94 years old on her New Year birthday, her memory is still amazingly complete. She can remember being drawn, when 2 or 3 years old, together with her sister.

> We discussed Sir Robert Gore-Booth, the new and the old Lissadell, also Ardtermon and the peculiarities of its bleak loneliness by the Atlantic shore. Jock maintains that Ardtermon was evacuated owing to the encroachments of the tide, however I had always been given to understand that Ardtermon was burnt down during the progress of a ball.

> The old Lissadell ... was a small structure [and] from accounts not held in very high repute as a dwelling. During the unsettled times, Jock tells me that a grave was dug in readiness [for Sir Robert] along somewhere by Crushmore. This grave was presumably never tenanted.

Hugh stayed overnight, and enjoyed a breakfast which included soda scones baked by Mary. This 'trusty servant who hails from Lewis' knew Sir James Mathieson, the former laird of the isle who, after spending upwards of half a million pounds (amassed while trading in opium in the far east) improving his property, then encountered financial difficulties 'that obliged him to part with his castle to Lord Leverhulme.' Hugh wrote that Sir Robert and Isabella, Jock's sister, had visited Mathieson on the Isle of Lewis 'when Sir Robert was accustomed to sail in these parts.' Isabella, it may be recalled, died while staying at Lissadell and was buried on the same day as her uncle, Sir Robert. On the second day of his visit, Hugh took the opportunity to probe Joanna's memory further, and she informed him that it was in the bedroom where he was accustomed to sleep at Lissadell that her sister, Bella, had died on the day after Sir Robert's death.

Most interesting of all, she unearthed a picture painted by Col. James Gore-

Booth, of Ardtermon, looking strangely awesome with Ben Bulben rearing its form in the background, and a huddled bunch of thatched cottages close to Rockly peninsula in the foreground. The indistinct outline of the former avenue of trees which led away from Ardtermon towards Sligo, seemed to hedge the background. Jock has promised to leave the watercolour to me in her will, should I survive her.

Hugh stayed with Joanna for a third day, during which he walked 'to Carbeth' [actually Carbeth House, about five miles away] to visit Col. Pollok-Morris, although Hugh wrote 'Pollard-Morris' who then brought him 'to Ardtermon.' His reason for going there is not explained, but while the property with a significant name had changed hands, Hugh seems to have been there on an earlier visit to 'Jock', and the obvious inference is that it had almost certainly been her father's residence before he disappeared to the far east. After all this, Hugh then returned to Oxford University where he took up his lecturing post in estate management, a position which he held for the next three or four years.

Hugh photographed in the uniform of the Royal Irish Fusiliers.

When the war commenced in September 1939, he was informed that he held a 'reserved occupation,' which meant that he would not be conscripted into the armed services. Despite this, Hugh felt it was his duty to do something to counter the evils of Nazism and decided to join the Royal Irish Fusiliers. According to Lt. Col. John Horsfall (who served with the 1st Battalion, Royal Irish Fusiliers for more than 12 years – and who wrote several books about the 38th (Irish) Brigade during the Second World War – it was common practice to refer to the regiment as the 'the Faughs.' The title had been adopted from their battle cry and motto, rendered as 'Faugh a Ballagh' (more correctly, Fág an Bealach), rather in the manner that the Royal Inniskilling Fusiliers and the Irish Guards were almost invariably referred to, respectively, as 'The Skins' and 'The Micks.' These pseudonyms prompted Horsfall to comment that the regiments were 'thereby preserving the Irish tradition of inconsistency in nomenclature.' Horsfall, an Englishman, spoke highly of his 'light hearted Irish soldiers,' describing how his battalion possessed 'a granite core of battle-hardened and experienced veterans who would stop at nothing.' Writing about the Faughs opinion of themselves as soldiers, Horsfell added that 'they have a superiority complex based on solid achievement in addition to the innate feelings of exclusive excellence which the Faughs and Inniskillings had always been prone to anyway.'

The Fusiliers regiment had been reconstituted two years earlier 'as a Regiment to include two regular Battalions as opposed to one, to be designated respectively, 1st Bn., and 2nd Bn. the Royal Irish Fusiliers (Princess Victoria).' Its origins dated back to 1790 as the old 87th Regiment. The 1st Battalion served in France during the opening months of the Second World War until the Germans overran that country. Most of the British troops managed to evacuate to England, where the battalion remained until 1943 when it was sent to north Africa. A few months after its formation in January 1938, the 2nd Battalion had sailed for overseas duty on the island of Malta and was still stationed there when Germany attacked Poland, precipitating World War II. It remained on the island until 1943.

Little is known about Hugh's first few years in the British Army apart from the fact that he was commissioned as a second lieutenant on May 11, 1940, just over three months after his brother, Brian, had been killed. He obtained the substantive rank of lieutenant on November 11, 1941, and underwent training in various parts of Britain prior to joining the main battalion at Malta. Most of what is now known about his service is derived from a detailed personal journal that he began to keep while at Malta from January 1943 onwards. There are hints in the journal that he was in the Suez Canal Zone prior to being stationed at Malta, but no details have survived and it is virtually certain that these referred to the roundabout journey then necessary to reach the island. The route, via the Cape of Good Hope and Egypt, resulted from the fact that the direct supply line through the Mediterranean was one of the most dangerous in any war zone due to the aggressive and concentrated use – by both sides – of bombers, surface warships, submarines and mines.

There is a description of Hugh's presumed route from England to Malta in Raymond Williams' book about the 'Faughs' at Malta. Williams joined the Fusiliers in December 1939, and after initial training at Holywood Barracks near Belfast, he and the other men of what was termed a 'holding battalion of the Fusiliers' learned that they were sailing to Liverpool where, after being issued with tropical kit, they boarded the P. & O. liner *Ormond*, bound for a then unknown destination. The timing of this despatch of reinforcements for the Faughs at Malta makes it highly probable that Hugh actually travelled with this contingent. Williams described how the liner headed out around the coast of Antrim where it joined a large convoy sailing due west into the Atlantic before turning south, presumably trying to avoid contact with German planes and U-boats. After three days the troops were informed that they were heading for South Africa.

In due course, after calling at Cape Town, the troops boarded the liner *Strathaird* which sailed up the east coast of Africa, arriving at Port Suez at the end of September after a voyage lasting a month and a half. The Faughs contingent was taken to Geniefa in the Suez Canal Zone, and it was here that the men heard for the first time that their ultimate destination was Malta, where they were taken by *HMS Liverpool* to strengthen the beleaguered island's garrison.

It might have seemed unlikely that so small an island in the central Mediterranean would play a crucial role in a global war, but Malta was situated at a point almost exactly where two vitally important supply lines of the western protagonists converged. For Britain it was an important staging post and base midway between Gibraltar and the Suez Canal; for the Italians, and later for the Germans too, it lay directly in their way between Italy and Tripoli.

Towards the end of 1940, the Italians suffered several humiliating defeats, first in Greece, followed by severe reverses in north Africa, forcing the Germans to take action to support them. As far as Malta was concerned, Hitler's most significant move at the time was the diversion of a large number of Luftwaffe planes from Norway to Sicily. This signalled the commencement of a systematic bombing campaign directed at Malta which was continued with an intensity and for a longer duration than that endured in any other theatre of war. During a single month in early 1942; over 1,000 tons of bombs were dropped on the island. Brigadier Low, of Hugh's battalion, wrote of the situation at the time: 'The strain on the men of this contingent was severe. Practically nobody for months on end ever got more than four hours sleep at a stretch, and the effect could be seen in their eyes.'

The German High Command then decided to do what the Italians had failed to do, that is, to rid themselves of this island nuisance from which British planes, surface warships and submarines were sinking so many of their ships while attempting to bring supplies to North Africa. But not for the first time, Hitler decided to override the advice of his generals and ordered the invasion of Crete instead, where a massive invasion force of surface ships, gliders and parachute troops received such a mauling that this alternative plan almost failed. For the Germans it proved a pyrrhic victory because, while it was considered to be a major disaster by the British at the time, the loss of Crete proved far less significant than the possible loss of Malta.

The two main drawbacks to Hugh's new posting were the regular air raids and the very severe shortage of food. This shortage had continued to worsen since the commencement of the island siege in 1941, and convoys attempting to get supplies to the island suffered such severe losses that, for a time, relief convoys ceased trying to get through. During one 20-month period, 33 out of 87 merchant ships trying to reach Malta were sunk. When conditions on the island became really desperate, an extra large relief convoy was despatched with a powerful naval escort comprising four aircraft carriers, two battleships, seven cruisers and 24 destroyers. The Germans and Italians repeatedly attacked this convoy using aircraft, warships and submarines which, between them, sank all but five of the 14 merchant ships, along with an aircraft carrier and two cruisers.

A flavour of what the sailors felt about Malta may be found in an account, privately published, by Eric Ranalow who, like many of the island's garrison at the time, was Irish. Ranelow had joined the British merchant navy in 1939 and described various attempts to break the Malta blockade. On one occasion, having dodged bombs and torpedoes, his ship managed to reach the island only to find it impossible to leave again. His ship then had to remain in Valetta for three months because 'the Mediterranean had become too dangerous for surface ships to move out.' So sustained was the bombing of the island at that time – especially the port – that the ship's crew had to disperse ashore. Coincidentally, in that same paragraph, Ranelow described the arrival at Valetta of the aircraft carrier, *HMS Illustrious*, which 'had limped in [to port] bombed, battered and almost sinking, having escorted a convoy of merchant ships with their valuable cargoes safely into Grand Harbour. Thousands of Maltese dock workers worked 24 hours a day for weeks to make her seaworthy again, all the time under continuous air attack.' On board this famous carrier throughout the war was Commander Con Glanton who, like Ranelow, came from County Cork and who, in the recent past, has kindly helped the author of this book by checking all the references to naval matters therein.

Hugh's battalion found itself taking part in various military exercises and maintaining and improving the island's anti-invasion defences. The coastal defences were described by Marcus Cunliffe in his history of the regiment as 'beach posts, strung out along the coastline behind belts of wire, each post consisting of a defensive position manned by seven or eight men with a Bren gun and a medium machine gun.' Although they were not to know it at the time, the expected invasion never materialised, but lying so close to both Sicily and enemy-held North Africa, the threat of a massive landing force must have seemed almost ever-present. Nowhere on the island was safe from bombing attacks but most of this activity was directed at the naval base and dockyards at Valetta and at the island's airports, and one of the battalion's regular duties was filling bomb-craters on the runways. On one occasion, when a company of the Faughs was engaged in repairing a damaged runway, the men were caught totally unprepared by an unexpected follow-up attack, described by one of the men:

> In the middle of the target area, with 50 or more bombers sailing towards you with anything but friendly attitude is hardly what the doctor ordered. It's amazing, however, how sympathetic even the smallest of holes can be on such occasions. They certainly were on this occasion, for though the bombs literally whistled on all sides, not a casualty was sustained by the Company. After it was all over, and the dust cleared away, heads began to peep up in all directions, and the only cries to be heard were the moans and groans over the amount of craters which now would have to be filled in.

* * *

Hugh began to keep a regular journal, presenting a first-hand insight not only into the activities of his battalion but also a picture of himself at the time. Fortunately, it has survived among the family papers, and the opening entry, written on January 1, 1943, reads:

> The dawning of another year as seen through the eyes of an officer serving in Malta. A discussion with my batman, Fusilier Dwyer (from Tipperary) suggests that the war may last 2 years and 6 months longer in his estimation, and 5 years and 8 months in my estimation.

Hugh's forecast was distinctly pessimistic while Dwyer's (June 1945) was to prove almost correct. Hugh appears to have been a quietly religious young man, frequently mentioning in his journal that he had cycled into Valetta to attend Morning Service in the Anglican Church.

His easy-going manner meant that Hugh usually got on well with the local people who for the most part liked the Irish soldiers, many of whom had already been stationed there for almost five years. The locals also became familiar with Irish tunes played by the battalion's band including '*The Rakes of Mallow, Let Erin remember, Oft in the Stilly Night*' and '*Killaloe*,' the regimental march of the Faughs. He enjoyed talking to the local people and he described his first expedition, to a nearby tiered valley where corn, globe artichokes, cabbage, carrots, peas, pumpkins and a few banana and orange trees grew. He arrived at a farm 'entirely contained inside a capacious limestone cave' where he introduced himself to an elderly couple who lived there together with a younger couple. He was anxious to supplement his platoon's rations, but most of the farmers were seriously short of food for themselves, so that tempting them to part with anything edible seemed next to impossible.

Around this time, for the first time during the war, there were signs that the peak of the successes of the Axis powers had passed. Six months earlier, the Germans and Italians in north Africa were almost at the gates of Cairo and in Russia, the former stood poised to take the significant prize of Stalingrad. Simultaneously, the Germans were also pushing south into the Caucasus and there was the breathtaking possibility that a breakthrough both there and at Suez might open the way for these two German forces to link-up. After months of fighting, the Russians counter-attacked north and south Stalingrad, effecting a huge pincer movement inside which the entire German Sixth Army was trapped.

It was against this background that Hugh learned that a platoon had to be made available to provide a Guard of Honour 'to celebrate the victories of the Red Army.' This began to make more sense when, a few days afterwards, Hugh was informed that a visit by a Russian 'Stalingrad' Colonel was expected. When the additional news – that he was reputed to believe in making soldiers live in the maximum discomfort – became known, Hugh noted in his diary that 'hence we have hidden all the comfortable mess furniture.'

After the Russian Colonel's visit, some of the British officers who had accompanied him were so impressed both by the bearing and the efficiency of the Royal Irish Fusiliers, and also by the mock battle specially staged by the battalion for the visitor, that Hugh was invited to organise a full-scale battle drill, involving commandos, landing craft and tanks. Hugh spent several weeks organising the affair with two fellow Irish colleagues, John Penny and Mike Rochford.

Further regular forays into the countryside in search of new food outlets by Hugh were met by the familiar reply: 'All feenish, all feenesh.' One day he saw a girl working with her father in the fields. She volunteered to summon a rather reluctant woman, her mother as it turned out, to the scene. Between them, 'persuaded by our usual tactics of expressing great hunger, promising great secrecy, an abundance of good money, and a faint hint of marriage held in the background, the goods were produced – several large cabbages, endives, kohl rabi and globe artichokes.' This cave, which Hugh had visited earlier to purchase fruit or vegetables, had been that family's home for generations and was not, as might be supposed, a war-time expedient resulting from the incessant bombing of the island.

Manning the island's beach posts was, perhaps, the most boring duty of all for the Malta garrison, involving men being posted on their own for long hours with nothing to do except look out to sea. Speaking to one of them, Fusilier McMahon told Hugh: 'I mind the time when [Fusilier] Dwyer had our post all decorated out with Shamrock and every class of national emblem.' Asked if he liked the time he was batman to the commanding officer, McMahon replied 'Well, sorr, betimes he was good to me – he'd give me £1 for Xmas and a glass of malt whiskey.' He told Hugh that he would be greatly surprised if he could see the amount of kit the C.O. carried about with him: 'He keeps nine boxes of kit below at St Andrew's. The boxes be full of old boots, shoes and civilian clothes. I'm sure the half of thim's gone rotten by now.' Soon after this, Hugh met the camp commander who introduced him 'to Mrs Dawson (née Paddy Kenlington, from Waterford and Dublin) who believes she once met Aideen [Hugh's sister] at the Adelaide [Hospital], Dublin.'

Hugh cycled with two of his colleagues, Mike Rochford and John Penny, to discuss 'field firing' and then met 'R.S. Cresswell' (about whom Hugh wrote 'was normally a Dublin lawyer') and they examined the guns and stores. Cresswell told him that 'Patrick Carey is running Mourne Grange [the County Down school Hugh had attended for his second-level education] as a co-educational establishment.'

Hugh organised a battle-drill for the battalion with the help of his two colleagues. On the morning of the exercise he began to get cold feet when he saw a large collection of important looking spectators assembled, including the whole officer personnel of 2 Infantry Brigade and N.C.O.s from his own regiment. His brigade major presented him to the brigadier who in turn introduced him to the General Officer Commanding Malta Troops, Major General Scobie. Then the 'battle' commenced:

> The Bren guns roared full belt until they were red-hot. One jammed and one broke a piston. The tempos, smoke and noise of the battle were so terrific that the [regimental] piper's attempt at playing the assault to the lilt of 'Patrick's Day' was completely obscured. The mortar men made some superb shooting: One two-inch 'high explosive' bomb landed on the roof of the blockhouse which was conspicuously decorated with the crooked cross of Nazism.

The 'grand finale' came with grenade bursts and smoke bombs as Bren and other groups rushed to the objective, and flags were mounted by each section to denote its position. Several senior officers congratulated Hugh on his careful preparations and even Major General Scobie telephoned that evening to say that the battle drill had raised 'the already high reputation and prestige of the Regiment.' Hugh's footnote to this episode reads:

> Meantime we are lying back and low, almost splitting ourselves in two with convulsions of laughter at the thought that three complete military ignoramuses like ourselves, who literally could not reach Lesson One in the rifle, should have been called upon to run the demonstration.

After this, Hugh was told 'some disquieting particulars about inter-company transfers, one affecting me: To go as 2nd i.c. [in charge] to A. Coy., a distasteful task to which I object.' In fact, he declined to accept this offer of promotion, almost certainly made in recognition of his battle drill initiatives, preferring to stay with his own company.

As a keen naturalist, Hugh continued to take every opportunity to go off alone in search of wildflowers and birds, and made detailed notes of many species of both., once observing 'a bunch of Willow Wrens [Warblers?]' in a garden at Cherubino, prompting his comment: 'They seemed to bring many pleasant recollection to mind – perhaps they will soon be warbling in the hedges by Drumcliff.' On another occasion his curiosity to identify a bird led him to the badly bomb-damaged Natural History Museum in Valetta where he found it to be a Blue Rock Thrush, the national symbol of the island.

March 5 was a national holiday so the battalion organised a dinner in Valetta. Hugh was among those at high table along with Brigadier Marshall, Father Anwell, Chaplain, and a variety of officers including a Maltese Liaison Officer who told Hugh that he recalled that in pre-war days the Irish Fusiliers had occupied this very building:

> The room is dimly lighted with black candles disposed in chandeliers on the table which is decorated with Regimentally coloured ribbons, and blood oranges in bowls. Pea soup is followed by fresh fish, frozen beef, cauliflowers and potatoes…. The band plays in the anteroom and three pipers in saffron Kilts, black or dark green braided tunics, stand by the door in attendance. They pipe round and round the table, *The Wearing of the Green*, *O'Neill's March*, and *Killaloe*. It all seems so weird. In the anteroom after dinner there is much hilarity – Boland is striking up *The Soldiers' Song* on the piano, everyone else is singing….

A story went round the battalion that when a visiting dignitary was being shown around the Faugh's encampment, he noticed the initials 'IRA' daubed on a wall and asked the accompanying officer what it meant. He was told 'the Irish Religious Association.' Richard Doherty, writing about the Irish generals in the Second World War, noted that the 'Faughs' were encouraged to learn and sing Irish songs and to learn Irish dancing. The regimental song book included '*Kevin Barry*,' '*Kelly the boy from Killane*' and '*The Sash*,' some of which, he wrote 'would have been guaranteed to cause a riot in Belfast or Dublin, but in the midst of war … they had a unifying rather than a dividing effect.'

The regiment's sister battalion, the 1st Battalion, Royal Irish Fusiliers, along with the Inniskillings, the London Irish and the Irish Guards had formed part of what was then the largest sea-borne invasion force deployed during the war, landing on the Atlantic and Mediterranean coasts of French north Africa and forcing the Germans there to fight on two fronts. Three of the Irish units involved had, on Churchill's insistence, been formed into the 38th (Irish) Brigade against the wishes of some of his generals and to the particular displeasure of John Andrews, Prime Minister of Northern Ireland. The Irish Brigade was to fight with considerable distinction all the way from Tunisia, through Sicily and Italy to Austria. Documenting the Brigade's progress, Henry Harris described how, after the fall of Rome, representatives of the Royal Irish Fusiliers, led by their pipes and drums, were welcomed to the Vatican by Pope Pius XII who told them how conscious he was 'of all the good the Irish did so far from their own land.' Afterwards, the band played Irish airs which echoed in the vast St Peter's Square and 'the innumerable Irish priests there kept shouting out for their favourite tunes, '*The Boys of Wexford* being the most popular.'

At the end of March, news came through to the troops on Malta that the Germans were now 'on the run' in Tunisia and it was only a matter of time before they were going to be defeated in north Africa. One morning in May 1943, Hugh arrived in Valetta and was surprised to see crowds waving flags, cheering and dancing in the streets, celebrating the stunning news that more than 200,000 Axis troops had just surrendered in Tunisia. Cycling back to base, Hugh passed some children parading with 'mock bands, waving tiny flags and beating mock drums fabricated from petrol cans.' He commented simply: 'Everyone bears a slightly festive air.' In fact, this was one of the turning points in the war, opening the way for the subsequent landings on Sicily that were to pave the way for the invasion of mainland Italy. Hugh described the celebrations subsequently organised by island garrison:

> A band is playing in the shade of some Palms and Norfolk Island Pines. The guests are assembling on a broad balcony approached by an ornate stone stairway from outside. As we mount the stairway I fall into conversation with Radcliffe. Sam Marshall, Landsbury and a great many other mutual acquaintances are on the balcony. The G.O.C., several Brigadiers, a savage looking Provost Marshall with an enormous moustache, some naval officers and a sparse sprinkling of Maltese and English women are among the throng.... Everyone is keyed up to an exceptional pitch pending the arrival of refreshments which, rumour has it, are to be supplied at the rate of 30,000 bottles of beer among 3,000 guests ... sandwiches are brought in ... we sip beer out of glasses – Mike recognises Gordon Duff. The Military Secretary, posted by a door, brings us forward and introduces me. G.D. remembers me quite distinctly from Llanover days [where Hugh had worked for a time after graduating] – we discuss angling on the Erne, the Spey, the Deveron and the Usk. He seems particularly interested in our Maltese bird findings ... "Talking about the Erne, is old Keenan

alive yet? It used to be wonderful white trout fishing down the Erne estuary –
I was stationed then at Finner Camp." I tell him that Jimmie Keenan has died
since, but I believe that Bob and others of the Keenans are alive yet. The
afternoon wore on in this fashion, nothing notable happening, everyone relaxing
in the sun with drinks and small talk.

Hugh's company organised its own victory celebrations later, with some
'entertainments' including a display of Irish dancing by a team of the
battalion's soldiers. Here and there in Hugh's personal journal there are
other brief references to some of the men in the battalion. He was
obviously especially interested to talk to men who came from Sligo:
'Fusilier Kilgallon, of 14 St Anne's Terrace, Sligo, came to speak to me
this evening – he has not visited Sligo for six and a half years.' Hugh did
not specifically comment upon his name, but this soldier may quite
possibly have been related to Thomas Kilgallon, the faithful valet who
sailed with Hugh's grandfather to the Arctic. Hugh also recorded a
conversation with 'Lance Corporal O'Dowd, who spoke to me on the
road a few days ago. His father used to live in one of the Temple House
gate lodges [the seat of the Percival family, friends of the Gore-Booths,
who lived near Collooney]. 'There's plenty of irons, I'm given to
understand, being passed among the boys at home, Sir. Ye know, Sir,
when they're talkin' of irons, it's what they name revolvers.'

* * *

Hugh recounted a meeting with two Maltese men who he met while out
for a walk with Mike Rochford.

I recognise them as two brothers who are accustomed to frequent the
neighbourhood of the cookhouse at our billets. We step out to meet them –
they smile broadly all over.
"Your home?" we inquire pointing to the windowless, fort like walls.
"My home, yes," replies the younger of the two.
"Where do you work?" We enquire further.
"At the Roadhouse," he ventures still smiling.
"How do you like the Irish?" we probe in cross-examination.
"Irish, all right Sir," he volunteers with obvious animation. "Irish and Maltese
all happy! Happy!" he reiterates several times with spontaneous pleasure. "We
all happy, one blood, one people, very happy, all right!" He repeats this over
and over again, linking his little fingers.
"How do you like the English?" we continue, by way of contrast.
"English all right." He pauses, with a slightly lustreless and unenthusiastic air,

"English and Maltese not so happy."

"How's that?" we ask him.

"Englishmen, he shout always at Maltese; Maltese not like."

"What does he shout," we enquire with an assumed air of surprise.

"He shout *Imshe* – get out – f*** off!" I reluctantly turn over in my mind an incident, which happened only this very morning, affecting an English Sgt. in our Battalion and one of the Maltese goat cart boys. The English Sgt. had, for no express reason at all, shouted at the Maltese boy in similar terms.

From time to time, Hugh mentioned how the Irish soldiers seemed to get along with the local people rather better than the men of the English regiments. Some of Hugh's journal entries also gave the impression that the Irish themselves felt that theirs was a more cohesive if not a better battalion than the others. He obviously disliked bombast from senior officers – especially those of the other regiments, some of whom seemed to him to be very close to stupid.

Not long after, word came through that the new General Officer Commanding, General Oxley, was on his way to see Hugh's Company. He arrived with an array of other officers, including Brigadier Brittorius. Hugh was surprised to find Oxley more elderly than he had expected: 'A man who seemed to speak to you and ask questions, the answers to which scarcely registered at all in his mind.' The top brass among the garrison had been greatly impressed by the efficient manner in which Hugh and a few of the other junior officers of the battalion had organised the recent assault courses, so both Hugh and Mike Rochford were summoned to Lascarras Barracks to appear before a senior officer whom Hugh described as:

a brusque, moustachioed old Etonian and Grenadier Guardsman.' He informed the pair that that he wanted them to organise another course because 'the G.O.C. is hot stuff on Battledrill; you have to mind your Ps and Qs.... You two will be instructors on the first courses, but you may need an extra instructor later. We are going to run officers' and sergeants' courses alternately ... I don't believe in mixing officers and sergeants, it always leads to trouble.

Hugh remonstrated as much as he dared, 'pointing out the good relations which had existed between our officers and sergeants on the last course.' 'Ah yes', he says, 'the trouble doesn't happen on the spot, it happens afterwards.' After telling Hugh and Mike they had ten days to organise the course, they were dismissed and, returning to their base, they called on Major Morris, whom Hugh noted came from Galway. Later, while making preparations for the course, they were 'invaded' by Brigadier Brittorius.

A florid gentleman with twinkling eyes and an enormous curly moustache, clad in K.D. [khaki drill] shorts. 'You want a haircut' was his spontaneous opening remark to Mike, and a few minutes later turned to his A.D.C., a rather pinched, miserable little Captain from the D.L.I. [Durham Light Infantry], and told him he had a fly button undone.

The course was to prove a success, and Colonel Kirby thanked the Fusiliers platoon for their keenness and their fine work on the course, but the G.O.C, who had been expected to attend, had actually driven past while the demonstration was going on and did not stop. However, the company commander subsequently wrote to Hugh and to Mike Rochfort congratulating them both and describing the course in glowing terms as a great success.

* * *

The preparations for an Allied landing on Sicily were now under way, the preliminary step that was to lead to the invasion of the Italian mainland. However, various ruses were adopted to keep the Germans guessing about possible landings on the south of France, Sardinia or Greece. Meanwhile, Colonel French called to see Hugh – who had been taken ill with bronchial pneumonia – and questioned him further about his earlier objections to the suggestion that he be transferred from C Company to A, despite the fact that this would have resulted in promotion:

I explain that I am only at present interested in remaining with my platoon – promotion or its possibilities hold no incentives for me, and I point out that there are other officers, senior to me, capable of doing the job. He winds up by promising to consider the question without promising anything. He asks if I would mind someone Junior to me being promoted over my head – I reply that it would be of no consequence to me whatever.

Early in June, the long expected news finally came that the battalion was being moved to a new theatre of war. Hugh described it as:

A Momentous Day in the History of the Irish Fusiliers. The time has arrived when, after five and a half years spent within Malta, the Battalion will leave the island. Our soldiers are astir at 4 o'clock – everything is packed and ready by 9 o'clock, and we move off to the docks in a fleet of 3-ton lorries at 9.30. Some most pathetic scenes followed, bearing witness to the very genuine affection the Maltese feel for our men. Groups of women, old and young, have gathered in the street corners in St. Julien's and Sleima – they are one and all, steadily weeping their hearts out as they wave to the passing convoy.

Some idea of the regard held by the Maltese for the Irish Fusiliers is indicated by the presentations made when it became known that the Battalion was leaving for a new posting. The town of Mosta presented the Battalion with a silver model of a Goza boat; Naxxar gave a silver model of a cannon, while Gargur presented two silver cups to mark the people's appreciation of the friendship that had existed between them and the Fusiliers during their five and a half year stay. Writing about the garrison troops stationed on the island during World War Two, the well-known author, Ian Hay, listed some of the regiments involved. They were, he wrote, 'mainly county regiments, the backbone of the British Army; men of Devon, Dorset, Lancashire, Kent, Durham and Cheshire.' It would appear that, as far as Hay was concerned, the Royal Irish Fusiliers just might as well have been stationed on St Helena when, in fact, they had been in Malta far longer than any of the others he named. Now, as they departed, Hugh described the scene:

This was June 11, 1943, and as the R.Ir.F. battalion boarded the troopship *HMT Neuralia* in Valetta's Grand Harbour as part of 234 Infantry Brigade, a band struck-up on the quayside and our own band replies from one of the forward decks, the pipes playing *Killaloe*, and the troops crowded into every available space along the sides and top of the ship…. The ship starts slowly … to pull out of the bomb shattered surrounds of the creek …. Our parting drama reaches its climax when the ship passes the various booms and approaches the lighthouse. The Governor's launch, with its highly polished brazen funnel, waits our departure, formed up in our starboard side like a marine sentinel. The Governor, His Excellency Lord Gort [another Irishman], stands with Gordon Duff in the stern sheets. As we slide past, the band strikes up again, the troops cheer and H.E. raises his red-banded hat exposing a conspicuously bald head. There is further cheering, with calls of 'Wan for the Faugh A Ballagh.' One can instinctively feel that he has a rising lump at the back of his throat. He is as fond of the Irish Fusiliers as if they were a family of his own. He has already written an appreciative letter to the Commanding Officer concerning our Regt.

Perhaps because of its age – it had seen service as a troop ship in the First World War – the *Neuralia* travelled at a slow speed, and despite the crowded, airless conditions, the men were in good spirits – excepting those (including Fusilier Sweeney) who had left Maltese wives behind. On the first evening, presumably to divert attention from thoughts about bombers and submarines, an entertainment was laid on which, Hugh thought, exposed:

a notable contrast between the behaviour of the English and Irish Troops aboard. Not a single Irishman has volunteered to perform to-night at the pre-arranged concert; on the other hand, in an impromptu concert resembling a Ceilidhe, and promoted on one of the after decks ... all the performers were Irish to a man.

When the convoy reached Alexandria, Hugh was among an advance party to the battalion's new camp which he described as 'a diminutive arid waste with a few palm trees,' but being close to the sea, Hugh, with Mike Rochfort, immediately went for a swim. The Faughs new base had no buildings, all the sleeping and other facilities being in tents. Hugh decided to seek a billet and went to nearby Iskenderia where he got Egyptian currency at the Mustafa Barracks and found an Officers' Rest Hotel. 'Inside there is [a] wide oak staircase, a bar, papers (including the *Scottish Field*, *La Libre France*, and *Life*), baths, a roof top for sun bathing, comfortable beds and a remarkable cuisine.' Hugh was invited to attend a private concert arranged by a wealthy Egyptian in Alexandria and, with some time on his hands, decided to explore part of the city with its evident contrasts.

The battalion soon evacuated their transit camp, and were driven in trucks 'to Wogburg' [Cairo] and then out into the desert to a new camp where Hugh was hospitalised with an attack of very unpleasant Sandfly Fever for more than a week. From his bed he watched a Hoopoe probing with his long beak in the lawn 'There are also some very familiar Black Kites, a bird which, according to Thompson, was first protected in Egypt by order of Lord Kitchener, and there are Carrion Crows.' From the hospital, Hugh was subsequently moved to a nearby house for convalescence. He made a number of forays to visit nearby libraries and museums and when he asked an Egyptian for directions to the Museum of Hygiene, he discovered that the man was Sub-Dean at the Faculty of Engineering at Giza University who told him that he had been educated in Dublin and Edinburgh.

What educational establishment did you visit in Dublin,' I enquired. 'Padraig Pearse's School, Rathfarnham – I was only there for a short while.' He expressed admiration for Pearse, 'and also strong Egyptian nationalistic sentiments, whose pattern had obviously been woven from the model seen in Ireland.' He recommended Hugh to visit Edfina, near Alexandria, to see the King's State Farm of 12,000 acres, and also invited him to visit his own faculty. Back in the convalescent home, a Scotsman from Galloway was surprised to hear from Hugh that he had worked on Jock Jardine's property in Dumfrieshire.

When news arrived about the invasion of Sicily, there was renewed speculation about future events. For the battalion, these latter began with an overnight train journey, and Hugh awoke to find a countryside with citrus and banana plantations which turned out to be somewhere between Haifa and Tripoli, the latter not to be confused with the city of the same name in Libya. Lebanese Tripoli lay about 150 miles north of Haifa on the coast.

Though the battalion did not arrive at their new camp-site until night time, the men were taken on a strenuous mountain exercise next day, followed by a nine-mile march through olive and mulberry groves the day after. Camping out overnight, the exercise continued with further mountain training at a higher altitude where Hugh noted 'stunted specimens of Cedar of Lebanon trees, Pinus Montana and Aleppo Cyprus [Cypress].' After one rest day, there followed yet another exhausting mountain exercise:

> We press onwards and upwards, starting to climb a steep rock and scrub-covered bank which rises to approximately 550 metres. I hear Riordan say in reference to the hills which hem us in: 'I wish thim wans over there were the Knockmealdown Mountains, and the wan over there was the Galtee More.' Corporal Devaney is humping the base-plate of the 3' mortar – he presses on with all the tenacity and stride of a mountainy man. I remember an account he once gave me about working for a sheep farmer up in Glenade [a dozen miles, as the crow flies, north-east of Lissadell].

Next day, Sunday, Father Anwell, one of the chaplains, conducted a column of trucks with members of the battalion to Nazareth, a few miles distant from their new base. Hugh was not impressed: 'Commercially speaking the home of our Lord gave every indication of having been exploited to the full. Such places as the Galilee Hotel, various restaurants and the street hawkers all strengthened this impression, the unpleasant nature of which was adequately described by one Fusilier who made the quite spontaneous remark, 'I don't know how Christ stuck this for thirty years.' The party swam in Lake Galilee, after which they sat drinking tea while listening to an orchestra playing at the Lido until it got dark. Hugh went to see an agricultural settlement, studying the combine harvesters, drills, harrows and multiple ploughs, and admired the Friesian and Ayrshire cattle in the byres, and the white Leghorns in the poultry department. On the way he noted the comfortable Jewish settlements with their cultivated fields, contrasting this with what he saw of the Arabs in their tents. When Mike Rochford called out a greeting in Arabic to a Bedouin woman at a well, she looked at him and spat contemptuously.

And so it went on, days on active training punctuated with rest days, during one of which Hugh learnt to drive a carrier under the supervision of Lance Corporal Byrne from Wexford. Hugh went to a Jewish settlement and spoke to Russians and Poles there, spending a whole evening with one family and returning a few days later to visit another. Meanwhile the Fusiliers were treated to a topographical and historical lecture about the area around the camp, an area that Hugh described as being situated in 'the plain of Eodraelon [Esdraelon] the scene of so many notorious encounters in Biblical and other times.' The Plain of Esdraelon was crossed by the highland route from Jerusalem to Galilee, and it was on the slopes of Mount Gilboa, a few miles to the south, that Saul and Jonathan were killed by the Philistines, their deaths prompting the lines in the Books of Samuel: "How are the mighty fallen, And the weapons of war perished."

In the morning, the Fusiliers' weapons of war, far from perished, were loaded onto trucks at the start of another move. The local Arab children cheered as the trucks drove through Jezreel, the scene of Jezebel's execution, to board a train which brought them overnight back to their earlier camp site near Lake Galilee. During a few days' respite, renewed rumours circulated that the battalion was 'for the high jump,' a forecast which seemed to have some substance when the men began to practice using landing craft. An inter-section assault course was likened by Hugh to an Irish race meeting. Soon after, yet another move brought the battalion back to the Suez Canal region. Now mid-August, the heat was almost unbearable – the temperature in the shade rose to 105° Fahrenheit but military exercises continued. That night, Hugh heard a piper marching through the camp playing what he thought, in his comatose state, was as he wrote it 'Fainne Gal na La [*Fáinne Geal an Lae*, the Dawning of the Day]'. He jumped up and began to dress until Company Sergeant Major Connor told him that the piper had just played 'Lights Out' [*Oft in the Stilly Night*]. He had an hour and a half of sleep before being roused for yet another landing-craft exercise by moonlight, after which the men were congratulated by Major Playtell-Bouverie. 'He rounded up his speech by expressing that the Faugh a Ballaghs deported themselves magnificently.'

Hugh was suddenly laid low with symptoms of tonsillitis, and diarrhoea, and spent several days fasting. Before he had fully recovered, the battalion moved on again. Travelling through the night to Ishmaliah, he tried to doze lying on the luggage rack. After a short stay, the train continued to Gaza. There, in total darkness, trucks arrived and brought the battalion to a camp in northern Syria, and as Hugh's condition had not improved during the arduous journey, he was sent to hospital in Sidon. Lying in his hospital bed, where he finished reading *David Copperfield* and began reading Maria Edgeworth's *Castle Rackrent*, he was told that the British Eighth Army had landed on mainland Italy. One of his visitors was a Rhodesian officer who had left his 1,500 acre farm in the care of a neighbour. He told Hugh that he had visited Lord Clarina's estate in County Clare [actually, it was in County Limerick] before the war.

While he was still convalescing at the hospital, Major Shepherd, one of the battalion officers, called to see Hugh. Writing about this sometime afterwards, Shepherd recalled that he had done so because he had just been informed that the Faughs had been ordered to prepare to leave that same day for a new posting which was going to involve action. He recalled that Hugh was 'very worried at not being with us – the hospital [staff] were firm in refusing his request to do so.' After 33 days in hospital, Hugh was ordered to spend a further 14 days on sick leave in Beirut, about 40 miles to the north. He stayed in the officers' club, 'a noisy, pretentious institution, seething with officers of all nationalities and descriptions.' Hugh availed of every opportunity for exercise, walking or hitch-hiking to places of interest nearby, or up into the mountains, which seemed to hold a special attraction for him because the wild flowers and bird life there were likely to be more interesting. Writing an account of one of these latter expeditions, he described how he reached a mountain village situated at an altitude of 3,000 feet, only to fall asleep so that he missed the returning bus. However, a large saloon car crammed with six occupants stopped and he was offered a lift but, with no room inside, he stood on the car's running board as it descended around 'many sharp bends with glimpses of perpendicular cliffs into deep ravines' – obviously a hair-raising ride. The journal continued: 'The car eventually halted at a hotel and one of the passengers, who was the owner of the establishment, invited me inside. [Later] while we continued our journey, I reclined beside a Lebanese student – a Police Officer rides in front beside the driver who is a …'

At this point, without explanation, Hugh's journal came to an abrupt end. The most likely reason for this sudden ending is that while he was writing this account, he was interrupted and told to prepare immediately to join a convoy about to leave Haifa with supplies and reinforcements for three Greek islands lying off the Turkish coast. He may not have been told until the convoy got under way that his precise destination was the island of Leros, to which his battalion had already been sent.

* * *

While Hugh had been convalescing, his battalion was stationed for several days at the foot of Mount Carmel before sailing from Haifa on board the destroyer *HMS Intrepid* as part of the 10th Infantry Division of the British Ninth Army. Apart from some officers, no one on board knew that their destination was a small Italian-occupied island about a dozen miles off the Turkish coast. Three other battalions which, like the Faughs had been training in mountain warfare, were also heading for the small Dodecanese Island of Leros and other units in the convoy were bound for two nearby islands, Kos and Samos. All three islands had been in Italian hands since 1911, and in light of the sudden Italian surrender, the British decided to occupy these islands before the Germans attempted to do so. Ominously, the Germans had already seized the much larger island of Rhodes with which, along with Crete, they had hoped to deny Allied access to mainland eastern Greece and the Dardanelles.

Despite this, Churchill saw the capture of the Dodecanese islands as a worthwhile diversionary tactic, and ignored American opposition as well as the advice of Alanbrooke and his Chiefs of Staff – who thought that all available resources in the region should have been concentrated on the Italian campaign. Churchill clung to the idea on the basis that the Germans were now in serious difficulties in Russia – being pushed back relentlessly and with huge losses by the Soviet Army. Additionally, the British and American landings on mainland Italy had caused the Italian government to surrender, forcing the Germans to deploy much needed men and materials to replace the Italian garrisons not only throughout Italy, but also in southern France, Albania, Greece and Yugoslavia. With their armies seriously stretched, the Germans were additionally forced to station very large numbers in northern France where they were expecting a major invasion – though this was not to materialise until the following year.

Churchill was thus determined to occupy three islands in the Aegean – hopefully without Italian resistance – thereby convincing the Germans that it was a prelude to landings on the Greek mainland, thus pinning down still more German troops. He gambled on several possible developments; first, that the Germans – so preoccupied with all their other problems – would not bother to intervene and second, that Turkey might see advantages for itself in joining the war at this stage on the Allied side. He was to be disappointed on both counts. Three years earlier, according to an account written by Neil McCart, a force of Swordfish flew off from the carriers *Illustrious* and *Eagle* and dropped 92 tons of bombs on the small airbase at Leros. Effectively, the base was put out of action, thus rendering the island defenceless against air attack. Crucially, this meant that if the Germans did attempt to react, Leros would have to be defended – as Churchill must have known – without air cover.

When the British convoy reached the three islands, the Italians stationed there put up no resistance, but efforts to persuade them to become part of the new garrison– especially those who were manning heavy artillery in strategic positions, met with an unenthusiastic response. As the Faughs and the other battalions settled in and commenced planning their defence strategy, another convoy was on its way; this was the one that Hugh had just managed to join, and was, in fact, the last to get through to Leros. As Major Shepherd of the battalion wrote later:

> just before the Germans attacked, great was the surprise and pleasure of the Bn. to see Hugh arrive one morning with our final reinforcements; he had managed the difficult job of reaching us, many others had failed. The Commanding Officer insisted on Hugh taking over 2nd. i/c. of C. Coy., which he did ... [and] carried out important work during the period ... in reconnaissance of likely landing beaches, minefields and Italian positions, which made him invaluable when the enemy landed on Apetici [hilltop] feature.

On November 3, six days after Hugh's last journal entry and a couple of days after he landed on Leros, the Germans vigorously attacked both Kos and Samos, about 30 miles south of Leros, and after a day's fighting, the British garrisons were overwhelmed and forced to surrender. The Luftwaffe then turned its deadly attention to Leros, carrying out almost non-stop bombing and straffing attacks – a softening-up process prior to the expected landings. The Irish battalion was given the task of covering the centre of Leros where the main town and its harbour lay. Their Commanding Officer, Lt. Col. Maurice French, was suddenly struck-down with Sandfly Fever, but he had already warned his battalion that, because of the island's heavily indented coastline, it would be foolish to commit all the men to coastal defence, especially as he felt quite sure that the Germans would deploy parachute troops. Perhaps because of Col. French's illness, GHQ in Cairo instructed Brigadier Robert Tinley to take overall command of the island's defences and Col. French and his fellow officers were dismayed when this gunnery officer, who knew little about the command of infantry, undid all of French's arrangements, deploying the defenders in small units around the coast and displaying special attention to the beaches.

On November 11, the Germans launched the long expected attack on Leros, making successful sea-borne landings in the north of the island and a single landing in the east. The former were effected, not at sandy beaches as Tinley expected, but along the rocky shores, while the eastern landing was close to Apetici Hill, just north of the Faughs' main positions. Critically, Tinley hesitated, thus allowing the Germans to consolidate their positions. Lt. Hugh Gore-Booth ordered his company forward and succeeded in driving the Germans back some distance, though they were unable to dislodge the enemy from the strategic hill position. The Germans called up more air support and the Fusiliers' lines were further bombed and straffed but their position was stabilised overnight. The German gun positions on Apetici continued to cause problems, and next morning Hugh carefully worked his way along the hillside with a small fighting patrol to try to surprise and dislodge them. The patrol crept around the hill's right flank, dotted with scrubby bushes and large boulders, and just as they hurled hand grenades at the gun post, it appears that they were spotted and subjected to murderous machine-gun fire. All but one of the members of the patrol were mortally wounded. Fusilier McKeever, who was only slightly injured, tried to help Hugh to get back, but to no avail. He died a short time later.

While all this was happening, Col. French's prediction came true when some 700 German parachute troops landed on the island. Unlike the situation at Kos and Samos where fighting lasted for only a matter of hours, the Leros garrison held out for five days against huge odds, during which the air bombardment never ceased. Indeed, on the third day the German command recorded that 'it seemed impossible that we should ever win the battle' and during one engagement, a member of the Faughs estimated German casualties at 40 per cent. However, it was their complete control of the air that turned the tables in their favour.

Hopelessly outnumbered, with no air support, and with no prospect of reinforcements or fresh supplies, a decision was made on November 16 to surrender. Because there had been some striking similarities (albeit on a different scale) between the Battle of Crete and that for Leros, it seems strange that the British did not appear to have learned several important lessons from the former – in particular, the importance of air cover and good communications. The lack of proper communications and Tinley's decision to spread the defences too thinly and in the wrong places played a crucial part in the failure to prevent the Germans from consolidating the all-important original footholds. For the Germans, the similarity between the two invasions lay in the cost of winning the battle. They suffered 3,000 casualties, lost 156 aircraft, 10 merchant ships, two troopships, one destroyer, and 20 small naval vessels, losses that seemed disproportionate to the importance of such a very small and a not especially strategic island. British fatal casualties on the island numbered less than 200 men, though they, like their opponents, suffered severe naval losses, and five regular battalions spent the remainder of the war in P.O.W. camps.

Royal Irish Fusiliers' casualties were relatively light, but Hugh Gore-Booth lay dead on the hillside where he fell, not far from where his commanding officer died a day later. Of the 14 Irishmen killed on the island, six came from the Republic and four from Northern Ireland and a further four apparently had no precise addresses. One of the fourteen had been the most senior officer on the island, Lieutenant Colonel Maurice French from Wellington Bridge, County Wexford (whose idea it had been to try to persuade Hugh to accept promotion at Malta). He was killed on the third day only a short distance from where Hugh had died.

In his *History of the Second World War*, Churchill devoted 16 sixteen pages to the Leros campaign which, considering its relative unimportance in a global conflict, seems somewhat excessive until it is recalled that he personally pushed ahead with the whole idea despite American opposition. Obviously he felt the need to justify the plan and much of his written detail concerned his attempts at the time to persuade his American allies that the assault on the Dodecanese Islands was strategically justifiable. In response to his pleas for American air support, Eisenhower reluctantly sent two groups of long-range aircraft which managed to wipe out an entire German support convoy and, on a second sortie, sank two German transport ships loaded with troops. Had this support been continued, the fate of Leros might have been different, justifying General Wilson's comment to Churchill that 'it was a very near thing between success and failure.' (Wilson had just been appointed Supreme Allied Commander Mediterranean). Churchill wrote that 'the withdrawal of the [American] fighters sealed the fate of Leros,' adding that the garrison had comprised: 'three fine battalions of British infantry.' Seething over the unenthusiastic help given by the Americans, his final comment was: 'Leros is a bitter blow to me … I was grieved that the small requests I had made for strategic purposes … should have been so obdurately resisted and rejected.'

As Chief of Imperial General Staff, Fermanagh-born Field Marshall Lord Alanbrooke was closer to Churchill than anyone else during World War II, and Britain owes him a huge debt of gratitude for his important role in throwing cold water on some of his Prime Minister's wilder notions about how to conduct the war. The high commands of both the German and Soviet forces must have wished for a similar 'watchdog' to dissuade Hitler and Stalin, respectively, from interfering with the direction of their campaigns. From his diary entries made after Kos and Samos had fallen, it appears that Alanbrooke had been unable to stop Churchill from proceeding with the Dodecanese campaign. Instead, he recorded: 'We discussed the desirability or otherwise of vacating Leros, a very nasty problem. Middle East [Command] … can neither hold nor evacuate Leros …'

* * *

Exactly one week after Hugh's death, a telegram arrived at Lissadell from the War Office informing the family that he had been reported missing. A week later, Sir Josslyn received a letter confirming the information already sent by telegram, with the detail that 'a notification has been received from the Military Authorities in the Middle East that your son, Lieutenant H. Gore-Booth was reported missing on the 12th November, 1943.' The War Office despatched another letter some three months afterwards giving some brief details received from Corporal J.M. Devaney, a member of Hugh's unit. The letter gave the information that: 'on the afternoon of 11th November 1943 [the actual date was the 12th] accompanied by three men, Lieutenant Hugh Gore-Booth went to attack an enemy machine-gun post. The party was fired on almost immediately and the informant adds that he saw your son fall and is almost certain he was killed.' More than seven months after Hugh had died, the family received a further letter stating that:

> The Department has no alternative but to accept with deep regret, [it had received] reliable evidence of your son's death in action on the island of Leros.

On the morning of the surrender of the island, on checking Company rolls, it was reported to his Warrant Officer by your son's Company Sergeant-Major, who is now a prisoner-of-war, that Lieutenant Gore-Booth had been killed, and that his body had been seen and identified by the Sergeant Major. It is consequently being officially recorded that Lieutenant Gore-Booth was killed in action between the 12th and 16th November, 1943.

The effect that this news had on the family, coming some two and a half years after the death of Brian, can only be imagined. To make matters worse, in both cases there had been the initial uncertainty of the situation, leading to hopes that each, in turn, might have survived after all. It had taken the family several weeks to come to terms with the fact that Brian had, indeed, died but in Hugh's case, the uncertainty continued for almost eight months. Sir Josslyn, already unwell, took to his bed, and the family remained convinced that he died of a broken heart five days after Hugh's death was finally confirmed.

Throughout late 1943 and into the early months of 1944, while the family's uncertainty about Hugh's fate continued, they went to great lengths to try to discover whether or not, as they hoped, he might have survived after all. Among the sources approached was the Vatican which had opened an Enquiry Bureau in London. The difficulty had been caused partly by the fact that the island was now in enemy hands and all Hugh's colleagues who had survived had been taken as prisoners-of-war to Germany. The matter was further complicated at the time because – although this was not then known – after he had 'gone missing,' a local fisherman, George Hadzimanoli, found Hugh's body and buried him and his colleagues on the mountainside where they lay. After the general surrender, the Germans organised parties of British soldiers to collect the bodies of their dead comrades and bury them together, but because Hadzimanoli had already buried Hugh, his body was not found. Altogether, 184 bodies were accounted for and after the war the British War Graves Commission erected headstones over each grave and enclosed the whole in a plot surrounded by ornamental trees. About three years later, the bodies of Hugh and those who died with him, were brought down from the hill where they fell and were re-interred side-by-side with their comrades, but because the bodies could not then be identified, each of the Italian marble headstones for this latter group bears the inscription, 'buried near this spot.'

A German Internet website concerning Leros, gives a four-paragraph description of this British military cemetery at Alinda, one of which is devoted entirely to Hugh Gore-Booth. A few months after the war ended,

Hugh's name was published in the *London Gazette* as having been Mentioned in Despatches for Distinguished Service.

His campaign medals included the 1939-45 Star; the Africa Star; Italy Star; the Defence Medal; War Medal, 1939-45; and the Oak Leaf Emblem. Had Hugh's attack on the German machine gun post proved successful it seems quite possible that he would have merited the award of the Military Cross in addition to the five other M.C.s gained by members of the battalion.

Hundreds of letters conveying expressions of sympathy continued to arrive at Lissadell over an extended period as the likelihood of his survival waned. Besides those from relations and close friends, there were very many from persons quite unknown to the family, sent by people who had met Hugh at some point in their lives and who remembered him with affection. A set of eight letters addressed by his mother to 'Lieutenant Gore-Booth, 2nd Batt. Royal Irish Fusiliers, M.E.F.' (Mediterranean Expeditionary Force) which were returned to Lissadell bearing a rubber-stamped message: 'It is regretted that this item could not be delivered because the addressee is reported missing,' represents a pathetic memento in the family archives of the loss of the family's second son. The returned letters have never been opened.

By the KING'S Order the name of
Lieutenant H. Gore-Booth,
The Royal Irish Fusiliers,
was published in the London Gazette on
13 September, 1945.
as mentioned in a Despatch for distinguished service.
I am charged to record
His Majesty's high appreciation.

J.J. Lawson

Secretary of State for War

Hugh's name was published in the *London Gazette* as having been mentioned in a despatch for distinguished service

Two months after the family had been informed that Hugh had, in fact, been killed, Major Shepherd of Hugh's battalion (who, it may be recalled had visited Hugh in hospital just before the battalion sailed for Leros), wrote to Lady Gore-Booth. This battle-hardened veteran told her in touching terms: 'the death of Hugh was a sad blow to us all in the Bn. May I offer, on behalf of all who had the honour to serve with him, our deepest sympathy; he was loved by all.' In the course of his letter, Shepherd recollected various aspects of Hugh's life including his refusal of an offer made by Colonel French to accept promotion to Captain because he wished to stay with his men. He also referred to Hugh's remarkable work organising 'battle drills' at Malta and, by contrast, his love of walking across the rocky Maltese countryside, and elsewhere, to study bird life. He told Hugh's mother that he had received information indicating that the bodies of all the soldiers killed on Leros had been removed to a small cemetery and he hoped to return to the island to see the situation for himself.

In December, 1944, Sgt Larkin wrote to Hugh's mother from Stalag 357, a prisoner of war camp in Germany, to tell her something of the circumstances of her son's death. After Hugh and his men had gone to destroy a German machine-gun nest, 'about two hours later there were a couple of explosions and then rifle and machine gun fire, then all went quiet again. A short period after this, one of the Fusiliers of that patrol staggered into one of my posts wounded in seven places. He told us the whole patrol was wiped out.' The sole survivor was, in fact, Fusilier J. McKeever from Lurgan, who had tried to rescue Hugh, and who also wrote to Hugh's mother seven months later:

> My Dear Lady, Major Shepherd desires me to write you and tell you all I know about your son, Lieut. Gore-Booth who was killed in action. Well my lady this letter will be as difficult for me to write as it will be for you to receive. I must say that your son was a fine soldier, and a very brave man. When your son was wounded I done my best under fire to carry him to safety and get him medical attention right away, but he died before I reached the First Aid Station, the only words he said to me was, to let his Superior Officer knew he had been wounded, this I done as soon as possible ….

Four years later, Captain R.J.Q. Ambrose of Hugh's battalion, wrote to Lady Gore-Booth to inform her he was about to visit Leros and, after going there he wrote again to let her know he was sending a report of his visit to Lt. Col. W.G. Findlater. He intended that it would be then forwarded to Lt. Gen. Templer, Vice-C.I.G.S. [Vice-Chief of General

Staff] at the War Office, who was also Colonel of the Royal Irish Fusiliers Regiment at the time. In this second letter, he described meeting George Hadzimanoli – the Leros fisherman who had found Hugh's body – who had told him that he had buried Hugh where he lay. He had led Captain Ambrose to the place and:

> we followed exactly the path taken by Hugh and his patrol [and we were] shown the exact spot where he had found a British Lieutenant and four British soldiers, and he is the person who tended this spot until 1946 when he guided the personnel of the [War] Graves Commission to the spot.

Captain Ambrose proposed that a fund be raised to provide a scholarship to the University of Athens on an annual basis for a young man from the island of Leros. He also suggested providing an outboard motor for George Hadzimanoli, the fisherman who had found Hugh's body and had tended the grave.

After the war both Angus and Bridget travelled (on separate occasions) to see their brother's grave and, 44 years after Hugh died, one of his colleagues in the Faughs wrote to Aideen, inviting her to join a party of almost 100 veterans and relatives who were about to visit the islands of Kos and Leros. As a result, Aideen became the third member of the family to do so, and later described how she saw Hugh's headstone in the well-kept cemetery, shaded by jacaranda trees, tamarisks and oleanders, surrounded by a pittosporum hedge. Aideen wrote in 1992 to Edward Johnson, a friend of Hugh's, in a further attempt to discover more information about her brother's death. Although unable to help, he replied that he had first met Hugh in Egypt, 'a quiet, happy person.' He recalled an incident involving an officer dressing down a junior officer and, happening to look at Hugh who was standing nearby, demanded: 'What are you smiling at, Mr Gore-Booth?' Back came the reply as quick as a flash: 'I'm not smiling, I just have a happy face.'

It will be recalled that when Hugh visited the Aran Islands in 1937, the poet, Máirtín Ó Direáin, had helped Hugh in his efforts to learn Irish. After Máirtín heard about Hugh's death, he wrote a touching Appreciation which appeared (during 1961) in a collection of personal reminiscences entitled *Feamainn Bhealtaine*. In his reminiscences, Ó Direáin recalled first meeting Hugh on the ferry going to the Aran Islands.

> I noticed a particular young man scrutinising the islands intently from the first moment he caught sight of them. He had a wholesome ruddy complexion, he was fair-haired and of just medium stature. He was wearing shorts and had a

haversack on his back. The fair hair, ruddy looks and shorts gave him a very youthful appearance. You would swear that you were looking at a youngster of seventeen years and I was surprised when he told me later that he was twenty-seven, the same age as myself at the time. His name was Hugh Gore-Booth, son of a brother of Countess Markievicz …. He had an interest in the Irish language and he had with him a [school text] book by Common Noun which had, I think, the title *Clocha Scail*.

He made a deep impression on me as a person, and he was so refined, so kindly and so courteous that I took an immediate liking to him. He was perceptive too and it did not take him long to notice the ways of the people …. We went through a lot of topics those evenings: the Irish question, the question of the islands and their people, the question of the war, which according to us, and to others besides, was near at hand. He didn't leave me in any doubt … which side he was on. He felt it was his duty to fight against Germany. He wrote to me later and sent me pictures he had taken on the island and said he was working away at the Irish with the help of '*Clocha Scail*.'

It didn't surprise me very much, afterwards, when I heard he was killed during the last war … fighting for what was right as he saw it. It surely saddened me. He is laid to rest in some lonely place far from Lissadell and from Sligo…

May God have mercy on his gentle soul.

During April 1951, a pair of stained glass windows in memory of Brian and Hugh was unveiled and dedicated during a special Service in Lissadell Church. An article published in the *Church of Ireland Gazette* described the windows as:

A beautiful and artistically executed piece of work, whose designer and executor was Miss K. O'Brien, of the Tower of Glass Stained Glass Works, Dublin. Its design is of two symbolic figures, Courage and Love, representing the Courage and Love which culminated in the Supreme Sacrifice. Below the feet of the two figures, the evil of the world is shown in the form of snakes and bats, with the Dove of Peace enmeshed in a net. This portion of the window is executed in dark and sombre tones. For contrast the figures are bright and colourful … and the background, particularly that of the sea, is a symphony of colour. In the extreme upper portion of the window the souls are seen rising to perpetual light.

Kathleen O'Brien had joined the Tower of Glass Studio at the invitation of Sarah Purser, R.H.A., who painted the well-known portrait of the young sisters, Constance and Eva. Purser had also been commissioned to design a stained glass window in memory of Eva for the Round House in Manchester. Dedicating the new window, the Bishop of

Kilmore quoted a passage from a letter written by Brian shortly before his death: 'I do not feel we are fighting only for victory but to exterminate all sorts of evil things … I know now some ancient truths I never knew before and. I have tasted the strength of leaving oneself in Other Hands.' The bishop described the words as 'a wonderful testimony, and a joyous comfort to those he left behind to mourn his loss. Here was Courage, here was Love. Both dedicated to the cause of Truth, and ready to pay the price of supreme human sacrifice.'

A pair of stained glass windows– designed by Kathleen O'Brien of the Tower of Glass studio – was installed in Lissadell church and dedicated to the memory of Brian and Hugh. – (*photo, The Irish Times*)

Mention has been made of Hugh's quiet religious faith, and in this connection it is interesting that his Malta diary recorded that on one Sunday he attended a service in Valetta Presbyterian Church, not St George's Anglican church. There is no record of him suggesting he had a particular interest in Presbyterianism, but the point is interesting because, while he was at Oxford University, it seems he attended St Columba's chapel, which was founded there as a Presbyterian Chaplaincy. Little or nothing of this would now be known were it not for the fact that Hugh's name is featured on the war memorial in the chapel.

* * *

The two brothers, Hugh and Brian lie, as Mairtín Ó Direáin wrote, 'far from Lissadell.' The deaths of the two brothers had devastating consequences for the family, then faced with the additional concern for the third brother, fervently hoping that he would not become one more victim of the war. Angus was serving with the Irish Guards whose regimental motto is '*Quis Separabit*,' an oblique but perhaps appropriate reminder of the deaths of two Old Testament figures, Saul and Jonathan, who died fighting the Philistines. As recorded in the Second Book of Samuel: 'Saul and Jonathan were lovely and pleasant in their lives, And in their death they were not divided.'

Brian and Hugh lost their lives fighting against Nazism, a regime of modern-day Philistines, and in death they, too, were not divided.

Gabrielle Gore-Booth (left) with her mother and the young Elizabeth Petch
who became a life-long friend of both Gabrielle and Aideen.

The sisters Gabrielle (above) and Aideen.

The Lissadell Affair, and after

Sir Josslyn's four daughters Bridget, Rosaleen, Aideen and Gabrielle lived, at least for the most part, quiet unobtrusive lives. Three of the four sisters never married, and only the latter two are now even vaguely remembered outside the family circle. Aideen is most likely to be remembered because, for many years, she personally conducted visitors on tours around Lissadell, while Gabrielle's name may be recalled because of her part in what became known as 'the Lissadell Affair.' Some may also recall the shadowy figure of their brother Angus, sitting quietly in the corner of the library, whose life, like that of Michael, had been blighted by the onset of schizophrenia.

Bridget, the eldest of the four sisters, was known as 'Biddy' in the family circle and resided for some years at Bundoran and later in various parts of England, eventually returning from Cumbria to live in Fintona, County Tyrone where she died in May 1992. A newspaper reporting her death recorded that she was:

> a noted painter and much of her acclaimed work was inspired by her Sligo background…. Although confined to a wheelchair in later years, Miss Gore-Booth continued to turn out paintings at a rate which belied her advancing years. Her works were featured in several exhibitions.

When Bridget left Lissadell to live in Bundoran, she was joined there for a time by Rosaleen who also spent some years in England before returning to Ireland where she lived with friends at Killeavy, Co. Armagh. Little is now known about her except that she shared her family's propensity for an interest in painting and a love of horses and, like her mother, she was an expert needle-woman. Rosaleen, who predeceased her older sister by one year, died on April 12 1991, and the two sisters were buried in the family plot at Lissadell church.

Their eldest brother Michael, who succeeded his father as the seventh baronet in 1944, had lived a fairly normal life until his late teens or early twenties when, as already mentioned, a mental condition began to become increasingly evident. Aideen was to recall that 'everybody was very upset, and there was no one to explain it, and I became very frightened and confused and could not concentrate any more.' She wrote in her memoirs, that he became ill 'at a time before people who suffered in this way could be cured, as they can now.' Like most people faced with a similar problem at that time, members of the family found it difficult to accept and state openly that the heir was mentally ill. Although there had been earlier symptoms, matters greatly worsened when, after attending Cambridge University, he had sat for a consular service examination and was placed last. He attended various psychiatric hospitals for treatment, including St Patrick's and St Edmundsbury in Dublin, from where he went on to Warneford Hospital near Oxford and subsequently to a home in York. His brother Hugh visited him at Oxford in 1942 and wrote a detailed letter to his parents about his condition and his treatment:

> M[ichael] suffered for 11 years from his complaint – he is now making a recovery – during which he suffered many setbacks. Its slow progress renders it none the less remarkable [and] it clearly commenced, according to all available data, when Dr. McInnes took over the management and reorganisation of the Warneford Hospital and it is to him and the staff who worked under him that we owe our deep gratitude.....

Hugh considered that moving him to this hospital had been a step in the right direction and had been the cause of 'convalescence after an abnormally protracted illness.' He thought Michael 'was obviously pleased with the change of surroundings, companions and diet, and with the trouble which has been taken to promote this change.' Although Hugh thought his brother's state would be 'a considerable shock for anyone who had known him previously,' nevertheless, 'much of what he has got to say is highly intelligent and even shrewd, although his delivery is noticeably weak.'

As a result of Hugh's letter, Lady Gore-Booth decided to travel to Warneford and, encouraged by what she then saw for herself, she wanted to bring Michael back home to Lissadell. Sir Josslyn became extremely concerned at this suggestion, thinking it would be more sensible to get a second opinion. Hugh thought that 'any attempt to move Michael home for at any rate some considerable time ahead, is quite out of the question, and might not only prove fatal to his recovery, but might also seriously prejudice the health of other members of the family [who] could not be expected to stand up to the additional strain which would thereby be cast on them.'

After Michael was moved to a home in York, Aideen visited him there on a number of occasions, invariably staying with her friend, Eileen

Goodbody, in Dublin en route, and other members of the family also went to see Michael from time to time. Sir Michael died at York on March 16, 1987 aged 78, and his body was brought back to Lissadell where the funeral took place four days later in the church built by his great grandfather. The attendance exceeded 300 including representatives of the Army, Sligo County Council and Sligo Corporation.

* * *

The foregoing provides the background against which Aideen's sister, Gabrielle, is now most likely to be recalled, because it was she who, in 1944, took on the responsibility of running the Lissadell Estate after her father died. Having had four brothers, Gabrielle could hardly have anticipated this turn of events brought about by the fact that the heir, Michael, was incapable of managing Lissadell, and his brother Hugh, who had trained in the business, had been killed during the war, as had Brian. Her remaining brother, Angus, was at the time serving in the Irish Guards but he, too, was to develop signs of mental instability. Even so, Gabrielle might have remained a little-remembered figure like her two older sisters, were it not for the part she played in the family's unequal struggle to retain Lissadell Estate intact, a long drawn-out saga spanning two and a half decades. 'The Lissadell Affair,' as it came to be known, was possibly the most distressing episode in the family's long history.

Because of his mental condition, Michael had been declared a ward of court, and the responsibility for the running of the estate was entrusted to Patrick Rutledge, a former Minister for Justice under Mr de Valera. As General Solicitor for the time being for Minors and Wards of Court, he then appointed Gabrielle to act as manager, and in the circumstances, this seemed to be the best possible arrangement. The High Court later agreed that Gabrielle, Aideen and Angus, as well as their mother, could continue to reside in what was then, legally, Sir Michael's house and this situation pertained throughout the following eight years. As Terence de Vere White wrote in *The Irish Times*:

> The Wardship began very happily. The ... worst ills of chancery were avoided by a sensitive arrangement which allowed the Gore-Booths not only to continue to live at Lissadell, but Lady Gore-Booth was empowered to draw cheques on a local bank to pay the current expenses of the estate.

In 1950, Mr Justice Cahir Davitt, was appointed President of the High

Court. Later in the same year it was he who proposed in that court that the Lissadell Estate be sold to the Land Commission. The proposal was opposed by Rutledge, who was continuing to act as Committee of the Estate of Sir Michael Gore-Booth, and the matter was dropped. When Rutledge died two years later, Davitt appointed Mr Justice Gerald Maguire to the position. Maguire immediately commenced making changes in relation to the administration of Lissadell, taking the view that Gabrielle had no idea how such a large estate should be managed because, as he stated, the family had run up a bank overdraft of £20,000. Gabrielle vigorously denied this allegation and counter-claimed that the overdraft had resulted from Maguire's actions.

Sir Michael Gore-Booth, Seventh Baronet who, although he succeeded to the title was declared a Ward of Court.

As time went by Gabrielle found it increasingly difficult to know the details of what was going on, because Maguire refused to allow her access to the estate accounts. Her anxieties mounted after she discovered that a payment made to Mr Maguire in connection with the sale of timber during the autumn of 1954 had not, by the year's end, been entered in the accounts. The matter was only rectified 13 months later after representations had been made on behalf of the family to the Registrar of Wards of Court, and as a result of this and other incidents, Gabrielle deeply distrusted both Maguire's policy of managing the estate and the accounting procedures that were being employed.

The scene was thus set for an all-out head-on confrontation between Mr Justice Maguire and Miss Gabrielle Gore-Booth, a confrontation which was, inevitably, unevenly balanced. Gabrielle believed (according to what her sister Aideen subsequently wrote) that she was dutifully carrying out her father's instructions given to her as he lay dying. However, Aideen's recollections, written in her old age, were not always accurate, and there is some doubt as to whether Sir Josslyn, on his deathbed did, in fact, instruct Gabrielle to manage the estate. Whatever about that, it certainly seems that Gabrielle believed it to be the case, and her subsequent actions were those of someone who was convinced she was acting solely for the good of the family. The consequences were to prove that she was seen by the other side to be disruptive and stubborn, and this almost certainly made matters worse.

Finding it impossible to deal with Gabrielle, Mr Justice Davitt then dismissed her and appointed Mr Charles Caffrey as manager of the estate instead. Gabrielle's earlier appointment to act as manager had been made by Mr Rutledge on an informal basis and, as Davitt pointed out, had not been sanctioned at the time by the courts. When, for some reason, Caffrey did not take up the post, the position was filled three months later by Mr John Costello, and after Gabrielle had unsuccessfully demanded to see Costello's references, her very pointedly defiant stance with Mr Justice Davitt and with Mr Justice Maguire became even more hardened. Matters went from bad to worse, and in March 1956 an order was made by Davitt to sell the estate to the Land Commission wherein it was stated that the Trustees of the estate had consented to the sale. This was hotly disputed by Gabrielle who claimed that one of the Trustees, Major Nicholls, had informed her that the contrary was the case, but the sale went ahead and 2,600 acres at Lissadell were sold to the Land Commission for £77,000 – roughly £30 per acre. Mr Justice Maguire then ordered the disposal of property and stock on the estate, on foot of which a commencement was made when a Mr McGarry, accompanied by three cattle drovers and a force of 20 Gardai and detectives arrived one morning at Lissadell. McGarry informed Gabrielle and Aideen that he had been authorised 'to proceed with all reasonable speed to effect the sale of the livestock, crops and farming implements on the estate.' *The Irish Times* reported what happened next:

> Miss Gabrielle Gore-Booth jumped across a hedge into the field and chased the cattle through the field. She was joined in the chase by her sister who entered the field through a gate. They were followed by Mr. McGarry and his drovers. The chase continued through the field for a few minutes, when the two sisters gave it up. The drovers brought the herd on to the road, where a lorry was waiting. Then Miss Gabrielle Gore-Booth said that two of the cattle belonged to an employee, Mr. Patrick Flynn [of] Lissadell, and that she would not permit any of the cattle to be loaded until Mr. Flynn had identified his own cattle. Mr. McGarry said that Mr. Flynn could identify his animals later.

According to the report, the drover then decided to move the cattle to the nearby village of Carney where they were loaded onto a lorry and driven away. An injunction was granted against the two sisters and their mother ordering them to cease taking part in or interfering with the management of the estate. Shortly after this, Maguire made an application in the name of Sir Michael Gore-Booth to commit Miss Gabrielle Gore-Booth and Miss Aideen Gore-Booth to prison for alleged contempt of court in connection with the recent incident concerning the cattle. This application for a committal order must have seemed one of the most bizarre occurrences during this whole lengthy saga, representing as it did a move, nominally made by a brother, to have two of his sisters sent to jail or, as Aideen pointedly expressed it, evicted. Commenting on this situation, Mark Bence-Jones, wrote: 'It would certainly have caused an outcry if the nieces of Constance Markievicz had been gaoled by the Republic for the sake of which she had herself endured prison.' Others may have taken the view that Constance herself would have had very little sympathy for the nieces of a family that she considered, as she told her brother Josslyn, were 'usurpers and tyrants.'

An affidavit was subsequently read on behalf of Gabrielle, stating that Maguire had put the figure for the net loss of the estate at £20,828, a figure which she had sworn was incorrect. She argued that the figure certified by the auditors, and which had been passed by the President of the High Court, was £15,302 on December 31, 1954. On that misstatement, as she called it, Mr Justice Maguire obtained an order from the President of the High Court on March 23, 1956, and claimed that neither she nor her sister had defied the court, but had believed that the order made on March 23 was made on false representations. In his judgment, Mr Justice Murnaghan said that it was impossible, when there were conflicting affidavits and without hearing evidence in the witness box, to say which figure was to be accepted but he preferred the account of these incidents given by Miss Gabrielle Gore-Booth. It seemed to him that the method adopted to move the cattle might have been different and he refused the application made to send the two sisters to prison.

Four months later, following an appeal, an injunction was granted against Gabrielle and Aideen and their mother forbidding them from interfering with the management of the estate. One of the three judges of the Supreme Court involved said that 'everybody had the greatest sympathy for these ladies, but was it because of that the Court was to be stultified?' When asked if he was in a position to say that his clients would not obstruct, counsel acting for the family replied that it was not fair to put them into a position of having to give an undertaking before there was any evidence of their having disobeyed the injunction.

Many years before his death, Sir Josslyn had planted large coniferous plantations – mostly Sitka Spruce – which had been carefully managed by a regular cycle of planting, thinning, maturing, felling, and replanting to provide a steady income for the estate. When the solicitors acting for the Gore-Booth family finally succeeded in obtaining copies of the estate accounts for the years 1956-59 (a year and a half later, in July, 1961), included were the figures for the sale of the more than 150 acres of timber for which Gabrielle considered the almost derisory sum of just over £18,000 had been paid. Lady Gore-Booth demanded an enquiry and the case was heard by Mr Justice Davitt, but after he stated that he had insufficient time to read the affidavits, the case was put back to the following December. He eventually heard the case on oral evidence more than three years later in October 1964 and reserved judgment, giving his judgment during March of the following year. In the course of this very lengthy document, Davitt stated that he thought it opportune at that stage to consider whether Miss Gore-Booth could be regarded as an unbiased witness:

> The following short resume of her activities at Lissadell during the years immediately preceding the events of 1957 is of some relevance in this context. During the period when the late Mr. Rutledge was Committee of the Estate of the Ward, she was allowed gradually to assume the functions of manager without any formal appointment or sanction of the Court. During the years 1944 to 1954 inclusive, losses on the running of the estate at Lissadell averaged £3,000

a year. In October 1954, after Mr. Maguire had become Committee, I had a meeting in my chamber at which he and Miss Gore-Booth were present together with the then Registrar, Dr. Webb.

After commenting upon the continuing losses which he had suggested to Maguire required economies (including reductions in staff and certain changes including the appointment of a manager), he outlined how Gabrielle had been obstructive:

> Although I had personally warned her of the consequences of such a course of conduct, she continuously refused to co-operate; not merely did she refuse to co-operate, she endeavoured in various ways to thwart and obstruct Mr. Maguire in his efforts to effect the economies and the changes which I had sanctioned. A situation developed in which strike action by the employees at Lissadell became imminent and which eventually resulted in their employment and hers being terminated.

However, he said, negotiations which then followed resulted in the reinstatement of the men, (41 had been dismissed), and the retention of Miss Gore-Booth 'in an office capacity,' and the appointment of a manager but, he added:

> She and her mother claimed, in effect, the right to veto any appointment which did not meet with their approval and made other unreasonable demands. Eventually, Mr. Maguire was faced with a situation in which the men refused to work under a manager except upon terms dictated by Lady and Miss Gore-Booth …. It was obviously impossible to carry on, and Mr. Maguire dismissed the whole staff at Lissadell and applied to the Court for directions as to the closing down of all operations there and the disposal of the property.

He then described how, by order of 22 March 1956, he had been given liberty to offer the lands at Lissadell for sale to the Land Commission, to let them temporarily in the meantime, and to sell off the livestock, crops, implements and chattels. He had subsequently been given liberty to institute proceedings for an injunction against Lady Gore-Booth and her daughters restraining them from interfering with the management of the estate. He noted that: 'the injunction was granted by Mr. Justice Dixon on 12 February, 1957, from whose judgement in the matter most of this resumé is taken.' He then drew particular attention to the following passage:

> The events of February and March of last year crystallised a position which has obtained essentially unchanged since then. Lady Gore-Booth and her daughters have remained in occupation of the lands, to which they have no

title, and have carried on the farming and other activities of the estate as if they were the owners of it. The men who were lawfully dismissed have been retained in employment except so far as a few men left voluntarily. The produce of the estate has been sold and the proceeds received by Miss Gabrielle in defiance of explicit directions.

Again in defiance of such directions, these proceeds have been partly applied in paying the wages of the men wrongfully retained in employment. The Committee has been excluded from effective control and management of the estate and has been denied the account books of the estate – which are, of course, the property of the Ward – or close inspection of them. Every Order of the Court has been ignored, evaded or defied … I can only regard all three defendants as combined in an agreement – what the law terms a conspiracy – to prevent the effective management and control of the estate by the proper authority and to render ineffective the lawful Order and directions in regard of the competent Court.

He felt it reasonable to conclude from the quoted brief that Miss Gabrielle Gore-Booth was not likely 'to form an unbiased opinion as to the way in which the property was being managed, or to give unbiased evidence on the matter.' He referred to the fact that she had received some support from an independent witness, Major Peter Hall, who had given evidence concerning three of the woods at Lissadell where felling had been carried out.

It had been Hall's opinion that the value of the timber extracted from one particular site had been sold for about 75 per cent of its true value, though this was a view that he had been unable to verify. Hall also claimed that another wood had been clear-felled although there was no licence for clear-felling, only a licence for cutting 435 Spruce trees, but the estate manager argued that this figure represented all that had remained standing after extensive storm damage.

In his opinion, Major Hall's evidence did little to support Gabrielle's case, and while he accepted that 'there may at least have been some laxity on the part of [whoever] was checking the loads of timber removed,' he was not satisfied that 'any such laxity has been satisfactorily established.' It was his opinion that the injunction had resulted in securing comparative peace at Lissadell, and while he was sensible of the limits which the injunction had placed upon Miss Gabrielle's 'activities,' he also noted that she had not ceased 'from meddling in matters which are no longer any legal concern of hers.' Stating that she had persistently complained to all and sundry in a manner likely to render the position of any estate manager at Lissadell 'utterly intolerable,' he went on:

Neither she nor her mother or sister have any legal right whatever to have any say as to how Lissadell is to be managed. They have no legal right even to be at Lissadell. They have been allowed to remain there because of the belief that if Sir Michael Gore-Booth were under no disability, it would be his wish permanently to extend the hospitality of his home to his mother and sisters.… As matters are they remain at Lissadell by permission of the Committee and the Court. I might say that their tolerance, as far as the Court is concerned, has been strained to the limit.

I do not accept Miss Gore-Booth's case as being established. I say her case because I believe she is really the moving party. I do not see it necessary for the Registrar to take any account or make any enquiries such as those sought for the Notice of Motion. I do not consider it necessary to direct [the manager to] discontinue the felling and sale of timber.… There is no necessity and I do not propose to make any Order or give any direction except to refuse the Motion.

Another three months elapsed before Mr Justice Davitt signed his judgment, following which an appeal was lodged. According to Gabrielle, it was not possible to obtain a copy of the judgment for a further five months until after Davitt retired when the decision to go ahead with the appeal was abandoned due to lack of funds. Gabrielle subsequently maintained that because of the injunction given against her it was extremely difficult for her to collect evidence without Judge Davitt taking the stay off the eviction order. Mr Quinn, who had been appointed Solicitor General for Wards of Court and who was Committee of the Estate of Sir Michael, died shortly after this.

The Irish newspapers covered the saga in the course of their normal court reporting, the details of which, so often couched in legal language, were not always easily understood by the general public. Despite (or because of) this, there was a growing sense – founded or otherwise – that a grave injustice had been done to the Gore-Booth family who appeared to be fighting a very unequal battle to retain the house and its estate intact for future generations. Indeed, it was rather more a prolonged war than a battle, for the whole episode lasted for more than two and a half decades.

The first newspaper to treat the matter as a 'general interest' story was the London based *Sunday Times* which strongly criticised the manner in which the State had intervened on Sir Michael's behalf. This was followed by decision by Radio Telefis Éireann to screen a '7 Days' television programme about 'The Lissadell Affair' thus bringing the whole matter freshly to the attention of a very wide audience. Reviewing television programmes for *The Irish Times* during May 1971, Ken Gray wrote about what he termed 'the careful and painstaking research and some skilful interviewing in the "7 Days" inquiry into the Lissadell Affair.' Posing the question: 'Management, negligence or sheer dishonesty?' he went on: 'There's plenty of mystery in the Lissadell story, much of it still unsolved, and a strong suggestion of injustice.' Gray concluded that the programme was challenging in its contention that 'Miss [Gabrielle] Gore-Booth has a strong case that cries out for further investigation.'

The renewed publicity about the matter was then raised in the Dáil by the Labour Party T.D., Mr Barry Desmond, who called for a tribunal of enquiry. Dr Noel Browne also raised the matter in the Dáil, asking the Minister for Lands, Mr Moran, whether the Land Commission intended proceeding with the acquisition or purchase of the Lissadell Estate. After a non-committal reply, he asked if, in view of the fact that the estate belonged to the heirs of the Countess Markievicz, would he [the Minister] take every precaution to see that their wishes in regard to the disposal of the estate are consulted? Although the Ceann Comhairle (Speaker) intervened to point out that the question impinged on a court case, Browne persisted in questioning: 'Is it a fact that there is in being an inter-departmental conspiracy to conceal the fact from the public that the estate has in fact been filched over the years by certain persons who were to supervise?' The Minister interrupted to say the matter was *sub judice* and he accused Browne of carrying out a campaign 'for his own purpose.' Browne replied that this was a scandalous statement, to which Moran retorted: 'I would be far more concerned about any relations of the Countess Markievicz than the Deputy or any of his antecedents.' After Dr Browne asked 'Are you able to look after them?' the matter was then dropped.

Detailed articles were published in *The Irish Times* on two consecutive days in December 1970 which were all the more interesting for having been written by its literary editor, Terence de Vere White, who was a former solicitor. He had travelled to Lissadell to see for himself what had been happening there. Commenting about the allegations that timber from the estate had been sold for less than the market value he wrote that 'Either the proper price was mis-appropriated – or the greater part of it – or else timber was sold for a song to timber merchants.' Denied access to the accounts and having discovered a number of discrepancies, he thought it seemed hardly surprising that Gabrielle Gore-Booth was certain in her own mind that timber and cattle were being sold off at a fraction of their true value. Continuing his article, de Vere White wrote that from the age of 16 he had lived in 'the world of judges and registrars and orders and summonses and affidavits and delays and adjournments.' The names of the legal parties mentioned by Gabrielle during their discussion were all well-known to him and, as he expressed it: 'I found incredulity mounting. One rogue? Possibly two? Not very likely. Three? I cannot believe it. Then again, supposing so many functionaries of the court were dishonest, why should they all lay into the Gore-Booth estate? There were others to pilfer.'

Gabrielle: 'She was always fair and wise with the workforce.'

Looking into the matter further, he reported that he had come across references to a curious episode relating to a typist who was employed by the General Solicitor. She had been accused of embezzling money, and in the course of her trial secured an order to inspect trust bank accounts opened by Maguire, the greater part of which related to the Lissadell estate. When the legal advisors acting for the accused typist proceeded to avail of the authority to inspect the bank accounts, they were informed that the State had entered a *nolle prosequi.* and the proceedings against her were discontinued.

This was not, however, quite the end of the matter, because Gabrielle's solicitors decided to submit questions to the Department of the Taoiseach, the Department of Justice and to the Attorney General's

Department. During this correspondence, a challenge was put to the authorities that they should have immediately instituted an investigation. In response, the reason given for dropping the case was that Maguire, the essential witness, who had been ill for some time, had died, and that there was no other reason for dropping it. However, a subsequent search in the Criminal Court records showed that although 14 months had elapsed from the instigation of proceedings to the date of Mr Maguire's death, no deposition had been taken from him, although a number of depositions had been taken from other parties.

De Vere White commented that during his legal career he had met many neurotic and mad people and suffered boredom and worse listening to their persecution fantasies but, he wrote, 'Miss Gore-Booth is not one of these.' He decided that it would have been irresponsible of a person such as himself, trained as a lawyer and practised as an officer of the court, not to check Gabrielle's story:

> I did so with her solicitor, Mr. Charles H. Browne of the firm of (alas that Dickens had never heard of it!) Argue and Phibbs of Sligo. I expected Mr. Browne, as man to man, to warn me that Miss Gore-Booth tended to exaggerate. Far from it. If she had laid about her with whips, Mr. Browne resorted to scorpions. He had even a tale to tell of attempted murder of a witness for the Gore-Booths....

Summing up, he wrote that it seemed to him that 'if timber merchants paid big sums for trees, surely there would be someone connected with them who would come forward and say so. But if they got the trees very cheap then the accusation lies that the Gore-Booths were sold up the river.' His view was that the wealth of accusations deserved an enquiry, but a judge had said no. 'That would have been enough for most people once upon a time. Is it to-day?' he asked in his article published nearly 30 years before the word 'Tribunal' was on everybody's lips in Ireland.

De Vere White's article resulted in a flood of letters to the editor being published in *The Irish Times* over a period of many months. The first of these was written by Mr Cahir Davitt who, although he had by then retired as President of the High Court, took the unusual step of writing in response to de Vere White's articles. Commenting that they had made 'distressing reading,' he felt he could not allow what had been written to go unchallenged. He began by making the point that in the normal course of events, a person is entitled to keep his personal affairs more or less private. The mere fact he had happened to become a ward of court should not expose that person to the risk of having his affairs become the subject of public controversy. After drawing attention to the provision in the Constitution that justice must be administered in public 'except in such special and limited cases as may be prescribed by law,' Davitt then made the point that these provisions included exceptions in the exercise of the jurisdiction of the High Court in Wards of Court matters.

> For the 20 years preceding my retirement as President of the High Court … I exercised that jurisdiction. Any information I may have gained as to the affairs of Sir Michael Gore-Booth has been acquired in my capacity as the judge in charge of such matters. Apart from my duties as such I would have no knowledge of them. My information is in my opinion privileged, and the privilege is Sir Michael's. Moreover, so long as he remains a Ward of Court his affairs continue to be sub judice. For these reasons I am not at liberty to engage in any controversy as to the facts of the matter which is the subject of Mr de Vere White's article.

Davitt, however, felt free to make a number of observations. He asserted that, in relation to the three persons who had acted successively in the position of Registrar of the Wards of Courts, as well as the two who had been General Solicitor for the same, he could recall no instance in which he had reason to be 'dissatisfied with the way in which [they] discharged their several and various duties, at times under difficult and even exasperating circumstances.' He was emphatic that allegations and insinuations of incompetence, negligence and even worse concerning the officers mentioned above were, as far as he was concerned, unbelievable.

> Listening receptively and perhaps uncritically, to one side of the story is not the best way to arrive at the truth and reality of the matter. He [de Vere White] has heard one side of the story … The whole story is, however, to be found in the Wards of Court Office … It would require a careful examination of these files, now extending back over a quarter of a century, and the exercise of much patient industry as well as legal skill and judgement to arrive at a sound conclusion as to the true facts of this tangled matter. Mr de Vere White has not, of course, made any such examination.

Four days later, a response from Gabrielle was published, and in the course of her letter to the editor she posed several questions:

> Why was there no trouble until Mr. Maguire came? Why did the legal costs of the Committee of the Estate which amounted to £418 for the years 1945 to 1952 when Mr. Ruttledge was there, go up to £8,668 for the years 1952 to 1960 when Mr. Gerald Maguire was Committee?

She concluded her letter with another question: 'If Judge Davitt is quite satisfied about everything, what evidence has he of the trees sold? I would like to share the knowledge with him even now.'

After an interval of four days, Judge Davitt's reply, which extended to a full column and a quarter, was published in the newspaper's letters columns. Stating that he was writing without the aid of notes about a matter going back over many years, he could not know whether or not Miss Gabrielle Gore-Booth's figures were correct. What he did know, he said, was that the trouble which eventually arose was caused by her refusal to co-operate and by her persistent attempts to oppose and obstruct him in the exercise of his duties. Some of the costs incurred during his own time in office had resulted from several proceedings which had to taken against her in the High Court, one of which had to be appealed (successfully) to the Supreme Court.

After dealing with various issues including the very confused matter about the sale of timber, Davitt referred to the fact that Gabrielle, along with her mother and sister, had decided to appeal to the Supreme Court against his decision. However, due to financial considerations (he understood), they had been precluded from doing so. He was surprised, as a consequence, to see that these protracted proceedings were described in de Vere White's article in the following words: 'And why, if there was such a tale of wrong-doing had it not been brought to court? But it had, and when an enquiry was asked for, the judge said there was nothing to enquire into.'

> Miss Gore-Booth has made full use of the communications media to tell her side of the story; with what degree of fairness may, perhaps, be judged from the foregoing instance. As I said in my previous letter the whole story is to be found in the files of the matter now extending back over twenty-five years. Part of the other side of the story can be found in my judgement ... Perhaps your readers [this remark was addressed to the newspaper's editor] would like an opportunity of hearing it. I have no objection to the judgement being fully reported should you, Sir, see fit to do so, and if the President of the High Court should give the necessary permission.

The Irish Times took the decision to publish Davitt's judgement in full about three weeks later – part of which has been already been quoted here, and during February 1971, the same newspaper carried a report about the inaugural meeting of the Solicitors Apprentices' Debating Society, at which the first woman auditor of the society for 50 years, Miss Elizabeth Ryan, gave an address on 'Ireland, its laws and its mentally ill.' Among the speakers was Dr Noel Browne, T.D., who said that a new Mental Treatment Act was needed because of changes in the general care for psychiatric patients.' Gabrielle had read the report, noting especially a paragraph stating that another speaker, Mr T.A. Finlay, S.C. (later to become Chief Justice), had referred to the publicity given to 'the Lissadell Affair.' In relation to this, he was reported as saying:

> It might well be that this publicity showed up some anachronism in the procedures of the administration of the Wards of Court. To lawyers like himself who knew the fierce integrity and abiding common sense of Mr. Justice Davitt, who tried the issues arising between the relatives of the Ward and the Committee in that particular case, it was unthinkable that the underlying suggestion of a perversion of justice in that case, as distinct from some frailty in the method of administration had any grounds at all.

This brief but interesting reference to Lissadell was, however, hardly more than an interjection, after which Mr Finlay went on to speak about other matters concerning mental illnesses and the law.

The correspondence columns of The Irish Times continued to feature letters about 'the Lissadell Affair' until June 1971 – almost all of them sympathetic to the family, including one from Frank Wynne, the President of the Yeats Society. Letters of a similar tone were also published in various other newspapers, notably in the *Sunday Press* and *Evening Press*, one of which, written by a Mr J. Murphy, appeared in the latter. In it he asserted that the Gore-Booths were 'an illustrious family with a long tradition of generous service to their local community', and added that it was from this same family that Constance Markievicz had sprung, 'a heroic leader in the struggle for national liberation. What had been a local indebtedness to the family was thereby broadened to encompass the entire nation.' Commenting on what had been happening in the courts, the writer went on:

> Thereafter, through mismanagement or something worse, the estate suffered grievous losses and gross neglect. Appeals to the courts were unavailing and, likewise, requests for an impartial investigation of the whole scandalous affair proved fruitless. The people of Ireland owe a debt of gratitude to the Gore-Booths ….

Not everyone agreed with such a benign view. Around the same time *The Sligo Champion* headlined a prominent news story 'Religious discrimination against Gore-Booth family challenged.' The item concerned Eugene Gilbride, a former Fianna Fáil T.D. and a member of Sligo County Council who, the report said, recalled that Constance Markievicz, whom he had known well, told him that 'her reason for going into public life in the first place was to atone for the misdeeds of her grandfather, Sir Robert. Her dearest wish was to see homesteads on the lands taken from the people by her ancestors.' Gilbride also criticised the R.T.É. television documentary which, he wrote, 'led the public to believe that Michael Davitt's son – Judge Davitt – was a crook and [that] Sir Robert Gore-Booth was a great patriot and a humanitarian..'

Gilbride was reacting to an editorial published in *The Sunday Times* three weeks earlier which had called on the Attorney General to agree to an enquiry into the affair. The article went on to state:

> If the North is ever to lie down with the South in Ireland, one of the fears that must first be allayed in the minds of Northern Protestants is exactly the suspicion aroused in them by this case, that lawyers and politicians in the South are prejudiced against Protestant holdings.

Noting that the Republic (unlike Northern Ireland) lacked either an Ombudsman or a system to support historic houses, the newspaper held the view that 'it would be a politic as well as a compassionate move on the part of the Irish Attorney General to agree to an inquiry.'

The journalist, Lorna Siggins, whose father's home was close to Lissadell, wrote several articles about the estate, first in the *Sunday Tribune* and subsequently in *The Irish Times*. She recalled that:

> The once thriving estate was now run-down, most of the livestock sold, the gardens destroyed and the outbuildings empty. Virtually the only sound of activity was the rasping sound of chain saws among the estate's plantations, and the roar of trucks hauling out the timber. The demesne, which had traditionally welcomed visitors with open gates was now surrounded by barbed wire and padlocks. The family members were virtually prisoners in their own home, isolated and seemingly powerless.

While the rights and wrongs of this family saga have never been resolved, it would be foolish to attempt to come down heavily on one side of the argument rather than the other as long as some of the details of the affair remain outside the public domain. Most of what is currently available lies in the files of the Wards of Courts office, about which the late Mr Justice Davitt wrote: 'It would require a careful examination of these files, extending over a quarter of a century, and the exercise of much patient industry as well as legal skill and judgement to arrive at a sound judgement as to the true facts of this tangled matter.' Perhaps the matter might be summed up by stating simply that Gabrielle and Aideen did their honest best, as they saw it, to protect the family estate, but were misguided in all sorts of ways. For his part, Mr Justice Maguire, in poor health, was faced with a difficult task, and the sale of the Lissadell timber was probably handled incompetently rather than fraudulently. Mr Justice Davitt not unreasonably believed the official side and it then became *res judicia* and could not be reopened as the appeal in the case had been dropped. The general public, relying mainly on the newspaper reports of the case had, rightly or wrongly, misgivings about various aspects of the affair, feeling that a grave injustice had been done to the family.

One person who certainly seems to have taken this view was Lord Louis Mountbatten, who as a result, asked Gabrielle to look after his forestry records at nearby Classiebawn. He subsequently appointed her as his Agent for the estate, thus providing her with a useful source of income. Mountbatten regularly spent a month there each year with his family, usually bringing a few relations and friends with him as well so, besides her other duties, Gabrielle made most of the necessary preparations for these visits and acted as his secretary at Classiebawn throughout the year. Three or four years after this, Gabrielle was diagnosed as having cancer and eventually had to relinquish her position at Mullaghmore, and throughout all this period Mountbatten regularly wrote friendly letters both to Gabrielle and to her sister Aideen.

In what appears to have been one final attempt to change matters at Lissadell, Sean McBride and Muireann Ní Bhriain, counsel for the Gore-Booths, completed a memorandum detailing all the claims made on behalf of the family which were then submitted to the Attorney General. It never reached consideration because, less than two months later, Gabrielle was dead. The youngest of the four sisters, she died in the Adelaide Hospital, Dublin on 30 June 1973 aged 55, and she was buried in the family plot, close to her father, mother, grandfather and grandmother. Apart from the two brothers who were killed during the Second World War, all her sisters and brothers died either in their seventies or their early eighties. Her death, at a comparatively early age, may well have been partly due to the stresses and strains resulting from her long campaign on behalf of the estate. After Gabrielle's death, her surviving sister wrote: 'I felt our "king-pin" was gone.' Aideen then made the following entry in her Memoirs.

She was one of the bravest and best of people, loyal to her parents and family, and always fair and wise with the 'Work Force.' I only remember her having one long holiday when she went to America to stay with Paul and Pat Gore-Booth. She loved music and played the organ in Lissadell Church and loved to practice the hymns every Saturday. Am glad to say the organ has been repaired in memory of her.… There was a beautiful Service to rededicate it.

* * *

Of all the Gore-Booths, the one member of the family most likely to be remembered by the general public is Aideen. Like her sister Gabrielle, she lived for most of her life at Lissadell, and many people who visited the old mansion still recall how she brought visitors on conducted tours of the house which, to put it mildly, had seen better days. Indeed, during her latter years all the indications were that the historic house was in a state of terminal decline, suffering from a leaking roof and an all-pervading odour of dampness and decay. Despite all this, few things gave her more pleasure than cheerfully regaling her visitors with tales about her ancestors, from Sir Robert to her Aunt Constance, all without any apparent trace of resentment or bitterness about the family's many misfortunes.

Among the carefully preserved family papers, there remain scores of letters thanking her for the trouble she had taken to make her guided tours so very interesting and entertaining.

As a young woman, she trained as a children's nurse, working for a time both in England and Ireland. She was a keen swimmer, often bathing twice daily even in her old age, usually preferring to swim at Bundoran rather than at Lissadell. Like her brother, Hugh, ornithology was a favourite pastime; and she once spotted an osprey close to the shore at Lissadell – a rare sight in Ireland. Aideen took an active part in parish activities and in community work and, well into her old age, she continued to drive around the neighbourhood and into Sligo town in her little Austin 'Mini' car which was as well-known in the area as she was herself.

Rather more is known about Aideen than her brothers and sisters, mainly because she wrote what she called her 'Memories,' 65 foolscap pages of typed details about events relating to the family and about herself. Some of the factual errors evident in her record may, perhaps, be explained because it was written in her old age but for all that, it provides interesting insights into the family story, some details of which might otherwise have been lost.

Aideen Joyce Gore-Booth was born in 1916, two months after the Rising in which her Aunt Constance played such a prominent part. Gabrielle, was born two years later and they were very close sisters for the whole of their lives, going on cycling tours around Ireland and also travelling to the continent together. She recalled her father going fishing for salmon and trout in the River Erne with the older boys.

> I often helped my mother make up sandwiches for them, and they would be away all day. It was exciting when they used to return with, perhaps, several salmon. The largest I remember was thirty-five pounds. Sometimes we would go with him and I still remember the charm of that river.

She remembered the names of some of the families who lived there in Cliff House, Laputa and The Mullens.

> All these places disappeared in the reservoir which was created to give electricity. I am glad father had died before this happened. He loved that river so dearly and all the pastime of the fishing. Alfred Paton, one of the ghillies, came by bus when my father was ill and walked the three miles from the main road to see him.

Aideen loved travelling with her father in the family car, a 1908 Wolseley, and when the weather was fine the hood would be taken down. She also liked going to tennis parties, with the Atkinsons of Cavan Garden and the Hamiltons of Brown Hall, near Ballintra, 'Sheila [Hamilton, who later moved to Coxtown], my contemporary, becoming a life-long friend.' As already noted, another friend, Eileen Goodbody, lived in Clonskeagh, Dublin, where Aideen often stayed, either when en route to York to visit Michael, or while attending the Dublin Horse Show.

When Aideen and her brothers and sisters were young, the family used to spend up to two months each year at their summer residence at the West End of Bundoran. Aideen recalled that it was about 100 yards from the cliff; and had a yard at the back with an old coach house, a stable and loft, while on the sea side there was a lawn and an oval pathway 'where I learnt to cycle.' She described in some detail the preparations for the family's annual stay:

> There would be two carts packed with all our goods and chattels. A man, usually Pat McElroy, led down a cow. My sisters Bridget and Rosaleen drove down with Titmouse, the Shetland pony, in the little dog cart with the dogs. We were all stuffed into the Wolseley. Then through time there was a man from Ballyshannon, Mr. Slevin, who had a Ford lorry, who used to transport everything instead of the carts, and several people travelled with him in the cab. He was

nicknamed "Paddy Go Easy." I remember being fascinated by the shops of that time and sometimes going with our Nanny to make small purchases. I can remember so clearly the shop assistants saying to Nanny "Aren't the Countess's nieces lovely" and Nanny would hastily remove us.

Later on, during the thirties, Mark Wynne's Play Company would perform every night in the Hamilton Hall and my mother would bring my sister Gabrielle, brother Angus and myself to these shows. I used to love their songs and plays and began to think I would fancy a life on the stage. I think I subconsciously learnt a lot of entertainer's tips from them, which came in very useful when, from 1966 – 1988, I showed the House to the public.

Aideen claimed – could this have been true? – that she could remember Gabrielle's christening although she herself was no more than about 26 months old at the time, and she also wrote that she remembered sitting on the family's newly acquired Shetland pony when she was three years of age. She also recalled Kate Maria Macey, the children's nanny at this time. The family loved Kate, and Lady Gore-Booth cared for her until her death at the age of 103. Other recollections included:

When I was six years of age I was sent to learn with the Governess in the schoolroom. The first was a Miss Abraham from Yorkshire. My mother thought a great deal of her, because she stuck to us during the hair-raising times of the Civil War. Apart from lessons, she made us pick blackberries for jam, and also plant daffodil bulbs which were being cast away and these still exist around the house. She was followed by a Miss Atwood, who had been governess to Edwina and Mary Ashley. The former married Lord Louis Mountbatten. Miss Atwood, used lipstick which was quite a sensation at Lissadell. I remember her as a kindly person, who taught a great deal of Grecian mythology….

After being tutored at home, Aideen went to a 'finishing school' in London, spending four terms there, during which time, Gabrielle was sent there too. Wishing to be in a position to earn her own living, Aideen went to the Norland Institute, a nursing college in London, to train as a children's nurse. This period made a deep impression on her and she described some of her experiences at the college in detail.

Before I left the Institute I took a number of interviews seeking a job but did not fancy any of them. The Norland training was very good and I never regretted going there. When the training was finished I went to South Wales to stay with my brother, Hugh who was land agent at Llanover, working for Major Herbert.

Her first paid job proved unsatisfactory, so she left and stayed with a friend in Worcestershire, Esme Howard, whose mother, she explained, was one of the Stewarts from Horn Head in Co. Donegal. It was she who advised Aideen to go to see Lady Plymouth who was looking for a companion for her daughter. After the interview, she returned to stay with the Howards again, convinced that she had no chance of being given what she considered would be an ideal posting. However, after dinner that evening Lady Plymouth telephoned to say she wanted Aideen to be companion to her 14-year-old daughter, Gillian, an appointment that was to give her great pleasure. There were four other children, the eldest son away at school, and a brother and sister younger than Gillian, and a baby. They lived about ten miles northeast of Worcester, in a house called Hewell Grange. The house and its grounds held many attractions for Aideen, one being the opportunity presented to go riding – usually with young Gillian – and she was also invited to join the local hunt. 'I have always been a lover of horses and riding, and I enjoyed it so much the days passed happily, and it was such a kindly household.'

Three months later, on Christmas Day, the family had invited many friends to join them for dinner and Aideen related how the guests arrived one after another, commencing with:

> Lady Plymouth's mother and father, Lady and Lord Weymss, her brother whose wife was dead, Guy Charteris, and Mary Rose and Hugo, his two younger children, Lord O'Neill and his wife Anne, who was Guy Charteris's eldest daughter. Her husband was a very nice man, he spoke so fairly about everyone in the north of Ireland where he lived. This struck me so much. He was brother of Terence O'Neill, who if people had been sensible, he and [Sean] Lemass [when Taoiseach] could have made the history of Ireland as different to what has happened in such a shameful way.

Lady Plymouth invited Aideen's brother Hugh to stay with them: 'He was very interested to meet all the family and glad that I was very happy.' Shortly after this, following a shooting party, Aideen was invited to join the guests for dinner and she was placed sitting next to an army officer who asked: 'What relation was that harridan Countess Markievicz to you?' Remembering something that her father had once told her, she answered: 'She was my aunt and she had the courage of her convictions.'

After she left the Plymouth family, Aideen went with Gabrielle to Germany. The visit, in 1938, was apparently prompted by the nanny employed by the Plymouths, who had earlier worked for Grafin [Countess] von Punckler-Limbourg in Silesia in eastern Germany, where she helped to rear four of the children. The eldest daughter, Mussi, was due to celebrate her twenty-first birthday and Miss Croxon arranged for two Gore-Booth sisters to visit the young woman's German home. There was an expectation that a return visit by Mussi and her sister might be possible the following year, but this never happened due to the outbreak of World War II. Aideen described how:

> [The family was] so friendly and Mussi was a tall beautiful girl with wheaten straw-coloured hair. Her mother was a very interesting woman, and would bring me for walks in the forest, and tell me that Hitler would ruin Germany as he was not a God-fearing man. [The family, assuming they survived, almost certainly lost their estate in 1945 when more than three million Silesian Germans were evicted from their properties]. We were young and light-hearted and certainly enjoyed ourselves. The [birthday] dance was held in a castle belonging to the grandmother. I forget her name. She had another unmarried daughter who belonged to what was a twisted religion. The Graf was nice old man and we had family prayers every morning. We made up a huge number of bouquets of flowers, and there were dances where the man gave them to whoever he wished to dance with. Some of the girls 'pinched' them if they did not receive any. Very strong etiquette was kept during the dancing. You danced for a short time but you must not sit out with your partner. Gabrielle was conversing with her partner after the dance and there was an awful fuss. She was a very shy person and was very embarrassed.

The family was once again staying in their Bundoran summer home when Britain and France declared war on Germany following the invasion of Poland. Hugh was with them on holiday too and, knowing the implications of this event for himself, he told Aideen that she 'must keep the home fires burning.' Meanwhile, she took a course of training in the Adelaide Hospital, Dublin to qualify for the Civil Nursing Reserve. Gabrielle told her father she wanted to go to England to do 'war work' but, not unexpectedly considering that three of his sons and two of this daughters were already over there, her father would not allow this. At the time the brothers were either working there or were at college, while Bridget and Rosaleen had recently gone to look after children who had been evacuated from the major cities to rural areas to get away from the German bombing raids. Early in 1940, while Angus was at home from England (and had brought a cousin, John L'Estrange, whom he had met in Oxford), there was 'a funny smell'. Aideen wrote:

> And suddenly Gabrielle realised there was a fire in the stable yard. I remember putting on old rubber boots, and a shower proof over my trabalco pyjamas which I had made, and rushing up to the stable yard to find there was a fire in the hardware store and another overhead in the Estate Office.

> I do not think they were joined. We had no phone then and I cannot remember

how Gabrielle contacted the Sligo Fire Brigade. They came very soon. There was a heavy frost, the water from the hoses freezing. We got the girls out of the building; they were office workers and their maid. I went to rouse the men in the farmyard, falling off my bicycle on the way. My father was in bed with bronchitis, and someone foolishly told him. It was a dreadful blow for him. Gabrielle, who was working for him, made the room in the mansion – where we now have our kitchen – into the Estate Office.

Irreplaceable records were lost in the fire which, because it started in two different places, caused the family to believe it was not accidental.

Aideen, who was once asked by a British army officer: 'What relation was that harridan Countess Markievicz to you?' Remembering what her father had taught her, she replied: 'She was my aunt and she had the courage of her convictions'.

Aideen was continuing with her Civil Nurse Training in Dublin when news of the sinking of the *Exmouth* was received at Lissadell. She recalled that just before this, she had suffered a fearful depression, and Rosaleen, who had returned to Lissadell from England, told her 'that Flip, the fox terrier – that she and Brian shared – howled and cried about the time Brian lost his life.' More than three years later, Aideen described how the family came to hear further dreadful news:

I was very strong in those days and in bad weather would carry hay on my back to our ponies who grazed in Anticliney. One day I had the job of working at the end of a [potato] drill with an old man called Andy McGowan ... and I asked him if he ever made a match for anyone. He said no, and I said I didn't believe him. Then he proceeded to tell me he had gone with this young fellow to this old man – to see if he could have his daughter. The father said he would give her away when he got the manure out of her. I, being rather simple, thought she was to have a dose of medicine, and Andy was very amused, when he meant she had to bring out the manure for the potatoes on her back. When I came back after lunch the men asked what Andy had said and they were in fits of laughter.

I was just writing this funny story to Hugh when the word came that he was missing. He was in Leros with the Royal Irish Fusiliers. Whatever way the message was sent, my father and I believed he would turn up. This was November 1943. Then [some months later] one of his companions came home ... and told us he had lost his life. My father died four days afterwards.

Aideen wrote in her *Memoirs* that her father had informed her that after his death, Michael was to be made a ward of court. Later, she wrote that on his death-bed he had asked Gabrielle to carry on the estate 'until a new man took over,' though, as has already been mentioned, there is some doubt about the veracity of this claim. Aideen then wrote in her journal that her sister 'promised she would do this. She was twenty-two years old, so she diligently kept everything going.'

In her *Memoirs* Aideen also referred to her several other appointments as a children's nurse or governess in England besides that with Lady Plymouth but did not mention any such posting in Ireland. In fact, just a few years after her father's death, she was governess to a family living at Ballybrack, Co. Dublin, where the eldest of three children was then about eleven years old.

More than 50 years later, Elizabeth Petch, who may have known Aideen better than anyone outside the family circle, remembers her as 'a wonderfully jolly person who loved her life at Lissadell and never complained when things were tough for her.' Elizabeth recalled that one of her most endearing characteristics was her almost childlike innocence, and her ability to get so much pleasure from simple things. 'She remained the same person all her life, warm-hearted, kind, full of fun and she fought with great courage to overcome all the difficulties and tragedies of her life.' Elizabeth subsequently spent a number of holidays at Lissadell which she still recalls as 'a magical place where the days were filled with riding, swimming, picnics – she made everything seem such an adventure.' She encouraged me to learn to ride, and also taught me much about country ways, and bird watching and flowers.' Aideen and Elizabeth subsequently became life-long friends and Elizabeth has no doubt that her own interest in breeding Connemara ponies, about which she has written a book, originated with her happy vacations at Lissadell.

Gabrielle and her mother were ill for a time, Lady Gore-Booth with a gall bladder problem, and Gabrielle was suffering from anaemia, while Aideen was having hip problems. She managed to get away on a brief holiday to Spain, only to receive a telegram from Gabrielle to say that her mother had suffered a slight stroke. When she arrived back, Aideen stayed with her mother at Ardeevin, the house on the Rosses Point road where she had lived since Sir Josslyn had died in 1944. When spring came, Lady Mary asked Aideen to 'bring her home' and their mother spent her last 27 months at Lissadell, where she died in 1968.

* * *

One topic mentioned several times in her *Memoirs* was the family's friendship with the Mountbattens who, every summer came over from their estate at Broadlands in Hampshire, to stay at Classiebawn Castle, near Mullaghmore, not far from Lissadell. Erected by the third Viscount Palmerston (who had been friendly with Sir Robert), and designed by J. Ranson Carroll, the castle was built of stone brought from Donegal, but when Palmerston died in 1865, it was still not completed. The property, which then included an estate of more than 6,000 acres, was left to his stepson, the first Lord Mount Temple for whom the building work was finished nine years later. It then passed to his nephew, the Hon. Evelyn Ashley-Cooper, whose son Colonel Wilfrid Ashley was the father of Edwina who married Lord Louis Mountbatten. Incidentally, Wilfrid, who later became Lord Mount Temple, is thought to have been one of Constance's many admirers when she was a beautiful young woman and the possible consequences, had this admiration developed further, are interesting to contemplate.

From the 1950s onwards, Mountbatten used to invite the Gore-Booth sisters and their mother 'for a glass of sherry' at Classiebawn, and he and his family would then invariably go to Lissadell 'for afternoon tea.' On one occasion, after Mountbatten had been to Lissadell along with his two daughters, Aideen wrote: 'It was so nice meeting them, and Lord Louis, as we called him, made so much fun. Maread McEvoy, who was helping us, was dreadfully disappointed that the Mountbattens were not wearing crowns!' Shortly after this he brought his sisters, Princess Alice and the Queen of Sweden, to visit Lissadell.

Mountbatten was well aware of the problems facing Lissadell because of the ward of court case and had noted how Gabrielle appeared to have grasped an intimate knowledge of forestry. He wrote to Lady Mary in April 1960 because his solicitor, Mr Browne of Argue and Phibbs in Sligo (who also acted for the Gore-Booths): 'says that your daughter, Gabrielle, is the greatest expert in timber in these parts.' He hoped that he might have her advice about selling timber at Classiebawn 'due to the death duties at 80 per cent, [following the death of his wife] which threaten the future of the estate. It is touch and go if I can keep Classiebawn but I mean to do so.'

Gabrielle accepted Lord Mountbatten's offer, and within a couple of years he appointed her his agent there, after which he again wrote to Lady Gore-Booth, telling her: 'What a tremendous load she [Gabrielle] is taking off my shoulders by looking after Classiebawn Estate. While Jules Bracken was alive and we were not letting the Castle there were no worries, but now that a series of American millionaires are coming over this summer I do not know what I would do without her to keep an eye on things.'

Despite his high profile, Mountbatten continued his annual Irish holiday notwithstanding the IRA campaign of paramilitary violence that had commenced in the 1960s. He was Chief of the Defence Staff, and had close connections with the British royal family (as a great grandson of Queen Victoria and grand uncle to Prince Philip). Although he and his extended family were conscious of the security problem posed by these visits, the only drawback that seemed to impinge upon Lord Louis was that he was unable to invite members of the royal family to join them as guests there. Mountbatten always looked forward to his annual stay at Classiebawn, and he seemed to be generally liked in the locality where he and the family and their guests moved easily and freely among the local people. Lord Louis regularly drove into Mullaghmore and to Grange to buy newspapers and groceries, places where he could be his natural self, indulging in simple pursuits like mackerel fishing, lobster potting, riding and, most especially, building sand castles with his grandchildren whom he adored. Indeed, so certain was he that the local people's friendship was genuine that he never altered his very predictable holiday arrangements in the slightest degree.

After Gabrielle died, Lord Mountbatten wrote to Aideen saying that Gabrielle had been 'so much on our minds, and we have talked about her so often since. All of us, including the grandchildren, will miss her very much indeed …' He asked Aideen if she would take on her late sister's job as his agent at Classiebawn, offering to pay 'really adequate fees for anything you can do to help us.' Although she was reluctant at first to do so, she eventually agreed and, like Gabrielle before her, she found herself each year making many of the arrangements for the annual Mountbatten holiday. For several months beforehand, letters would arrive almost every other day as Mountbatten remembered something else that he required to be done.

By the early 1970s, various additional security steps were being taken by the British and Irish authorities, notably by the latter which provided police escorts while the family travelled by car, and a police presence at the castle. The visits continued until 1979, and in July of that year Lord Louis wrote the usual series of letters to Aideen in connection with the various arrangements. The final one confirmed that he and the family and some friends would be travelling on the Liverpool–Dublin ferry on August 5, and would be met by the British ambassador with whom they were to have breakfast. From there the party would, as usual, travel on to Sligo. He also confirmed that 'the usual arrangements had been made by the security forces and the Garda Commissioner.'

Classiebawn castle, north of Lissadell. Lord Mountbatten employed Gabrielle – and subsequently Aideen – to act as secretary to his Mullaghmore estate.

At Classiebawn, the Mountbattens indulged in all the usual holiday pursuits and there was nothing to suggest that it was to be other than just one more carefree vacation. And so it was, until the fifth last day when Lord Louis decided, as he so often did, to inspect the lobster pots which he had set in the bay on the previous evening. He drove down to the little harbour at Mullaghmore, accompanied by his daughter Patricia and her husband, Lord Brabourne, and the latter's aunt. Also in the party were Lord Brabourne's eighty-three year old mother, his teenage twin sons, and another boy, Paul Maxwell from Enniskillen, who had a summer job looking after Lord Mountbatten's boat.

They all piled into *Shadow V* and a few minutes later, as they approached the first of the lobster pots, there was a fearful explosion that hurled bodies and debris into the air. The IRA thought that killing Mountbatten would be a blow for Ireland's cause and, as happened before and was to happen many times after, it mattered little to them that there were others close to their target who were likely to be killed or gravely injured. Writing about this in his book about Sligo, John Cowell referred to the perpetrators as 'murdering outsiders' as a result of whose action: 'distress and disgrace gripped the villagers, for Mountbatten was their friend, as was Edwina, his wife … [who] celebrated with them in the local pub, as she mourned with them at their funerals.' Lord Mountbatten died instantly, as did one of his twin grandsons and the little Enniskillen boat boy. The old Lady Brabourne, suffering from terrible injuries, survived for two days before she died in spite the heroic efforts made by the staff at Sligo General Hospital. Aideen was at Lissadell when she heard the news:

> It was a terrible time … Peter Nicholson 'phoned me to say Shadow V was bombed and Lord Louis and Paul Maxwell dead. I immediately wrote a note that the house [Lissadell] was closed owing to the bomb … I went to Mullaghmore and met two ambulances, and then I saw John Maxwell, Paul's father, and he told me all. Lord and Lady Brabourne were badly injured. Also, Tommy, Nicholas's twin. I went to Classiebawn and it was so sad.

* * *

A few years later Aideen, who had not been well for some time, was informed she had cancer and spent a period in hospital. When she got back to Lissadell, she had an opportunity to take up one of her favourite pastimes again – horse riding. One of the last entries in her journal records an invitation by Maggie Hedges, the owner of a newly established riding school at Moneygold, to school a four-year-old cob 'with a nice drop of cart-horse blood.' Having 'got on famously', she was encouraged to take the horse to the Royal Dublin Horse Show where she was awarded a third prize.

A description of a visit to Lissadell, written by Mary Maher, appeared in *The Irish Times* during the 1966 annual Yeats Summer Festival. She reported that a group of 50 people attending the event went to see the house on a very wet August day:

> We filed off [the bus], our wellington boots squeaking, to see the home of Countess Markievicz. The Gore-Booth family still lives here and annually opens the house to visitors from the Yeats Summer School.... We trouped into the small room reserved for everyday family use, and were received by a smiling Miss Gore-Booth. We dripped on her rugs and gazed curiously at family photographs, pictures of smiling children with one or two snapshots tucked into the frames. Propped on the mantelpiece under some framed oil paintings were two prints of the Irish countryside. This is the house that Sheelah Kirby 'in The Yeats Country' said was a symbol of ordered and gracious living, which she found fitted in with ideas about personal fulfilment and achievement.

Diana Norman was another visitor to Lissadell who, in her biography of Constance, described how she was welcomed by Miss Aideen who then personally conducted her as well as a party of schoolchildren on a tour of the house. Afterwards, watching the children depart, Norman wrote:

> It was just a house they left, interesting, but not very much, that somebody had built in another age. It was not necessary and it did not occur to them that they should even shake its dust off their trainers. They were nice children, and why should they say 'the hell with it'? But they didn't have to; a daughter of the house had done all that on their behalf a long time ago.

Other visitors – the overwhelming majority – recall with pleasure going to see Lissadell and being welcomed by Aideen Gore-Booth before she guided them through the old mansion, describing its contents and recounting something of the family's history. For most of them, their recollections are probably mainly of a house that was a shadow of its former days – as John Ardagh wrote: 'a strange, melancholy house, more than a little run to seed. Cluttered with bric-a-brac and family memorabilia.' Lorna Siggins, who was one such visitor, described in *The Sunday Tribune* how people who went to the house were met by

Aideen, 'muffled in Aran cardigan and grey wool skirt; she is small and sprightly with more than a sparkle of humour and wit.'

Mary Lappin reported in the *Irish Press* how the house was 'a veritable museum of paintings, china and unfinished needlepoint' which, 'despite minimal upkeep … has salvaged enough dignity to hint at its former glory.' Another writer, John Waters, writing about six years before Aideen died, described her as 'no longer young [and] without staff, cleans the house herself, opens it to the public every weekday afternoon and gives the only guided tour of a house in Co. Sligo.' Ann Morrow, in her book about the Anglo-Irish, described how Aideen locked up the house after the last visitors of the day departed:

> Looking like any landowner's wife, sister or aunt in Hampshire or Sussex who might be saying goodbye to helpers and guides.… But this is Ireland and Miss Gore-Booth is sole custodian, helper, cook, guide, mechanic and aesthete. [She] turns a giant key in the door of the shuttered house, her heels echoing in the hall. On the way … she stops to answer the question whether she thinks she is Irish or Anglo-Irish. Without a moment's hesitation, she replies: 'I think of myself as a mongrel.'

For almost 22 years after Gabrielle died, Aideen continued to show visitors over the house, looking after the family home virtually unaided. Throughout this period, living an almost hand-to-mouth existence, she remained there – sometimes alone, sometimes with her brother, Angus. With inadequate funds, the house was largely unheated and for much of the time maintenance was concentrated on trying to keep the roof watertight. Visitors at the time remember the odour of dampness that pervaded everywhere, which did little to help her in her struggle against failing health. She died in 1994 and was buried beside Gabrielle in the family plot at Lissadell church.

Ardtarmon Castle photographed while still in ruins.
It was the first of three Gore-Booth residences in the Lissadell area

EPILOGUE

The rest of the story about the Gore-Booths of Lissadell is quickly told.

With an ever-worsening roof problem and the resulting serious problems caused by damp, it was not until Sir Angus' son, Josslyn, became responsible for Lissadell House that any significant work could be undertaken. Although born, educated and working in England, he had known Lissadell since boyhood, and spent many holidays there. The responsibility became his, as he explained in an article published in the 2002 summer edition of the *Irish Arts Review*:

> When a final attempt was made by the General Solicitor for Wards of Court to sell the estate … with the blind optimism of youth, I resisted this initiative. The High Court resolved the issue by handing over the estate to me, together with its liabilities, existing and contingent. My motivation was a mixture of filial duty, sentimental attachment and a feeling that there was something about [Lissadell] which demanded its preservation.

Even at that early stage, Sir Josslyn, the ninth baronet, realised that Lissadell could never again be self-supporting. The sale of 2,600 acres to the Land Commission (during the wardship of court period) had reduced the estate to just 400 acres, much of it non-productive. Fortuitously, the setting-up of the National Heritage Council provided Sir Josslyn with an extremely productive partnership which led to grant funding which enabled him to tackle the critical and very expensive roof problems. Local craftsmen were then employed under the supervision of Nicholas Prins, the estate manager. All the lead valleys and parapet gutters were replaced and the very large skylights that illuminate the hall and gallery were rebuilt and strengthened with metal plates. This vital work was then followed by a long process of drying out the entire building to eliminate the all-pervading odour of dampness that had for so long been a feature of the house. Only then was it possible to make a start, stripping-out the old plumbing, replacing the electric wiring, and then embarking on a programme of general refurbishment with a view to transforming the old mansion into a comfortable family home.

Few people were aware of the work then in hand. Sir Josslyn regularly travelled to Lissadell from his home in Durham to oversee the work in progress and as it progressed he and his family stayed there for longer periods. It was around this time that Hugh Montgomery-Massingberd and Christopher Sykes wrote that Sir Josslyn's 'sympathetic restoration of the great house promises to breathe new life into this extraordinarily atmospheric place without losing any of its potent poetry.'

Although much still remained to be done, the family settled at Lissadell during April 2002. This move, along with the continuing restoration work, was effected so unobtrusively that the general public continued to be unaware not only of what had already been achieved, but also of the fact that Gore-Booths were actually living once again at Lissadell. However, an announcement in the press less than two months later quickly brought the family into the news.

One of the many problems facing Sir Josslyn and Lady Jane was the fact that the contents of the old house resembled that of a museum rather than a family home. The clutter of furniture and memorabilia left little space to make the house more comfortable, forcing the family to make difficult decisions about disposing of surplus furniture, etc. During May 2002, Mealy's of Castlecomer held a two-day fine art and antique sale at which more than one third of the items offered for auction came from Lissadell House. Much of what was to be sold was described as bric-a brac, but some concern was expressed about the imminent dispersal of some of the original contents, including part of the important collection of furniture, most of which had been ordered in one single lot by Sir Robert Gore-Booth when the house was nearing completion in 1835. All of it had been specially made for Lissadell House by Williams and Gibton, a well-known Dublin firm that had supplied furniture for a number of important State buildings, including Dublin Castle and the Vice-Regal Lodge, so that the collection at Lissadell was probably unique. Not unexpectedly, the auction attracted considerable interest, an interest that was reflected in the bidding.

With the mansion reorganised to the family's taste it seemed that Lissadell was now secure for the foreseeable future. While there was much work yet to be done within, much more remained to be tackled without, where there were extensive outbuildings, many in a very poor state of repair. Further expenditure would be required to tarmacadam several miles of badly pot-holed driveways and, as if all that was not enough, a final decision had to be made concerning his grandfather's gardens, once considered to be one of the finest in Ireland. To assess the situation, Sir Josslyn had already commissioned two well-known specialists in this field, Terence Reeves-Smith and Belinda Jupp. They produced a very detailed survey (actually covering more than just the gardens) running to two volumes that made bleak reading. In the Wood Garden, apart from some old iron railings, they found just a few other remaining elements, and they reported that there was absolutely no trace at all of the former Old Garden area. Some of the old trees in the two-acre Upper Garden had survived but here again Nature had taken over and the range of green houses and the potting sheds had fallen into ruin. One of the worst aspects of the deterioration of the estate had resulted from the decision – made over the heads of the family during the Wardship of Court period – to plant forest trees almost right up to the side of the house. Sir Josslyn had them felled and the stumps removed at considerable expense in order to restore the park-land surrounding the house, but the sheer scale of all the other work likely to be involved in attempting to restore the gardens was so daunting that nothing further was done about it.

As time went by, Sir Josslyn became ever more concerned about the demands being made on his financial resources until matters reached the point where he decided he could go no further. As he expressed it, he had neither the energy nor the resources to continue the work, and there were family considerations as well. While it had been his ambition to live at Lissadell, it was only when he had moved there that the full impact of what still remained to be done had become apparent. He told a reporter from *V.I.P.* magazine that even if he had the resources to complete the restoration work, it would have been done at the cost of enormous unhappiness to himself and the family. As he expressed it: 'Had [Lady] Jane been totally happy about it … then the story might have been different,' adding that 'we, sadly, have no close relatives in Ireland at all.' He also had to consider the impact the move had had upon his two daughters 'who had left their school friends behind.'

His subsequent announcement, made during May 2003, that he had decided to sell Lissadell took almost everyone by surprise and was widely reported in the news media, generating a long-running correspondence in the letters columns of *The Irish Times*. Most of this correspondence was sympathetic to the family, expressing a general concern for the future of the estate and a hope that the State would intervene to purchase the property for the nation. As John Ducie, chairperson of An Taisce wrote: 'Once again the family of one of the great houses has decided to sell up.' He went on to predict that the State was unlikely to purchase it, given that, in contrast to the rest of Europe, the Republic of Ireland 'has no national trust-type legislation to help the voluntary sector to own and manage heritage properties for the people.' However, An Taisce has, since then, established the National Trust for Ireland Heritage Foundation, aiming 'to attract donations and legacies specific to properties and to pursue acquisitions.'

Lord Altamont, who was having problems at Westport, also expressed concern about the lack of State support for heritage sites such as Lissadell which, as he pointed out, along with Clonalis House and his own Westport House constituted the only three showplaces in the whole of Connacht. As Desmond Fitzgerald, President of the Irish Georgian Society commented: 'One cannot blame developers, or owners who sell, if there is no viable alternative for the survival of the house.'

In the course of a statement he had prepared for the press, Sir Josslyn expressed regret at having come to the conclusion that Lissadell should be sold, explaining that:

> The house is now, following further repair work, in a stable condition and we have been considering where to go from here … and my own feelings for the house have prompted me to maintain it in so far as was possible.… I have [also] been happy to pay the running costs on the estate out of income, and to invest additional capital in the restoration, but I have concluded that, to do the job properly, it will require greater resources than I can justify in the future. It has often been remarked that few of the Big Houses of Ireland remain in the hands of their families and I regret that my decision will reduce their number. But I am now confident that Lissadell will have a brighter and different future in other hands.

The asking price for the house and its 400 acres was thought to be around €3.5 million, a figure that was generally seen as 'not excessive,' but in a period of serious economic downturn, the Fianna Fáil-led administration found itself faced with a very uncomfortable dilemma. The government had to make a decision mindful not only of the need for fiscal rectitude, but also conscious that it did not wish to be seen as turning its back on the home of Constance Markievicz, a founder member of the party. This latter point raised some hopes that the property would indeed be secured by the State, even if there had been some concern that the government appeared to take no action – despite having been appraised of the impending sale several months before the intention to sell became common knowledge. Hopes were further renewed when Minister Ó Cuív declared that he had 'a huge emotional attachment to Lissadell House' which he went on to describe as 'a very exceptional property attached to an incredible woman who is a major national and international figure.' Matters looked even better when another Minister, Martin Cullen, after he had been (somewhat belatedly) requested by the government to make a preliminary appraisal of the situation, declared that the house was in good condition.

Several weeks elapsed – during which time support for the idea of State ownership grew stronger – before a surprise announcement from the cabinet indicated that the acquisition could cost up to €30 million. This figure was met with widespread disbelief, especially when it transpired that the government was not willing to provide a detailed breakdown of the costings in order to explain the significant difference between the asking price and this latest calculation. One of the details that did emerge was that the sum announced included provision for ongoing expenditure up to the year 2009. The government decided that it was unable to proceed further on its own but suggested that the property might be acquired 'in a partnership from the voluntary or private sector' but no suitable partner came forward and no specific joint offer was made for the property.

Then, in mid-August, Sir Josslyn announced that Lissadell had been sold to a private purchaser who was Irish and who intended to use it as a family home but was prepared to continue to open the house to visitors. It later transpired that the new owners were Edward Walsh, SC, and his wife Constance Cassidy, SC, who, after making an unsuccessful bid to secure the remaining contents of the mansion, appealed to the government to save the contents for the nation, an appeal that elicited no response. A few weeks later, in a gesture that some thought hinted at a degree of contempt for Lissadell, the government announced its decision to purchase Durrow Abbey estate for €3 million, not much less than the asking price for the Lissadell estate and far higher than the figure to be realised at the subsequent auction of the Lissadell contents.

The contents' sale was held at the end of November 2003, conducted jointly by Hamilton Osborne King of Dublin and Christies of London. An illustrated catalogue was produced to a standard that made it an attractive souvenir of what the old house looked like before most of its contents were scattered far and wide. Included in the auction was most of the remaining furniture commissioned by Sir Robert when the house was being built, about which James Peill noted in the sale catalogue that 'Lissadell remains the only house in Ireland still to retain its original Williams and Gibton furniture and its importance as such cannot be overstated.' There were those for whom the sale of such a unique collection was a matter of serious concern but the government's inaction made its dispersal virtually inevitable. The short catalogue article ended with the suggestion that the auction would provide 'an opportunity not only to see this furniture, possibly for the last time, *in situ* in the rooms for which it was intended, but also to buy and take home a souvenir of this superlative "Grecian" tradition.' Some nine months later the *Irish Examiner* reported that the new owners estimated that the total cost of refurbishment at between €3 and €5 million. Commenting on this the newspaper pulled no punches:

> Having wrung its hands at the prospect of spending €30 million refurbishing Lissadell House ... it now transpires that the cost of refurbishing the stately home was overestimated by a whopping €25 million.... The only plausible explanation [for the disparity] is that the Government never really wanted the house [and] the cost was deliberately inflated as an excuse not to buy.

It was unfortunate that the new owners were unable to purchase outright the contents of the house. Instead, as Heather White wrote in the *Ulster Tatler*:

> the accumulated belongings of the Gore-Booths over such a long time – furniture, paintings, ceramics, glass, silverware, Grand Tour artefacts, items from Sir Henry's Artic (sic) collection, jewellery, books, linen, lace, fishing rods and croquet sets – even down to cooking utensils from the kitchen. The highest sale of the day ... was the double portrait of Constance and Eva Gore-Booth which was bought by an Irish collector for €239,000.

With an attendance of over 1,000, not surprisingly, the auction proved hugely successful.

It must have been a period of mixed emotions for Sir Josslyn – regret at having to sell the property after having made considerable progress in halting the decline of the mansion; and relief that a heavy burden had been lifted from his shoulders. Like so many of his forebears he is a very private person and shuns publicity, so that the intense media interest focussed upon him at the time was hardly to his liking. With the completion of the sale of the house and its contents, there was nothing left but to turn the key in the door for the last time as the Gore-Booths departed, leaving Lissadell forever.

*   *   *

Given that they were an Anglo-Irish landlord family it was inevitable – rightly or wrongly – that they were often viewed as little better than the worst of that class. This was all part of what Roy Foster called 'the institutionalised debasement of popular history.' Happily, as he noted: 'by the 1960s the work of a whole generation of scholars has exploded the basis for popular assumptions [including] the record of landlordism.'

One of the scholars that Foster almost certainly had in mind was Professor J.C. Beckett who, writing in the 1970s, noted that the most popular general assumption was that all landlords, without exception, cruelly cleared their estates of unwanted tenants. As he expressed it: 'Public opinion made few distinctions or allowances and the landlord class as a whole fell under a general condemnation.' The responsibility for this thinking may well have resulted from the decision made by the government in 1847 to change the Poor Law so that the staggering costs of famine relief fell on the estates rather than upon itself. The so-called logic of that move, as Julian Moynahan noted:

> was that an expiring tenantry should pay for its own relief by paying its rents, which of course it could not do. Under this law, many of the proprietors were rendered bankrupt, and naturally it was the more generous in organising famine relief on their own properties who went under in the largest numbers ... [while] the least charitable of the existing landlords reaped the cash benefit [derived from] the disappearance of the millions of peasants...

The landlords had opportunities for leadership and self-sacrifice but, as Moynahan also noted, all too often their response was 'a sort of moral if not a physical absenteeism.'

Where did the Gore-Booths stand in all this? Were they, as landlords, just as bad as the worst ones? Or did they take some half-hearted measures to help their tenants? Or is it really true that they made a point of knowing each of their tenants personally, fed them during the famine years, and did not rack-rent them? On several occasions during the nineteenth century, assurances were given to the family by both the local clergy and the local newspapers that the record of their deeds would never be forgotten, yet few people today have any knowledge of what they actually did. That record will not be found in Irish history books but in the yellowing pages of the vast family archive currently stored in the Public Record Office in Belfast.

Constance was the exception – much more is known about her than all the other family members put together. She has been the subject of no less than seven biographies and her name was invoked in virtually every exhortation made to the government to save *her* home for the nation.

In a statement made shortly before leaving Lissadell, the present baronet, Sir Josslyn, wrote: 'My family, for good or ill, has played a part in Irish history.' In typical Gore-Booth fashion he left it to others to arrive at a final judgement.

SELECT
BIBLIOGRAPHY

Akenson, Donald Harman, *If the Irish ran the World*, 1997
Alexander, Angela, *Catalogue* (preface) re. Auction of Surplus Contents, Lissadell, 2002
Alldritt, Keith, *The Man and the Milleau* (W.B. Yeats), 1996
Anderson, R. A. *With Plunkett in Ireland*, 1983
Ardagh, John, *Ireland and the Irish*, 1994
Ash, Marinell, *This Noble Harbour*, (Invergordon), 1991
Ball, C.F., *Botanizing in Bulgaria*, (*Journal of the R.H.S.*, Vol. XXXIX), 1913
Ball, Stephen (ed.) *A Policeman's Ireland*, 1996
Barone, Roseangela, *The Oak Tree and the Olive Tree*, 1991
Barton, Brian, *From Behind a Closed Door*, 2002
Beckett, J.C. *The Anglo Irish Tradition*, 1976
Bence-Jones, Mark, *Life in an Irish House*, 1976
Bence-Jones, Mark, *Irish Country Houses*, 1988.
Bowen, Elizabeth, *Collected Impressions*, 1942
Bowen, Elizabeth, *The Shelbourne*, 1958
Boyce, D. George, and O'Day, Alan, (eds), *The Making of Modern Irish History*, 1996
Boylan, Henry, *Dictionary of Irish Biography*, 1998
Broderick, Marian, *Wild Irish Women*, 2001
Cardozo, Nancy, *Lucky Eyes and a High Heart*, (Maud Gonne), 1979
Caulfield, Max, *The Easter Rebellion*, 1961
Chambré, Sophia, *Lissadell ... , the Country House, an architectural discourse* (Thesis), 1997
Churchill, Winston, *History of the Second World War*, 1951
Clarke, Kathleen, *Revolutionary Women*, 1991
Colum, Mary, *Life and the Dream*, 1958
Connolly, James, *Labour in Ireland*, 1944
Connolly, S. J. (ed.), *The Oxford Companion to Irish History*, 1998
Coogan, Tim Pat, *1916: The Easter Rising*, 2001
Coogan, T.P. and Malcolmson, G, *The Irish Civil War*, 1999
Coote, Stephen, *W.B. Yeats, a Life*, 1997
Costello, Francis, *The Irish Revolution and its Aftermath*, 2003
Coulter, Henry, *The West of Ireland*, 1862
Cowell. John, *Land of Yeats' Desire*, 1997
Coxhead, Elizabeth, *The Daughters of Erin*, 1979
Craig, Maurice, *The Architecture of Ireland from Earliest Times to 1880*, 1982
Craik, Mrs, *An Unknown Country*, 1880
Crawford, E.M. *The Hungry Stream*, 1997
Cunliffe, Marcus, *The Royal Irish Fusiliers, 1793-1950*, 1975
Cullen, L. M., *The Emergence of Modern Ireland*, 1981
Cullen, Mary and Luddy, Maria (eds), *Female Activists, Irish Women and change, 1900-1960*, 2001
Curtis, Liz, *The Cause of Ireland*, 1994
Danchev, Alex and Todman, Daniel, (eds) *War Diaries of Field Martial Lord Alanbrooke*, 2001
Davies, Norman, *God's Playground: a History of Poland*, 1981
Davies, Norman, *The Isles, a History*, 1999
Davies, Norman, *Microcosm*, 2002
Davis, John, ed., *Rural Change in Ireland*, 1999

Denison, Alan (ed.), *Letters from A.E.*, 1961

De Vere White, Terence, *Kevin O'Higgins*, 1948

Dicks, Brian, *The Greek Islands*, 1986

Doherty, Richard, *Clear the Way*, 1993

Doherty, Richard, *Irish Generals*, 1993

Drummond, John, *The Bride wore Black*, 1940

Dudgeon, Jeffrey, *Roger Casement, The Black Diaries*, 2002

Durand, Stella, *Drumcliff, the Church of Ireland parish*, 2000

Edwards, Kenneth, *The Mutiny at Invergordon*, 1937

Eichacker, Joanne Mooney, *Irish Republican Women in America*, 2003

Elwes, Henry John and Henry, Augustine, *The Trees of Great Britain and Ireland, 1906-13*

Fingall, Lady, *see* Hinkson, Pamela.

Finnegan, T.A. *Sligo, Sinbad's Yellow Shore*, 1977

Foster, R.F., *Paddy and Mr Punch, Connections in Irish and English History*, 1993

Foster, R.F., *W.B. Yeats, a Life*, 1997

Foster, R.F., *The Irish Story*, 2002

Fox, R.M. *Rebel Irishwomen*, 1935

Foy, Michael, and Barton, Brian, *The Easter Rising*, 2000

Frazer, James, *Handbook for Travellers in Ireland*, 1859

Fulford, R. *Votes for Women*, 1958

Gaughan, J. Anthony, *Thomas Johnson*, 1980

Gibbon, Monk, *The Living Torch*, 1970

Godley, General Sir Alexander, *Life of an Irish Soldier*, 1939

Goodwin, Francis, *Domestic Architecture*, 1834

Gore-Booth, Eva, *The One and the Many*, 1904

Gore-Booth, Eva, *Broken Glory*, 1917

Gore-Booth, Eva, *The Sword of Justice*, 1918

Gore-Booth, Sir Paul, *With Great Truth and Respect*, 1974

Grafton, Anthony, *The Footnote: A Curious History*, 2003

Green, Alice Stopford, *The Making of Modern Ireland and Its Undoing*, 1988

Gregory, Adrian and Pašeta, Senia, (eds), *Ireland and the Great War*, 2000

Griffith, Kenneth, and O'Grady, Timothy, *Curious Journey*, 1998

Hamilton, Michael, *Down Memory Line, the SLNC Railway*, 1997

Harper, Marjorie, *Adventures and Exiles: The Great Scottish Exodus*, 2003

Harris, Henry, *The Royal Irish Fusiliers*, 1972

Hart, Peter, *The IRA at War, 1916–23*, 2003

Hartland, William Bailer, *The Little Book of Daffodils*, 1884

Haverty, Anne, *Constance Markievicz, an Independent Life*, 1988

Hay, Ian, *The Unconquered Isle, Malta*, 1944

Hinkson, Pamela, *Seventy Years Young*, (Lady Fingall's memoirs), 1937

Hobson, Bulmer, *Ireland, Yesterday and To-morrow*, 1968

Hogan, Richard, *Dictionary of Irish Literature*, 1979

Hogan, Robert, and Kilroy, James, *The Abbey Theatre*, 1978

Hopkinson, Michael, *The Last Days of Dublin Castle*, 1999

Hopkinson, Michael, *The Irish War of Independence*, 2002

Howe, Stephen, *Ireland and Empire*, 2000

Inglis, Brian, *Roger Casement*, 1975.

Inglis, H. D., *A Journey throughout Ireland*, 1834

James, Dermot, and Ó Maitiú, Séamas, *The Wicklow World of Elizabeth Smith*, 1996

James, Dermot, *John Hamilton of Donegal, This Recklessly Generous Landlord*, 1998

Jeal, Tim, *Baden-Powell*, 1989

Jeffery, Keith, (ed) *The Sinn Fein Rebellion as They Saw It*, 1999

Johnson, Edward B.W., *Island Prize*, 1992

Johnston, Tom, *Orange Green and Khaki*, 1992

Jones, Winston Guthrie, *The Wynnes of Sligo and Leitrim*, 1994

Kennedy, Liam, *Colonialism, Religion and Nationality in Ireland*, 1996

Kenny, John, *History of World Exploration* (Royal Geographical Society), 1991

Kenny, Mary, *Good-bye to Catholic Ireland*, 1997

Kiberd, Declan, *Inventing Ireland*, 1996

Kilgannon, Tadg, *Sligo and its Surroundings*, 1949

King, Carla (ed), *Famine, Land and Culture in Ireland*, 2000

King-Harman, Anthony, *The Kings of King House*, 1996

Kirby, Sheelah, *The Yeats Country*, 1977

Kissane, Noel, *The Irish Famine, a Documentary History*, (undated)

Konarsky, Szymon, *O heraldyce i 'heraldycznym' snobizmie*, 1967

Krause, David, *Sean O'Casey, the Man and his Work*, 1983

Lamb, Keith and Bowe, Patrick, *A History of Gardening in Ireland*, 1995.

Lapisardi, Frederick S., *The Plays of Eva Gore-Booth*, 1991

Lee, J.J., *Ireland, 1912–1985*, 1989

Levinson, Leah, *With Wooden Sword*, 1983

Levitas, Ben, *The Theatre of Nation, 1890-1916*, 2002

Lewis, Samuel, *Topographical Dictionary of Ireland*, 1837

Lewis, Gifford, *The Years Flew By*, 1974

Lewis, Gifford, *Eva Gore-Booth and Esther Roper*, 1988

Lissadell Nursery Catalogues, 1905-55

Luddy, Maria, *Women in Ireland*, 1995

Lyons, F.S.L., *Ireland since the Famine*, 1996

Macardle, Dorothy, *The Irish Republic*, 1937

McBride, Lawrence W., *Images, Icons and the Irish Imagination*, 1999

McCart, Neil, *The Illustrious and Implacable Classes of Aircraft Carrier*, 2000

McCoole, Sinead, *No Ordinary Women ...*, 2003

McCormick, Donal, *The Incredible Mr. Kavanagh*, 1960

McGowan, Joe, *In the shadow of Benbulben*, 1993

McGowan, Joe, *Constance Markievicz, the People's Countess*, 2003

McHugh, Roger, *Dublin 1916*, 1966

McInerney, Michael, *The Riddle of Erskine Childers*, 1971

McTernan, John, *Historic Sligo*, 1965

McTernan, John, *In Sligo Long Ago*, 1998

McTernan, John, *Here's to the Memory*, 1992

Magris, Claudio, *Danube*, 1990

Maher, Jim, *Harry Boland*, 1998

Malcolmson, Dr. A.P.W., and ors., Lissadell Papers (at P.R.O.N.I.), 1997

Marreco, Anne, *The Rebel Countess*, 1967

Martin, F.X. and Byrne, F.J., *The Scholarly Revolutionary, Eoin McNeill*, 1973

Moody, T.W. and Martin, F.X., *A New History of Ireland*, 1980

Moriarty, Mary and Sweeney Catherine, *The Rebel Countess*, 1991

Morrow, Ann, *Picnic in a Foreign Land*, 1989

Morgan, Austen, *James Connolly, a Political Biography*, 1988.

Moynahan, Julian, *Anglo-Irish*, 1994

Moynihan, Maurice, *Speeches and Statements by Éamon De Valera*, 1980

Mulholland, Marie, *The politics and relationships of Kathleen Lynn*, 2002

Mullins, Edward and Bowe, Patrick, *Irish Gardens and Demesnes*, 1980

Murphy, James H., *Abject Loyalty*, 2001

Murphy, William M., *Family Secrets*, 1995

Murphy, William M., *Prodigal Father, John Butler Yeats*, 1978

Neeson, Eoin, *Birth of a Republic*, 1998

Ni Éireamhain, Eibhlin, *Two Great Irishwomen*, 1971
Norman, Diana, *A Terrible Beauty, a life of Countess Markievicz*, 1967
Novick, Ben, *Conceiving Revolution*, 2001
O Broin, Léon, *Revolutionary Underground*, 1976
O Broin, Léon, *W.E. Wylie and the Irish Revolution*, 1989
O Broin, Léon, *Protestant Nationalism in Revolutionary Ireland*, 1985
Ó Céirin, Kit and Cyril, *The Women of Ireland*, 1996
O'Donnell, E.E., *The Annals of Dublin*, 1998
O'Dowd, Mary, *Power Politics and Land*, 1991
O'Faolain, Sean, *Countess Markievicz*, 1934
O'Grady, John, *The Life and Work of Sarah Purser*, 1996
Ó Glaisne, Risteárd, *Cosslett Ó Cuinn*, 1996
Ó Glaisne, Risteárd, *De Bhunadh Protastúnach*, 2000
O'Reilly, Seán, *Irish Houses and Gardens*, 1998
O'Rorke, Terence, *History of Sligo Town and County*, 1890
O'Toole, Fintan, *The Ex-Isle of Erin*, 1996
O'Toole, Fintan, *The Irish Times Book of the Century*, 1999
Padfield, Peter, *War Beneath the Sea*, 1995
Pakenham, Thomas, *The Boer War*, 1979
Pakenham, Valerie, *The Big Houses in Ireland*, (undated)
Pankhurst, E.Sylvia. *The Suffragette Movement*, 1977
Paseta, Senia, *Before the Revolution*, 1996
Pattinson, William, *Mountbatten and the Men of the [HMS] 'Kelly'*, 1986
Peatling, G. K., *British Opinion and Irish Self-government, 1865-1925*, 2001
Plunkett, Horace, *Ireland in the New Century*, 1904
Potterton, Homan, *Rathcormick*, 2001
Power, Bill, *White Knights, Dark Earls*, 2000
Prebble, John, *The Highland Clearances*, 1963
Prebble, John, *Scotland*, 1984
Pugh, Martin, *The Pankhursts*, 2001
Purchas, F. H., *Some Interesting Experiments on Sir Josslyn's Lissadell Estate…*, 1908
Purchas, F. H., *Estate Magazine*, Vol. Viii, 1908
Purvis, June, *Women's History in Britain, 1850-1945*, 1995
Pyle. Hilary, *Jack B. Yeats, a Biography*, 1970
Pyle, Hilary, *The Red Headed Rebel* (Susan Mitchell), 1998
Quinlan, Carmel, *Genteel Revolutionaries*, 2001
Ranelow, Eric, *A Corkman at Sea*, 1999
Reeves-Smith, Terence, and Jupp, Belinda, *Lissadell Demesne, Co. Sligo*, 1998
Roberts, David, *Shipwrecked on top of the World*, 2004
Roper, Esther, *The Collected Poems of Eva Gore-Booth*, 1929
Roper, Esther, *The Prison Letters of Countess Markievicz*, 1929
Roskill, Stephen, *The Navy at War, 1935-45*, 1960
Russell, George (A.E.), *New Songs*, 1932
Russell, George, *The Living Torch* [Monk Gibbon (ed)], 1937
Ryan, Deirdre, *The Lissadell Estate of Sir Robert Gore-Booth, 1845-47*, (Thesis), 1996
Ryle-Dwyer, T., *De Valera, The Man and the Myth*, 1991
Scannell, Mary, and Synnott, Donal, *Census Catalogue of the Flora of Ireland*, 1987.
Snoddy, Theo, *Dictionary of Irish Artists of the 20th Century*, 1998.
Spooner, Tony, *Supreme Gallantry, Malta, 1939-45*, 1960
Sprinks, Neil, *Sligo, Leitrim and Northern Counties Railway*, 2001
Step, Edward, *Wayside and Woodland Trees*, 1948
Stocks, M.D., *Fifty Years in Every Street, (The Manchester University Settlement)*, 1945
Summerfield, Henry, *That Mystical Minded Man* (*George Russell*), 1975

Sweetman, David, *The Medieval Castles of Ireland*, 1999
Swords, Liam, *In their own Words*, 1991
Tierney, Michael, *Eoin McNeill; Scholar and Man of Action*, 1980
Thomson, David, *Woodbrook*, 1974
Took, Roger, *Running with the Reindeer*, 2003
Van Hoek, Kees, *An Irish Panorama*, 1946
Van Voris, Jacqueline, *Constance de Markievicz in the Cause of Ireland*, 1967
Wakefield, E., *Ireland, Statistical and Political*, 1812
Ward, Margaret, *Unmanageable Revolutionaries*, 1983
Ward, Margaret, *In their own Voice*, 1995
Ward, Margaret, *Hanna Sheehy Skeffington, a Life*, 1997
Watney, John, *Ireland*, 1989
Webb, D. A., Parnell, J., and Doogue, D., *An Irish Flora*, 1996
Welch, Robert, (ed.), *The Oxford Companion to Irish Literature*, 1996
White, J. and Wynne, M., *Irish Stained Glass*, 1963
Williams, Raymond, *The Defenders of Malta*, 1975
Wood-Martin, W. G., *History of Sligo, County and Town, 1882-92*
Wright, Arnold, *Disturbed Dublin*, 1914
Wynne, Maud, *An Irishman and his Family*, 1937
Ziegler, Philip, *Mountbatten*, 1985
Zweiniger-Bergielowskia, Ina, *Women in Twentieth Century Britain*, 2001

(- - - -), *Polski slownik biograficzny*, 1975

NEWSPAPERS AND PERIODICALS

Belfast Telegraph; Daily Mail; Evening Mail; Evening Post; Evening Press; Evening Standard; Daily Express (Dublin); Daily Mirror; The Freeman's Journal; Irish Examiner; Irish Independent; Irish News; Irish Press; The Irish Times; Manchester Guardian; Manitoba Daily Witness; Montreal Free Press; Morning Post; The Nation; New York Times; Sligo Champion; Sligo Chronicle; Sligo Guardian, Sligo Independent; Sligo Journal; Sunday Press; Sunday Times; Sunday Tribune; The Times; The Times Literary Supplement; Whitehaven News; Women's Labour News.

The Author; Bean na hÉireann; Church of Ireland Gazette; Country Life; The Farmer and Stockbreeder; Farmers' Home Journal; Fishing Gazette; Game and Gun; Gardeners' Chronicle; Illustrated London News; Irish Arts Review, Irish Homestead; The Landmark; The Living Torch; Nodlaig na bhFianna; Pall Mall Gazette; Poetry Review; Quarterly Review; Riding Magazine, St. James's Gazette, The Saturday Review, The Times Literary Supplement; Tygiel Kultury, Ulster Tatler; Vanity Fair; V.I.P. Magazine; The Vote; The World; The World of Fashion; Yachting World.

INDEX